RED *and* BLUE
NATION?

RED *and* BLUE NATION?

Characteristics and Causes of America's Polarized Politics

PIETRO S. NIVOLA

DAVID W. BRADY

editors

HOOVER INSTITUTION ON
WAR, REVOLUTION AND PEACE
Stanford University

BROOKINGS INSTITUTION PRESS
Washington, D.C.

Red and Blue Nation? Characteristics and Causes of America's Polarized Politics
may be ordered from:
BROOKINGS INSTITUTION PRESS
c/o HFS, P.O. Box 50370, Baltimore, MD 21211-4370
Tel: 800/537-5487; 410/516-6956; Fax: 410/516-6998

Library of Congress Cataloging-in-Publication data
Red and blue nation? : characteristics and causes of America's polarized
politics / Pietro S. Nivola and David W. Brady, editors.
    p.   cm.
Summary: "Considers the extent to which polarized views among political leaders
and activists are reflected in the population at large. Pays particular attention to factors
such as the increased influence of religion and the changing nature of the media and offers
thoughtful analyses of the underlying problems"—Provided by publisher.
  Includes bibliographical references and index.
  ISBN-13: 978-0-8157-6082-5 (cloth : alk. paper)
  ISBN-10: 0-8157-6082-5 (cloth : alk. paper)
  ISBN-13: 978-0-8157-6083-2 (pbk. : alk. paper)
  ISBN-10: 0-8157-6083-3 (pbk. : alk. paper)
1. Political parties—United States. 2. Party affiliation—United States. 3. Polarization
(Social sciences) 4. United States—Politics and government. I. Nivola, Pietro S.
II. Brady, David W. III. Title.
JK2261.R28 2006
324.273—dc22   2006034595

9 8 7 6 5 4 3 2 1

The paper used in this publication meets minimum requirements of the
American National Standard for Information Sciences—Permanence of Paper
for Printed Library Materials: ANSI Z39.48-1992.

Typeset in Adobe Garamond

Composition by Circle Graphics
Columbia, Maryland

Printed by R. R. Donnelley
Harrisonburg, Virginia

For **TINO** *and* **BIRDIE**

Who both knew truly polarized politics

Contents

Preface   ix

1 *Delineating the Problem*   1
   William A. Galston and Pietro S. Nivola

2 *Disconnected: The Political Class versus the People*   49
   Morris P. Fiorina and Matthew S. Levendusky

   COMMENTS
   Disconnected, or Joined at the Hip?
   Alan I. Abramowitz   72
   Gary C. Jacobson   85
   Rejoinder: Morris P. Fiorina and Matthew S. Levendusky   95
   Rejoinder: Alan I. Abramowitz   111

3 *Polarization Then and Now: A Historical Perspective*   119
   David W. Brady and Hahrie C. Han

   COMMENTS
   Polarization Runs Deep, Even by Yesterday's Standards
   James E. Campbell   152
   Carl M. Cannon   163

4 *Polarized by God? American Politics
   and the Religious Divide*   175
   E.J. Dionne Jr.

   COMMENTS
   Myths and Realities of Religion in Politics
   Alan Wolfe   206
   Andrew Kohut   214

5 *How the Mass Media Divide Us*   223
   Diana C. Mutz

   COMMENTS
   Two Alternative Perspectives
   Thomas Rosenstiel   249
   Gregg Easterbrook   255

6 *Polarizing the House of Representatives:
   How Much Does Gerrymandering Matter?*   263
   Thomas E. Mann

   COMMENTS
   Why Other Sources of Polarization Matter More
   Gary C. Jacobson   284
   Thomas B. Edsall   290

Contributors   301

Index   303

Preface

Nearly everyone agrees that the politics of the United States in recent decades have become in some respects more polarized, but there is far less agreement on precisely which respects. Nor is there consensus on whether the phenomenon afflicts only the so-called political class or runs deeper into the mass electorate. In addition, while some observers view the current partisan divide as noteworthy by historical standards, others are not so sure. And in any event, the causes and consequences of the country's political polarization, to say nothing of possible remedies, are a matter of intense debate.

In collaboration with the Hoover Institution at Stanford University, the Governance Studies program at Brookings has embarked on a concerted effort to make sense of this complex subject. From a series of seminars and scholarly papers written by several of the nation's leading social scientists and journalists in the field, Brookings and Hoover have compiled two conference volumes that promise to shed light on our understanding of the sources and implications of America's polarized politics.

In this, the first of those two books, William A. Galston and Pietro S. Nivola of the Brookings Institution begin by framing the alleged problem of polarization. In their assessment, the partisan polarity today—though hardly a culture "war"—is more pronounced and deep seated than it was nearly a generation ago. While not all the effects of polarization are cause for concern, Bill and Pietro submit that at least four arenas have suffered: a firm foreign policy, a responsible long-range fiscal policy, a sound process of appointing judges to the federal bench, and a healthy quotient of public trust in government—these are at risk in a political climate less hospitable to bipartisan accommodation.

In the book's second chapter, Morris P. Fiorina of Stanford and Matthew S. Levendusky of Yale University contend that the country's polarized elites elevate elected officials whose ideological stances tend to be sharply at odds with mainstream public preferences—a thesis challenged, at least in part, by two discussants of the authors' essay: Alan I. Abramowitz of Emory University and Gary C. Jacobson of the University of California–San Diego.

Chapter 3 examines the current contours of partisan polarization in historical perspective. David W. Brady of Stanford and Hahrie C. Han of Wellesley College argue that today's partisanship is hardly exceptional, or especially acute, when compared with the party conflicts during much of the nation's past. James E. Campbell of the State University of New York–Buffalo and Carl M. Cannon of the *National Journal,* the two discussants of this paper, are less inclined to view the current situation as relatively unremarkable.

E.J. Dionne Jr. of Brookings writes about the much-discussed ascent of religious voters in contemporary U.S. politics. He observes in chapter 4 that observant religious voters have played an increasingly significant role in differentiating the Republican Party's posture from the Democratic Party's. Yet, religion has not displaced long-standing determinants of voter preferences such as race, class, and geography. Alan Wolfe of Boston College and Andrew Kohut of the Pew Research Center mostly concur with E.J.'s conclusion.

Diana C. Mutz of the University of Pennsylvania explores the alleged polarizing influence exerted by the mass media in chapter 5. Professor Mutz makes a good case that the media are part of the problem, though at least one of her discussants, Thomas Rosenstiel of the Project for Excellence in Journalism, is more skeptical—and in any case, a second commentator, Brookings visiting fellow Gregg Easterbrook, stresses that whatever the media's complicity, not much, if anything, can be done about it.

Finally, another Brookings scholar, Thomas E. Mann, contests the conventional view that the gerrymandering of congressional districts accounts for the marked decrease in competitive elections for seats in the U.S. House of Representatives. He suggests in chapter 6 that other factors account for more of the increasingly polarized alignment of the parties in the House. Thomas B. Edsall of Columbia University and Gary C. Jacobson agree and add texture to what those factors have been.

The book, in sum, supplies a rich collection of topics and analytical perspectives that will prove valuable to policymakers as well as students of politics, members of the press, and the interested public in disentangling fact from fiction about the forces shaping America's present political landscape. The volume's editors wish to acknowledge the excellent assistance they received from Gladys Arrisueño, Lisa Bonos, Erin Carter, Bethany Hase, Andrew Lee, Richard Walker, and Adam Wolfson.

The Brookings-Hoover project would not have been possible without the generous support of the John D. and Catherine T. MacArthur Foundation and the Rockefeller Brothers Fund.

RED and BLUE NATION?

1

Delineating the Problem

William A. Galston
Pietro S. Nivola

W hat do people mean when they say that politics in the United States are polarized? Polarized in what sense? How pervasively? How much more than in the past? For what reasons? Why should we care? And what, if anything, ought to be done about it? In the fall of 2005, the Governance Studies Program of the Brookings Institution, in collaboration with the Hoover Institution at Stanford University, set out to explore such questions. This book is the first of two volumes resulting from our joint venture.

It should be stressed at the outset that these volumes are not meant to embellish rarified and inconclusive academic debates about the phenomenon called polarization. Rather, we are interested in getting to the bottom of the subject because a great deal of conventional wisdom presupposes not only that the nation's political divisions run deep, but also that they are wreaking great havoc.

We begin by enumerating some important points on which scholars and political observers generally agree. The U.S. Congress is more polarized ideologically than it was just a generation ago. In the House of Representatives, ideological overlap between the political parties has all but disappeared, and the rise of "safe" districts with partisan supermajorities has tended to push representatives away from the center. Activists in both parties have long been extremely polarized, and there are indications that the gap between them has widened even more in recent decades. Technological and regulatory changes in the past two decades, since roughly the mid-1980s (including the repeal of the fairness doctrine, which prohibited broadcast news programs from engaging in overt editorializing), have revolutionized the mass media, with the result that the country's news outlets have become more numerous, diverse, and politicized.

With these realities widely recognized, what—if anything—is left for analysts to argue about? The principal bone of contention is the extent to which polarized views among political leaders and activists are reflected in the population at large. Even here there is some agreement on meaningful trends. While there is no evidence that the electorate's overall ideological balance has changed much over the past three decades, voters are being sorted: fewer self-identified Democrats or liberals vote for Republican candidates than they did in the 1970s, fewer Republicans or conservatives vote for Democratic candidates, and rank-and-file partisans are more divided in their political attitudes and policy preferences. Also, religiosity (not to be confused with the denominational hostilities of the past) has become a telling determinant of political orientations and voting behavior. All else equal, individuals who attend church frequently are more likely to regard themselves as conservatives and vote Republican.

The unsettled questions are how far these trends go and how much difference they ultimately make. Do substantial segments of the mass electorate, not just political elites, tend to cluster consistently into opposing ideological camps that differentiate the respective agendas and candidates of the political parties? Put simply, in a polarized America most Democratic and Republican voters are, if not increasingly segregated geographically, decidedly at odds over a number of salient policy issues. While the severity of the country's "culture wars" is overstated, the preponderance of evidence does suggest that some significant fissures have opened in the nation's body politic, and that they extend beyond its politicians and partisan zealots.

The fissures are interesting in themselves, but only up to a point. What can make them important is the harm they might do to the quality of political discourse and public policies, or even to the stability of American democracy. The actual extent of that harm is even more debatable than the nature and depth of the root causes, but many fear the worst. We hear that polarization accounts for gridlock over major national priorities—such as better budgetary balance, long-range reform of social insurance programs, a new generation of environmental programs, sensible immigration policy, the capacity to mount and maintain a forceful foreign policy, and more.[1] We are told that the nation's politics and government are becoming less engaging, less responsive, and less accountable to the citizenry. We are warned that the health of vital public institutions—the Congress, the courts, the executive bureaucracy, the news media—is endangered. We are informed that rampant incivility threatens established norms of pragmatic accommodation, or worse, that civil strife may be just around the corner.[2] We are led to believe, in short, that the Republic has been rendered "dysfunctional."[3] A central aim of our study is to determine how these claims and imputations stand up under scrutiny. For without that determination, there is no way of knowing whether the country has a serious problem, never mind how to correct it.

We cannot make progress toward that end until we disentangle the phenomenon of polarization from other things with which it is often confused. As Morris P. Fiorina of Stanford University has observed, polarized politics are one thing, close division or partisan parity quite another. An election may be closely divided without being deeply polarized, as it was in 1960, or deeply polarized without being closely divided, as it was in 1936, or neither, as seems to have been the case in the famous "Era of Good Feeling" between the war of 1812 and Andrew Jackson's arrival on the presidential stage. The conventional wisdom is that the electorate has been both deeply *and* closely divided during most of the national elections of the past decade. We argue that this proposition is valid to an extent. Its proponents often go on to claim, however, that the interaction between *deep* and *close* division is bound to create inertia. But as George W. Bush's first term demonstrated, a president elected with a minority of the popular vote and working with only a razor-thin margin in Congress could achieve legislative successes even amid polarized politics—at least as long as the majority party was purposeful and unified.

Here is another important distinction: "polarization" is not synonymous with "culture war." Intense political conflict can occur along many different dimensions, of which cultural issues form only one. When Franklin D. Roosevelt

1. Here is how one of our colleagues, Thomas E. Mann of the Brookings Institution, summarized the situation in remarks at the conference "The Polarization of American Politics: Myth or Reality?" at Princeton University, December 3, 2004: "Party polarization and parity have consequences: for policy (difficulty enacting reasonable, workable, sustainable policies that are congruent with public preferences and needs); for the policy process (demise of regular order in Congress, a decline of deliberation, a weakening of our system of separation of powers and checks and balances); and for the electoral process (limited scope of competition, evermore egregious partisan manipulation of the democratic rules of the game)."

2. Hunter (1994, p. 4).

3. Rivlin (2005).

took dead aim at "economic royalists" at the height of the New Deal, his politics polarized American society. But an economic crisis, not a cultural one, was at the root of the polarization. In the election of 2004, the salience of cultural questions, although significant, was less than exit polls and media reports suggested. Nonetheless, other considerations—such as the Iraq war and America's role in the world—still divided much of the electorate. Political turmoil or tranquility, in other words, is not just a function of the extent of society's "cultural" tensions.

Of course, to say that culture is not the only possible dimension of polarization is not to deny its conspicuousness in recent analyses of American politics. For more than a decade, few objects of social commentary have stirred more hyperbole than the supposed culture clash. The nation's elections no longer are described as contests between two highly competitive political parties, but rather as a kind of holy war between red and blue states, pitting the devotees of "moral values" against their doubters.

Immediately after the balloting in 2004, for example, the prevailing journalistic story line was that morality had been a "defining issue," cited by Americans more often than any other reason for their support of President George W. Bush.[4] This interpretation came naturally. It conformed to years of oversimplifications— from candidates who perceived a "religious war" going on in our country, as well as pollsters and political operatives who spoke darkly of an evenly divided America that "inflames the passions of politicians and citizens alike"[5] and of "two massive colliding forces," one "Christian, religiously conservative," the other "socially tolerant, pro-choice, secular."[6]

The notion of a great cultural collision has also drawn sustenance from scholarly tracts. James Davison Hunter's *Culture Wars,* published in 1991, found a chasm between "orthodox" and "progressive" factions: each "can only talk past the other."[7] In a more recent book, *The Values Divide,* John Kenneth White sees "two nations." In the 2000 election, says White, their respective inhabitants cast ballots primarily on the basis of how disparately they "viewed the country's moral direction."[8]

Finally, when assessing polarization, we would sound a cautionary note: beware of visual gimmickry. The red-versus-blue election maps—an artifact of

4. See, for instance, Katharine Q. Seelye, "Moral Values Cited as a Defining Issue of the Election," *New York Times,* November 4, 2004.

5. Greenberg (2004, p. 2).

6. Republican pollster Bill McInturff was quoted in "One Nation, Fairly Divisible, Under God," *The Economist,* January 20, 2001.

7. Hunter (1991, p. 131).

8. White (2003, p. 164).

the Electoral College—are static images using rough aggregates. Underneath, partisan differences may be widening on key issues, and more voters may be choosing to live in neighborhoods and counties dominated by people with whom they agree. How to chart such changes without either oversimplifying or understating them is no easy undertaking.

Some Preliminaries

A plurality of the U.S. electorate continues to profess moderate political persuasions. In 2004, 21 percent of the voters described themselves as liberals, 34 percent said they were conservatives, and fully 45 percent were self-described moderates.[9] These numbers were practically indistinguishable from the average for the past thirty years (20 percent liberal, 33 percent conservative, 47 percent moderate).[10] Contrary to an impression left by much of the overheated punditry, the moderate middle swung both ways in the 2004 election. Both presidential candidates amassed support from these voters. Fifty-four percent of them went to the Democratic nominee, John Kerry, 45 percent to George W. Bush. In fact, the reelection of President Bush was secured chiefly by his improved performance among swing voters such as married women, Hispanics, Catholics, and less frequent church attendees—not just aroused Protestant fundamentalists.

Nor did a widely anticipated "values" Armageddon materialize over the issue of same-sex marriage. President Bush endorsed the concept of civil unions in the course of the campaign, and about half of those who thought this solution should be the law of the land wound up voting for him. Initiatives to ban same-sex marriages were on the ballot in three battleground states, yet John Kerry still managed to carry two of the three. Political scientists Stephen Ansolabehere and Charles Stewart III carefully examined county-level election returns and discovered an irony: by motivating voters and boosting turnouts, initiatives to ban gay marriage ended up aiding Kerry more than Bush.[11]

With respect to the most persistent wedge issue—abortion—there have been some unexpected twists as well. In the midst of the continuing partisan schism, a recent analysis shows that Republicans are consistently winning among those

9. Galston and Kamarck (2005, pp. 3).

10. These numbers are based on exit polls. The National Election Studies (NES) suggest that the percentage of moderates has remained stable over the past three decades, while the percentage of both liberals and conservatives has risen modestly. Complex methodological debates among the authors in this volume cloud the conclusions we feel confident about drawing from these data. Suffice it to say that there has not been a huge swing away from the center since the 1970s.

11. Ansolabehere and Stewart (2005).

voters (more than 60 percent of the electorate) who believe that policy on abortion should be more selective. Republican presidential candidates carried this group in 1996, 2000, and 2004—despite the fact that a clear majority of the group leans pro-choice and prefers that abortion be "mostly legal" rather than "mostly illegal." The staunchly pro-life Republican Party seems to be persuading millions of moderately pro-choice voters that its positions on specific abortion policies are reasonable.[12]

In the 2004 election, moral values turned out to be the leading concern of just 22 percent of the electorate—at most.[13] (When the Pew Research Center surveyed the voters with an unprompted open-ended formulation, instead of pigeonholing them with a fixed list of choices, only 14 percent of the respondents volunteered some version of "values" as their first concern.)[14] For the overwhelming majority of voters, a combination of other issues—such as the Iraq war and the threat of terrorism—were more salient. In fact, the percentage of moralists appears to have been, if anything, lower in the 2004 election than in 2000 and 1996.[15]

And what about the TV maps that depict "red" America clashing with "blue"? They are colorful but crude. Plenty of states ought to be purple.[16] There are red states—Oklahoma, Kansas, North Carolina, and Virginia, for instance—

12. Kessler and Dillon (2005).

13. Curiously, in spite of this relatively modest share, many a seasoned political analyst insisted that the "values" cleavage dominated the election. Greenberg and Carville (2004, p. 1), for example, concluded that Bush won the election largely because of the "attack on Kerry on abortion and gay marriage and the extreme cultural polarization of the country." Yet their own poll numbers indicated that the "most important issues" were Iraq, terrorism, and national security, which formed a combined total of nearly 40 percent, whereas "moral values" accounted for just under 20 percent.

14. Pew Research Center for the People and the Press, "Voters Liked Campaign 2004, but Too Much 'Mud-Slinging,' " November 11, 2004 (people-press.org/reports/display.php3? ReportID=233).

15. "The Triumph of the Religious Right," *The Economist,* November 13, 2004. Twenty-two percent of the voters in 2004 cited moral issues, according to the prevailing exit poll estimates. But 35 percent had placed moral/ethical issues at the top in 2000, and fully 40 percent had done so in 1996. Naturally, one has to take all these figures with a large grain of salt. The figures vary with the exact survey instruments used. Nonetheless, the available numbers decidedly do not suggest that "moral values" had surged to new heights by 2004.

16. Estimates of "purple" states vary considerably according to the methodology employed. Abramowitz and Saunders (2005) provide a tally of only twelve, but other estimates suggest a near plurality of states. For example, seventeen states fell into the category according to a preelection analysis that weighed (a) the percentage margin of victory in the 2000 and 1996 election, (b) whether a state voted consistently for one party in the past four presidential elections or swung back and forth, and (c) whether trends in the previous two presidential elections made a state significantly more competitive or less. See also Richard S. Dunham and others, "Red vs. Blue: The Few Decide for the Many," *Business Week,* June 14, 2004.

that have Democratic governors, just as the bright blue states of California, New York, and even Massachusetts have Republican governors. Some red states, such as Tennessee and Mississippi, send at least as many Democrats as Republicans to the House of Representatives. Michigan and Pennsylvania—two of the biggest blue states in the last election—send more Republicans than Democrats. North Dakota is blood red (Bush ran off with 63 percent of the vote there), yet its entire congressional delegation is composed of Democrats. On election night, Bush also swept all but a half-dozen counties in Montana. But that did not prevent the Democrats from winning control of the governor's office and state legislature—or stop, we might note, the decisive adoption of an initiative allowing patients to use and grow their own medicinal marijuana.[17]

In sum, just as the actual configuration of public attitudes in the United States is more complex than the caricature of a hyper-politicized society torn between God-fearing evangelists and libertine atheists, the country's actual political geography is more complicated than the simplistic picture of a nation separated into solidly partisan states or regions.

To these prefatory observations one more should be added: for all the hype about the ruptures and partisan rancor in contemporary American society, the strife pales in comparison with much of the nation's past. There have been long stretches of American history in which conflicts were far worse. Epic struggles were waged between advocates of slavery and abolitionists, between agrarian populists and urban manufacturing interests at the end of the nineteenth century, and between industrial workers and owners of capital well into the first third of the twentieth century. Yet what those now nostalgically pining for a more tranquil past remember are the more recent intervals of consensus.

Yes, there have been interludes when it was possible to speak of "the end of ideology," in Daniel Bell's famous phrasing, but those periods have been the exception more than the norm. Of all these periods, the two decades between the end of World War II and the mid-1960s may have been the most exceptional of all. It could not last, and it did not. The relative harmony between the parties on international affairs in the 1950s collapsed amid the antiwar protests of the 1960s. A complacent entente on race gradually gave way with the Supreme Court's intervention in *Brown* v. *Board of Education* and the civil rights movement. By 1964, emerging differences between the parties had triggered a Republican surge for Senator Barry Goldwater's candidacy in the South, a harbinger of even bigger

17. The Montana Medical Marijuana Act won the approval of 61.8 percent of Montana voters, faring 3.5 percentage points better than Bush, according to statewide election data.

things to come. President Dwight D. Eisenhower's "Modern Republicanism" brought a period of relative partisan peace on the central question of how government should manage the economy (recall Nixon's famous admission, or boast, that "We are all Keynesians now"). The ceasefire ended, however, just a few years later with rising rates of inflation and of marginal taxation. Supply-side economics made its debut, and the Republicans, once fiscally conservative, morphed into the party of lower marginal tax rates secured by permanent (as distinct from strictly countercyclical) tax cuts.[18]

Any serious exploration of today's political polarities has to be placed in historical context. We have to ask: compared to what? Four decades ago, cities were burning across the United States. A sitting president, one presidential candidate, and the leader of the civil rights movement were assassinated. Another sitting president was driven from office, another presidential candidate was shot, and a hail of bullets felled antiwar demonstrators at Kent State University. George W. Bush is, by current standards, a "polarizing president." But in comparison with, say, Abraham Lincoln or Lyndon Johnson, the divisions of the Bush era appear shallower and more muted.

Polarization in Perspective

Badly in need of a reality check, popularized renditions of the polarization narrative were subjected to a more systematic assessment a couple of years ago in a book provocatively titled *Culture War? The Myth of a Polarized America*. In this intriguing study, rich with survey data, Stanford's Fiorina and his associates reaffirmed the oft-obscured fundamental fact that most Americans have remained centrists, sharing a mixture of liberal and conservative views on a variety of presumably divisive social questions. Ideologues of the left or right—that is, persons with a *Weltanschauung*, or whose politics consistently form an overarching world view that tilts to extremes—are conspicuous on the fringes of the two parties and among political elites, but scarcely among the public at large. Indeed, sentiments there appear to be moderating, not polarizing, on various hot-button issues. To cite a couple of striking examples, the authors found notable increases in social acceptance of interracial dating and of homosexuality.[19]

---

18. In a series of papers, Geoffrey C. Layman and Thomas M. Carsey have shown that rather than one dimension of conflict diminishing or displacing prior dimensions, most have been layered on top of one another since the 1960s, a process they call "conflict extension." See especially Layman and Carsey (2002a, 2002b).

19. Fiorina, Abrams, and Pope (2006, pp. 109–26).

Moreover, the authors argued, the moderate consensus seems almost ubiquitous. The inhabitants of red states and blue states differ little on matters such as gender equity, fair treatment of blacks in employment, capital punishment, and the merits of environmental protection.[20] Majorities in both places appear to oppose outlawing abortion completely or permitting it under all circumstances, and their opinions have changed little over the past thirty years.

Fiorina's findings squared with earlier research by several social scientists. In an important article published in 1996, Princeton sociologist Paul DiMaggio and coauthors John H. Evans and Bethany Bryson found little empirical evidence for supposing that social attitudes had become more polar in the U.S. population.[21] On the contrary, gaps among groups over race and gender issues, crime, sexual morality, and the role of the welfare state had either remained constant or narrowed over time. Similarly, after studying eight communities in depth, Alan Wolfe of Boston College concluded in his book, *One Nation, After All,* that Americans had grown more, not less, tolerant and united on such issues.[22]

That said, the central motif of Fiorina's work is not that signs of polarization are *nowhere* to be found. Again, the argument is that they exist, but principally amid the parties' most active antagonists, while the rest of the population mostly looks on. That observation is scarcely novel or controversial. For years, other scholars had been observing the tendency of the political class to grow more partisan.[23]

DiMaggio and his associates discerned a pattern of "depolarization" among Americans when classified by age, education, sex, race, region, and even religion. The main exception was persons who clearly identified themselves as political partisans. These had drawn apart, and according to more recent data have continued to do so.[24]

No knowledgeable observer doubts that the American public is less divided than the political agitators and vocal elective office-seekers who claim to represent it. The interesting question, though, is, how substantial are the portions of

20. Fiorina, Abrams, and Pope (2006, p. 16).

21. DiMaggio, Evans, and Bryson (1996).

22. Wolfe (1998, p. 320). For additional support of this general proposition, see Baker (2005); Davis and Robinson (1996).

23. See Poole and Rosenthal (1984, 2001); King (1999); Layman and Carsey (2000).

24. Evans (2003). In Evans's words, "political activists are becoming more polarized over the issues that have been of concern to politically active religious conservatives." For a contrary perspective, see Collie and Mason (1999).

the electorate that heed their opinion leaders, and thus might be hardening their political positions? Here, as best we can tell, the tectonic plates of the nation's electoral politics appear to be shifting more than Fiorina and his coauthors were willing to concede.

Even though the mass electorate has long formed three comparably sized blocs (29 percent identifying themselves as Republicans, 33 percent as Democrats, and almost all the rest as independents), the attributes of the Democratic and Republican identifiers have changed. They are considerably more cohesive ideologically than just a few decades ago.[25] In the 1970s it was not unusual for the Democratic Party to garner as much as a quarter of the votes of self-described conservatives, while the GOP enjoyed a nearly comparable share of the liberal vote. Since then, those shares have declined precipitously.[26] In 2004 Kerry took 85 percent of the liberal vote, while Bush claimed nearly that percentage among conservative voters.

Further, as their outlooks tracked party loyalties more closely, Democratic and Republican voters became far less likely to desert their party's candidates. As Princeton University political scientist Larry Bartels has demonstrated, party affiliation is a much stronger predictor of voting behavior in recent presidential elections than it was in earlier ones.[27] In 2004 nearly nine out of every ten Republicans said they approved of George W. Bush. A paltry 12 percent of Democrats concurred. In an earlier day, three to four times as many Democrats had held favorable opinions of Ronald Reagan, Gerald Ford, Richard Nixon, and Dwight Eisenhower.

25. Pew Research Center for the People and the Press, "Democrats Gain Edge in Party Identification," July 26, 2004 (people-press.org/commentary/display.php3?AnalysisID=95). These shares have varied over time, but those in 2004 were almost identical to those in 1987. Some analysts stress that within the three-part division, the fastest growing group has been persons registering as independents or "other." Even if everyone in this category were a genuine centrist—a big "if"—the main thing to remember is that most registered voters continue to identify as either Democrats or Republicans, and, as we shall show, their views are diverging in a number of important respects. Moreover, in a significant recent analysis, Keele and Stimson (2005) show that the share of "pure" independents (voters who do not consider themselves closer to one party than to the other) has fallen by half since the early 1970s, from 14 percent of the electorate to just over 7 percent. More than three-quarters of self-declared independents now admit to being closer to one party than to the other.

26. Galston and Kamarck (2005, p. 45). A generation ago, party identification and ideology were weakly correlated. Now the two are much more tightly intertwined. See also Abramowitz and Saunders (1998, 2004).

27. Bartels (2000).

Deepening Disagreements

Of course, the use of the terms liberal and conservative can be squishy—and if, at bottom, there is still not much more than a dime's worth of difference (as the saying used to go) between the convictions of Democrats and Republicans, the fact that partisans are voting more consistently along party lines says little about how polarized they might be. What counts, in other words, is the *distance* between their respective sets of convictions.

On the issues that mattered, the distance was considerable. Consider the main one: national security and foreign policy. The Pew Research Center's surveys found, for example, that while almost seven in ten Republicans felt that the best way to ensure peace is through military strength, fewer than half of Democrats agreed.[28] In October 2003, 85 percent of Republicans thought going to war in Iraq was the right decision, while only 39 percent of Democrats did.[29] When asked whether "wrongdoing" by the United States might have motivated the attacks of September 11, a *majority* of Democrats, but just 17 percent of Republicans, said yes. Democrats assigned roughly equal priority to the war on terrorism and protecting American jobs (86 percent and 89 percent, respectively). By comparison, Republicans gave far greater weight to fighting terrorism than to worker protection.[30]

Popular support for the Iraq war has sagged since these surveys were taken. Yet, as of March 2006, nearly seven out of ten Republicans still perceived the U.S. military effort in Iraq as going well, while only three out of ten Democrats agreed. Two-thirds of Democrats (but only 27 percent of Republicans) felt the United States should bring its troops home as soon as possible.[31] Not surprisingly, fully 76 percent of the electorate saw important differences between the parties in 2004, a level never previously recorded in modern survey research.[32]

28. Pew Research Center for the People and the Press, "2004 Political Landscape: Evenly Divided and Increasingly Polarized," November 5, 2003 (people-press.org/reports/display.php3?ReportID=196).

29. By December 2003, the percentage of Republicans holding this view rose to 90 percent. The percentage of Democrats went up to 56 percent, before dropping back again later on. Pew Research Center for the People and the Press, "After Hussein's Capture . . . ," December 18, 2003 (people-press.org/reports/display.php3?ReportID=199).

30. Pew Research Center for the People and the Press, "Foreign Policy Attitudes Now Driven by 9/11 and Iraq," August 18, 2004 (people-press.org/reports/display.php3?ReportID=222).

31. David Kirkpatrick and Adam Nagourney, "In an Election Year, a Shift in Public Opinion on the War," *New York Times*, March 27, 2006. The polling data reported in this article were also based on Pew surveys that queried respondents on whether the war was going "very well or fairly well."

32. For data on this going back to 1952, see the American National Election Studies (www.umich.edu/~nes/nesguide/toptable/tab2b_4.htm).

Among so-called active partisans, who represent a nontrivial fifth of all voters, the gap was even more dramatic.[33] Reviewing 2004 National Election Study data, Alan I. Abramowitz of Emory University and Kyle Saunders of Colorado State University report that 70 percent of Democrats, but just 11 percent of Republicans, typically favored diplomacy over the use of force. On major questions of domestic policy, the difference was only a little less pronounced. The issue of health insurance, for example, ranked high for 66 percent of the Democrats, but for only 15 percent of the Republicans.[34]

Then there is the matter of abortion. Following the Supreme Court's *Roe* v. *Wade* decision, no domestic issue has been more contentious. And no other issue has played a bigger role in mobilizing observant religious voters (a force about which we will have more to say later). A majority of Americans accept abortion under various circumstances. But the majority wobbles when abortion is framed as an absolutely unrestricted right to choose. The persistence of this dichotomy is noteworthy. Fiorina and his colleagues, in fact, provide perhaps the most emblematic evidence of the ongoing rift. When people were asked in 2003 whether abortion should be called an act of murder, 46 percent said yes and exactly 46 percent demurred.[35] No doubt, if the question had been directed only at persons who identified themselves as Republican or Democratic loyalists, the percentages would have been even higher, and the underlying passions even more polar.

Redder Reds, Bluer Blues

In assessing these deepening disagreements we must also consider the territorial contours of today's polarization. The question is of importance because if voters tend to migrate geographically toward like-minded voters, the resulting political segregation of Democrats and Republicans could increasingly lock in their differences: a person's partisan inclinations seem more likely to deepen and endure if he or she is spatially surrounded by fellow partisans.

According to Fiorina and his associates, no wide gulf separates the residents of Republican-leaning (red) states and Democratic-leaning (blue) states. But states are large aggregates in which the minority party almost always obtains one-third or more of the vote. This raises the question of what constitutes a sig-

33. Active partisans are defined as voters who are engaged in two or more political activities other than voting.
34. Abramowitz and Saunders (2005).
35. Fiorina, Abrams, and Pope (2006, p. 81).

nificant difference among states. Consider some of the data Fiorina himself presents from the 2000 election. In red states, Republican identifiers slightly outnumbered Democrats, but in blue states, Democrats enjoyed an edge of 15 percentage points. In red states, the share of the electorate that was conservative was 20 points larger than the share characterized as liberal. Blue state residents were 15 points less likely to attend church regularly, 11 points more supportive of abortion rights, 12 points more likely to favor stricter gun control, and 16 points more likely to strongly favor gays in the military.[36] Polarization exists to some extent in the eye of the beholder. We think, though, that these and other quantitative differences between red and blue states are large enough to make a qualitative difference.

The results of the 2004 election only reinforced this judgment. Using a slightly different definition of red and blue states (namely, states that Bush or Kerry won by at least 6 percentage points), Abramowitz and Saunders find differences in excess of 20 points along numerous dimensions, from church attendance to gun ownership to attitudes on hot-button social issues such as abortion and gay marriage.[37]

There are indications, moreover, that red states have gotten redder and blue states bluer, at least in this sense: presidential vote tallies in more states in recent years have strayed from the national norm. To be sure, this pattern of differentiation could be subject to change. Suppose, as a thought experiment, a presidential election were held as of this writing (in the spring of 2006), and that Bush was an incumbent seeking another term. With his popularity at its present lows and solid majorities of residents in states he had carried in 2004 now expressing disapproval, quite a few "red" states might more accurately be colored pink or even pale blue.[38] But at least as of 2004, it was clear that the presidential candidates' margins of victory in more and more states had widened.

In 1988 there were only fifteen states in which George H. W. Bush won with a vote share greater than 5 percentage points above his national average, and only nine states in which his share was more than 5 points below his national average. Put another way, twenty-six states were within a 5 point range of his 53.4 percent share of the national vote. By contrast, in 2004, George W. Bush carried twenty states with a share of the vote more than 5 points above his

36. Fiorina, Abrams, and Pope (2006, pp. 43–44).
37. Abramowitz and Saunders (2005, p. 13).
38. See Richard Morin, "Pink Is the New Red," *Washington Post,* April 17, 2006.

national share, in twelve states he ended up more than 5 points below it, and in just eighteen states his share fell within the 5 point range.[39]

These results are not an artifact of an arbitrary selection of elections. In the election of 1960, which produced a near tie in the popular vote between John F. Kennedy and Richard Nixon, a remarkable thirty-seven states yielded results within 5 percentage points of the national margin. In 2000, another election year with a razor-thin popular vote margin, only twenty-one states ended up within this range. These results do not reflect only the polarizing consequences of George W. Bush's campaign and style of governance. In the 1996 race between Bill Clinton and Bob Dole, only twenty-two states were within 5 points of the national margin, nearly identical to the 2000 result. In fact, the past three presidential elections have produced three of the four most polarized state results in the past half-century. (The Reagan-Carter election of 1980 is the fourth.)[40]

There also has been evidence of increasing dispersion at the substate level. One way to get closer to developments on the ground is to examine the share of the population living in places where voters sided with one party or the other by lopsided margins. Compare the three closest elections of the past generation. In 1976, when Jimmy Carter beat incumbent Gerald Ford by a scant 2 percentage points, only 27 percent of voters lived in landslide counties (where one candidate wins by 20 points or more). In 2000, when Al Gore and George W. Bush fought to a virtual draw, 45 percent of voters lived in such counties. By 2004, that figure had risen even further, to 48 percent.[41]

39. Galston and Kamarck (2005, p. 54). Using a different methodology, Abramowitz and Saunders (2005) reach a parallel conclusion. Comparing two presidential elections (1976 and 2004) with nearly identical popular vote margins, they found that the average state margin of victory rose from 8.9 percentage points to 14.8 percentage points, the number of uncompetitive states (with margins of 10 points or more) rose from nineteen to thirty-one, and the number of competitive states (with margins between 0 and 5 points) fell by half, from twenty-four to twelve. Not surprisingly, the number of electoral votes in uncompetitive states soared from 131 to 332. These numbers merely confirm what every contemporary presidential campaign manager instinctively understands: in normal political circumstances, when neither party has suffered a major reversal (a big-time scandal or policy failure, for instance), the actual field of battle has tended to be small and concentrated in the Midwest.

40. William A. Galston and Andrew S. Lee; tabulations on file with the authors.

41. Bill Bishop, "The Great Divide," *Austin American-Statesman*, December 4, 2004. See also Bill Bishop, "The Cost of Political Uniformity," *Austin American-Statesman*, April 8, 2004; Bill Bishop, "Political Parties Now Rooted in Different Americas," *Austin American-Statesman*, September 18, 2004; Bill Bishop, "The Schism in U.S. Politics Begins at Home," *Austin American-Statesman*, April 4, 2004.

In 2004 fully 60 percent of the nation's counties handed supermajorities of 60 percent or more to either Bush or Kerry. The corresponding figure for the 2000 election was 53 percent, and for the 1996 race it was just 38 percent.[42] As far as we can tell, the 2004 percentage was exceeded only once in the past half-century, when Richard Nixon routed George McGovern in 1972. In the earlier close elections of 1960 and 1976, landslide counties represented 48 and 37 percent, respectively, of the total. The figures from 2000 and 2004 thus strike us as significant.[43]

To be sure, depicting the political landscape exclusively on the basis of vote tallies for presidential candidates is not wholly satisfying—and again, 2008 could conceivably alter much of the terrain we have described. As we remarked earlier, more evidence would be needed to demonstrate the significance of the country's partisan geographic divide. For example, one would need to show that elective offices down the line—Senate and House seats, governorships, state legislatures—are also now falling like dominos into the hands of one party or the other.

While we do not attempt so laborious an analysis here, this much is relatively easy to see: the number of congressional districts that voted for different parties in presidential and congressional contests has declined. Typically, this number decreases between a presidential election and the following midterm. But just the opposite happened between 2000 and 2002, yielding the fewest split districts in at least half a century. In 2004 a mere fifty-nine congressional districts went in opposite directions in presidential and House elections. Compare this low figure to 2000, when there were eighty-six such districts, or 1996 and 1992, when there were more than a hundred.[44] Or compare the 2002 midterm figure of sixty-two with the three previous midterms, which averaged almost precisely twice that number.[45]

These trends have not been confined to the House. In 2004 the percentage of states won by the same party in that year's Senate and presidential races rose to a level not seen for forty years, and the percentage of Senate seats held by the party winning that state in the most recent presidential election rose to the highest

42. Mark Mellman, "Americans Are Voting as a Bloc," *The Hill,* January 19, 2005.

43. Galston and Lee; tabulations on file with the authors. For the methodological debate sparked by the initial county-level findings, see Klinkner (2004); Bishop and Cushing (2004). Klinkner and Hapanowicz (2005) acknowledge an increase in landslide counties between 2000 and 2004.

44. Dan Balz, "Partisan Polarization Intensified in 2004 Election," *Washington Post,* March 29, 2005.

45. Jacobson (2003a, p. 12).

level in at least half a century. As one might infer from these results, by 2004 the percentage of partisans voting for the other party's House or Senate candidates had fallen to levels not seen since the early 1960s.[46]

In sum, although these data hardly paint a complete picture, they do suggest that sizable blocs in the national electorate have not been conducting centrist business as usual. Like the elections of 1960 and 1976, those of 2000 and 2004 were closely contested. Unlike the elections of 1960 and 1976, the past two were slugged out primarily in a small handful of states. Elsewhere, larger shares of voters seem to have gotten sorted into states more strongly predisposed to one side or the other. And the predispositions seem rooted in appreciably different characteristics. We are inclined to concur with Fiorina that such contrasts fall well short of proving that Americans are mostly a bunch of "culture warriors." But we also suspect that where there is smoke there may be, if not exactly a four-alarm fire, some significant friction.

Sorting

What has happened in the electorate has much to do with how sharply political elites have separated along their respective philosophical and party lines. That separation is not in doubt. In the 1970s, the ideological orientations of many Democratic and Republican members of Congress overlapped. Today, the congruence has nearly vanished. By the end of the 1990s, almost every Republican in the House was more conservative than every Democrat. And increasingly, their leaders leaned to extremes more than the backbenchers have. Outside Congress, activists in the political parties have diverged sharply from one another in recent decades. Meanwhile, interest groups, particularly those concerned with cultural issues, have proliferated and now ritually line up with one party or the other to enforce the party creed. Likewise, the news media, increasingly partitioned through politicized talk-radio programs, cable news channels, and Internet sites, amplify party differences.

These changes, the reality of which hardly anyone contests, raise an important scholarly question with profound practical implications: what are the effects of elite polarization on the mass electorate? One possibility raised by Fiorina and others is that the people as a whole are not shifting their ideological or policy *preferences* much. Rather, they are being presented with increasingly polarized *choices,* which force voters to change their political behavior in ways

46. Jacobson (2005, pp. 208–10).

that analysts mistake for shifts in underlying preferences.[47] A plausible inference is that if both parties nominated relatively moderate, nonpolarizing candidates, as they did in 1960 and again in 1976, voters' behavior might revert significantly toward previous patterns. Another possibility is that changes at the elite level have communicated new information about parties, ideology, and policies to many voters, leading to changes of attitudes and preferences that will be hard to reverse, even in less polarized circumstances.

Both processes can occur. On the one hand, there is no reason to believe that today's voters are unresponsive to changes in choices that the parties offer. The Democratic Party's decision to nominate more moderate presidential candidates in 1960, 1976, and 1992 (in the wake of more liberal but failed candidacies) did shift mass perceptions and behavior. A 2008 presidential contest between, say, Senator John McCain (R-Ariz.) and a Democratic nominee seen as more moderate than Gore and Kerry would almost certainly change the dynamics of party competition.[48]

On the other hand, there is evidence suggesting that as party hierarchies, members of Congress, media outlets, and advocacy groups polarize, so gradually does much of the public. Voters become more aware of the differences between the parties, they are better able to locate themselves in relation to the parties, and they care more about the outcome of elections. As a result, their partisan preferences become better aligned with their ideological and policy preferences.[49] Marc J. Hetherington of Vanderbilt University has shed light on how this mass "sorting" takes place. Voters (especially the attentive ones) exposed to the drumbeat of partisan and ideological disputes among opinion leaders eventually pick up their messages.[50] The partisan polemics at the elite level signal what it means to be a Democrat or a Republican, and hence help voters align with the party whose position best approximates their own. Abetting people's receptivity to political cues is the increased influence of education. In 1900

47. See Fiorina, Abrams, and Pope (2006, pp. 165–86).

48. Indeed, the evidence suggests that the shift between George W. Bush's relatively moderate 2000 campaign and a more conservative line in 2004 had the effect of further polarizing the electorate. There is little evidence, however, that underlying public attitudes on most basic issues shifted dramatically and durably in the course of these four years. See Abramowitz and Stone (2005).

49. For evidence and discussion on these points, see Brewer (2005); Jacobson (2003b); Baumer and Gold (2005).

50. Hetherington (2001). See also Abramowitz and Saunders (1998); Layman and Carsey (2000); McCarty, Poole, and Rosenthal (2006, p. 44). In an important book, Zaller (1992) began to explore how elite opinion affects mass opinion.

only 10 percent of young Americans went to high school. Today, 84 percent of adult Americans are high school graduates, and almost 27 percent have graduated from college. "This extraordinary growth in schooling," writes James Q. Wilson, "has produced an ever larger audience for political agitation."[51]

The interaction between elite cues and voter responses is complex and varied. A recent analysis suggests that voters who have positioned themselves clearly on an issue, care intensely about it, and see important differences between the parties over it choose sides accordingly. For other voters who care less about a given issue, party identification is the primary driver: When their party changes its position, they tend to change as well. And those voters who do not perceive differences between the parties (a diminishing share of the electorate) will likely change neither their party nor their position on the issue.[52]

Thus far we have discussed issue-induced or partisan shifts among voters with prior positions. But elite polarization has another dimension—namely, its effects on young adults entering the electorate without fully formed preferences and attachments. In an important analysis of 1972–2004 National Election Study data, M. Kent Jennings and Laura Stoker find evidence that the increasingly polarized parties and their activists tend to polarize young adults whose attitudes, once formed, are likely to remain stable over a lifetime. Jennings and Stoker also find evidence that, for young adults, new dimensions of polarization add to rather than displace older divisions; that is, race, gender, culture, and religion do not erase the impact of New Deal–based divisions about the role of government in the economy.[53] Especially in the case of the young, partisan polarization not only sorts but also shapes basic political orientations and party allegiances.

The cue-taking that has helped fuse ideology with party loyalty at the grass roots, in turn, reinforces the hyper-partisan style of candidates for elective office and their campaign strategies. Given the increasing proportion of the electorate that is sorted by ideology, mobilizing a party's core constituency, rather than trying to convert the uncommitted, looks (correctly or not) more and more like a winning strategy.[54] And that means fielding hard-edged politicians appealing to, and certified by, the party's base. This electoral connection—and not just endogenous partisan incentives within institutions such as the House of Representatives—may help account for the increasingly polarized Congress of recent decades. And,

51. See James Q. Wilson, "How Divided Are We?" *Commentary,* February 2006, pp. 15–21.
52. Carsey and Layman (2006).
53. Stoker and Jennings (2006).
54. Levendusky (2005).

as Gary C. Jacobson has suggested, it may even account for a tendency of Democrats and Republicans to move further apart the longer they stay in office.[55]

It would be a mistake, however, to see only one-way causality in the relation between changes at the elite and mass levels. History supports Jacobson's contention that political elites in search of a winning formula anticipate voters' potential responses to changed positions on the issues and are therefore constrained to some extent by that assessment. The Republican Party's southern strategy reflected a judgment that Democratic support for civil rights had created an opportunity to shift voters and (eventually) party identification as well. The Democrats' transition from a moderate stance on abortion in 1976 to a less nuanced one by 1984 rested on a judgment that this move would attract the better-educated, younger, more upscale voters who had been activated politically by Vietnam and Watergate.[56]

A feedback loop that mutually reinforces polarized comportment up and down the political food chain has at least a couple of important implications. For one, the idea that self-inspired extremists are simply foisting polar choices on the wider public, while the latter holds its nose, does not quite capture what is going on. While it is possible to distinguish conceptually between polarization and sorting, the evidence suggests that over the past three decades these two phenomena cannot be entirely decoupled. Polarized politics are partly here, so to speak, by popular demand. And inasmuch as that is the case, undoing it may prove especially difficult—and perhaps not wholly appropriate.

Root Causes

Underlying the sharper demarcation of Democratic and Republican identities, from top to bottom, is a broad assortment of systemic forces, forces that will be the focus of several chapters in this volume. For now, a few of the main markers can be sketched. They include certain large historical transformations, the changing role of religion, the mass media, and the way representatives are elected to Congress.

HISTORICAL TRANSFORMATIONS

First on the list has to be the regional realignment of the parties.[57] After Barry Goldwater carried five states in the Deep South in 1964, it became clear that the

---

55. See Jacobson (2000, 2003b, 2004). Importantly, Jacobson's findings apply to both the House and the Senate.
56. Jacobson (2000).
57. Stonecash, Brewer, and Mariani (2003).

Democratic Party's lock on the region had loosened. The Republican ascent in the South accelerated in the wake of the 1965 Voting Rights Act, which mobilized black voters and drove additional white conservatives out of the Democratic Party.[58] As the Democrats lost their conservative southern base, they consolidated strength among more liberal constituencies prominent elsewhere—in particular, much of the Northeast and eventually California. At the same time, Republican moderates began losing their traditional foothold in regions such as New England, diminishing the party's internal ballast against harder-line conservatives. The GOP, now anchored in the South and West, became more orthodox.[59]

The famous *Roe* v. *Wade* decision exacerbated party divisions. In 1972, the year before *Roe,* neither party's platform even mentioned abortion. In 1976 both parties held moderate (and nearly interchangeable) positions. Over the next two presidential cycles, however, activists in the two parties moved farther away from one another, and by 1984 the party platforms had settled into the polarized paradigms that have persisted over the past two decades.[60]

Ronald Reagan further clarified the Republican agenda, championing bold tax cuts, retrenchment of the welfare state, and, not least, a much more muscular national defense than the Democrats advocated. The latter consideration warrants more attention than has been paid by much historiography on the transformative events defining modern American party politics.[61] The Vietnam War, and later the lowering of East-West tensions, shattered the bipartisan unity that had prevailed in foreign policy during much of the cold war. The Democrats moved left. The party's standard-bearer in 1972, it should be recalled, proposed slashing the U.S. defense budget by one-third. Soon after, the Democratic majority leader in the Senate was to be the author of a legislative proposal calling for drastic reductions of U.S. forces in Europe. By 1983, when the Reagan administration was determined to deploy Pershing missiles in Europe to counterbalance the Soviet Union's provocative deployment of its intermediate-range missiles, Democratic majorities in the House of Representatives were adopting resolutions supporting a nuclear freeze. Deviations like these signaled to the party bases a growing contrast—one that would reach its starkest manifestation seven years later, when Iraq invaded Kuwait and most Democratic senators declined to approve the use of force against the aggressor.

58. Rohde (1992).
59. See Black and Black (2002).
60. For a more detailed account of this change, see Galston (2004).
61. On what follows, see Nivola (1997, p. 250).

The end of the cold war ushered in what one of us has called "the age of low politics."[62] Relieved of the need to pull together in the face of a great external threat, the political parties now could afford to pull apart—and to wrangle about every manner of domestic issue, regardless how parochial, petty, or picayune. Thus, luxuriating in their holiday from foreign affairs, the congressional parties indulged in long and bitter quarrels over matters such as raising the minimum wage by a few cents or the Clinton-Lewinsky scandal. (For all but four House Republicans in 1998, impeaching the president had become an idée fixe. One wonders whether their zest for it would have been quite so unsparing if the fall of 1998 had been, say, the fall of 1962, when the country and the world stood at the brink of nuclear annihilation.)

Intensifying the partisan squabbles has been the extraordinary parity of the competitors. With the parties evenly matched, unusually small margins now make the difference between winning and losing the presidency, the House, or the Senate. With so much riding on marginal changes in party support, it is not surprising to see both sides clawing to gain an edge by whatever means are deemed effective. Hence, if the GOP can add a few seats to its majority in the House by manipulating congressional district lines in Texas, it seizes the opportunity without hesitation. When the Democratic opposition spots a chance to trip up a Republican president's judicial nominees, it rarely seems to hesitate either. When competing in a dead heat, anything goes.

The news media thrive on the perpetual feuding because partisan machinations, stridency, and acrimony make good copy. This calculation, of course, is not new, but several factors appear to have heightened it in recent times. The mainstream media—the three old-line broadcast networks and the national newspapers—have more rivals. The number of Americans receiving their news from network television or daily newspapers has been declining steadily.[63] Internet outlets, talk-radio stations, and cable channels pitching to narrow cultural and politically attentive audiences have proliferated. This niche-oriented industry increasingly resembles a high-tech cousin of the combative partisan press of the nineteenth century—a development further facilitated by the repeal of the fairness doctrine.

Of course, it is far from self-evident which side—politicized journalism or its audience—is the principal agent driving deeper wedges. The new media are

62. Nivola (2003).
63. Project for Excellence in Journalism (2005).

cultivating their particular partisan and ideological markets but are also responding to the emergence of those markets.[64] The latter, in turn, reflect changes under way in the mass electorate.

THE ROLE OF RELIGION

One such change pertains to the role of religious voters. To be sure, religion has always played a prominent part in U.S. politics, and we would be hard-pressed to claim that its significance today is more notable than the sectarian political currents in the past. At one time, denominational distinctions—Christians and Jews, Protestants and Catholics, Baptists and Lutherans—had a strong partisan cast. Those patterns have waned. But a new one has clearly emerged: the contrast between the voting behavior of the most active worshipers and everybody else in the past four presidential elections has widened when compared with modern historical levels. From 1952 through 1988, Democratic presidential candidates tended to fare only about 2 percentage points worse among regular churchgoers than among voters who attended church infrequently or not at all. Starting in 1992, the religion gap grew to an average of nearly 12 points.[65] The most religiously observant voters, almost irrespective of denomination, leaned to the Republican standard-bearer in the 2000 election, and even more so in 2004.

The reason is straightforward. Religious observance and political preference now are powerfully correlated. More than half of those who attend church weekly call themselves conservatives, four times the percentage of those who regard themselves as liberals. What has sent regular churchgoers to the right is the undeniable impact (on them) of the abortion issue most notably, but also other social and cultural concerns such as sex education and school prayer.[66]

---

64. See Hamilton (2006).

65. Galston and Kamarck (2005, pp. 43, 47–48). For parallel findings based on white voters only, see Fiorina, Abrams, and Pope (2006, pp. 132–34).

66. Bartels (2005) finds that the impact of social issues on party affiliation and presidential preference among regular churchgoers has more than doubled since 1984. Abortion remains the great wedge issue, splitting frequent church-attending white voters and those who seldom or never attend. According to Abramowitz and Saunders (2005), the former oppose legal abortion by 69 percent, the latter by only 22 percent. On how polarization between self-described conservatives and liberals seems to have broadened to encompass additional cultural issues, see Evans (2003, pp. 16–18, 30–32).

We are not yet convinced that faith-based forces have polarized the political parties more than other factors have.[67] The divorce between the adherents of "hard" and "soft" stances on questions of national security, for example, strikes us as no less consequential. Notice, moreover, that potent faith-based constituencies do not *always* skew a party's policies to the right. Religious conservatives in the Republican ranks, for example, have favored increasing antipoverty programs (even if they mean more debt or higher taxes), stricter environmental standards, and foreign aid (to combat problems such as HIV/AIDS).[68]

Also, pure polarization implies a symmetrical dynamic, in which more or less equally robust blocs of voters on *both* sides of the political spectrum are gravitating toward the poles. But while religious traditionalists appear to be flocking to the Republican Party, the "true loyalists" (pollster Stanley Greenberg's phrase) of the Democratic Party include more than secularists.[69] Millions of Protestants, "modernist" evangelicals, Vatican II Catholics, and non-Orthodox Jews regularly vote Democratic. Indeed, while losing the evangelical Protestant vote by more than three to one, John Kerry and George W. Bush split the mainline Protestant vote precisely down the middle.[70] This reality probably constrains the party from embracing a maximally secular agenda, even though the Democratic base is certainly loaded with staunch secularists.

Nonetheless, the concentration of fervent fundamentalists at the core of the Republican Party unquestionably matters. At a minimum, it has ensured that key symbolic issues—*Roe* v. *Wade,* end-of-life decisions, "intelligent design," bioethics, and so forth—form a distinct partisan fault line. And the valence effect of such issues for the party bases seems unlikely to diminish anytime soon.

---

67. Some multivariate analysis does suggest, though, that church attendance has had an increasingly distinct impact on voting. This appears to have been particularly true in 2004. See Pew Research Center (2005, p. 29). On the other hand, it turns out that white born-again Christians are even more polarized by income than are other white voters. For born-agains, the gap between high-income and low-income Republican Party identification is more than 30 percentage points, compared to only 20 points for other white voters. See McCarty, Poole, and Rosenthal (2006, pp. 100–01).

68. The Pew Research Center has developed a three-part classification of respondents with GOP allegiances. One of the groups, characterized by frequent attendance at church, Bible study, or prayer group meetings, appeared to be overwhelmingly (80 percent) in favor of the proposition that "the government should do more to help needy Americans even if it means going deeper into debt." Pew Research Center for the People and the Press, "Beyond Red vs. Blue," May 10, 2005 (people-press.org/reports/display.php3?ReportID=242).

69. Greenberg (2004).

70. See Green and others (2004).

Of course, these issues could recede somewhat if cross-cutting concerns that traditionally animated voters—perhaps, most notably, economic ones—regain their former dominance.

Although voting behavior continues to correlate with income levels, the dominance of pocketbook issues has declined relative to various other issues.[71] Indeed, there is considerable debate now about the actual political weight of economic concerns.[72] As both parties became "Keynesians" and learned to tame the business cycle, unemployment faded somewhat as a determinant in American elections. In the twenty-two years that spanned November 1982 and election day 2004, the U.S. economy was in recession a mere one-twentieth of the time. The political economy was altogether different in the four decades preceding 1982, when recessions afflicted the electorate more than one-fifth of the time. We might thus expect cultural themes with their religious overtones to remain prominent. On the other hand, Nolan McCarty, Keith T. Poole, and Howard Rosenthal find a suggestive correlation between the rise in polarization over the past three decades and the increase in economic inequality during that period. By contrast, in the years after World War II, when the New Deal coalition was alive and well, income and partisanship were only weakly correlated.[73]

HOW CONGRESS GETS ELECTED

In each of the first fifteen elections for the House of Representatives following World War II, either the Republicans or the Democrats gained an average of twenty-nine seats. In the past fifteen elections, the average switch was thirteen seats. By 2004, less than 10 percent of the House was being seriously contested. When the votes were counted, the composition of even gigantic delegations, such as California's, proved immutable. (None of California's fifty-three seats changed parties in 2004.) Competitive districts are vanishing.[74]

---

71. See Fiorina, Abrams, and Pope (2006, p. 136).

72. Bartels (2005) argues that white voters in the bottom third of the income distribution remain reliably Democratic, presumably because these voters remain preoccupied with long-standing economic concerns. Still, perceptions of economic self-interest, and the total shares of voters choosing a party affiliation for reasons of economic insecurity or risk-averseness, may not be quite the same in the post-Keynesian age.

73. McCarty, Poole, and Rosenthal (2006, chap. 3).

74. Earlier in this essay, we noted that a number of red-state congressional delegations are composed of Democratic as well as Republican members. A caveat: a few of these Democrats hold safe seats, in carefully contoured minority districts. Thus, the state delegations can appear to be more mixed than they otherwise would be.

Exactly what has eroded the competitiveness of congressional elections is the subject of much scholarly debate. One school of thought points to the way districts are delineated. Increasingly sophisticated computer software has refined the ability of political cartographers to map with pinpoint precision the spatial distribution of voters needed to maximize partisan advantage, and then to gerrymander the boundaries accordingly. Another school stresses the power of incumbency: The unmatched capacity of House incumbents to bankroll their reelections is at an all-time high.[75] Still another emphasizes the dynamics of political segregation, whereby politically homogenized districts develop when voters tip the balance by moving to be near fellow partisans.[76]

The alternative explanations hinge in part on methodological subtleties. To assess the impact of gerrymanders on the relative competitiveness of districts, for example, Alan Abramowitz has looked at the normalized presidential vote within districts before and after each redistricting (following each decennial census). He surmises that if partisan redistricting were the reason for the decline in competitive races, the number of competitive districts should have fallen every time. Finding no such decrease in 1992, he argues that other factors must be at work in the long-term loss of competitiveness.[77] Complicating Abramowitz's inference, however, is the effect of a significant third-party candidate, Ross Perot, in the 1992 election. Perot drew down the vote shares for both major-party candidates, thus making it seem as if more districts had been contestable.

Whatever the source of noncompetitive elections, a profusion of one-party districts drives moderates out of Congress.[78] In such districts, candidates have little incentive to reach out to voters across party lines. The imperative instead becomes to appeal to the base and preempt possible primary challenges from the extremes. The direct primary (or threat thereof), not the general election, becomes the defining political event. In theory, in a simple two-party electoral system the natural tendency of candidates competing for single-member districts is to move toward the center of the spectrum. But the balloting in primaries

75. Ornstein, Mann, and Malbin (2006).

76. See, for instance, Oppenheimer (2005). Also see Bill Bishop, "The Schism in U.S. Politics Begins at Home," *Austin American-Statesman,* April 4, 2004.

77. Abramowitz, Alexander, and Gunning (2005). Similarly, McCarty, Poole, and Rosenthal (2006, pp. 63–67) find that the curve representing party vote shares by congressional district virtually coincides with the curve representing vote shares by county, the boundaries of which are not much subject to political manipulation. This suggests that the congressional districting process contributes little to polarization.

78. For a contrary view, see King (1999).

often discourages this convergence. The electorate in these contests tends to be small (under 18 percent now, even in presidential primaries), unrepresentative, and highly motivated. Candidates protect their flanks by positioning themselves further to the left or right of the general public on issues that the primary clientele regards as litmus tests.[79]

The number of Democratic Party primaries for House seats remained about the same in the thirty years from 1962 to 1992, but on the Republican side the number rose steeply, and the dreaded *chance* of being ousted in a primary, however long the odds, now chills would-be centrists in both parties. The unintended consequences of this institution in American elections have given pause to political scientists ever since V. O. Key began calling attention to its risks some fifty years ago. Particularly where interparty competition is lacking (as in many congressional districts), the direct primary stokes the process of polarization.

So What?

When all is said and done, the developments we have reviewed to this point are only cause for serious concern if they can be demonstrated to imperil the democratic process or the prospects of attending to urgent policy priorities. That demonstration is anything but unambiguous or simple to supply.

To begin with, some of what passes for dysfunctional polarization actually may be little more than the downside of unified party control of the executive and legislative branches. Unified government—as in the first six years of the Bush presidency but also the first two of the Clinton presidency—permitted partisans to move their political agendas further to the left or right than would have been possible otherwise. Divided party control of government, on the other hand, compels accommodation. The GOP's victory in 1994, for example, pushed Clinton toward the center. If the Democrats had regained at least one chamber of Congress in 2004, the result almost certainly would have been to force Bush toward middle ground in his second term. Divided government, in short, can temper a "polarizing" president.

Whether such tempering is always for the best is debatable. (Try to picture, hypothetically, a tempered Abraham Lincoln "triangulating" with a Democratic

---

79. While this "primary threat" thesis is intuitively plausible, the direct evidence supporting it is mixed at best. Much rests on the extent to which incumbents act preemptively to ward off challenges that would otherwise occur. Only sophisticated interviewing can document these "non-events." See, however, Burden (2001).

House or Senate in 1862.) Partisan polarization can have advantages, not just liabilities. Inasmuch as the Democratic and Republican parties differ more visibly, they offer voters "a choice, not an echo," to borrow Goldwater's words. There is something to be said for that clarification. Was the public philosophy of the Democrats more intelligible in the days when the party had to accommodate the likes of southern segregationists under its big tent? For years political scientists had lamented the lack of a "responsible" party system in the United States. Now, with the political parties more coherent, centralized, unified, and disciplined—in sum, a bit more reminiscent of the majoritarian style in some European parliamentary regimes—analysts and pundits rhapsodize about the days of Tweedledum and Tweedledee and their old incongruous ad hoc coalitions, deference to seniority and debilitating filibusters, weaker legislative party leadership, and often sloppy bipartisan compromises.[80]

Accountability

But what if a good deal of the public agenda is being hijacked by the polarized militants that rule the parties or, at any rate, densely populate their bases? Surely, as many critics have argued, there have been glaring episodes of this sort. The Clinton impeachment imbroglio was one. In December 1998 the House of Representatives voted to sack the president, with 98 percent of the Republican members concluding that Clinton's conduct rose to the level of high crime. But this verdict of "the people's house" did not align with the views of the people. From the eruption of the sex scandal in January 1998 through the end of the Senate trial in February 1999, every national poll showed the public opposed to impeachment and conviction, typically by margins of two to one.[81] In 2005 congressional intervention in the Terri Schiavo case provided another unsettling illustration of how Congress could lurch in one direction while lopsided majorities in public opinion polls leaned the other way.

Occasionally, the policy outcomes have seemed disconnected from prevailing public preferences in less ephemeral controversies as well. For quite a few years, passage of national energy legislation was held hostage in part by an unresolved dispute of far greater interest to strict environmentalists than to average motorists:

---

80. Just how cohesive and disciplined the congressional parties really are as of this writing is a very debatable matter. After Tom DeLay ceased to be the Republican majority leader, House Republicans began resembling, at crucial times, the disheveled majorities of yore—unable even to agree on a federal budget in the spring of 2006, for instance.

81. Jacobson (2000, p. 10).

namely, whether to permit exploration for oil and gas anywhere in the Arctic National Wildlife Refuge. Similarly, a minority view presently governs stem cell research. As much as 58 percent of the public would prefer to allow research that might result in new cures for diseases than to preserve the human embryos used in the process.[82] Yet so far, the opponents have held the upper hand, limiting government-funded research only to existing cell lines from embryos that have already been destroyed.

Exhibits like these are proof perfect to many critics that the political process is now routinely out of touch and unaccountable. But is it? So sweeping a verdict remains unwarranted unless the data supporting it can be taken to scale. A much wider range of policy debates has to be parsed, including truly big-ticket items, not primarily smaller-bore questions like the Schiavo controversy or even the Clinton impeachment fracas.

A recent attempt to do just that is the engaging book *Off Center: The Republican Revolution and the Erosion of Democracy* by political scientists Jacob S. Hacker and Paul Pierson. In this ambitious treatise, the authors argue that mainstream popular sentiments failed to inform, much less decide, virtually every major policy initiative of the GOP during the George W. Bush presidency.[83] According to Hacker and Pierson, for example, the prescription drug bill, Bush's energy legislation, and the proposed reform of Social Security—and more— were pushed relentlessly on a nonconsenting public.

Arguably, however, just the opposite was the case. The addition of prescription drug benefits to Medicare was a Bush campaign promise in 2000. More than anything else, its inspiration came from his strategy of "compassionate conservatism"— an effort to attract middle-of-the-road voters by co-opting the Democrats on an issue dear to them. The Bush administration's energy proposals reflected, for the most part, precisely what American consumers *really* demand—namely, continued production of low-cost energy, and no meaningful pressure to conserve it. Hacker and Pierson claim that strong majorities preferred something called "conservation."[84] But an expressed preference for that slogan signifies next to nothing. The effective method for saving fuel is a rising price, either induced by free-market forces or by taxes, both of which are inimical to most voters. Bush's

---

82. Pew Center for the People and the Press, "The 2004 Political Landscape: Evenly Divided and Increasingly Polarized," November 5, 2003 (people-press.org/reports/display.php3? ReportID=196).

83. Hacker and Pierson (2005).

84. Hacker and Pierson (2005, p. 83).

Social Security plan went nowhere, partly because it met unified resistance from the Democrats, but more fundamentally because most Americans were opposed to it.[85] As for Bush's foreign policy, the Iraq project—in fact, the president's whole approach to foreign affairs—was basically put to a referendum in the elections of 2002 and 2004. Realistically assessed, none of these initiatives turns out to have been an affront to popular sovereignty.

Gridlock?

Maybe the critique of policymaking in a polarized political environment has to take a different tack: the trouble is not that the government is out of step with the people, but that it is not getting much done in their interest, whether they like it or not.[86]

The public may not relish the hard choices that are needed to ensure the solvency or soundness of the Social Security system, but serious policymakers have to see them through anyway. The public may not welcome the pain that a genuine energy conservation plan inflicts—a stiffer excise tax on gasoline, say—but policymakers do society a disservice if they perennially chicken out. It may well be that intensely partisan politics throws up additional roadblocks to certain *un*popular measures that a responsible government ought to take for the sake of the public good in the long run. We will circle back to this important consideration shortly. Beforehand, though, we urge caution against the conventional supposition that political polarization (at least to its present extent) is necessarily a recipe for policy paralysis.

Whatever else the overall legislative record of recent years may show, sclerosis has not been a distinguishing characteristic. Reform of the welfare system, substantial tax reductions, big trade agreements, a great expansion of federal intervention in local public education, important course corrections in foreign policy, reorganization of the intelligence bureaus, a significant campaign finance law, new rules governing bankruptcy and class-action litigation, a huge new cabinet department, massive enlargement of Medicare—for better or worse, all these milestones, and others, were achieved despite polarized politics.

85. Interestingly, the Bush Social Security venture might have stirred less public skepticism if it had been sold in a stealthier manner. Bush did *not* claim that private accounts would fix the program's eventual insolvency. That bit of honesty was commendable, but it led people to wonder why the privatization was a pressing imperative in the first place. We are indebted to our Brookings colleague Peter Orszag for this insight.

86. For evidence that elite polarization leads to some forms of policy gridlock, see McCarty, Poole, and Rosenthal (2006, pp. 175–89).

Some of these exploits probably were only possible *because* of disciplined ("polarized") voting by the congressional majority party, as the work of David W. Brady and Craig Volden suggests.[87] (That was certainly true of the 2003 tax reduction bill, for example.)[88] Several, though, occurred because partisan polarities, though significant on many issues, were not consistently so dramatic and all-encompassing as to cause the wheels of government to grind to a full stop. It is not always easy, as a matter of fact, to find brilliant daylight between the official postures of the political parties.

Take the Republicans. There was a time when limited government was a distinguishing aspiration of Republican presidents and congressional leaders. That austere orientation lost allure after January 1996, with the debacle of the government shutdown. Today, big spending and big bureaucracy are hallmarks of the politically chastened GOP. Witness the party's complicity in the largest expansion of an entitlement program (the Medicare prescription drug benefit) in forty years, the profligacy of the Republican-controlled Congress on everything from highways and farm subsidies to reconstruction assistance for the Gulf states inundated by Hurricane Katrina, the king-sized Department of Homeland Security, the stiff statism of the USA Patriot Act, and the No Child Left Behind law's federal tutelage of local education policy.[89] By the time President Bush delivered his State of the Union address in January 2006, some of his themes (the nation's "addiction to oil," for example, and the need to bolster America's "competitiveness") sounded as if they had been lifted from the scripts of Democratic administrations and congressional leaders in decades past.

The Democrats, to be sure, have dissented on more than a few high-profile matters—for example, by defending the status quo for Social Security, second-guessing the Bush administration's policy on Iraq, and preferring to nationalize end-of-life rules for fetuses but not for the sources of embryonic stem cells or for patients in vegetative states. But more than is commonly acknowledged, the two

87. Brady and Volden (2006).

88. The Republican vote on this second round of Bush tax reductions was 224 to 1 in the House, and 48 to 3 in the Senate.

89. To quote Representative Jeff Flake (R-Ariz.), "the material that [now] comes from the Republican caucus is not to call for the elimination of this program or that, it's to brag that we have increased the budget for education by 144 percent." See Sheryl Gay Stolberg, "The Revolution That Wasn't," *New York Times,* February 13, 2005. The 2005 transportation bill was larded with 6,000 pet projects at a cost of $286 billion. In the fall of 2005 the supposedly disciplined Republican-led House proved unable to reduce the growth in mandatory government spending by even as little as one-tenth of 1 percent.

parties also appear to have crawled toward common ground on a number of sensitive issues.

However hard it was for many Democrats to swallow, say, welfare reform or the North American Free Trade Agreement (NAFTA) in the mid-1990s, these once-defining disputes had cooled by the end of the decade.[90] Similarly, the crime issue, which the Republicans had exploited so effectively in the 1988 election, subsequently lost much of its partisan luster. Helpfully, crime rates declined, but also the Democrats inoculated themselves by enacting a far-reaching anti-crime bill in 1994.

In the 2004 election cycle, no serious contender for the Democratic presidential nomination campaigned to overturn the 1996 welfare law or NAFTA. For all their gripes about "tax cuts for the rich," the Democrats effectively embraced much of Bush's tax reduction. True, Senator Kerry favored bringing the top tax rate on incomes above $200,000 back up to 39.6 percent, but that would still have been a far cry from the 70 percent rate that Ronald Reagan had slashed. The Democrats fumed that, over the ensuing ten years, a $1.35 trillion deficit loomed on account of the Bush administration's fiscal policies, but Kerry's proposed tax and spending package was estimated to spill almost the same amount of red ink ($1.3 trillion).[91] Bush came out against same-sex marriages—but so did Kerry. And later, on the red-hot issue of immigration policy, key liberal Democrats such as Senator Edward M. Kennedy (of Massachusetts) sought and shared middle ground with George W. Bush.

There has been enough partisan convergence (albeit selective, tenuous, opportunistic, or episodic) to secure key pieces of legislation. Lest we forget, the 2001 tax cut would not have passed if an abundance of Democratic senators

90. The decline of various divisive issues, and the partisan convergence on some of them, has been observed by Dionne (2004, pp. 17–19), among others. Dionne notes that welfare reform was clearly one such issue for the Democrats. The earned income tax credit was one for the Republicans. Concurring with President Clinton's expansion of that program, Bush in 2000 affirmed that slowing its payments would "balance the budget on the backs of the poor." For his part, Al Gore wound up endorsing government assistance, within limits, to the work of religious charities. And the Republicans at the end of the Clinton years were proposing nearly as much federal spending on education as the Democrats.

91. Jonathan Weisman, "Kerry's Dueling Promises on Economy," *Washington Post,* August 25, 2004. The composition, of course, was different. Kerry proposed more than $770 billion in new spending over the course of the decade, Bush much less. Bush's tax cuts were estimated to reduce revenue by more than a trillion dollars; Kerry's tax plans represented about half a trillion dollars in reduced revenue. See also Robert Pear, "Two Rivals Push Domestic Plans, But Say Little of Big Price Tag," *New York Times,* October 13, 2004.

had not voted for it.[92] That fall, a total of 193 Democratic lawmakers joined 260 Republicans in embracing the Patriot Act. One hundred and twenty-nine Democrats sided with 255 Republicans to create the Homeland Security behemoth. Fifty-two Republicans voted with 246 Democrats to enact the McCain-Feingold campaign finance reform. In both chambers, Republicans and Democrats voted in almost equal numbers to adopt the No Child Left Behind scheme.[93] In July 2002, the Sarbanes-Oxley rules for corporate governance were enacted almost unanimously by both chambers.[94]

Displays of bipartisanship, often yielding decidedly centrist results, have not stopped there. With enough Republican defections, majorities in both chambers declined to approve a constitutional amendment barring gay marriages.[95] The Central American Free Trade Agreement (CAFTA) would not have been ratified comfortably in the summer of 2005 if eleven Democratic senators had not voted with the Republican majority.[96] A nearly unanimous Senate voted to set new limits on the interrogation of detainees suspected of terrorism.[97] Liberal interest groups and evangelicals have teamed up to lobby for projects like the Aspire Act, an antipoverty bill cosponsored by Senators Jon Corzine (D-N.J.) and Rick Santorum (R-Pa.).[98] The Republican-led House—a body alleged to be the wholly owned subsidiary of the Christian right—passed a stem cell research bill more liberal than the Bush administration's policy.[99]

92. Twelve Democrats sided with forty-six Republicans.

93. This roll call was particularly striking. In the House, 198 Democrats and 183 Republicans voted for the Bush No Child Left Behind bill. In the Senate, the bill garnered the votes of forty-three Democrats and forty-four Republicans.

94. The vote on Sarbanes-Oxley, on July 25, was unanimous in the Senate and 423 to 3 in the House.

95. In the House, for example, twenty-seven Republicans voted against the amendment with 158 Democrats and one independent. The vote fell forty-nine short of the required two-thirds for adoption. The twenty-seven GOP defections were enough to confirm that the gay-marriage ban would not come down to a neat party-line vote.

96. Reflecting the enduring residue of the NAFTA debate as well as heightened partisan divisions, however, only a handful of House Democrats supported CAFTA. Even normally pro-trade "New Democrats" voted against it in droves.

97. Forty-six Republicans, forty-three Democrats, and one independent supported the bill.

98. Ray Boshara, "Share the Ownership," *Washington Post,* February 8, 2005.

99. Fifty Republicans sided with 187 Democrats. The bill would allow stem cells to be derived from human embryos that have been donated from in vitro fertilization clinics, were created for the purposes of fertility treatments, or exceeded the clinical need of the individuals seeking such treatments.

Congress: Hell's Kitchen?

Even if the contemporary Congress has been productive, its deliberative process has not been pretty—and some prominent scholars are convin .ed that the sausage-making activities, if not the sausages themselves, are uglier now than they used to be. Lawmaking by "stealth," these writers submit, has become standard operating procedure, resulting in less transparency, more cooking of cost estimates and budget numbers, greater use of sleepers tucked into omnibus packages, closed rules, the drafting of legislation in oligarchic conference committees, and, in most instances, imperious exclusion of the parliamentary minority.[100]

One presumably simple gauge of the impact of heightened partisanship on congressional deliberations is a measurable increase in petulance. In floor debates, for instance, the number of words ruled either out of order or "taken down" rose after 1985.[101] The incivility is vexing, yet surely some of what Democrats regard as uncivil conduct by their congressional adversaries these days simply has to do with the Democratic Party's uncustomary minority status.[102]

Arguably, a good deal of procedural fairness has been lost in the contemporary Congress. When the Democrats were in power, they were known to stretch roll calls in the House from the customary fifteen minutes to thirty in order to marshal the votes needed to pass the party's preferred budget legislation. Republicans, including then representative Dick Cheney, deplored this practice and called it a serious abuse of power. Since 2001, however, House Republican leaders have sometimes held votes open for hours.[103] Republicans may have felt powerless in conference committees when Democrats were the ruling majority, but these days the Republican majority has gone a step further, sometimes excluding Democratic members almost entirely. Still, some of the Democrats' grievances are reminiscent of those harbored by the old House Republicans who spent professional lifetimes marginalized before 1995.[104] The parallels aside, an unfamiliar

100. See, for example, Hacker and Pierson (2005, pp. 154–55); Quirk (2005); Mann and Ornstein (2006); Sinclair (2006).

101. Jamieson and Falk (2000, p. 106).

102. Expressing the views of many Democrats, Representative David Price (D-N.C.) declared that party discipline enforced by the Republican leadership has "gone beyond its proper bounds." Quoted in David S. Broder, "The Polarization Express," *Washington Post,* December 12, 2004.

103. Norman Ornstein and Thomas E. Mann, "If You Give a Congressman a Cookie," *New York Times,* January 19, 2006.

104. Connelly and Pitney (1994).

degree of majority-party cohesion, discipline, bicameral coordination, and central control is bound to beget a discontented minority.[105]

There is, of course, some irony in this situation. Unhappy Congress watchers nowadays sometimes lament the same "new" institutional practices that liberal observers fifty years ago would have welcomed. The end of the seniority system for committee chairmanships, for instance, is presently seen as regrettable. Ambitious members seeking these jobs tend to be hardliners who have ingratiated themselves with the party leadership. A half-century ago, though, the complaint among progressives was that Congress could not move priorities such as civil rights legislation because party leaders and caucuses were powerless to dislodge obstructionist southern chairmen of the House Rules Committee and the judiciary committees.

The minority in the 109th Congress, in any event, was not entirely enfeebled under the new order of things. Showing unusual solidarity, Democrats successfully thwarted Bush's Social Security plan. And in the House, the Democrats, like the Republicans, empowered their leadership to discourage dissent. Stray members inclined to work too closely with the GOP were threatened with the loss of committee seats.[106]

A crucial component of the deliberative activity of Congress is the oversight function. Congressional oversight of the executive branch has faltered in the past half-dozen years.[107] Some missteps by the intelligence agencies and bureaus charged with homeland security, for instance, might have been averted if congressional watchdogs had performed their duties more assiduously. Yet how much of this neglect can be imputed to "polarization," rather than simply the effects of unified party control of both branches, is by no means an easy call. It is inaccurate, furthermore, to portray the Republican-controlled Congress as invariably supine. Early in 2006, for example, an investigating committee of the House issued a report on the executive branch's response to the Hurricane Katrina disaster. A more blistering congressional critique of executive mismanagement in modern times would be hard to find.[108]

105. On institutional changes that have facilitated party discipline over time, see, for instance, Rohde (1991).

106. Jim VandeHei and Charles Babington, "Newly Emboldened Congress Has Dogged Bush This Year," *Washington Post,* December 23, 2005.

107. See, for instance, on this point, Sinclair (2005, p. 251).

108. U.S. House of Representatives (2006). In another indication that Congress was reaffirming its oversight responsibilities in 2006, the Senate Intelligence Committee, led by Senator Pat Roberts (R-Kans.), broke with the Bush administration's approach to its domestic eavesdropping program.

It is said that partisan polarization prevents lawmakers from adequately scrubbing, sanitizing, or simplifying their legislation. The Medicare prescription drug provisions are cited as a particularly egregious example. But how does this charge stack up against the counterfactual? Suppose the half-trillion-dollar drug bill had not been flogged by GOP powerbrokers but crafted instead in a convivial bipartisan fashion. It might well have emerged just as flawed—and almost certainly more extravagant.

Today's sorry legislative stories should be benchmarked by yesterday's. Think back to the Carter years and the convoluted National Energy Act of 1978, or further back to Lyndon Johnson and his Great Society's Community Action Program and the Model Cities law. Those enactments were legendary for their unanticipated complications and consequences.[109] It is easy, in other words, to commit what could be called the "Golden Age fallacy" about Capitol Hill. The entrenched Democratic barons who dominated the legislative branch four or five decades ago were just as capable of making a hash of congressional projects (as they did, with fatal consequences later on, in the flood planes of Louisiana, for instance).[110]

All this suggests that, at a minimum, the much-bewailed partisan divide in American politics may not have impaired the democratic policy process quite as consummately as many believe.

Four Risks

To say that the impairment has been exaggerated is not to conclude, however, that there is none at all. Increased polarization of the political parties carries at least four risks. First, it complicates the task of addressing certain long-range domestic policy problems, particularly the big ones that cannot be solved without altering the established distribution of benefits in the modern welfare state. Second, it can mar the implementation of a steady, resolute foreign policy and national security strategy. Third, partisan excesses can do lasting damage to vulnerable institutions, most notably the judiciary. Finally, there is the distinct possibility that partisan antagonisms, and especially

109. On the Community Action Program, see, for example, Moynihan (1970). On the Carter energy legislation, see Nivola (1986).

110. For an eerie reminder of this epoch and its underside, see the extraordinary account by Michael Grunwald and Susan B. Glasser, "The Slow Drowning of New Orleans," *Washington Post,* October 9, 2005.

the slash-and-burn tactics that polarized parties routinely adopt, erode public trust in government.[111]

Restructuring Entitlements: From Tall Order to Mission Impossible

The United States, like many other countries, will not be able to sustain the impending demographically induced bulge in the cost of extant social insurance programs without either rethinking them or, alternatively, imposing draconian tax increases or sacrificing a multitude of basic public obligations, starting with national defense.[112] One-party forays are ill-suited to the challenge of meaningfully addressing social entitlements. In the past dozen years, major presidential initiatives of that sort have repeatedly faltered. With no buy-in from the GOP, Clinton's proposed overhaul of the nation's health care system crashed and burned. For want of any Democratic support, Bush's effort to modify the Social Security program fared no better. If these debacles are what members of Congress have in mind when they assert "now we've got gridlock," they are right.[113]

Projects like updating Social Security or health insurance—or for that matter reforming farm subsidies, the national tax structure, and most other large, institutionalized claims on the federal fisc—tend to encounter popular skepticism and so require political cover for their proponents. Bipartisan cooperation is essential to face these daunting tasks. Inasmuch as the vendettas of polarized politicians now frustrate even the faintest semblance of bipartisan deal-making, the nation will be the worse off because of them.

When Politics No Longer Stops at the Water's Edge

The same can be said for the thankless job of U.S. international relations. Ostensibly, no great difference on foreign policy sundered the parties in the 2004 campaign. On fighting terrorism, the Democratic platform sounded stout: The government should "take all needed steps."[114] On Iraq, the Democratic

---

111. Based on their analysis of the interaction between increases in inequality and immigration, McCarty, Poole, and Rosenthal (2006) find a correlation between intensifying polarization and diminishing support for policies (such as a higher minimum wage) that supposedly reduce inequality. Along with other aspects of their carefully argued book, the assessment of this claim awaits scrutiny by other scholars with comparable methodological sophistication.

112. Rivlin and Sawhill (2004).

113. Senator James Jeffords (independent of Vermont), quoted in David von Drehle, "Political Split Is Pervasive: Clash of Cultures Is Driven by Targeted Appeals and Reinforced by Geography," *Washington Post*, April 25, 2004.

114. Democratic National Committee (2004, p. 18).

presidential candidate (in his words) was "not talking about leaving," but "about winning."[115] Scratch the surface, however, and a wide breach could be discerned. As we reported earlier, with respect to how the United States should respond to the security threats posed by rogue states and Islamic extremism, perceptions by the party bases were worlds apart.[116]

The message emanating from leading advocacy groups in Democratic circles has been that military action to oust dangerous despots and regimes that harbor terrorists is counterproductive. Here, according to Peter Beinart of the *New Republic,* was how the most prominent liberal organization, MoveOn, viewed a U.S. attack on Afghanistan after September 11: "If we retaliate by bombing Kabul and kill people oppressed by the Taliban, we become like the terrorists we oppose."[117]

The Democratic establishment, to be sure, never went that far. In the murkier dilemma of how to handle Saddam Hussein, twenty-nine Democratic senators (and the leading Democratic candidate in the 2004 race) voted with forty-eight Republicans in October 2002 to authorize the use of force. Yet the main thing to note about such glimmers of bipartisanship is their inconstancy. Three years later, with the armed forces conducting a high-stakes counterinsurgency in Iraq, Senate Democrats voted overwhelmingly to develop a timetable for withdrawing the troops.[118] It turns out, in short, that now these members *were* "talking about leaving"—and not "about winning."

The purpose of these reflections is not to side with one group or another about whether it was wise to invade Iraq or Afghanistan, or about other fateful policy determinations in the post-9/11 context. Our point is only that stability and perseverance in the pursuit of a foreign policy are as necessary in today's treacherous world as during the showdown with fascism in the 1940s and with communism afterwards. A course of action buffeted by polarized politicians, and tugged in contradictory directions, is no course whatsoever.

115. "Transcript: The First Presidential Debate," *Washington Post,* September 30, 2004.

116. In May 2005, the Pew Research Center came to this blunt conclusion: "Foreign affairs assertiveness now almost completely distinguishes Republican-oriented voters from Democratic-oriented voters. . . . In contrast, attitudes relating to religion and social issues are not nearly as important in determining party affiliation." Pew Research Center for the People and the Press, "Beyond Red vs. Blue," May 10, 2005 (people-press.org/reports/display.php3?ReportID=242).

117. Peter Beinart, "A Fighting Faith: An Argument for a New Liberalism," *New Republic,* December 13, 2004.

118. The vote on this amendment to a 2006 appropriations bill, November 15, 2005, counted thirty-eight Democratic senators, one Republican, and one independent in favor. Only five Democrats joined the fifty-three Republicans voting "nay."

Abusing the Judiciary

There is reason to fear that if partisan contestation is unrestrained it can wreck more than decorum in the legislative branch; it could weaken other parts of the government—sensitive executive agencies and, above all, the federal bench.

A polarized Congress and its retinue of strident advocacy groups are bruising the bureaucracy and the courts in a number of ways. The new interpretation of senatorial advice and consent, seemingly held by much of the parliamentary opposition, was summed up by Senate minority leader Harry M. Reid (D-Nev.) in 2005: "The president is not entitled to very much deference in staffing the third branch of government, the judiciary."[119] The grueling and often acrimonious process of confirming presidential appointments has increased vacancy rates in several judicial circuits.[120] Under George W. Bush, rates of confirmation for appellate court nominees have been the lowest of the past half-century.[121] Bracing for pitched battles over Supreme Court nominees, the White House repairs to stealth candidates—ones with unknown views or zipped lips. At least one recent nominee (Harriet Miers) had a paper trail so thin that her basic qualifications for the job were a mystery to many.[122]

On top of this deterioration, the nature of rhetorical assaults on the judiciary took in 2005 an inflammatory turn not heard in a long while. A member of the Senate leadership referred to one of the Supreme Court justices as "a disgrace."[123] At another point, House majority leader Tom DeLay (R-Tex.) threatened unspecified retribution against judges involved in the Terri Schiavo case, and declaimed that Justice Anthony Kennedy should be held "accountable" for using international law in deciding a recent death-penalty case.[124] Utterances like these signaled a degree of partisan distemper increasingly careless about the separation of powers. "Our independent judiciary is the most respected branch of our government, and the envy of the world," cautions Theodore B. Olson. It is also a delicate one, not to be trifled with.

---

119. *Congressional Record,* daily ed., September 20, 2005, p. S10214.

120. Binder and Maltzman (2005).

121. Sarah A. Binder, Forrest Maltzman, and Alan Murphy, "History's Verdict," *New York Times,* May 19, 2005.

122. See Stuart Taylor Jr., "Opening Argument: Does Miers Have What It Takes to Excel on the Bench?" *National Journal,* October 15, 2005.

123. Theodore B. Olson, "Lay Off Our Judiciary," *Wall Street Journal,* April 21, 2005.

124. Charles Krauthammer, "Judicial Insanity," *Washington Post,* April 22, 2005.

More Distrust

One way to regard the current state of America's political parties is that their polarization tends to alienate and exclude ordinary citizens. "Most Americans," says Fiorina, "are somewhat like the unfortunate citizens of some third-world countries who try to stay out of the crossfire while left-wing guerrillas and right-wing death squads shoot at each other."[125] But another way to view the belligerents is that they actually interest and engage *more* voters—including more of the average sort, not just fanatics of the left and right.[126]

Inclusion of the fanatics is itself a possible net benefit. Better to pitch partisan tents inclusive enough for society's keenly ideological tribes than to further radicalize them by freezing them out. As Jonathan Rauch, a Brookings guest scholar and correspondent for the *Atlantic Monthly,* conjectured in a brilliant article in 2005, "On balance it is probably healthier if religious conservatives are inside the political system than if they operate as insurgents and provocateurs on the outside." When "the parties engage fierce activists" even at the risk of eclipsing some "tame centrists," Rauch concludes, "that is probably better for the social peace than the other way around."[127]

Even if the polar party system overrepresents, more than domesticates, the most fervid activists, it has not bored everybody else. The hotly contested 2004 election produced an impressive turnout, 59 percent—nearly 5 percentage points more than four years earlier. Fired-up party organizations managed to generate the remarkable increase in participation, often through old-fashioned get-out-the-vote methods (face-to-face contact between campaign workers and prospective voters) not seen on so large a scale since the heyday of the old party machines.[128] Both sides worked feverishly. The Democratic vote increased from 51 million in 2000 to 57 million. The Republican vote surged from 50.5 million to nearly 61 million. Figures of that magnitude suggest that a lot of average voters, not just those at the extremes, were successfully mobilized.[129]

125. Fiorina, Abrams, and Pope (2006, p. 8).
126. On how issue polarization helped explain the 2004 increase in voter turnout, see Abramowitz and Stone (2005).
127. Jonathan Rauch, "Bipolar Disorder," *Atlantic Monthly,* January/February 2005, p. 110.
128. Michael P. McDonald, "The Numbers Prove That 2004 May Signal More Voter Interest," *Milwaukee Journal Sentinel,* November 27, 2004.
129. The figures are all the more remarkable considering the massive mobility of the U.S. population. With more than 39 million Americans changing their place of residence over the previous years, the negative implications for voter registration could have depressed turnout well below the 59 percent level.

If polarized parties are what can get 120.3 million Americans to cast ballots—the largest number in U.S. history—why worry? Because a healthy civic culture ought to do more than bestir voters; it should build their trust in the nation's political institutions. It is in this respect that, alas, querulous partisanship can become corrosive. An abundance of nasty campaign advertising, negative news media slants, and outbursts by truculent politicians does not necessarily discourage people from voting, but a citizenry ingesting a steady diet of partisan vitriol may nonetheless grow disenchanted and cynical.[130] The fact that bodies such as the U.S. Congress consequently operate under a cloud of public mistrust is far from ideal.[131]

Conclusions

The politics of the United States today are organized by two parties that exhibit somewhat greater clarity and cohesion than they did through most of the second half of the twentieth century. While the policy distinctions between them at the programmatic level are often a lot less bright than many onlookers like to proclaim, the distinctions are plain enough where it counts: on particular issues that motivate the opposing sets of active partisans and also bond significant blocs of ordinary voters more faithfully to one side or the other. Not only that, but the two camps are showing signs of territorial differentiation, so that the ideological proclivities in the electorate and the political geography seem increasingly entwined. In these respects, it is correct to say the nation is more polarized than it has been in roughly a generation.

To call these conditions a culture war, however, is melodramatic, a point that Morris P. Fiorina and Matthew S. Levendusky revisit in this volume. A plurality of the electorate continues to be politically moderate and unaligned. Few if any states resemble the homogeneous polities of years past (the old one-party South, for example). For every defining issue that separates Democrats from Republicans at present, there seem to be almost as many that have long ceased to be sources of discord. And certainly the contemporary "war" between the parties is, by historical standards, a mild one—particularly in comparison with the maelstroms of the nineteenth century. Then, it was not uncommon for the backers of a presidential candidate to publicly accuse a rival of being an

---

130. See Dionne (2004).

131. See Hibbing and Theiss-Morse (1995, pp. 1–3); King (1997). In a more recent book, Hibbing and Thiess-Morse (2002) link public distrust to the perceived level of political controversy.

alcoholic, having a bigamist wife, or committing serial murders (to cite just a few slurs circulated by the pamphleteers for Andrew Jackson and John Quincy Adams in the election of 1828).[132] The tone of the current times can be disagreeable, but frankly, it sounds tame in comparison with the rants that, say, John Adams's supporters hurled at Thomas Jefferson in 1796; they would "blister the hairs off a dog's back," as Bill Clinton put it. The importance of placing today's partisanship in proper historical context is spelled out later in this book in an essay by David W. Brady of Stanford University and Hahrie C. Han of Wellesley College.

Moreover, the amount of mischief actually caused by political polarization in recent years should be kept in perspective. Mainstream voters have not stayed home in disgust in recent elections. On the contrary, they have turned out in greater numbers. True, their preferences have sometimes received short shrift amid the partisan altercations in Washington (there is no other way to describe, for example, the Clinton impeachment fight or the Bush administration's stance on stem cell research). But such departures aside, we are not persuaded that the overall supply of public policy in the current climate has been unrelated to popular demand, or that the supply has been meager.

The reasons we reach this conclusion are straightforward. For all the angst about paralytic polarization, the volume of policy items on which the parties have come to considerable consensus over the years is too often underestimated. Bipartisanship is stumbling these days, but occasionally it still happens, and continues to get some significant things done. Polarized though they are, the political parties remain locked in tight competition. Inevitably, their parity means that presidential candidates on both sides simply cannot be oblivious to voters in the malleable middle all of the time. There is just no other logical way to account for key policy initiatives such as Bush's expensive prescription drug benefit. (Yes, the legislation itself was adopted on "polarized" party-line votes. The original inspiration, though, was a calculated appeal to the electoral center.)

Parity also means that moderates in Congress, though an increasingly endangered species, retain considerable leverage. The arithmetic is elementary: no matter how polar the parties may be, an evenly divided legislature enables even a dwindling band of centrists to hold the balance of power. Clearly, the moderates have kept polarized politics from deadlocking the Senate; their pivotal role,

132. Paul Johnson, "Once upon a Time," *Wall Street Journal,* October 20, 2004.

for instance, shelved parliamentary tactics that, in the end, might have brought most legislative business to a standstill.[133]

Even with all these reassurances in mind, however, some implications of partisan polarization are sobering. We fear that the current pattern will delay, perhaps indefinitely, serious work on the fiscally exacting social programs such as Social Security, Medicare, and Medicaid over the ensuing decades. Discharging that politically perilous responsibility will almost certainly call for a greater measure of bipartisan comity than has been mustered in the past dozen years. We fret, also, that sustaining a steady national security posture and foreign policy may become infeasible when partisan dissension knows no bounds. And we are uneasy with the way Washington's polemicists of both the right and left take liberties with fragile institutions such as the independent judicial branch and abet a general loss of trust in the nation's public life.

It is crucial, therefore, to gain a better understanding of how these problems arose. The rest of this volume offers some leads. E. J. Dionne Jr., a senior fellow at the Brookings Institution, provides a chapter on the increasingly important impact of religious voters and groups. Diana C. Mutz, a professor at the University of Pennsylvania, explores the influence of the news media. Thomas E. Mann, another veteran Brookings scholar, probes the implications of gerrymanders, primary challenges, and safe congressional seats.

Following each of these contributions (and those mentioned earlier by Fiorina and Levendusky and by Brady and Han) are commentaries by other authorities who offer additional viewpoints on the causes of polarization. Andrew Kohut, director of the Pew Research Center for the People and the Press, and Alan Wolfe of the Boisi Center for Religion and American Public Life at Boston College provide reflections on Dionne's assessment of the role of religious voters. Gregg Easterbrook, a visiting scholar at the Brookings Institution, and Thomas Rosenstiel, director of the Project for Excellence in Journalism in Washington, suggest that the media do not polarize the public as much as they reflect the polarization already present. Professor Gary C. Jacobson of the University of California, San Diego, takes up Mann's essay on the role of congressional redistricting, and Thomas B. Edsall of Columbia University discusses alternative sources of polarization.

---

133. We refer here, of course, to the "gang of 14's" compromise, in 2005 and 2006, on the Senate majority's so-called "nuclear option" to bar minority filibusters against Supreme Court nominees. This rule change would have triggered a countertactic by the Democratic opposition: shutting down the progress of practically all other Senate business.

Jacobson and Alan Abramowitz debate Fiorina and Levendusky's conclusion that the level of political polarization is modest in the U.S. electorate. Carl M. Cannon of the *National Journal* and James E. Campbell, a political scientist at the University of Buffalo, review Brady and Han's chapter.

From these accounts, scholars, policymakers, and interested citizens will learn more about how to locate and assess the political system's malfunctions, and what remedies might be worth considering.

References

Abramowitz, Alan I., Brad Alexander, and Matthew Gunning. 2005. "Incumbency, Redistricting, and the Decline of Competition in U.S. House Elections." Paper prepared for the annual meeting of the Southern Political Science Association, New Orleans, January 6–8.

Abramowitz, Alan I., and Kyle Saunders. 1998. "Ideological Realignment in the U.S. Electorate." *Journal of Politics* 60 (3): 634–52.

———. 2004. "Rational Hearts and Minds: Social Identity as Party Identification in the American Electorate." Paper prepared for the annual meeting of the American Political Science Association, Chicago, September 2–5.

———. 2005. "Why Can't We All Just Get Along? The Reality of a Polarized America." *The Forum* 3 (2): Article 1.

Abramowitz, Alan I., and Walter Stone. 2005. "The Bush Effect: Polarization, Turnout, and Activism in the 2004 Presidential Election." Paper prepared for the annual meeting of the American Political Science Association, Washington, August 31–September 3.

Ansolabehere, Stephen, and Charles Stewart III. 2005. "Truth in Numbers." *Boston Review* 30 (February/March): 40.

Baker, Wayne. 2005. *America's Crisis of Values: Reality and Perception.* Princeton University Press.

Bartels, Larry M. 2000. "Partisanship and Voting Behavior, 1952–1996." *American Journal of Political Science* 44 (1): 35–50.

———. 2005. "What's the Matter with *What's the Matter with Kansas?*" Paper prepared for the annual meeting of the American Political Science Association, Washington, August 31–September 3.

Baumer, Donald C., and Howard J. Gold. 2005. "Party Images and Partisan Resurgence." Paper prepared for the annual meeting of the American Political Science Association, Washington, August 31–September 3.

Binder, Sarah A., and Forrest Maltzman. 2005. "Half-empty or Half-full? Do Vacant Federal Judgeships Matter?" Paper prepared for the annual meeting of the Midwest Political Science Association, Chicago, April 7–10.

Bishop, Bill, and Robert Cushing. 2004. "Response to Philip A. Klinkner's 'Red and Blue Scare': The Continuing Diversity of the American Political Landscape." *The Forum* 2 (2): Article 2.

Black, Earl, and Merle Black. 2002. *The Rise of Southern Republicans.* Harvard University Press.

Brady, David W., and Craig Volden. 2006. *Revolving Gridlock: Politics and Policy from Jimmy Carter to George W. Bush.* Boulder, Colo.: Westview Press.

Brewer, Mark. 2005. "The Rise of Partisanship and the Expansion of Partisan Conflict within the American Electorate." *Political Research Quarterly* 58 (2): 219–29.

Burden, Barry C. 2001. "The Polarizing Effects of Congressional Primaries." In *Congressional Primaries and the Politics of Representation,* edited by Peter F. Galderisi, Marni Ezra, and Michael Lyons, pp. 95–131. Lanham, Md.: Rowman & Littlefield.

Carsey, Thomas M., and Geoffrey C. Layman. 2006. "Changing Sides or Changing Minds? Party Identification and Policy Preferences in the American Electorate." *American Journal of Political Science* 50 (2): 464–77.

Collie, Melissa P., and John Lyman Mason. 1999. "The Electoral Connection between Party and Constituency Reconsidered: Evidence from the U.S. House of Representatives, 1972–1994." In *Continuity and Change in House Elections,* edited by David Brady, John Cogan, and Morris Fiorina, pp. 211–34. Stanford University Press.

Connelly, William F., Jr., and John J. Pitney. 1994. *Congress' Permanent Minority? Republicans in the U.S. House.* Lanham, Md.: Rowman & Littlefield.

Davis, Nancy J., and Robert V. Robinson. 1996. "Are the Rumors of War Exaggerated? Religious Orthodoxy and Moral Progressivism in America." *American Journal of Sociology* 102 (3): 756–87.

Democratic National Committee. 2004. "Strong at Home, Respected in the World: The 2004 Democratic National Platform for America." Washington.

DiMaggio, Paul, John Evans, and Bethany Bryson. 1996. "Have Americans' Social Attitudes Become More Polarized?" *American Journal of Sociology* 102 (3): 690–755.

Dionne, E. J., Jr. 2004. *Why Americans Hate Politics.* New York: Simon & Schuster.

Evans, John H. 2003. "Have Americans' Attitudes Become More Polarized?—An Update." *Social Science Quarterly* 84 (1): 71–90.

Fiorina, Morris P., Samuel J. Abrams, and Jeremy C. Pope. 2006. *Culture War? The Myth of a Polarized America.* 2d ed. New York: Longman.

Galston, William A. 2004. "Incomplete Victory: The Rise of the New Democrats." In *Varieties of Progressivism,* edited by Peter Berkowitz, pp. 59–85. Stanford, Calif.: Hoover Institution Press.

Galston, William A., and Elaine C. Kamarck. 2005. *The Politics of Polarization.* Washington: ThirdWay.

Green, John C., and others. 2004. "The American Religious Landscape and the 2004 Presidential Vote: Increased Polarization." *Fourth National Survey of Religion and Politics,* University of Akron, November–December.

Greenberg, Stanley B. 2004. *The Two Americas: Our Current Political Deadlock and How to Break It.* New York: St. Martin's Press.

Greenberg, Stanley, and James Carville. 2004. "Solving the Paradox of 2004: Why America Wanted Change but Voted for Continuity." Washington: Greenberg Quinlan Rosner Research.

Hacker, Jacob S., and Paul Pierson. 2005. *Off Center: The Republican Revolution and the Erosion of Democracy.* Yale University Press.

Hamilton, James T. 2006. *All the News That's Fit to Sell: How the Market Transforms Information into News.* Princeton University Press.

Hetherington, Marc J. 2001. "Resurgent Mass Partisanship: The Role of Elite Polarization." *American Political Science Review* 95 (3): 619–31.

Hibbing, John R., and Elizabeth Theiss-Morse. 1995. *Congress as Public Enemy.* Cambridge University Press.

———. 2002. *Stealth Democracy: Americans' Beliefs about How Government Should Work.* Cambridge University Press.

Hunter, James Davison. 1991. *Culture Wars: The Struggle to Define America.* New York: Basic Books.

———. 1994. *Before the Shooting Begins: Searching for Democracy in America's Culture War.* New York: Free Press.

Jacobson, Gary C. 2000. "Party Polarization in National Politics: The Electoral Connection." In *Polarized Politics: Congress and the President in a Partisan Era,* edited by Jon R. Bond and Richard Fleisher, pp. 9–30. Washington: CQ Press.

———. 2003a. "Terror, Terrain, and Turnout: Explaining the 2002 Midterm Elections." *Political Science Quarterly* 118 (1): 1–22.

———. 2003b. "Partisan Polarization in Presidential Support: The Electoral Connection." *Congress and the Presidency* 30 (1): 1–36.

———. 2004. "Explaining the Ideological Polarization of the Congressional Parties since the 1970s." Paper prepared for the annual meeting of the Midwest Political Science Association, Chicago, April 15–18.

———. 2005. "Polarized Politics and the 2004 Congressional and Presidential Elections." *Political Science Quarterly* 120 (2): 208–09.

Jamieson, Kathleen Hall, and Erika Falk. 2000. "Continuity and Change in Civility in the House." In *Polarized Politics: Congress and the President in a Partisan Era,* edited by Jon R. Bond and Richard Fleisher, pp. 96–108. Washington: CQ Press.

Keele, Luke J., and James A. Stimson. 2005. "Polarization and Mass Response: The Growth of Independence in American Politics." Paper prepared for the annual meeting of the American Political Science Association, Washington, August 31–September 3.

Kessler, Jim, and Jessica Dillon. 2005. "Who Is Winning the Abortion Grays?" Washington: ThirdWay.

King, David C. 1997. "The Polarization of American Political Parties and Mistrust of Government." In *Why People Don't Trust Government,* edited by Joseph S. Nye, Philip Zelikow, and David C. King, pp. 155–78. Harvard University Press.

———. 1999. "Congress, Polarization, and Fidelity to the Median Voter." Paper prepared for the Massachusetts Institute of Technology Conference on Parties and Congress, Cambridge, Mass., October 2.

Klinkner, Philip A. 2004. "Red and Blue Scare: The Continuing Diversity of the American Electoral Landscape." *The Forum* 2 (2): Article 2.

Klinkner, Philip A., and Ann Hapanowicz. 2005. "Red and Blue Déjà Vu: Measuring Political Polarization in the 2004 Election." *The Forum* 3 (2): Article 2.

Layman, Geoffrey C., and Thomas M. Carsey. 2000. "Ideological Realignment in Contemporary American Politics: The Case of Party Activists." Paper prepared for the annual meeting of the Midwest Political Science Association, Chicago, April 27–30.

———. 2002a. "Party Polarization and 'Conflict Extension' in the American Electorate." *American Journal of Political Science* 46 (4): 786–802.

———. 2002b. "Party Polarization and Party Structuring of Policy Attitudes: A Comparison of Three NES Panel Studies." *Political Behavior* 24 (3): 199–236.

Levendusky, Matthew S. 2005. "Sorting in the U.S. Mass Electorate." Paper prepared for the annual meeting of the American Political Science Association, Washington, August 31–September 3.

Mann, Thomas E., and Norman J. Ornstein. 2006. *The Broken Branch: How Congress Is Failing America and How to Get It Back on Track.* Oxford University Press.

McCarty, Nolan, Keith T. Poole, and Howard Rosenthal. 2006. *Polarized America: The Dance of Ideology and Unequal Riches.* MIT Press.

Moynihan, Daniel Patrick. 1970. *Maximum Feasible Misunderstanding.* New York: Macmillan.

Nivola, Pietro S. 1986. *The Politics of Energy Conservation.* Brookings.

———. 1997. "Commercializing Foreign Affairs? American Trade Policy after the Cold War." In *U.S. Foreign Policy after the Cold War,* edited by Randall B. Ripley and James M. Lindsay, pp. 235–56. University of Pittsburgh Press.

———. 2003. "Can the Government Be Serious?" In *Agenda for the Nation,* edited by Henry J. Aaron, James M. Lindsay, and Pietro S. Nivola, pp. 488–94. Brookings.

Oppenheimer, Bruce I. 2005. "Deep Red and Blue Congressional Districts: The Causes and Consequences of Declining Party Competitiveness." In *Congress Reconsidered,* 8th ed., edited by Lawrence C. Dodd and Bruce I. Oppenheimer, pp. 135–57. Washington: CQ Press.

Ornstein, Norman J., Thomas E. Mann, and Michael J. Malbin. 2006. *Vital Statistics on Congress 2005–2006.* Washington: National Journal Group.

Pew Research Center. 2005. *Trends 2005.* Washington.

Poole, Keith T., and Howard Rosenthal. 1984. "The Polarization of American Politics." *Journal of Politics* 46 (4): 1061–79.

———. 2001. "D-NOMINATE after 10 Years: A Comparative Update to Congress." *Legislative Studies Quarterly* 26 (1): 5–29.

Project for Excellence in Journalism. 2005. *The State of the News Media: An Annual Report on American Journalism.* Washington.

Quirk, Paul J. 2005. "Deliberation and Decision Making." In *Institutions of American Democracy: The Legislative Branch,* edited by Paul J. Quirk and Sarah A. Binder, pp. 314–48. Oxford University Press.

Rivlin, Alice M. 2005. "Are We Too Polarized to Make Public Decisions?" Speech delivered at Indiana University, School of Public and Environmental Affairs, October 27.

Rivlin, Alice M., and Isabel Sawhill, eds. 2004. *Restoring Fiscal Sanity: How to Balance the Budget.* Brookings.

Rohde, David W. 1991. *Parties and Leaders in the Postreform House.* University of Chicago Press.

———. 1992. "Electoral Forces, Political Agendas, and Partisanship in the House and Senate." In *The Postreform Congress,* edited by Roger H. Davidson, pp. 27–47. New York: St. Martin's Press.

Sinclair, Barbara. 2005. "Parties and Leadership in the House." In *Institutions of American Democracy: The Legislative Branch,* edited by Paul J. Quirk and Sarah A. Binder, pp. 224–54. Oxford University Press.

———. 2006. *Party Wars: Polarization and the Politics of National Policy Making.* University of Oklahoma Press.

Stoker, Laura, and M. Kent Jennings. 2006. "Aging, Generations, and the Development of Partisan Polarization in the United States." Working Paper WP2006-1. Institute of Governmental Studies, University of California, Berkeley.

Stonecash, Jeffrey M., Mark D. Brewer, and Mack D. Mariani. 2003. *Diverging Parties: Realignment, Social Change, and Political Polarization.* Boulder, Colo.: Westview Press.

U.S. House of Representatives. 2006. *A Failure of Initiative.* Hearings before the Select Bipartisan Committee to Investigate the Preparation for and Response to Hurricane Katrina. 109 Cong. 2 sess. Government Printing Office.

White, John Kenneth. 2003. *The Values Divide: American Politics and Culture in Transition.* New York: Chatham House.

Wolfe, Alan. 1998. *One Nation, After All.* New York: Viking.

Zaller, John R. 1992. *The Nature and Origins of Mass Opinion.* Cambridge University Press.

2

Disconnected: The Political Class versus the People

Morris P. Fiorina
Matthew S. Levendusky

D uring the last decade of the twentieth century, the belief that American political life had become highly polarized attained the status of conventional wisdom. At the 1992 Republican National Convention, candidate Pat Buchanan declared the outbreak of a culture war, "a war for the soul of America." And in the midterm elections of 1994, the story line held that "angry white males"—upset with gays, gun control, immigration, affirmative action, and Hillary Clinton—put an end to more than forty years of Democratic Party dominance of the House of Representatives. Although the angry talk subsided a little in the following years, the firestorm erupted again in 1998 with the Monica Lewinsky scandal and the subsequent impeachment of President Bill Clinton.

So far, the 2000s have brought no respite. The decade began with the contested presidential vote in the state of Florida and the razor-thin victory of Republican candidate George W. Bush, sealed by the decisions of a Republican secretary of state and a conservative-controlled Supreme Court. The episode left many Democrats bitter, unwilling even to acknowledge the legitimacy of the Bush presidency. Following an interlude of muted partisanship after the terrorist attacks of September 11, 2001, President Bush reversed his campaign pledge and chose to govern as a divider not a uniter, implementing political adviser Karl Rove's strategy of winning reelection by maximizing support among core Republican groups.

More recently, the president and vice president have argued vigorously for exceptional interpretations of executive power, while their Democratic adversaries in Congress strongly contest such interpretations.

Thus, at some levels the contention that political life has become more polarized is not in dispute. Nor is Pat Buchanan alone among public intellectuals in seeing an ongoing cultural conflict in America.[1] Other conservatives have characterized the conflict in similarly bellicose terms:

> The competition is not a battle of interests but, as in late antiquity, a battle of worldviews. . . . What is at stake is not simply how much wealth is to be redistributed . . . but all of the values and beliefs of a culture. With the answers to such basic questions as "what is just?" "what is good?" and "what is evil?" now a matter of debate, the term "culture wars" has appropriately been used to describe the scene in contemporary American politics. And just as pagan Rome died and gave way to the new culture of Augustinian Christianity, so is Tocqueville's America dying and giving way to the new culture of expressive individualism.[2]

> There is no "after the Cold War" for me. So far from having ended, my cold war has increased in intensity, as sector after sector of American life has been ruthlessly corrupted by the liberal ethos. It is an ethos that aims simultaneously at political and social collectivism on the one hand, and moral anarchy on the other.[3]

Of course, intellectuals are by definition a small and unrepresentative slice of American life, so few would take such pronouncements as an accurate reflection of what is happening in the country at large. More convincing evidence of polarization comes from studies of the political class—public officials, party and interest group leaders, activists, financial contributors, and members of the political infotainment community. This evidence documents a dramatic rise in congressional polarization since the mid-twentieth century, as well as the existence of significant differences in the political views held by the various segments of the political class.[4]

---

1. Sociologist James Davison Hunter is generally credited with inspiring Buchanan's call to arms. See Hunter (1991).

2. Dworkin (1996, p. xi).

3. Kristol (1995, p. 486).

4. For references to this literature, see the citations in the essay by David W. Brady and Hahrie C. Han in chapter 3 of this volume.

Yet there remains a critical missing piece in the prevailing portrait of a polarized American political order—the American people. Until very recently, polarization of the electorate was assumed to be one of the most important factors in explaining the polarization of the political class. As Bush reelection strategist Matthew Dowd stated in 2003, the president had not tried to expand his electoral base because "you've got 80 percent to 90 percent of the country that look at each other like they are on separate planets."[5] Why should a candidate bother trying to appeal to the middle if there are no voters left there? Thus the campaign strategy of "mobilizing the base" would seem to have supplanted the traditional strategy of "moving to the center" with good reason: in today's political climate there are no more "swing voters" that a move to the center might appeal to.

The only problem, however, is that recent academic research contradicts the belief that there is no longer a middle ground in American politics. In the late 1990s, both qualitative and quantitative studies found little evidence that Americans were highly polarized, or that they were becoming more so.[6] On the contrary, Princeton University sociologist Paul DiMaggio, with coauthors John H. Evans and Bethany Bryson, conducted an exhaustive analysis of General Social Survey and National Election Studies data from the years 1972 to 1994 and found that the political views of Americans had become more *similar,* not more different. (This conclusion also held when the study was updated through 2000 by Evans.)[7] A study by University of Michigan sociologist Wayne Baker, who examined twenty years of World Values Survey data, found not only little evidence of a culture war in the United States, but also that most Americans held a mix of the traditional and modern views that were supposedly at war.[8] More recently, Morris P. Fiorina, Samuel J. Abrams, and Jeremy C. Pope found that attitudinal differences between residents of the so-called red and blue states were greatly exaggerated in 2000—a conclusion that was reaffirmed when the analysis was updated through 2004.[9]

In other words, while systematic evidence indicates that American politics as conducted by the political class is increasingly polarized, the evidence also suggests that this development is not simply a reflection of an increasingly polarized electorate. The result is a disconnect between the American people and those

5. Quoted in Ron Brownstein, "Bush Falls to Pre-9/11 Approval Rating," *Los Angeles Times,* October 3, 2003.

6. The most notable qualitative study is by Wolfe (1998). The most notable quantitative study is by DiMaggio, Evans, and Bryson (1996).

7. DiMaggio, Evans, and Bryson (1996); Evans (2003).

8. Baker (2005a).

9. Fiorina, Abrams, and Pope (2006).

who purport to represent them—a disconnect that political scientist Keith T. Poole has called "the central puzzle of modern American politics."[10] Contrary to a half-century of theory and research on the centrist tendencies of two-party politics, American politics today finds a polarized political class competing for the support of a much less polarized electorate.[11]

So why, then, has the idea of a polarized electorate attained the status of conventional wisdom? As it turns out, the exaggerated picture of popular polarization is easier to explain than the disconnect between representatives and the represented. Many in the journalistic community forgot, never learned, or have chosen to ignore a half-century of research contrasting the mass public and political elites.[12] The result has been that the media have lost sight of critical differences between the two groups. People who are active in politics know a lot and care a lot about politics and public policy, and their views are organized according to ideological frameworks. In contrast, most ordinary voters have less knowledge about politics, care less about it, and are largely nonideological. Moreover, people who are active in politics tend to have more extreme views than ordinary voters. Yet because political elites constitute the public face of politics, the media naturally portray this unrepresentative slice of America as the norm rather than the exception—a tendency that is undoubtedly exacerbated by the media's preference for stories that stress conflict over agreement.

Nevertheless, it does a journalist no great harm to believe that the country is polarized when it is not. But candidates running for office—as well as the people who work for and bankroll them—have a great personal interest in getting things right. They run too great a risk of wasting their investments by operating on the basis of false information—such as the idea that "80 to 90 percent of the country look at each other like they are on separate planets." So what, then, would prompt members of the political class to act on the erroneous presumption that the mass public is as polarized as the political class?

Party Sorting vs. Polarization

We do not think there is a simple answer to this question, so we will focus instead on a development that many believe is a major factor in a more complicated answer.[13] Commentators and pundits look at the electorate today and see

10. Remarks by Keith T. Poole at the History of Congress Conference, Stanford University, Spring 2004.

11. See Downs (1957).

12. See McCloskey, Hoffman, and O'Hara (1960); Converse (1964).

13. See, for example, Jacobson (forthcoming 2007).

Table 2-1. *Party Sorting without Increasing Aggregate Polarization in a Hypothetical Electorate*

Ideology	Period 1	Period 2
Liberals	60 Democrats, 40 Republicans	90 Democrats, 10 Republicans
Moderates	100 Independents	100 Independents
Conservatives	40 Democrats, 60 Republicans	10 Democrats, 90 Republicans

Source: Compiled by the authors.

two ideologically distinct camps, and they label that polarization. But polarization implies that the political opinions and attitudes of the public—in the aggregate—have been pushed away from moderate, centrist positions to the liberal or conservative extreme. When the electorate is highly polarized, the middle ground literally vanishes—but that is not the case today.

Instead, over the past generation, party sorting—the process by which a tighter fit is brought about between political ideology and party affiliation—has occurred in American politics. As recently as the 1970s, liberals and conservatives could each find a comfortable home in either the Democratic or the Republican Party. But nowadays the Republican Party is much more likely to be the home of ideologically conservative voters, while the Democratic Party is home to most liberals. The relative numbers of conservatives and liberals may not have changed all that much, but their party affiliation certainly has.[14]

The distinction between party sorting and polarization is fairly easy to see with an example. Consider the hypothetical electorate depicted in table 2-1. At any point in time, the electorate consists of 100 liberals, whose party affiliation can be either Democratic or Republican; 100 moderates, who are political independents; and 100 conservatives, whose party affiliation, like the liberals', can be either Republican or Democratic. In Period 1, liberals are slightly more likely to be Democrats and conservatives are slightly more likely to be Republicans, but both parties contain significant numbers of liberals and conservatives. Knowing a voter's party affiliation in Period 1, then, provides relatively little information about her political ideology.

Between Period 1 and Period 2, the parties sort themselves along ideological lines. The great preponderance of liberals are now affiliated with the Democratic

14. While scholarly awareness of party sorting has been evident for some years, and a number of excellent focused studies have appeared, there has been relatively little work tracing the issues that are most closely associated with sorting, the groups in which sorting has most clearly occurred, and other specific features of the sorting process. For a review of the evidence for party sorting on abortion, see Adams (1997). For sorting on women's issues, see Sanbonmatsu (2002).

Party, and a similarly large proportion of conservatives are now Republicans. The result of this party sorting is that, in Period 2, the parties are far more ideologically homogeneous. Knowing a voter's party affiliation now provides a great deal of information about her ideology.

The most important point of this example, however, is that between the two periods the aggregate ideological distribution remains unchanged. At all times there are exactly 100 liberals and 100 conservatives (along with the 100 moderates). Despite changes in the numbers of conservative Democrats and liberal Republicans, the aggregate level of polarization in the electorate is unchanged.

Some analysts prefer to refer to the developments shown in table 2-1 as "partisan polarization." But we think this term only confuses the discussion. We prefer the term "party sorting," reserving the term polarization for bimodal distributions of opinion, or movements toward a bimodal distribution of opinion: voters are polarized on an issue if more of them cluster at the extremes than locate themselves in the center, or if they are moving from centrist positions toward the extremes. As we show in the body of this chapter, the party sorting that has occurred over the past generation has moved the parties further apart from one another, but has not produced bimodal distributions of aggregate opinion. Sorting, rather than polarization, is a more accurate label for the changes we have seen over the past quarter-century.

Given the political changes that have occurred in the United States since the mid-twentieth century, it would be extremely surprising if there had *not* been some party sorting. Consider the political realignment of the South. Forty years ago, the Democratic Party had a much larger proportion of identifiers in the South—many of whose racial and social attitudes and views on national defense were more conservative than those of the national Democratic Party. Later, as Democratic identification fell in the South (particularly among white males), one would logically expect the Democratic Party as a whole to become more homogeneously liberal.

Surprisingly, however, survey data do not register major effects from these political changes. For example, between 1987 and 2003, according to a 2003 survey by the Pew Research Center, the average difference between Republicans and Democrats on twenty-four political and policy items increased by only 5 percentage points (from 12 percent to 17 percent), and the average difference on seventeen social and personal attitudes increased by only 4 percentage points (from 7 percent to 11 percent).[15] These seem like rather small increases,

15. Pew Research Center for the People and the Press, "The 2004 Political Landscape: Evenly Divided and Increasingly Polarized," November 5, 2003 (people-press.org/reports/display.php3?ReportID=196).

especially because on some issues—such as capital punishment—the official positions of the parties are significantly different, but majorities of both parties are in favor. In light of this, the amount of sorting at the level of ordinary voters hardly seems commensurate with the sorting of Democrats and Republicans at the elite level.

Sorting and Ideology

Party identification and ideology are more closely related today than they were in the recent past, and there is general agreement that this closer relationship reflects the relatively greater differentiation of the two parties at the elite level.[16] Some observers have suggested that the election of Ronald Reagan began a period of increasingly sharp differentiation between the two parties at the elite level. Since that time, the positions of the Democratic and Republican parties on key issues such as taxes, abortion, and national defense have become more clearly defined. Furthermore, the strategies used by both parties in Congress to control the legislative agenda have pushed the parties further apart in their public positions.[17] With the parties' elites becoming more differentiated during the 1980s, it would be reasonable to expect to find that ordinary voters cued off these changes (to some degree) and aligned themselves with the party that more closely represented their ideological positions. In other words, when confronted with a clear choice between two increasingly polarized parties, we might expect to see an increasingly strong correlation between the public's ideology and party identification.

Since the early 1970s, the National Election Studies (NES) surveys have asked a nationwide sampling of Americans to classify their political views on a seven-point scale from extremely liberal to extremely conservative and to classify their party identification, also along a seven-point scale, from strong Democrat to strong Republican. Figure 2-1 plots the correlation of these responses for the period 1972 to 2004. Interestingly, the correlation between party and ideology increases almost linearly over this entire period, with sharp increases from the early 1990s to 1996 and again in 2000. But the Reagan years (1981–89) do not particularly stand out.

Yet if party sorting has been taking place in response to elite polarization, we would expect to see an even tighter relationship between partisanship and ideology among voters who are more aware of the differences between the parties'

16. See, for instance, Adams (1997); Abramowitz and Saunders (1998).
17. Roberts and Smith (2003).

Figure 2-1. *Party Identification and Ideology Correlations, 1972–2004.*

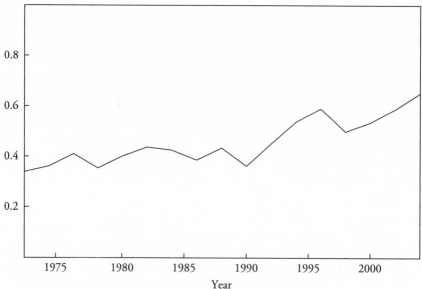

Source: Calculated from the National Election Studies cumulative data file.

elites. To check this proposition, we extended the comparison to two groups of survey respondents in the National Election Studies: those who claimed to see important differences between the Democratic and Republican parties, and those who did not.[18] Figure 2-2 compares the two groups.

Both groups exhibited similar trends of an increasingly strong relationship between partisanship and ideology over the thirty-two-year period. But in every election, respondents who saw important differences between the parties displayed a much stronger relationship between party identification and ideology than those who did not. It may seem odd that the subgroup trends in figure 2-2 are somewhat weaker than the overall pattern in figure 2-1. The explanation is that people have been shifting out of the "see no difference" category into the "see important differences" category. As shown in figure 2-3, the percentage of respondents who claimed to see important differences between

18. The text of the NES question reads, "Do you think there are any important differences in what the Republicans and Democrats stand for?"

Figure 2-2. *Party Identification and Ideology Correlations by Awareness of Elite Polarization, 1972–2004.*

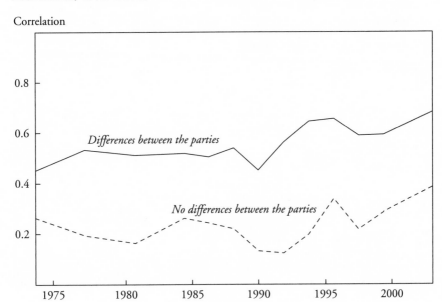

Source: Calculated from the National Election Studies cumulative data file.

the parties has increased steadily over the years—peaking at a stunning 76 percent in 2004.

This much of the story thus sits on solid evidence: as elites became more ideologically distinctive over the past quarter-century, ordinary voters recognized this development and then changed their positions, bringing their party identification and ideology more into alignment with each other.[19] Importantly, however, the pattern among ordinary voters is much weaker than among political elites: while there is almost a total separation between Democratic and Republican members of Congress, the pattern among ordinary voters is somewhat weaker. There has been some party sorting in the mass public in response to elite polarization, but the mass public is not nearly as ideologically divided as party elites.

19. Of course, one cannot draw conclusions about individual voters from aggregate analyses. Levendusky (2006) confirms this inference with an analysis of individual-level panel data, and also finds that conversion (rather than partisan replacement) is most consistent with the observed changes.

Figure 2-3. *Percentage of Respondents Who Saw Important Differences between the Political Parties, 1972–2004.*

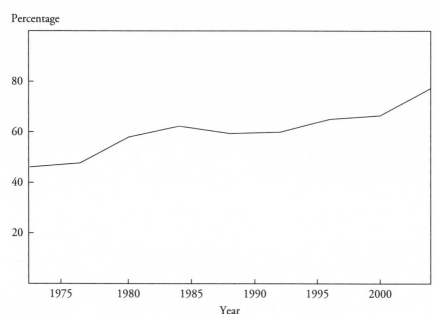

Percentage

Source: Calculated from the National Election Studies cumulative data file.

Sorting and Policy Areas

What if we look for evidence of party sorting below the level of ideology?[20] After all, political scientists have long known that voters are not very ideological.[21] In the typical National Election Studies survey, for instance, one-quarter to one-third of respondents decline even to position themselves ideologically. And when analysts measure ideology alternatively as a statistical constraint among specific issue positions, the usual finding is that the electorate is not very constrained—the simple fact is that people exhibit liberal positions on some issues and conservative positions on others. Perhaps, then, more sorting could be found below the level of broad ideology.

Each election year, the NES surveys Americans' attitudes and views in several policy areas. Policy areas are clusters of related issues, such as social welfare

20. This is similar to earlier works that looked for issue consistency across a variety of different issues. See, for example, Nie, Verba, and Petrocik (1979).
21. The locus classicus is Converse (1964).

issues, race-related issues, foreign policy and defense issues, and so forth. Previous studies have indicated that more people take consistent positions *within* a specific policy area than *across* areas.[22] Here we look at four of the most prominent policy areas discussed in the literature: New Deal social welfare issues, social and cultural issues, racial issues, and defense and military policy issues.[23]

What should we expect to find? First, we might expect the correlation between New Deal issue positions and party identification to show little change over time—or even show change in the direction of less party sorting. The basic "role of government in the economy" questions that make up the New Deal issue area have been around since the 1930s, and the relationship to party sorting may have become muted by the time our data begin in 1972. Indeed, the relationship to partisanship may have even declined as racial and social issues increased in prominence.[24]

Second, we would expect that Democratic and Republican voters have become better sorted on race issues. Carmines and Stimson have shown that party elites became increasingly differentiated on these issues after the 1958 elections, and they suggest that the sorting of ordinary voters followed.[25] However, they also suggest that the change among ordinary voters would occur only with a significant lag, as new generations of voters take the place of older generations. We therefore might expect to see some increased sorting in the thirty-year period we examine, but nothing very dramatic.

22. Carmines and Layman (1997); Layman and Carsey (2002).

23. We constructed indexes by taking several items relating to an issue area and calculating each respondent's average position across those issues. For New Deal issues, we used the following NES items: government provision of health insurance (VCF0806); government's role in securing everyone a good job and a standard of living (VCF0809); the government spending/services tradeoff (VCF0839); the amount of government spending on the poor (VCF0886); and government spending on welfare (VCF0894). For racial items, we used whether or not the civil rights movement pushes too fast (VCF0814); whether or not the government should ensure school integration (VCF0816); whether students should be bused to promote school integration (VCF0817); support for Affirmative Action in hiring or promotion (VCF0867A); whether or not the government should ensure that African Americans receive fair treatment in jobs (VCF9037); and how much the government should help minorities (VCF0830). For cultural issues, we used abortion attitudes (VCF0837/VCF0838); school prayer attitudes (VCF9043); attitudes regarding whether or not women and men deserve an equal role (VCF0834); attitudes toward laws protecting homosexuals from discrimination (VCF0876A); attitudes toward homosexuals in the military (VCF0877A); and attitudes toward adoption by homosexual couples (VCF0878). For defense-related items, we used attitudes toward cooperation with the Soviet Union (VCF0841) and attitudes toward defense spending (VCF0843). All two- and four-point items were made into seven-point-scales, and only white respondents were used to construct the racial policy items.

24. Edsall and Edsall (1991); Frank (2004).

25. Carmines and Stimson (1989).

Third, social issues such as equal rights for women, abortion, and school prayer, which were orthogonal to partisan debate a generation ago, have moved to the center of the debate between party elites.[26] Thus we might expect these issues to move from being largely unrelated to partisanship in the early years of our data to being more strongly related to party identification today.

Finally, ever since the Vietnam War, Republicans on balance have been the more hawkish party on matters relating to defense and military policy. We would therefore expect to see a strong correlation between defense-related issue positions and party identification over the entire three-decade period. By 2004, however, foreign policy and defense issues had cast the parties' elites into particularly sharp relief, so we may also expect to see a jump between 2000 and 2004.[27]

Figure 2-4 displays the relationship between partisanship and voter positions in the four policy areas. In each area, there is evidence of a strengthening relationship between the electorate's issue positions and party identification. Given our expectations, it is perhaps surprising to find that over the entire thirty-year period the trend is even more pronounced on New Deal economic issues (as shown by the higher correlation values across the board) than on issues of culture or race. That New Deal issues are increasingly correlated with party identification is strong evidence that popular commentators have overstated the diminished importance of these issues to the electorate.[28] For defense-related items, there is little change in the relationship until 2004, suggesting a sharp change in response to the contentious debate over the Iraq war, Afghanistan, and the war on terror.

But while there has been some sorting on the various issue areas, it is (again) important not to exaggerate the change that has occurred. Even in 2004,

26. Layman (2001).

27. For example, in the 2004 NES cross section, respondents were asked to rank themselves on a seven-point scale on the issue of whether the United States should attempt to deal with foreign crises via diplomacy or military action. The correlation between self-placement and party ID was 0.43, suggesting a fairly strong relationship between attitudes toward foreign policy and party ID in the most recent election.

28. While the stronger relationship between partisanship and New Deal positions is contrary to the claims of commentators such as Frank (2004), it is consistent with recent research indicating that economic issues have shown no decline as an important cleavage in U.S. elections. See Gelman and others (2005); Ansolabehere, Rodden, and Snyder (2006); Bartels (2006). The lack of sorting on the racial dimension is consistent with Abramowitz's critique of Carmines and Stimson's issue evolution thesis. See Abramowitz (1994).

Figure 2-4. *Party Identification and Voter Positions in Four Policy Areas, 1972–2004.*

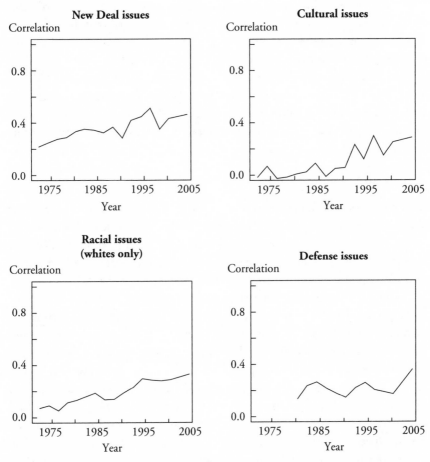

Source: Calculated from the National Election Studies cumulative data file. (For details on how these scales were constructed, see note 23 in the text.)

the correlations between partisanship and the racial, social, and defense policy areas were still much closer to zero than to one—numbers that seem a bit shy of "the great sorting-out" discerned by Democratic Party activists William A. Galston and Elaine C. Kamarck.[29] The simple fact is that on a variety

29. Galston and Kamarck (2005).

of issues many partisans take positions that are at odds with their party's national stance.[30]

However, it would be possible for even relatively small increases in sorting on specific policy areas to cumulate into more significant sorting if the individual dimensions somehow became more closely related to one another. To check this possibility, we correlated respondents' positions on the four policy areas with one another. (These patterns are displayed in figure 2-5.) While New Deal attitudes are more strongly related to both racial and cultural attitudes today than they were a generation ago, cultural and racial issues show no sign of a closer relationship.[31] Again, the evidence tends to support the sorting thesis, but the patterns are not especially strong.

Sorting and Specific Issues

Even if there is not strong evidence of sorting on the level of general ideology or in broad issue areas, it is possible that voters have sorted on one or two important issues. For example, Democrats and Republicans could be quite far apart on abortion yet have very muted differences over women's equality.[32] Sorting could be occurring on different issues, at different times, and among different groups, and averaging everything together may obscure significant trends and differences.

To get a sense of whether specific issues might be driving party sorting, we examined six issues in the NES surveys—three New Deal economic issues (whether government should provide health insurance, whether it should ensure jobs and a good standard of living, and how government should balance spending and services), two social issues (abortion and school prayer), and a race issue (whether the government should provide economic assistance to blacks and minorities). Given the trends observed for each of the broad policy areas, we would expect that positions on some of these issues must be more strongly related to partisanship today than a generation ago.

But how should we measure sorting on these specific issues? Because the individual items vary in question format (and therefore reliability), comparing correlations across items is inappropriate here.[33] Therefore, to measure sorting

30. See Hillygus and Shields (2005). One other point worth noting here is that the sorting evident in specific policy areas is not as linear as that shown by the more general ideology measure. In particular, figure 2-4 suggests that the spike in those seeing no difference between the major political parties in 1996 (in figure 2-2) may owe a lot to the volatility in the relationship between partisanship and the New Deal and cultural issue positions.

31. Comparisons on racial items are based on analysis of white respondents only.

32. See Sanbonmatsu (2002).

33. Krosnick and Berent (1993).

Figure 2-5. *Correlations between Voter Positions in Four Policy Areas, 1972–2004.*

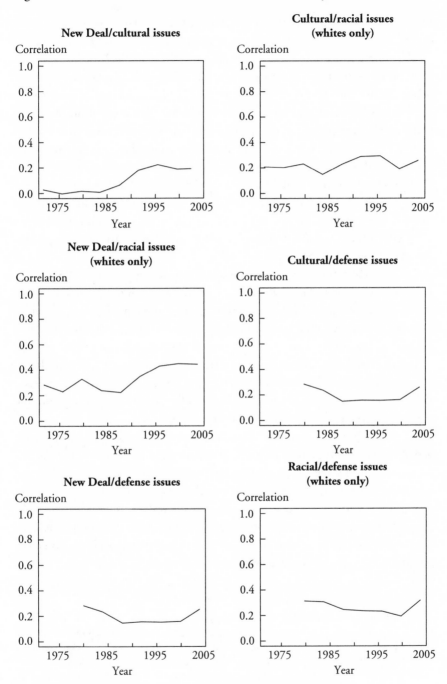

Source: Calculated from the National Election Studies cumulative data file.

across issues, we calculated the percentage of respondents who shared their party's national position on each issue.[34] The results are summarized in the graphs in figure 2-6. The most notable feature of the graphs is the lack of clear patterns. On some issues there appears to have been little sorting, and on other issues the sorting appears to be limited mostly to one party. On the issue of government-provided health insurance, for instance, there is not much sorting going on in either party—in the aggregate, the mass parties look more or less as they did thirty years ago. But on the issue of whether the government should ensure jobs for its citizens and provide a social safety net, Republicans have become somewhat more inclined to share their party's view that government should let each person get ahead on his or her own. Democrats exhibit no trend (unless the uptick in 2004 is the start of one). The tradeoff between more government services and lower taxes shows Democrats becoming better sorted and Republicans becoming somewhat less well sorted.

On the long-standing issue of whether or not the government should help minorities, we limited our analysis to the responses of white respondents, since that is where we would expect partisan sorting to occur. Over time, white Republicans have become better sorted on the issue, with a large majority now in agreement with the party position that blacks and other minorities should help themselves. But Democrats' views are almost unchanged over the thirty-year period. Even as the South realigned, white Democrats did not become any more liberal—and a majority of Democrats, in fact, remain out of step with the party position that government should provide assistance.

Of the issues we examined, the results for abortion and school prayer were perhaps the most interesting. Arguably, there has been no single issue in American politics during the last generation that has attracted as much attention and created as much controversy among party elites as abortion. Indeed, abortion has become a "litmus test" candidates must pass in order to advance to the highest ranks of their party. Not surprisingly, the graph for the abortion issue indicates that as the parties became more clearly identified with pro-life or pro-choice positions at the elite level, the mass public followed suit.

---

34. All but two of these items are measured using seven-point scales. For simplicity, on the seven-point scales a Democrat takes her party's position if she takes a position to the left of the midpoint, and a Republican takes her party's position if she takes a position to the right of the midpoint. For the school prayer item, we assume that the Democratic position is one of the two more liberal answers and that the Republican position is one of the two more conservative answers. For the coding of the abortion item, see note 36.

Figure 2-6. *Percentage of Respondents Who Took Their Party's Position on Various Issues, 1972–2004.*

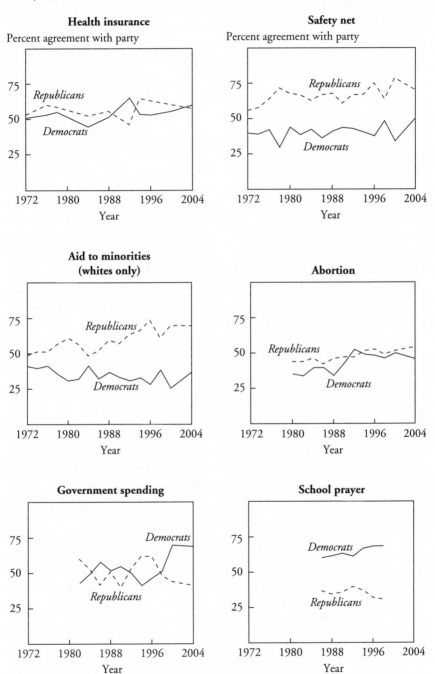

Source: Calculated from the National Election Studies cumulative data file.

Table 2-2. *Responses to the Question, When Should Abortion Be Permitted?*
Percent

Response	Strong Democrats	Strong Republicans
Never permitted	10	22
Only in case of rape, incest, or when the woman's life is in danger	23	37
For a clear need	13	18
Always as a personal choice	54	23

Source: 2004 National Election Study.

But here, too, we encounter the limits of the sorting thesis. As previous studies have shown, the abortion issue shows evidence of sorting for both parties.[35] Yet sorting at the mass level still falls far short of that among party elites. In the 2004 NES surveys, more than 40 percent of self-described "strong Republicans" and "strong Democrats" did not support the stated positions of their party's elites on abortion—and just about the same percentage of strong Republicans say abortion should always be a legal, personal choice as the percentage who said it should never be legal.[36] Thus, even for citizens who claimed the strongest attachments to their political parties (and who were therefore most likely to be aware of their party's position), there was considerable heterogeneity on this issue of abortion. This can be seen in the data in table 2-2.

While the Republican Party platform is staunchly pro-life, Republicans in the larger electorate are far from unified on the issue. And while Democrats are less divided than Republicans (a majority of strong Democrats say abortion should always be legal), it seems fair to conclude that more than one-third of them believe that abortion laws should be more restrictive than those favored by the national party. Even though abortion has caused a significant amount of sorting to occur in both parties, adherents of the two parties remain internally divided.[37]

35. See Adams (1997); Fiorina, Abrams, and Pope (2006, chap. 5).
36. The NES item gives the respondent four options: (1) by law, abortion should never be permitted; (2) the law should permit abortion only in the case of rape or incest, or when the woman's life is in danger; (3) the law should permit abortion for reasons other than rape, incest, or danger to the woman's life, but only after the need for the abortion has been clearly established; (4) by law, a woman should always be able to obtain an abortion as a matter of personal choice. We assume that the official Republican position is that abortion should never be permitted or be permitted only in cases of rape, incest, or a threat to the life of the woman, and we assume the Democratic position is that abortion should always be allowed.
37. Fiorina, Abrams, and Pope (2006, chap. 5) show that this conclusion does not depend on the NES survey item.

The issue of school prayer is interesting because, here, we encounter a surprising countertrend. Over time, Democrats became more accepting of their party's position (opposition to mandatory school prayer), while Republicans became less accepting of their party's position (support for school prayer). In each election year survey, a majority of respondents—including a majority of Republicans and a near-majority of Democrats—supported a moderate position: "The law should allow public schools to schedule time when children can pray silently if they want to." Even if party elites remained sharply divided over school prayer, the mass public did not.

The issue of equal rights for women exhibits a pattern similar to that for school prayer. Figure 2-7 shows the percentage of self-identified Republicans and Democrats who stated a position on the liberal end of the scale ("women and men should have an equal role" as contrasted with "women's place is in the home"). By 2004, support for equality for women had become the clear position in both parties—by huge majorities. In other words, over the past twenty-five years or so, Americans have moved toward a consensus on this once-contentious issue.

Figure 2-7. *Percentage of Respondents Who Took a Liberal Position on the Issue of Women's Equality, 1972–2004.*

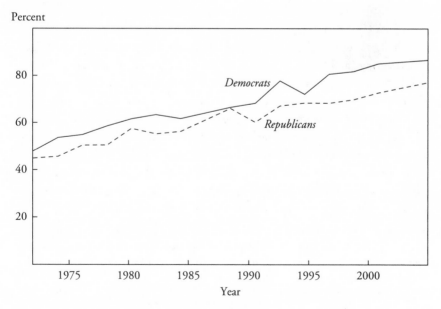

Source: Calculated from the National Election Studies cumulative data file.

Figure 2-8. *Percentage of Respondents Who Express Support for Same-Sex Relations, 1972–2004.*

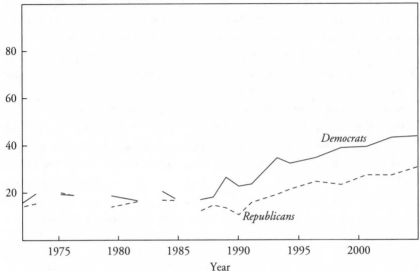

Percent supporting

Source: Calculated from the General Social Surveys.

Finally, consider the issue of gay rights. In 2004, same-sex marriage in Massachusetts and San Francisco was a hot-button issue on the campaign trail. While survey organizations have begun to ask people about gay marriage only recently, the General Social Surveys include a long-time series on the public's attitudes on same-sex relations. Figure 2-8 plots the percentages of Democrats and Republicans who stated that same-sex relations are "only wrong sometimes" or "not at all wrong." Among adherents of both parties there is a noticeable trend toward acceptance of the morality of homosexual relationships. Even if Americans are still divided on the issue of gay marriage, there seems to be growing agreement that gays and lesbians deserve equal treatment.[38]

38. The GSS also asks about support for homosexual civil liberties (whether or not the respondent would allow a homosexual to teach in a college or university, allow a homosexual to give a speech in the local community, or allow a book written by a homosexual in favor of homosexuality to remain in a public library). Analyses of these items not reported here find the same patterns. Fiorina, Abrams, and Pope (2006, chap. 6) document a similar pattern of growing tolerance for homosexuals in various spheres of American life.

In sum, abortion is the only social issue we examined that still exerts a strong push on party sorting. The other cultural issues—school prayer, women's rights, and gay rights—are ones on which the partisan attitudes of ordinary citizens seem to be converging rather than diverging. Far from party sorting contributing to a culture war organized around these issues, an increasing number of ordinary Americans appear to be walking away from the conflicts that characterize the party elites.[39]

Conclusion

Survey data reveal some evidence of party sorting over the past generation in U.S. politics. The party attachments of ordinary Americans have become more closely associated with their ideological self-classifications and with their positions on some issues. Moreover, several broad policy areas have become more closely related to one another. But the same data also show that the increase in sorting over the three decades has been modest, contrary to what is often asserted. This extended consideration of sorting in the mass electorate does not ultimately take us very far toward an explanation of the polarization among political elites.

Our findings contradict any simple assumption that the polarization of America's political class is a direct reflection of a similarly polarized mass electorate, even considering that the electorate is now better sorted than it was a generation ago. While superficially puzzling, common expectations about a tight relationship between constituents and their representatives overlook the intervening role of institutions in the American electoral process. Public officials are not elected by a direct popular vote of the country at large, as our national fixation with polling implicitly suggests. Public officials are instead elected by the electorates of fifty states, 435 congressional districts, and thousands of other local jurisdictions. Within jurisdictions, candidates must win

39. There is always the possibility that sorting may only have occurred for some demographic subgroups. To double-check the patterns (and non-patterns) reported on the six issues, we examined the percentage of respondents in various subgroups who supported their party's positions. We considered three obvious comparisons: men vs. women, Southerners vs. non-Southerners, and whites vs. African-Americans. While subgroups differ in expected ways (women tended to be more liberal than men, whites more conservative than blacks, etc.), the differences are small and the general findings are the same, so in the interest of space we do not include those figures here. The important point is simply that sorting does not seem to differ much by demographic subgroups.

primary elections, where turnout is often extremely low and less representative than in general elections. And in both primary and general elections, candidates sorely need both money and organizational backing in order to appeal to their electorates.[40] We think that research on popular political preferences points inexorably to the conclusion that the impact of a higher degree of internal party homogeneity is magnified by electoral arrangements. Once again, institutions matter.

The boundaries of political jurisdictions are subject to change and political manipulation (except those for statewide offices). Both academic and popular commentators have pointed an accusing finger at partisan redistricting as a source of elite polarization. The logic of the accusation seems plausible enough: Creating districts that are safe for one party or the other reduces the incentive for candidates to take moderate positions. But as Thomas E. Mann of the Brookings Institution discusses in his essay in this volume, the evidence (however plausible) that partisan gerrymandering is the major culprit in the polarization of the political class seems quite weak.

Our (tentative) view is that primaries are a more likely arena in which to find explanations of political polarization. As noted previously, turnout in primary elections is usually very low, so a few score committed supporters (at least on the lower rungs of the electoral ladder) can be a critically important foundation for a campaign. And, as Matthew S. Levendusky has demonstrated, committed supporters—those who will give money to a candidate or a party, attend a meeting or a rally, or get involved in other ways—are more likely to be found in the ranks of the politically sorted.[41] In the 2004 elections, for example, more than 80 percent of those who engaged in three or more campaign activities (a standard definition of "campaign activist") were sorted. The structure of American electoral institutions amplifies the influence of such voters—and their impact is felt most in primary elections.

Even though few incumbents face serious primary challenges, it would be a mistake to conclude that primary elections are unimportant. In all likelihood, incumbents act strategically to preclude primary challenges. Even if they are unlikely to face a challenge, candidates take special pains to maintain the support of their party's hard-core voters. One of us has offered this phenomenon as a possible explanation for the Clinton impeachment vote:

---

40. The primary election loss of Senator Joseph I. Lieberman (D-Conn.) to a political neophyte in August 2006 comes to mind.
41. Levendusky (2006).

When moderate House Republicans announced that they would vote to impeach President Clinton in the winter of 1998, it was widely interpreted as party pressure, since most such incumbents had indicated they personally favored censure rather than impeachment. The media clearly favored this interpretation, and certainly there was enough bluster within Congress to suggest that it was operating. But it is also very plausible, and consistent with my observation of a few of these members, that they were making a calculation of the following sort: "If I do not vote for impeachment, I will antagonize the hard-core partisans in my district. That certainly may hurt me in the primary, and even if I get by that, it will hurt me in the general election."[42]

If members anticipate potential challenges from the ideological poles, they will act preemptively to diminish the chances of that occurring. As sorting occurs, more and more candidates find themselves in such circumstances. Because sorting produces a more homogeneous and a more extreme primary electorate, the pressure increases for candidates to take consistently liberal or conservative positions on most issues, even when moderation would be more helpful in the general election. Thus sorted partisans move candidates toward noncentrist positions.[43] And it is not a large leap to presume that these same voters pressure members to support noncentrist policies after being elected.[44]

The interaction between party sorting and primary elections may go some way toward explaining the disconnect between voters and candidates in contemporary American politics. At first glance, it is puzzling that masses and elites look so fundamentally different—a disconnect that contradicts basic assumptions political theorists make about representation. But even if the majority of Americans remain largely centrist, an increasing number of citizens line up on the same end of the spectrum as their party, and these sorted citizens play a critical role in campaigns and elections. Candidates must respond accordingly.[45]

---

42. Fiorina (2001, p. 157).

43. Aldrich (1995).

44. Brady, Han, and Pope (forthcoming 2007) show that members of Congress whose positions diverge from those of their primary electorates are more likely to attract primary challengers, even if they are more attuned to the sentiments of their districts as a whole.

45. We also believe that candidates today are more personally extreme than they were in previous eras of American politics, perhaps because they emerge from the many cause groups that have joined more traditional groups and organizations on the political scene. Candidates more personally committed to policy positions may be willing to take greater electoral risks than others who value holding office relatively more highly than making policy. Although we think this a very important subject for further research, there is no denying that systematic research in the area is difficult.

Disconnected, or Joined at the Hip?

COMMENT

Alan I. Abramowitz

According to Morris Fiorina and Matthew Levendusky, American politics in the twenty-first century is characterized by "a disconnect between the American people and those who purport to represent them." A narrow "political class" made up of public officials, party and interest group leaders, activists, financial contributors, and media commentators is deeply divided in its political views. However, contrary to what they claim is the conventional wisdom among pundits and political commentators, the American public is not deeply divided.[1] Using language that could have been taken directly from Philip E. Converse's seminal study of American public opinion in the 1950s, Fiorina and Levendusky argue that ordinary voters in the United States remain "largely nonideological."[2]

But if the public is not deeply divided, what explains the increasing polarization of the political class? This is the major puzzle that Fiorina and Levendusky address. The solution they propose is "sorting," by which they mean a growing alignment between partisanship and issue positions among the public. This alignment can result from citizens choosing a party based on their issue positions, or from citizens changing their issue positions to bring them more into line with those of their preferred party. Nevertheless, Fiorina and Levendusky insist that sorting is not the same as polarization. Moreover, they argue that this process of

---

1. This idea was developed in Fiorina, Abrams, and Pope (2006). In fact, Fiorina's claim that only the "political class" is polarized has been widely—and favorably—cited by pundits and political commentators since the publication of the first edition of *Culture War?* For instance, see Elizabeth Auster, "U.S. Divided, but Analysts Don't Expect Culture War," *Cleveland Plain Dealer,* November 14, 2004; Eric Mink, "Exploding the Myth of Deep Divisions," *St. Louis Post-Dispatch,* October 20, 2004; Jane Eisner, "Americans Staying on the Sidelines of Political Showdown," *Philadelphia Inquirer,* May 29, 2005; David Brooks, "The More Things Change . . ." *New York Times,* October 23, 2004; John Tierney, "A Nation Divided? Who Says?" *New York Times,* June 13, 2004; Robert J. Samuelson, "The Politics of Self-Esteem," *Washington Post,* November 10, 2004; Susan Page, "What's a Governor Like You Doing in a State Like This?" *USA Today,* May 23, 2005. The recent publication of a very positive article in *The Reader's Digest* by William Beaman ("A Fractured America?" November 2005) suggests that Fiorina's thesis has now become the conventional wisdom. For an analysis of media reaction to the first edition of *Culture War?* see Baker (2005b).

2. See Converse (1964).

sorting has actually been very limited and that differences between rank-and-file Democrats and Republicans on most issues remain fairly small.[3]

But if sorting has been as limited as Fiorina and Levendusky claim, how can it explain the intense polarization that characterizes the political class in the United States? This kind of limited sorting cannot by itself explain why members of Congress and other elected officials—whose positions depend on maintaining the support of their constituents—are so deeply divided. Some additional explanation is required and, at the end of their chapter, Fiorina and Levendusky argue that "the impact of an increased degree of internal party homogeneity is magnified by electoral arrangements." Specifically, Fiorina and Levendusky point to primary elections as the culprit: "even if the majority of Americans remain largely centrist, an increasing number of citizens line up on the same end of the spectrum as their party, and these sorted citizens play a critical role in campaigns and elections. Candidates must respond accordingly."

I believe that while Fiorina and Levendusky are on the right track, they do not go far enough. There is evidence that the American public has become more polarized in its political views over the past twenty years. And while polarization is indeed greatest among the most politically engaged citizens, these engaged citizens are not, as Fiorina and Levendusky claim, a small and unrepresentative fringe group. Politically engaged citizens constitute a substantial portion of the American electorate. Moreover, sorting is not a process separate from polarization—it is a major contributor to polarization. On a wide range of issues, rank-and-file Democrats and Republicans are much more divided today than in the past—and the sharpest divisions are found among the politically engaged partisans who constitute the electoral bases of the two parties.

Political Engagement in the American Public

According to Fiorina and Levendusky, American society is made up of two distinct groups: a tiny political class that is deeply polarized and a mass public that is largely uninterested in politics and nonideological. In reality, the American public is far from homogeneous when it comes to political interest, knowledge, and activity. There are many gradations of political interest and involvement among the public. Some Americans have little or no interest in politics, while

3. A lengthier explanation of the distinction between polarization and sorting can be found in Fiorina, Abrams, and Pope (2006, chap. 4).

Figure 2-9. *The Politically Engaged Public, 1956–2004*

Percent of Public

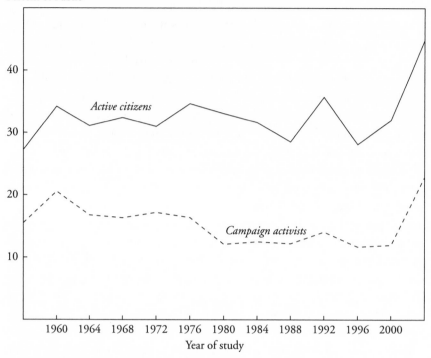

Year of study

Source: Calculated from the National Election Studies cumulative data file.
Note: Active citizens engaged in at least one activity beyond voting; campaign activists engaged in at least two activities beyond voting.

others care deeply about political issues. Some Americans seldom or never go to the polls, while others not only vote but also try to influence how their friends and neighbors vote, contribute money to candidates, and work in political campaigns. And while the number of Americans who engage in specific political activities varies over time, active citizens usually constitute a substantial share of the public.

Figure 2-9 displays the trend between 1956 and 2004 in the proportion of Americans who engaged in political activities beyond voting according to data from the National Election Studies (NES). Active citizens are defined as those who engaged in at least one activity beyond voting while campaign activists are defined as those who engaged in at least two activities beyond voting. The data show that the proportion of Americans who engaged in at least one activity beyond voting varied between 25 percent and 35 percent, while the proportion who engaged in at least two activities beyond voting varied between 12 percent and 20 percent. In 2004, however, the proportion of active citizens reached 45 percent, and the proportion of campaign activists reached 23 percent. Both of these figures were all-time highs.

Despite (or perhaps because of) the intense polarization of the American electorate over President George W. Bush and his policies, the 2004 presidential campaign produced a dramatic increase not just in voter turnout, but also in the number of people who engaged in political activities beyond voting. Various measures of political interest and involvement indicated that the American public was more engaged in the 2004 campaign than in any presidential campaign in the past half-century. A record 78 percent of respondents in the 2004 NES survey said that they perceived important differences between the two major parties—and a record 85 percent said that they cared "a good deal" about who won the presidential election. These figures appear to undermine Fiorina and Levendusky's assumption that ordinary Americans do not generally care much about politics. Ordinary Americans cared a great deal about the outcome of the 2004 presidential election.

The Growth of Polarization in the American Public

Fiorina and Levendusky argue that polarization and sorting are two distinct processes. They define polarization as a shift in the underlying distribution of policy preferences within the public and sorting as an increase in the association between policy preferences and partisanship. As noted earlier in this comment, I view sorting as an important component of polarization. But even by Fiorina and Levendusky's restrictive definition of polarization, the American public has become more polarized over the past twenty years.

It is difficult to find comparable measures of polarization for the American public over an extended period of time. For example, the seven-point issue scales currently used in the NES surveys were first introduced during the 1970s and 1980s. However, seven questions dealing with policy issues were included in every NES presidential election survey between 1984 and 2004. These questions asked about liberal vs. conservative identification, abortion policy, government aid to blacks, defense spending, government vs. personal responsibility for jobs and living standards, government vs. private responsibility for health insurance, and the tradeoff between government services and spending. I coded

Table 2-3. *Polarization on Seven-Item Policy Scale by Political Engagement,*
1984–2004
Standard deviations

	1984	1988	1992	1996	2000	2004	Percentage change (1984–2004)
Nonvoters	2.52	2.52	2.44	2.60	2.68	2.67	+6
Voters	2.89	3.13	3.15	3.39	3.31	3.60	+25
Active citizens	3.15	3.50	3.48	3.70	3.59	3.89	+23
Campaign activists	3.74	3.50	3.50	4.10	3.71	4.27	+14

Source: National Election Studies cumulative data file.

Note: Entries are standard deviations of scores on a seven-item policy scale. Items included in the scale are liberal-conservative identification, defense spending, abortion, government aid to blacks, jobs and living standards, health insurance, and government spending vs. services. Scores on the scale range from −7 (consistently liberal) to +7 (consistently conservative). Active citizens engaged in at least one activity beyond voting. Campaign activists engaged in at least two activities beyond voting.

responses to each of these questions according to whether a respondent was on the liberal side, the conservative side, or neither side (which included those in the middle and those with no opinion) and combined them into a fifteen-point liberal-conservative policy scale with scores ranging from −7 for respondents who took the liberal side on all seven issues to +7 for respondents who took the conservative side on all seven issues.

The standard deviation of the scores on the liberal-conservative policy scale can be used to measure the extent of ideological polarization within a group— the larger the standard deviation, the greater the dispersion of scores around the mean and, therefore, the greater the degree of polarization. Table 2-3 displays the standard deviation of scores on the liberal-conservative policy scale in 1984, 1988, 1992, 1996, 2000, and 2004 among four groups with varying levels of political engagement: nonvoters, voters, active citizens, and campaign activists.

The data in table 2-3 show that in all six election years campaign activists were the most polarized group, followed by active citizens, voters, and nonvoters. In addition, between 1984 and 2004, all four groups showed some increase in polarization. However, the increase in polarization among nonvoters was very slight, while the increases among voters and active citizens were much larger. According to these results, voters and active citizens were considerably more polarized in 2004 than they were in 1984.

To get an idea of the significance of the increase in polarization between 1984 and 2004, figure 2-10 displays the distribution of scores on the liberal-conservative policy scale among voters in each year. The two distributions look quite different. In 1984, 41 percent of voters were located within one unit of the center of the scale and only 10 percent were located near the left (−7 through −5) and right (5 through 7) extremes. In 2004 only 28 percent of voters were located within one unit of the center and 23 percent were located near the left and right extremes. These results indicate that even by the restrictive definition of polarization proposed by Fiorina and Levendusky, the 2004 electorate was considerably more polarized than the 1984 electorate.

Political Engagement and Ideological Polarization in 2004

While the 2004 electorate was considerably more polarized than the 1984 electorate, ideological divisions were much greater among some types of voters than others. Figure 2-11 shows the distribution of four groups of respondents—nonvoters, voters, active citizens, and campaign activists—on the seven-item liberal-conservative policy scale. For the purpose of clarity, in this figure the original fifteen-point liberal-conservative scale has been collapsed into a five-point scale: the five groupings are consistent liberals (those scoring −7 through −5 on the original scale), moderate liberals (−4 though −2), inconsistents (−1 through +1), moderate conservatives (2 through 4), and consistent conservatives (5 through 7).

The percentage of respondents located at the center of the liberal-conservative scale ranged from 47 percent among nonvoters to 31 percent among voters, 26 percent among active citizens, and 19 percent among campaign activists, while the percentage of respondents located at the left or right extremes of the scale ranged from 8 percent among nonvoters to 18 percent among voters, 29 percent among active citizens, and 35 percent among campaign activists. Thus, as Figure 2-11 shows, ideological polarization was greatest among the most politically engaged members of the public in 2004.

Fiorina and Levendusky's characterization of the American public as non-ideological actually appears to apply to only one of these four groups—nonvoters. Among the minority of Americans who did not vote in 2004, centrists outnumbered consistent liberals and conservatives by a four-to-one ratio. However, among the much larger group of active citizens, consistent liberals and conservatives outnumbered centrists. Among campaign activists—a group that comprised almost one-fourth of the public in 2004—consistent liberals and conservatives outnumbered centrists by a ratio of almost two to one.

Figure 2-10. *Polarization of Voters on a Seven-Item Policy Scale, 1984 and 2004*

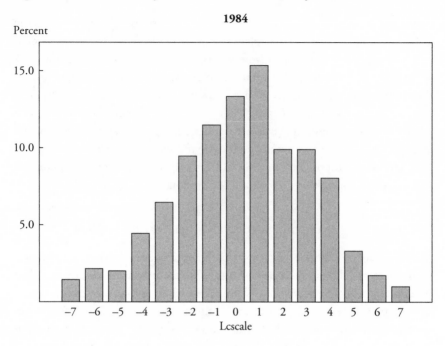

1984

Percent

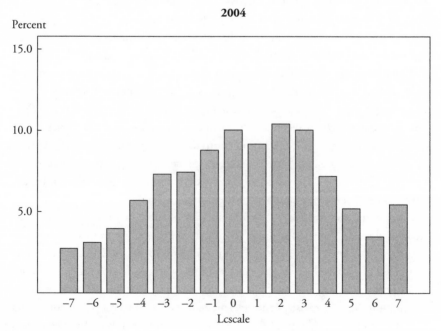

2004

Percent

Source: Calculated from the National Election Studies cumulative data file.

Figure 2-11. *Polarization on a Seven-Item Policy Scale by Level of Political Engagement, 2004*

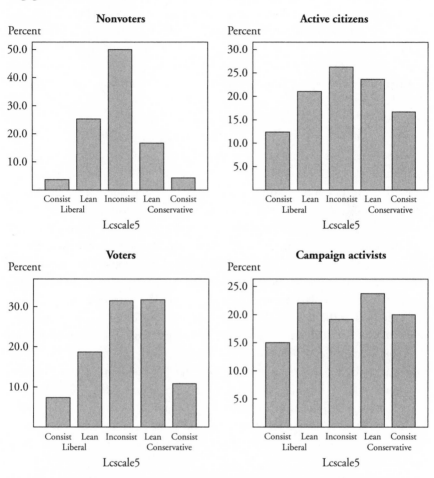

Source: Calculated from the National Election Studies cumulative data file.

Sorting and Partisan Polarization Among the American Public

Fiorina and Levendusky's attempt to distinguish sorting from polarization is based on a misunderstanding of the role played by political parties in a democratic political system. In a representative democracy, political parties set the policy agenda and organize the policymaking process. Polarization therefore depends not just on the intensity of ideological and cultural conflict in society, but also on the extent to which these conflicts are expressed through political parties. Partisan polarization makes it much more likely that ideological and cultural conflicts in society will be expressed politically.

The process that Fiorina and Levendusky refer to as sorting has contributed to a dramatic increase in partisan polarization in the United States. One of the main reasons Democratic and Republican candidates and officeholders are more deeply divided than they were thirty or forty years ago is because Democratic and Republican voters, opinion leaders, and activists are more deeply divided than they were thirty or forty years ago. Far from being disconnected from the public, Democratic and Republican candidates and officeholders are polarized precisely because they are highly responsive to their parties' electoral bases. And, as we will see, the Democratic electoral base is decidedly liberal while the Republican electoral base is decidedly conservative.

Fiorina and Levendusky argue that partisan "sorting" among the public has been quite limited and that the American public remains rather poorly sorted (when compared with political elites). It is indisputable that partisan polarization is greater among political elites than among the American public. Yet by some measures, partisan polarization has increased more rapidly among the voting public than among political elites in recent years. Figure 2-12 compares the trends in partisan polarization between 1972 and 2004 in two groups: voters and members of the U.S. House of Representatives. For voters, polarization is measured by the difference between the average scores of Democratic and Republican identifiers on the seven-point liberal-conservative scale. For House members, polarization is measured by the difference between the average scores of Democrats and Republicans on the first dimension of the DW-nominate scale.[4] The figure indicates that between 1972 and 2004 partisan polarization among members of the House of Representatives increased by about 50 percent. During the same period, however, polarization among the voting public more than doubled.

Moreover, differences between rank-and-file Democrats and Republicans have increased dramatically over the past thirty years on a wide variety of specific issues. Figure 2-13 displays the trends on four questions that have been included in NES surveys since 1980 or earlier: liberal-conservative identification, government aid to blacks, defense spending, and abortion. On all four of these questions, there has been a substantial increase in partisan polarization over time. On the ideology question, the difference in conservative identification between

---

4. Polarization scores in 1972 are used as a baseline for both groups.

Figure 2-12. *Trends in Partisan Polarization among Elites and Voters, 1972–2004*[a]

Ratio

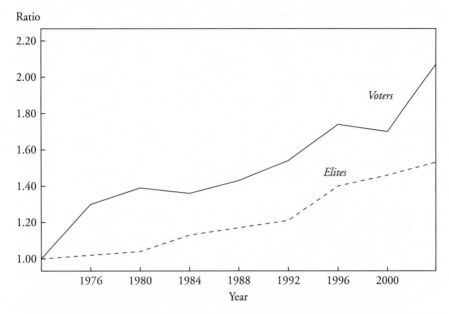

Sources: National Election Studies cumulative data file; DW-nominate scores compiled by Keith T. Poole (voteview.com/dwnomin.htm).

a. The trend in polarization among voters is based on the difference between mean scores of Democratic and Republican identifiers and leaners on the seven-point liberal-conservative scale. The trend in polarization among elites is based on the difference between mean scores of Democratic and Republican members of the U.S. House of Representatives on the first dimension DW-nominate scale. Polarization scores from 1972 are used as a baseline for both series.

Democratic and Republican voters increased from 31 percentage points in 1972 to 64 percentage points in 2004. On the question of government aid to blacks, the difference in opposition to government aid between Democratic and Republican voters increased from only 11 percentage points in 1972 to 38 percentage points in 2004. On the issue of defense spending, the difference in support for increased defense spending between Democratic and Republican voters increased from only 6 percentage points in 1992 to 45 percentage points in 2004. Finally, on the issue of abortion, the difference in support for the pro-choice position between voters of the two parties increased from only 3 percentage points in 1980 to 25 percentage points in 2004. This evidence indicates that partisan polarization has increased on a wide range of issues over the past few decades. On all four issues, in fact, the differences between Democratic and Republican voters in 2004 were the largest ever recorded.

Figure 2-13. *Trends in Partisan Polarization on Various Issues*[a]

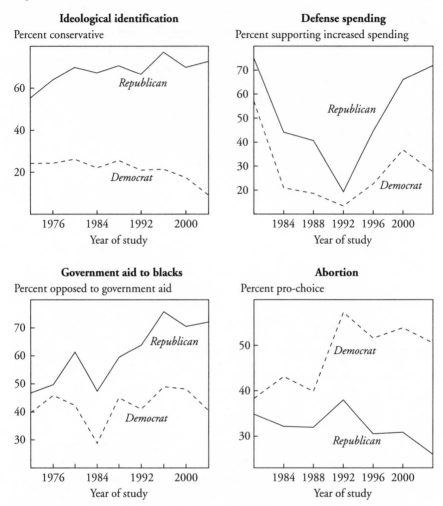

Source: Calculated from the National Election Studies cumulative data file.
a. Based on all voters identifying with or leaning toward a party.

Within the 2004 electorate, moreover, polarization was greatest among the most politically engaged partisans. Figure 2-14 illustrates the degree of partisan polarization on a ten-item liberal-conservative policy scale in the 2004 NES survey among nonvoters, voters, active citizens, and campaign activists. The ten items included in the scale were ideological identification, abortion, government aid to blacks, defense spending, health insurance, jobs and living standards, gay

Figure 2-14. *Partisan Polarization by Level of Political Engagement, 2004*[a]

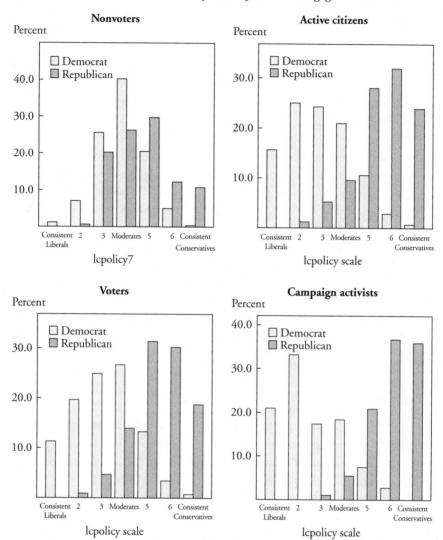

Source: Calculated from the National Election Studies cumulative data file.

a. The scale is based on ideological self-identification, abortion, government aid to blacks, jobs and living standards, health insurance, gay marriage, death penalty, government spending vs. services, defense spending, and diplomacy vs. military force.

marriage, diplomacy vs. military force, government spending vs. services, and the death penalty. On each item, respondents' answers were coded as liberal, moderate/undecided, or conservative. The scores were then summed to create a twenty-one-point scale ranging from −10 (consistently liberal) to +10 (consistently conservative). This twenty-one-point scale was then collapsed into a seven-point liberal-conservative scale to simplify the presentation of results. Each set of graphs in Figure 2-14 displays the distribution of Democratic and Republican identifiers, including leaning independents, on the collapsed seven-point liberal-conservative policy scale.

Once again, only the least engaged of the four groups—nonvoters—seems to fit Fiorina and Levendusky's description of a nonideological American public. Only among nonvoters do we find substantial overlap between the Democratic and Republican distributions. Voters, active citizens, and campaign activists were much more polarized. Ideologically consistent partisans (liberal Democrats and conservative Republicans) made up only 41 percent of nonvoters compared with 68 percent of voters, 74 percent of active citizens, and 82 percent of campaign activists. Moderate partisans made up 35 percent of nonvoters, 20 percent of voters, 15 percent of active citizens, and 12 percent of campaign activists. Finally, ideologically inconsistent partisans (conservative Democrats and liberal Republicans) made up 24 percent of nonvoters but only 12 percent of voters, 11 percent of active citizens, and 6 percent of campaign activists.

Conclusions

Fiorina and Levendusky's characterization of the typical American voter as disinterested, uninformed, and nonideological might have been accurate during the 1950s era studied by Philip Converse in 1964. But it is not an accurate description of the American electorate in the first decade of the twenty-first century. For one thing, the American electorate today is far better educated than the public of the 1950s. In 1952, 62 percent of American adults had not finished high school and only 15 percent had received any college education. In 2004 only 9 percent of American adults had not finished high school and 62 percent had received at least some college education. As a result of this dramatic rise in education levels, a much larger proportion of today's electorate is capable of understanding and using ideological concepts. In addition, the ideological cues provided by party leaders are much clearer now than in the 1950s. Today, only the most politically inert segment of the public—nonvoters—can accurately be described as disinterested, uninformed, and nonideological. This description clearly does not apply to voters, much less to active citizens or campaign activists.

The evidence presented here indicates that the ideological orientations of politically engaged partisans are very similar to the ideological orientations of Democratic and Republican candidates and officeholders. Among active citizens and campaign activists, very few Democrats are found to the right of center and very few Republicans are found either in the center or to the left of center. There is almost no overlap between the two distributions.

Nor are these politically engaged partisans a small and unrepresentative fringe group—they constitute a substantial proportion of the American electorate. In 2004, active citizens made up 46 percent of all Democratic identifiers and 49 percent of all Republican identifiers. Campaign activists made up 25 percent of all Democratic identifiers and 24 percent of all Republican identifiers. They are the citizens who vote in primaries, contribute money to parties and candidates, work on campaigns, and pay attention to the actions of their elected representatives. While their support may not be enough to win an election, no candidate or elected official can afford to ignore them.

COMMENT

Gary C. Jacobson

In *Culture War? The Myth of a Polarized America,* Morris P. Fiorina (with coauthors Samuel J. Abrams and Jeremy C. Pope) argued that the increasing polarization observed in American political life over the past several decades is almost entirely confined to a narrow political class—politicians, activists, commentators, journalists, and other political junkies. In his view, popular polarization—or at least the aspect of it characterized as a "culture war"—is a myth. He reads the survey evidence to show that the distribution of Americans' opinions on cultural issues such as abortion, homosexuality, and gun control has not become measurably more polarized, except among the minority of citizens most visible in politics as candidates, activists, and professional observers. Ordinary citizens, according to this argument, do not share the passion or extremism of the active stratum but are forced into what appear to be polar camps because the alternatives offered by political elites exclude centrist options.[5]

5. Fiorina, Abrams, and Pope (2006, chaps. 4–7).

Fiorina recognized one important exception to his analysis—that on some issues Americans had become modestly more polarized along party lines. This was not taken to undermine his main point, however, as he demonstrated that shifts in policy positions taken by the parties or the emergence of a new issue dimension could divide the electorate even if individuals' opinions did not change at all.[6] But this important distinction between polarization in general and *partisan* polarization raised the possibility that, even with no change in the distribution of mass opinion (or even increasing signs of consensus on some formerly divisive issues), opinion cleavages might be occurring increasingly along party lines, fueling a more polarized national politics.[7]

In this volume, Fiorina and Matthew S. Levendusky consider whether ordinary Americans have in fact responded to elite polarization by sorting themselves more consistently into the appropriate party, given their ideological stances and positions on enduring national issues. They find that such sorting has occurred but conclude that "the increase in sorting over the three decades has been modest" and that "extended consideration of sorting in the mass electorate does not ultimately take us very far toward an explanation of elite polarization" and thus cannot solve what Keith Poole has called the "central puzzle of modern American politics," which is the "disconnect between the American people and those who purport to represent them."

In reaching this conclusion, I think the authors downplay their own evidence of popular polarization. For example, in discussing the issue of same-sex relations, they seem to regard the increase in its acceptance among identifiers of both political parties as evidence that "partisan attitudes . . . seem to be converging rather than diverging" despite the emergence (visible in their figure 2-8) of a substantial partisan gap on this question since the late 1980s. Of course, this may mean only that people with different priors can read this kind of visual evidence differently. But less amenable to suggestion is the evidence presented in Alan I. Abramowitz's critique, which shows that respondents vary widely in political interest, sophistication, and activity, and that the higher their scores on these dimensions the more they have sorted themselves into the appropriate party. Moreover, the proportion of active and sophisticated voters is substantial, so sorting (and thereby partisan polarization) has extended to a much larger share of the electorate than implied by Fiorina and Levendusky's analysis. I would offer similar evidence and arguments

6. Fiorina, Abrams, and Pope (2006, chap. 9).
7. See Evans (2003).

Figure 2-15. *Ideological Differences between Partisan Voters and Their Parties,*
1972–2004

Mean difference on 7-point liberal-conservative scale

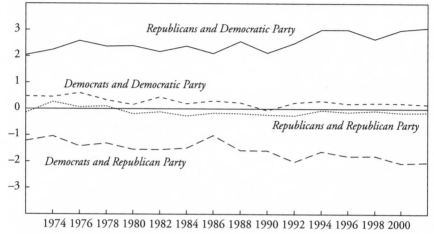

Source: National Election Studies cumulative data file.

had Abramowitz not saved me the trouble.[8] Because he has, I can proceed to
three additional points:

1. A first-order solution to Fiorina and Levendusky's puzzle is easy. National
politicians, while growing increasingly divided along partisan and ideological lines,
have not grown more distant from their supporters. At least as measured by the sub-
jective estimates of ordinary partisans, there is no "disconnect" to explain.

If elite polarization were separating representatives from the more moderate
citizens who elect them, we would expect the distance between respondents'
self-described ideological locations and those they estimate for their party and
its candidates to grow over time. But this has not happened. Figure 2-15 displays the difference between the self-placement of partisan voters and their
placement of the parties on the seven-point liberal-conservative scale in
National Election Studies (NES) surveys from 1972 through 2004.[9] Democrats
have tended to place themselves slightly to the right of their party, and Republicans slightly to the left of theirs—but the distance between partisans and their

8. Indeed, I have offered similar evidence and arguments in the past. See, for example, Jacobson
(2000).

9. The scale ranges from 1 (most liberal) to 7 (most conservative), with 4 as the middle point.

Figure 2-16. *Ideological Differences between Partisans and House Candidates,*
1978–2004

Difference on 7-point liberal-conservative scale

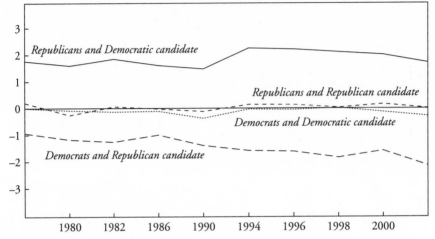

Source: National Election Studies cumulative data file.

own parties is small and, more important, did not increase at all over this
period. In fact, among Democrats the distance has narrowed a bit. What has
changed is the gap between partisans' self-placements and the perceived locations of the rival party, which has grown by a full point on the scale for both
Republican and Democratic voters.[10]

Similarly, the mean distance between perceived ideological locations of partisans and their own party's House candidates has been modest all along and does
not increase over time (figure 2-16). Moreover, Republicans place themselves on
average slightly to the *right* of their candidates, and Democrats place themselves
slightly to the *left* of theirs. Again, the ideological gap widens only between partisan voters (especially Democrats) and the other party's candidates (although it is
not as wide for candidates as for parties). Elite polarization has not, by this evidence, separated representatives from their own supporters, but leaders and parties have come to be viewed as notably more distant ideologically by those on the
other side. Thus the only voters who might have reason to be alienated by the

10. Both trends are significant at .001. The same results hold even if nonvoters are included in the
analysis, although the degree of change in perceived distance from the rival party is slightly smaller.

Table 2-4. *Ideological Extremism and Approval of Senators' Performance*

	Republicans		Democrats		Independents	
	Coefficient	Standard error	Coefficient	Standard error	Coefficient	Standard error
Republican senators						
Ideological extremity[a]	4.97**	1.77	−12.74***	3.35	−6.50***	1.78
Constant	75.88***	2.25	29.07***	2.78	43.03***	2.26
Adjusted R^2	.13		.41		.21	
Number of cases	48		48		48	
Democratic senators						
Ideological extremity[a]	−12.63***	3.26	−1.34	2.94	−4.45	2.67
Constant	30.16***	3.45	71.41***	3.14	51.55***	2.86
Adjusted R^2	.25		−.02		.04	
Number of cases	43		43		43	

Source: The dependent variable (percent approving of the senators' performance) is from the average of nine monthly polls taken between May 2005 and January 2006 by SurveyUSA (www.surveyusa.com/50StateTracking.html).

a. Log of absolute DW-nominate score.

**$p < .01$.

***$p < .001$.

growing extremism of their representatives are those who did not support them in the first place.

Additional evidence on this point is supplied by a new set of statewide polls, which ask, among other things, whether respondents approve of the job performance of each of their state's senators.[11] Table 2-4 lists the results of regressing partisans' approval ratings on the senators' ideological extremity (measured as the log of their absolute DW-nominate scores).[12] Ideological extremism had a large negative effect on approval ratings offered by people who identified with the party opposite a given senator. The coefficients indicate that approval was about 35 percentage points lower for the most ideologically

11. In May 2005, SurveyUSA, a polling firm whose main clients for its political surveys are local news media, began conducting monthly statewide automated telephone surveys of approximately 600 respondents in all fifty states. Among the questions asked are party identification and job performance approval of each state's senators. For a description and assessment of these data, see Jacobson (2006).

12. DW-nominate scores range from −1 (most liberal) to +1 (most conservative). Extremity is measured as the distance from the center, or 0. I use a log transformation because it provides a better fit to the data; linear results support the same substantive argument. Data are not available for the nine senators first elected in 2004, so they are omitted from the analyses reported in the table.

extreme senator than for the least extreme senator in either party. In contrast, ideological extremism had a significant *positive* effect on Republicans' approval of Republican senators (approval of the most conservative Republican is estimated to be 14 points higher than of the most moderate) and no effect at all on how Democratic respondents rated Democratic senators. More extreme senators received lower marks from independents, but in the case of Republicans the loss was almost completely offset by the gain among their own partisans. For Democrats, the effect fell short of statistical significance. Again, ideologues in office may alienate rival partisans, but they do not appear to displease their own partisans in the least.

2. Fiorina and Levendusky's analysis also ignores how sorting may have strengthened partisan sentiments, for either that or some other process is required to explain increasingly divergent partisan responses to national politicians and issues.

Fiorina and Levendusky refer to events such as the Clinton impeachment and the Florida election debacle as sources of the "conventional wisdom" that "American political life had become highly polarized" during the 1990s without acknowledging that partisan polarization on these issues was by no means limited to elites. Ordinary citizens were also fundamentally divided by party in their responses to these events.[13] They mention Karl Rove's strategy of mobilizing the Republican base to ensure the reelection of President George W. Bush without noticing that its very success demonstrates the widespread susceptibility of ordinary voters to partisan and ideological appeals. Partisan sorting has not only produced more ideologically coherent rival electoral coalitions; it has evidently left a large proportion of ordinary citizens primed to respond in partisan terms at the slightest provocation.

Partisan priming is of course most visible in the public's responses to President Bush and virtually anything connected to him. In the eighty-nine Gallup Polls taken between January 2004 and April 2006, his approval rating among Republicans has averaged 88 percent, among Democrats 14 percent. This 74 percentage point difference makes Bush the most polarizing president on record by a wide margin.[14] Partisan divisions extend to (and have been reinforced by) the president's policies. Between World War II and the March 2003 invasion of

13. Jacobson (2007, pp. 19–20, 61–65).

14. Before Bush, party differences in presidential approval ratings never exceeded 70 percentage points in any single Gallup Poll and never averaged more than 63 points for any one quarter. The gap for Bush exceeded 70 points in sixty-four of the eighty-two Gallup surveys taken between January 2004 and February 2006, surpassing 80 points in six of them, with quarterly averages ranging from 71 to 79 points and an overall average of 72 points. See Jacobson (2007, pp. 5–8).

Iraq, partisan differences in support of U.S. military actions were relatively small. The partisan gap averaged about 5 percentage points for Vietnam, between 11 and 12 points for Korea, Kosovo, and Afghanistan, and about 20 points for the Gulf War in 1991. Partisan differences in support of the Iraq war, in contrast, have averaged 58 points since the beginning of 2004, with an average of 79 percent of Republicans but only 21 percent of Democrats supporting the venture. Virtually every question concerning the Iraq war, its premises and its consequences, now produces widely divergent partisan responses.[15]

On a host of domestic issues—taxes, Social Security reform, energy development—surveys also find substantial partisan divisions that grow even wider when Bush's name is attached to any of the policy alternatives. For instance, one poll taken in March 2005 found that 42 percent of Democrats supported "a plan in which people who chose to could invest some of their Social Security contributions in the stock market," but only 11 percent said they supported "George W. Bush's proposals on Social Security." Seventy-seven percent of Republicans backed the stock market option and 74 percent supported "Bush's proposals," so the mention of Bush increased the already notable partisan gap from 35 to 63 percentage points in the survey.[16] More recent examples come from public responses to questions about the administration's warrantless wiretaps, with partisan gaps exceeding 50 points on some questions.[17]

There are, of course, some issues that produce only small partisan divisions. For instance, large majorities in both parties panned Congress and the president's intervention in the Terry Schiavo case, supported Bush's education reforms, and favored spending billions of dollars to rebuild New Orleans. But large party differences have become so common that it now makes little sense to analyze survey data on political questions *without* paying attention to the partisan breakdowns.

The influence of popular partisanship is not confined to opinions about politicians and issues. In line with the classic psychological conception of party identification, political perceptions and beliefs are also now strongly shaped by

15. Jacobson (2007, pp. 131–38, 223–32).
16. Jacobson (2007, pp. 214–16).
17. A CBS News/*New York Times* poll, conducted February 22–26, 2006, asked two forms of a question on whether respondents approved of the wiretaps. In the version that mentioned the threat of terrorism as a reason, 83 percent of Republicans but only 33 percent of Democrats approved. When terrorism was not specifically mentioned, 76 percent of Republicans but only 22 percent of Democrats approved. CBS News, "President Bush, the Ports, and Iraq," February 27, 2006 (www.cbsnews.com/htdocs/pdf/poll_bush_022706.pdf).

partisanship. Between mid-2004 and mid-2006, for example, an average of 76 percent of Republicans—but only 27 percent of Democrats—viewed the Iraq war as going somewhat or very well. Similarly, an average of 76 percent of Republicans but only 29 percent of Democrats believed the war has made the United States safer from terrorism.[18] As late as March 2005, long after unchallenged official reports had concluded otherwise, 79 percent of Republicans still believed that Saddam Hussein's Iraq possessed weapons of mass destruction just before the U.S. invasion, while only 37 percent of Democrats held this view. Republicans were also much more likely to believe—again, contrary to the highly publicized findings of official investigations—that Saddam was complicit in the terrorist attacks of 9/11 (an average of 46 percent among Republicans and 27 percent among Democrats).[19]

The Iraq war, like its initiator, has provoked unusually strong partisan responses, to be sure, but the same divergence in perceptions of reality applies to other domains as well. For example, partisan differences in perceptions of how the economy is performing have become just as wide as those regarding the Iraq war (see figure 2-17). From the beginning of 2004 through April 2006, the gap between those who rated the economy as "good" or "very good" has averaged 48 points higher among Republicans than Democrats. Class differences in the party coalitions may have something to do with this gap (economic circumstances improved more for upper-income than lower-income groups), but not enough to account for such sharply divergent readings of economic conditions by ordinary Democrats and Republicans.

It is these regular manifestations of partisan division—along with record-high levels of party-line voting in recent elections—that make it hard to believe that mass partisan polarization is illusory or that partisan polarization is limited to a narrow segment of the electorate. To be sure, the degree of polarization varies across voters, as Abramowitz demonstrates, as well as across political leaders and issues. (However, no senator or governor is as polarizing as Bush—and a few even receive higher marks from rival partisans than from their own.)[20] Nonetheless, that ordinary citizens are now so ready to respond in sharply divergent partisan terms to such a variety of political stimuli is, I think, strong evidence that underlying partisan divisions are strong, genuine, and widespread.

18. Jacobson (2007, pp. 224, 232).
19. Jacobson (2007, pp. 140–41).
20. Jacobson (2006).

Figure 2-17. *Rating the Performance of the Economy, by Party Identification, 2001–05*

Percent who said economy was "good" or "very good"

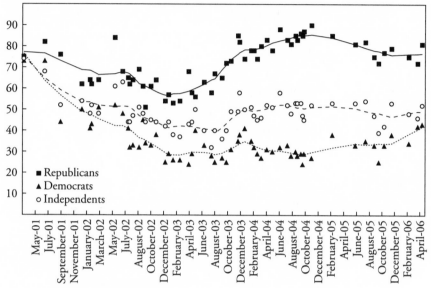

Source: CBS News/*New York Times* polls.

3. These underlying partisan divisions have a substantial cultural component; if they are not necessarily indicative of a "culture war," they do provide a popular basis for plenty of partisan conflict on cultural issues.

Consider the results shown in figure 2-18 of a study of religion and political behavior in 2004 reported by James L. Guth, Lyman A. Kellstedt, Corwin E. Smidt, and John C. Green.[21] Regardless of denomination, religious traditionalists—defined by orthodox or fundamentalist beliefs, regular participation, and identification with religious movements—are overwhelmingly Republican. Of the 26 percent of respondents Guth and his associates classified as religious traditionalists or Latter Day Saints (LDS/Mormons), 69 percent identified themselves as Republicans, but only 20 percent as Democrats. Of the 36 percent who were classified as modernist in religion, unaffiliated, Jewish, or "other," 50 percent

21. Guth and others (2005).

Figure 2-18. *Religion and Party Identification, 2004*[a]

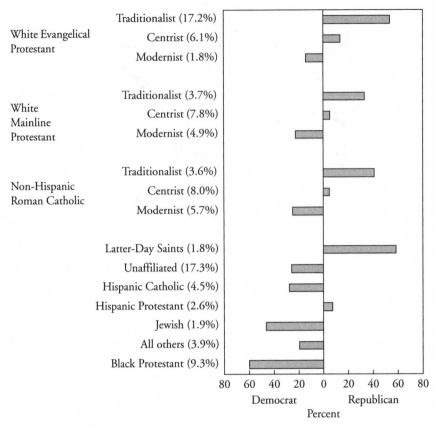

Source: Guth and others (2005, table 3).

a. Percentages given after each group indicate the proportion of those who self-identify as traditionalist, centrist, or modernist within the overall religious affiliation noted.

identified themselves as Democrats, but only 25 percent as Republicans. Democrats also held a wide lead among minorities (except Hispanic Protestants), while religious centrists (22 percent of respondents) gave Republicans an edge, 45 percent to 38 percent.

Restated in terms of party coalitions, 45 percent of Republicans were religious traditionalists or LDS, and only 22 percent were from the modernist/unaffiliated/ Jewish/other categories. Twenty-five percent of Republicans were religious centrists, and only 8 percent were minorities of any kind. In contrast, 44 percent of Democrats were from the modernist category, 24 percent were minorities, 20 percent were religious centrists, and only 13 percent were religious traditionalists or LDS.[22] Thus the largest factions in each party were at polar opposites on the religious-cultural divide, and the parties also had very different ethnic compositions. It would be surprising, then, if issues touching on these divisions—abortion, same-sex marriage, stem-cell research, "intelligent design" in science classes, assisted suicide, sex education, faith-based delivery of social services, affirmative action, immigration—did *not* provoke clear partisan differences.

REJOINDER

Morris P. Fiorina and Matthew S. Levendusky

We appreciate the attention given to our analysis by Alan I. Abramowitz and Gary C. Jacobson. In this rejoinder we will address a number of points of disagreement, as well as some questions that remain open for further research.

Response to Abramowitz's Comments

Alan Abramowitz's critique seems aimed at both *Culture War?* and our chapter in this volume. He makes two arguments: First, the extent of popular polarization is much larger than argued in *Culture War?* and the extent of party sorting is much greater than we argue in our paper. Second, the highly engaged portion of the electorate (which we all agree is more polarized than the larger mass of unengaged citizens) is much larger than we assume. In this rejoinder we show that the first claim is incorrect, and the second is highly contestable.

Before addressing his arguments, we offer one preliminary observation: Even if one were to accept Abramowitz's procedures and analyses uncritically (which we do not), much of the temporal change that he finds is due to sudden changes in many of the variables that occurred in 2004. Consider a modified version of Abramowitz's table 2-3 (see table 2-5). As shown in the last two columns, the change from 2000 to 2004 accounts for 40 percent of the total change among voters since 1984, 40 percent of the total change among "active citizens," and

---

22. Percentages total 101 because of rounding.

Table 2-5. *Polarization on the Abramowitz Scale: The Importance of 2004*
Standard deviations

	1984	2000	2004	Change 1984–2004 (percent)	Change 1984–2000 (percent)
Nonvoters	2.52	2.68	2.67	6	6
Voters	2.89	3.31	3.60	25	15
Active citizens	3.15	3.59	3.89	23	14
Campaign activists	3.74	3.71	4.27	14	−1

Source: Drawn from Abramowitz, table 2-3 in this volume.

all of the change among "campaign activists," who show virtually no change at all between 1984 and 2000. If Abramowitz had penned this critique before the 2004 election, when the first edition of *Culture War?* was written, he would have a much weaker case. Perhaps 2004 will prove to be a representative election from a new era—and perhaps it was just a blip. But let us take a closer look at Abramowitz's analysis.

How Much Polarization?

Abramowitz tracks responses on seven issue scales included in the National Election Studies (NES) since 1984. Each question asks respondents to place themselves at one of seven positions running from extremely liberal to extremely conservative. Abramowitz's procedures—which involve categorizing, aggregating, and categorizing again—systematically exaggerate differences and changes in the response patterns. First, he converts fine-grained measures to categorical measures by recoding everyone to the left of the scale's midpoint as a liberal and everyone to the right as a conservative, thereby equating "slightly liberal" (or "slightly conservative") responses with "extremely liberal" (or "extremely conservative") responses. As figure 2-19 shows, this recoding makes public opinion on a given issue look more polarized than before the recoding.

Next Abramowitz aggregates the seven scales and recategorizes the sum into a five-category measure that runs from "consistent liberal" to "consistent conservative." Consider a respondent with the following vector of responses on the seven-point scales that underlie the data in his tables and figures: (4, 4, 4, 4, 4, 5, 5). That looks like a quite moderate response pattern to us—five "middle-of-the-road" responses plus two "slightly conservative" responses. But Abramowitz's procedures (number of conservative positions minus number of liberal positions)

Figure 2-19. *The Abramowitz Recoding Exaggerates Polarization*

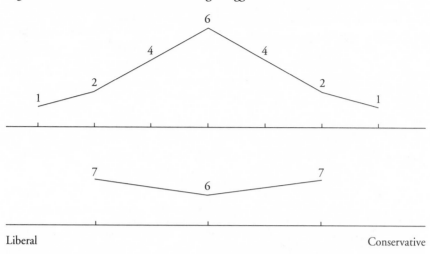

Liberal   Conservative

Source: Drawn by the authors.

assign this person a 2, which puts her in his "moderately conservative" category.[23] Similarly, (3, 3, 4, 4, 4, 4, 4) becomes −2, a "moderate liberal." Differences of a single scale position *on different issues* suffice to separate these respondents by half the maximum possible distance on Abramowitz's five-category scale.

Now, looking at change over time, if the first respondent becomes slightly more conservative on three issues, resulting in (4, 4, 5, 5, 5, 5, 5), she would now score 5 on Abramowitz' aggregate issue index, which makes this moderate conservative a "consistent conservative," the same as a person who puts himself at position 7 on all seven scales. Similarly, with a slight leftward movement on three issues, resulting in (3, 3, 3, 3, 3, 4, 4), the formerly moderate liberal respondent becomes a "consistent liberal," the same as someone who puts herself at position 1 on all seven scales. In sum, we believe that recoding the data, adding it up, and recoding it again exaggerates both the amount of division and the increase in division.[24]

23. Also note that a response vector like (1, 1, 1, 4, 7, 7, 7) gets assigned the same score (0, or moderate), as the response vector (4, 4, 4, 4, 4, 4, 4), although the first vector would seem an unlikely response pattern.

24. Abramowitz has asserted that because he uses the same procedures at all times, the changes he identifies are real. Our point is that the changes are exaggerated because marginal changes in the underlying scale positions can push respondents across the boundaries between his larger categories.

Table 2-6. *Changes in Policy Views, 1984–2004*
Percentage point change on scale from liberal to conservative

	Extremely liberal - - - - - - - - - - - - - -→ Extremely conservative						
Polarization							
Jobs/standard-of-living scale	2	1	0	−2 (−7)[a]	0	1	3
Liberal-conservative scale	0	2	3	3 (−7)	−1	3	1
Left shift							
Health insurance	6	2	3	0 (−9)	0	−2	−2
Spending/services	5	4	5	−3 (−5)	−3	−3	−2
Right shift							
Aid to blacks	0	−2	−5	−5 (−7)	−1	6	8
Defense spending	−5	−4	−3	−5 (−4)	8	4	2
No change							
Abortion	1	−1			3		−1

Source: Calculated from the National Election Studies cumulative data file.

a. Numbers in parentheses are percentage point changes when "don't knows" are treated as middle-of-the-road.

How much do Abramowitz's manipulations exaggerate polarization? Consider the raw data. Table 2-6 shows the percentage point differences between the responses on the seven issue items asked in 1984 and 2004 (the rows do not sum to zero because of rounding). Ignore sampling error, declining response rates, and other complicating factors—assume these numbers are exact. On two scales—liberal-conservative and government responsibility for jobs and standard of living—there is a slight polarization pattern: between 1984 and 2004 there is a single-digit decline in the number of people placing themselves in the exact center of the scale and a marginal increase in the number placing themselves on the left and right. (On the liberal-conservative scale, the number of self-identified moderates is actually 3 percentage points *higher* in 2004 than in 1984, but the number of people who declined to classify themselves at all is 10 percentage points lower in 2004 than in 1984. Abramowitz treats these "decline to classify" respondents as moderates, so we do too. But others may wish to distinguish between moderation and ignorance or uncertainty.)

Four other scales do not show increasing polarization. On each scale the number of respondents in the exact middle declines by single digits, but on the issues of government vs. private health insurance and lower public spending vs. more public services, there is also a decline in the number of conservatives—the population shifts to the left, increasing its support for active government. Conversely, on defense spending and aid to African Americans, there is a decline in the number of liberals—the population shifts to the right, in favor of more defense spending and less aid to African Americans. (As was the case with the liberal-conservative scale, all of the decline in moderates on the health insurance scale and five-sevenths of the decline on the jobs scale reflect a decline in respondents who do not classify themselves rather than a decline in self-placed moderates). On the four-point abortion item the middle is ambiguous, but there is essentially no change.

Now, when each of these scales is reduced to three categories (as in figure 2-19) and they are added up and recategorized, Abramowitz finds somewhat more people in the liberal and conservative categories and somewhat fewer people in the exact middle in 2004 than was the case in 1984. But as table 2-6 shows, only a minor share of this marginal movement reflects true polarization—the extremes gaining respondents at the expense of the middle. Rather, the population has gotten more liberal and less conservative on some issues, but more conservative and less liberal on others. No matter how much one slices, dices, and stews these data, we cannot see how it can support a case for a significant increase in polarization.

In light of the preceding discussion, we stand by our argument that the American electorate is not highly polarized now, and that it has not become appreciably more so in the period for which we have data. Our data show that the extent of partisan sorting varies across issues and parties. Some issues show greater sorting than others, and on some issues one party has become more homogeneous while the other remains unchanged or has become less homogeneous. In particular, contrary to a great deal of contemporary political commentary, party identifiers remain better sorted on New Deal economic issues than on social-cultural issues. To understand these patterns more fully, future work will need to examine the patterns of elite conflict on these issues more carefully; such work is beyond the scope of this essay. The more general point remains, however, that Abramowitz's analyses reflect artifactual exaggerations of differences, as explained above.

A Dramatically More Engaged Electorate?

Abramowitz believes that Philip E. Converse's 1964 portrait of a politically disengaged public is seriously outdated: in 2004, he writes, "the proportion of active citizens reached 45 percent, and the proportion of campaign activists reached 23 percent. Both of these figures were all-time highs." In addition, he cites record numbers of voters who perceived party differences in 2004 (as we note in our essay), and who cared a good deal about the outcome: "These figures appear to undermine Fiorina and Levendusky's assumption that ordinary

Figure 2-20. *Voters Who Worked for a Party or Candidate, 1952–2004*

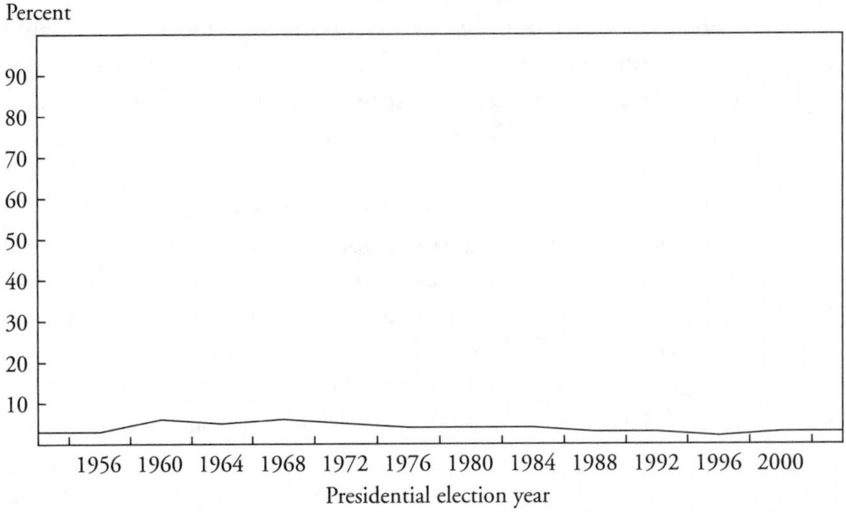

Percent

Source: National Election Studies cumulative data file.

Americans do not generally care about politics. Ordinary Americans cared a great deal about the outcome of the 2004 presidential election."

In fact, the case is much less clear than Abramowitz asserts. Consider his figure 2-9, which illustrates his claim that the proportion of active citizens and campaign activists reached all-time highs in 2004. Then recall our earlier point about the special nature of the 2004 election. Without the 2004 data, there is no increase in activity levels. In fact, there appears to be a decrease in campaign activism until 2000. But, for purposes of argument, we will set that point aside.

How does one rise from the category of mere voter to "active citizen" in Abramowitz's analysis? By engaging in one campaign activity beyond voting. So, what precisely did Americans do to set an all-time record for political engagement in 2004? Did they go out and ring doorbells, distribute leaflets, and in other ways work for a party or a candidate? No. As figure 2-20 shows, the number of people who engaged in such acts in 2004 was in the same low single-digit range that it has been for the half-century history of the NES. Did these suddenly newly engaged citizens give up an evening or Saturday afternoon to attend a meeting or rally? No. As figure 2-21 shows, the number of Americans who did so fell in the same high single-digit range typical of the past half-century. Figure 2-22 shows that the record increase in the active public arose nearly

Figure 2-21. *Voters Who Attended a Political Meeting, 1952–2004*

Percent

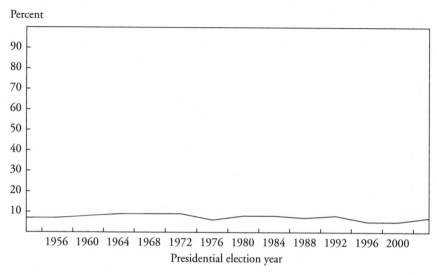

Presidential election year

Source: National Election Studies cumulative data file.

Figure 2-22. *Voters Who Tried to Influence How Others Voted, 1952–2004*

Percent

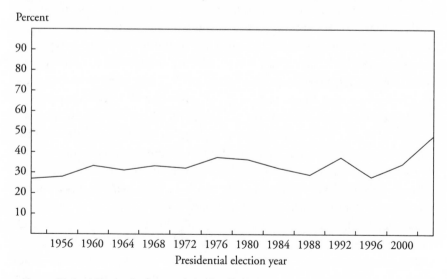

Presidential election year

Source: National Election Studies cumulative data file.

Figure 2-23. *Voters Who Gave Money to Help a Campaign, 1952–2004*

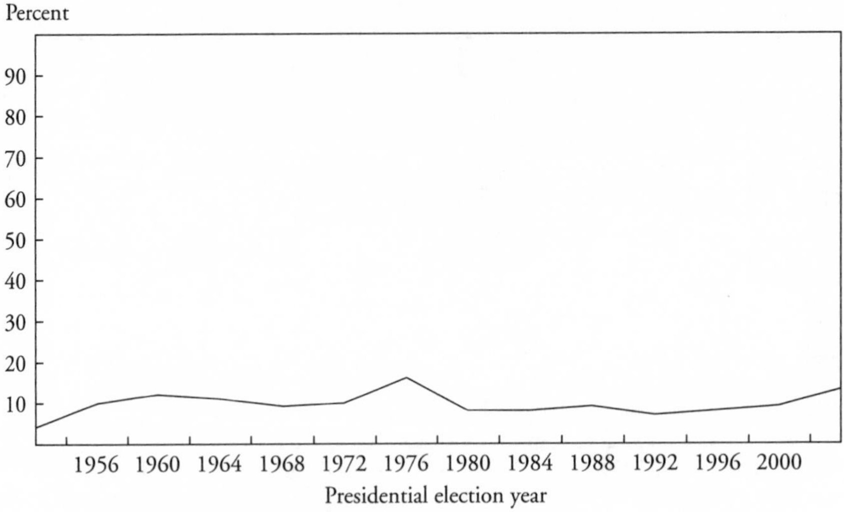

Percent

Source: National Election Studies cumulative data file.

entirely from talk—the number of people who reported trying to convince others how to vote rose 14 percentage points in 2004. A husband and wife discussing Bush vs. Kerry was sufficient to gain admission to "active citizen" status.

Now consider how such "active citizens" ascend to the higher category of "campaign activist." This ascension required one more activity. For a few people this meant writing a check. As shown in figure 2-23, the number of Americans who reported giving money to a campaign rose about 4 percentage points in 2004, the first time the percentage of contributors hit double-digits since the not-so-polarized 1976 election. Most campaign activists achieved their exalted status, however, by wearing a button or putting a bumper sticker on their car. As figure 2-24 shows, the number of Americans who publicly expressed their political preferences in these ways rose about 11 percentage points from the norm since 1984 to reach a level not seen since 1960.

But does such participation necessarily signify increased engagement? Recall that the parties have been much more active in the past two elections, mobilizing grass-roots supporters and returning to old-fashioned get-out-the-vote activities. Such increased party activity shows up clearly in the party contact reports among NES respondents. As figure 2-25 shows, there has been a steady increase in reported party contact since 1992, with an 8 percentage point jump

Figure 2-24. *Voters Who Wore a Button or Put a Sticker on a Car, 1956–2004*

Percent

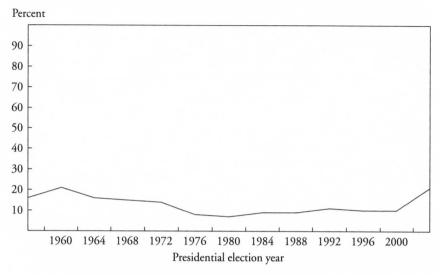

Presidential election year

Source: National Election Studies cumulative data file.

Figure 2-25. *Voters Who Were Contacted by Either Major Party, 1956–2004*

Percent

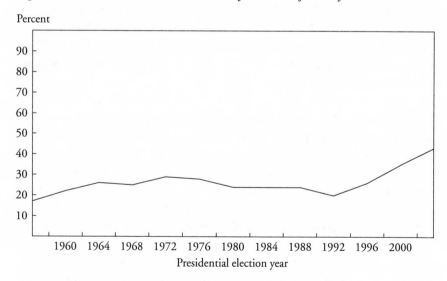

Presidential election year

Source: National Election Studies cumulative data file.

Figure 2-26. *Voters' Interest in Current Campaign, 1952–2004*

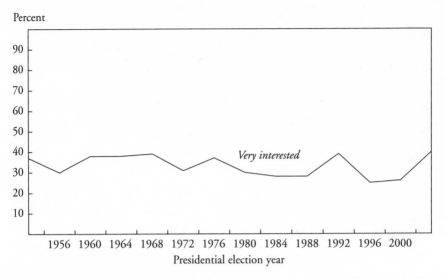

Percent

Source: National Election Studies cumulative data file.

in 2004. The parties may simply have passed out more buttons and stickers in 2004. Similarly, the 5 percentage point increase in presidential turnout that occurred between 2000 and 2004 does not necessarily indicate increased psychological engagement among citizens; it may only reflect increased mobilization activities by the parties. Abramowitz simply ignores this alternative explanation.

This is not the place to make an extensive argument about psychological engagement vs. party mobilization in 2004, but additional data bear even more directly on the question than the preceding figures. According to the NES, although a record number of Americans reported that they cared about the outcome, reading about the campaign in the newspapers and following it on TV were down in 2004. As shown in figure 2-26, interest in the campaign was about the same as in 1992, well within sampling error of 1976, and about the same as in 1960–68 (and it is a reasonable presumption that declining response rates yield a somewhat more politically interested sample today than in previous decades). Increased activity without increased interest or knowledge is consistent with a mobilization argument. Contrary to what Abramowitz asserts, a record numbers of Americans may not have jumped into the political arena in 2004—they may have been pushed.

Counter to Converse's portrait of a nonideological electorate, Abramowitz also contends that "the American electorate today is far better educated than the public of the 1950s. . . . As a result of this dramatic rise in education levels, a much larger proportion of today's electorate is capable of understanding and using ideological concepts." Despite "this dramatic rise in education levels," Michael X. Delli Carpini and Scott Keeter report that Americans are no better informed than they were a generation ago.[25] And in a new book, *Is Voting for Young People?* Martin P. Wattenberg reports that younger, better-educated cohorts of Americans are in fact the least well informed.[26] The communications revolution has generated an explosive increase in the number of information sources, but at the same time has made it easier for people to avoid them.[27] The old adage about leading a horse to water comes to mind.

Of course, if people have become sorted into highly correlated partisan and ideological categories, they may not need to know any details about politics. Partisan and ideological heuristics may now encapsulate their latent issue preferences. But as we have argued, the sorting process is much less perfect than many assume. Recent research reinforces this point.

Christopher Ellis and James A. Stimson examine the economic and social issue preferences of liberals and conservatives with surprising findings.[28] As figure 2-27 illustrates, the minority (about 20 percent) of Americans who categorize themselves as liberals have a reasonable resemblance to people "capable of using and understanding ideological concepts." More than 60 percent of them are liberal on both economic welfare issues and the newer social-cultural issues. Another 20 percent of them are old-time New Deal liberals who are left of center on economic welfare issues, but not on social issues. Self-described conservatives are another matter entirely.

About one-third of Americans call themselves conservatives. But as figure 2-28 shows, only one in five of those who adopt the conservative label have issue stances that are right of center on both economic welfare and social-cultural issues. Somewhat more than a quarter of self-described conservatives are social conservatives only, about 15 percent are economic conservatives only, and, most surprisingly, a third of those who adopt the conservative label express conservative

---

25. Delli Carpini and Keeter (1996).
26. Wattenberg (2006).
27. Prior (forthcoming 2007).
28. Ellis and Stimson (2005).

Figure 2-27. *Issue Liberalism of Self-Identified Liberals, 2004*

Percent

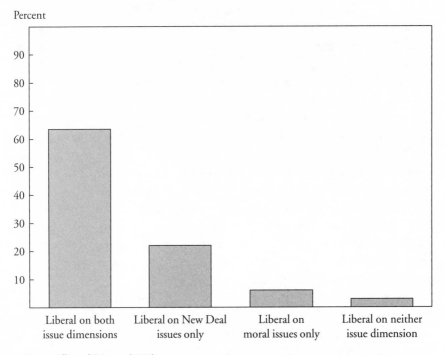

Source: Ellis and Stimson (2005).

views on *neither* economic nor social issues.[29] Such findings do not seem terribly consistent with an electorate that now understands and utilizes ideological concepts. In a related analysis, Edward G. Carmines reports that in contrast to members of Congress, whose roll-call votes on all manner of issues fall on a single left-right continuum, the positions of voters are spread across all four quadrants created by crossing economic and social issue positions (conservatives, liberals, populists, libertarians).[30] As we would expect from a generation of work dating back to Converse, American attitudes are multidimensional, and most

29. Together, the social conservatives and nonconservatives (Ellis and Stimson call them "conflicted conservatives") comprise a clear majority of self-identified *conservatives*. In this light it is easy to understand why President Bush's Social Security privatization proposal went nowhere.

30. Remarks by Edward Carmines at the 2006 annual meeting of the Midwest Political Science Association, April 20–23, summarizing an ongoing research project with Michael Ensley.

Figure 2-28. *Issue Conservatism of Self-Identified Conservatives, 2004*

Percent

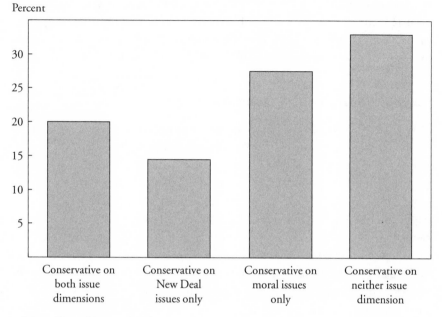

Conservative on both issue dimensions   Conservative on New Deal issues only   Conservative on moral issues only   Conservative on neither issue dimension

Source: Ellis and Stimson (2005).

Americans cannot reasonably be called ideologues. Of course, we do not consider this a fault of the electorate; rather, the electorate does not oversimplify and distort a complex reality as political elites do.

Popular Polarization vs. Party Sorting

Abramowitz remains unpersuaded by our distinction between polarization and sorting. We all agree that the electorate has become better sorted into parties, but Abramowitz prefers to use the term partisan polarization to describe the increase in party distinctiveness. Why do we prefer to maintain a conceptual distinction between sorting and polarization? Social science proceeds best when concepts are clear. Confusing the distinction between changing marginals— the proportion of liberals, moderates, and conservatives (polarization)—and changing correlations within relatively constant marginals (sorting) contributed to the misconceived belief in a culture war. Similarly, conflating partisan and aggregate polarization confuses the matter here. Using the term "sorting"— and avoiding the term "partisan polarization"—promotes conceptual clarity.

Even more important, the sorting/polarization distinction matters because the processes have significantly different implications. If polarization has occurred, the middle has vanished, and society has split into two opposing camps. If sorting has occurred, two opposing camps exist, but a middle remains to referee or reject their conflict. This point brings us to Jacobson's comments.

Response to Jacobson's Comments

Gary Jacobson makes several observations that provide us with an opportunity to clarify some of our arguments. First, consider his remark that "a first-order solution to Fiorina and Levendusky's puzzle is easy. National politicians, while growing increasingly divided along partisan and ideological lines, have not grown more distant from their supporters." His figure 2-15 shows that own-party voters see themselves as about as close to their representatives as they have been for a generation, but other-party voters see themselves as increasingly distant. Note that the latter finding is consistent with the demonstration in *Culture War?* that as the parties move toward their bases they move away from every member of the other party, whereas they move away from some members of their own party while they move toward others.[31]

But we would emphasize Jacobson's own characterization as a "first-order solution." Candidates are no further from their supporters today than a generation ago, but who is, and who is not, a supporter is partly endogenous—it depends on the choices that are offered. People who feel increasingly distant from their party may exit—either join the other party or decline to vote—thus leaving the category of partisan supporters made up of those who continue to feel close to their party.

As one of us has previously pointed out, there has been a "hollowing out" of the electorate during the past generation. Strong partisans now make up a larger share of the active electorate and weak partisans and independents a smaller share. The result is an actual electorate (as opposed to an eligible electorate) that is considerably more ideological than the electorate of a generation ago.[32] It is not surprising that this smaller, more ideological electorate is equally happy with its preferred candidate today as the larger, less ideological electorate of a generation ago. Thus, while we agree with Jacobson's observation that today's politicians can manage to get elected by today's smaller, more ideological electorates, we are

31. The net effect on own-party identifiers will depend on the shape of the party distribution and the positions the candidates move to. See Fiorina, Abrams, and Pope (2006, pp. 28–29).
32. Fiorina (2002).

not willing to exclude from consideration the preferences of the two-fifths of the eligible electorate that does not vote in presidential elections and the three-fifths or more that does not vote in off-year or state and local elections.

When we refer to a "disconnect" between the American citizenry and the political class, we are referring to something more general than whether today's politicians are less liked by those who continue to vote for them than were yesterday's politicians. For a half-century both academic political science and popular political commentary accepted the notion that two-party competition generated centrist policies. Maurice Duverger pointed out in a classic study that, empirically, two-party systems were characterized by "catch-all" parties, broad coalitions of disparate interests, whereas multiparty systems were more likely to have ideologically pure parties.[33] Downs demonstrated the logic of centrist competition theoretically.[34] Many Americans who were active in politics did not like this situation, decrying "me-too" parties, but few denied that it characterized American politics in the mid-twentieth century. By the late 1990s, however, changes were apparent.[35] The question that concerns us is why, with relatively little change in the general shape of voter preferences, did the nature of party competition experience a much larger change? And we think that answering that question is far from "easy."

Jacobson makes a second observation that, if not sorting, some other process must be identified to explain "increasingly divergent partisan responses to national politicians and issues." We agree, and we consider this an important question for future research. However, we suspect that highly divergent partisan responses relate much more closely to politicians and performance than to voters' positions on issues. That is, diverging response patterns between Democrats and Republicans owe more to the positions *elites* take and the things *elites* do than to where *ordinary citizens* stand. As shown in our chapter, partisan differences on the issues are less than often assumed even if the differences in evaluations of Bush (or the Iraq war) diverge greatly. And as Jacobson points out, "no senator or governor is as polarizing as Bush—and a few even receive higher marks from rival partisans than from their own." This evidence highlights the role of Bush *qua* Bush as a polarizer. If polarized evaluations of Bush stemmed from deep polarization of attitudes, then evaluations of rival governors and senators should follow the same pattern of deep polarization. But this is not the pattern we

33. Duverger (1954).
34. Downs (1957).
35. Fiorina (1999).

observe. Faced with less divisive choices, voter choices and evaluations are less divided. Evidence that Bush is a polarizing figure does not imply that the electorate has become *more polarized.*[36]

A recent study of the Iraq war issue in the 2004 voting nicely illustrates this argument. Philip A. Klinkner contrasts the views of Democrats and Republicans on U.S. foreign policy goals (for example, advance human rights, combat terrorism) and finds that the contrasts are significantly different in a statistical sense, but not large.[37] Contrasting the views of partisans on the means that the United States uses to carry out foreign policy (for example, military power, diplomacy), Klinkner again finds differences that are statistically different but not substantively large. The same is true for partisan attitudes on national defense issues like the importance of a strong military and partisan attitudes on patriotism and national affect. But when it comes to partisan attitudes toward President Bush, Klinkner reports the same huge partisan divide that Jacobson has so well described.[38] Bush is clearly a polarizer, even if Democrats' and Republicans' positions are not nearly as divided as their evaluations.

One could posit any number of idiosyncratic reasons for the strong reaction to Bush—visceral reaction to his Texas mannerisms, facial expressions, refusal to admit mistakes, and so forth, but the deeper question that requires an answer is how partisans can differ on seemingly factual matters, such as whether Saddam Hussein actually had weapons of mass destruction or was involved in the attacks on 9/11. But we should bear in mind that partisan differences in the perception of "objective" facts do not begin with Bush. As Larry M. Bartels has pointed out, partisans differed sharply on factual matters even in the 1980s (for example, on whether or not the budget deficit grew during the tenure of Ronald Reagan).[39] An explanation of partisan bias should not focus solely on Bush, but on patterns of elite politics more generally. In addition, part of the answer very likely has to do with the previously discussed decline in public attentiveness to political affairs, coupled with the perceived decline in the objectivity of the mainstream media, which together allow increasing numbers of Americans to choose their own facts. But we agree with Jacobson that this large and important question needs attention.

Finally, Jacobson notes the increased correlation between partisan divisions and religion. Here again, we think the key is the behavior of elites. Why

36. Fiorina, Abrams, and Pope (2006, pp. 25–32).
37. Klinkner (2006).
38. Jacobson (2007).
39. Bartels (2002).

should religion have related to partisan attitudes when both parties nominated (apparently) happily married heterosexual candidates who professed belief in God, went to church on Sundays, and in other ways hewed to conventional morality? But when Republican economic elites ally with religious traditionalists, and Democratic elites grow more secular, religion becomes relevant to the voters who must choose.

REJOINDER
Alan I. Abramowitz

Fiorina and Levendusky make four major criticisms of my response to their essay on party sorting in the American electorate. They argue that (1) my finding that there was a significant increase in ideological polarization between 1984 and 2004 is an artifact of the way that I recoded the seven National Election Studies (NES) items used to create the liberal-conservative policy scale; (2) greater political activism among the public in 2004 was a result of greater mobilization by the parties, not any increase in the underlying level of political involvement among citizens; (3) there has been no significant increase in ideological thinking among the public; and (4) "sorting" is not the same as polarization—just because Americans are now better sorted into parties based on ideological labels doesn't mean that they are more polarized.

I believe that all of these criticisms are mistaken or misleading. In fact, the American public is more polarized today than it was thirty years ago, Americans were more engaged in the 2004 presidential election than in any election since the end of World War II, the level of ideological thinking among the public is substantially greater today than in the past, and the process that Fiorina and Levendusky call "sorting" has been one of the most important sources of polarization in American politics.

Measuring Polarization

Fiorina and Levendusky claim that my finding of increased polarization among the public between 1984 and 2004 is an artifact of the way that I recoded the individual items used to construct the seven-issue liberal-conservative scale. This claim is clearly incorrect, however, since I recoded these items identically in both years. Therefore my recoding cannot possibly explain the change in the shape of the distribution of opinion on the seven-item scale between 1984 and 2004.

Fiorina and Levendusky go on to argue that because the distribution of opinion on the individual items used to construct the seven-item scale did not change between 1984 and 2004, one cannot conclude that the public became more polarized during this time period. But the increase in polarization between 1984 and 2004 was not due to increased polarization on the individual items but to increased consistency in responses across items. For example, the correlation between the jobs-and-living-standards scale and the health-insurance scale increased from .28 in 1984 to .49 in 2004. This means that these two items, which had only 8 percent of their variance in common in 1984, had 24 percent of their variance in common in 2004. As a result of increased consistency in responses to different issues, the proportions of consistent liberals and consistent conservatives in the electorate both increased between 1984 and 2004. Finally, while the NES data indicate that polarization peaked in 2004, these data also indicate that polarization has been increasing for three decades. With regard to polarization, the 2004 results were not a break with the past but a continuation of a long-term trend.

Political Activism and Engagement

The increased level of activism among the public in 2004 was not simply a result of increased mobilization by the parties, as Fiorina and Levendusky suggest. Among NES respondents who were not contacted by either political party, the proportion who tried to influence the vote of a friend, relative, or coworker increased from 28 percent in 2000 to 44 percent in 2004, and the proportion who displayed a button, bumper sticker, or yard sign increased from 6 percent in 2000 to 14 percent in 2004. Furthermore, increased mobilization by the parties also does not explain why the percentage of Americans who reported that they cared a great deal about who won the presidential election set an all-time record in 2004.

Fiorina and Levendusky note, correctly, that most of those who engaged in campaign-related activities in 2004 simply talked to a friend, relative, or coworker about the election or displayed a button, bumper sticker, or yard sign. Relatively few Americans took the time to engage in more difficult and time-consuming activities like attending a political rally or working on a campaign. But my point is not that vast numbers of Americans suddenly became hard-core political activists in 2004. My point is that the large group of Americans who engaged in these activities were quite polarized in their political views—active Democrats were quite liberal and active Republicans were quite conservative—and that these were the sorts of voters to whom candidates and officeholders paid close attention.

Ideological Thinking in the American Public

I strongly agree with Fiorina and Levendusky on one point: very few Americans are liberal or conservative ideologues. However, I strongly disagree with their claim that ideological thinking in the public has not increased over time. One piece of evidence on this score is the fact that the proportion of Americans unable to place themselves on the NES liberal-conservative scale fell from 30 percent during the 1970s and 1980s to only 18 percent during 2002–04. At the same time, the correlations between the liberal-conservative identification scale and specific issue scales increased. For example, the correlation between the liberal-conservative scale and the health-insurance scale increased from .28 in 1972 to .41 in 2004, while the correlation between the liberal-conservative scale and the abortion scale increased from .12 in 1972 to .37 in 2004. The correlations among issue scales also increased. For example, the correlation between the health-insurance scale and the jobs-and-living-standards scale increased from .33 in 1972 to .50 in 2004. Both increased awareness of ideological concepts and increased constraint indicate that ideological thinking is more prevalent than in the past.

Fiorina and Levendusky claim that liberal-conservative identification is not a meaningful measure of ideology because even though self-identified liberals usually take liberal positions on specific policy issues, self-identified conservatives frequently do not take conservative positions on specific policy issues. However, data from the 2004 National Exit Poll indicate that, on average, self-identified conservatives were as likely to take conservative positions on specific issues as self-identified liberals were to take liberal positions.

For example, 71 percent of self-identified conservatives (vs. 17 percent of self-identified liberals) wanted abortion illegal in all or most cases; 61 percent of self-identified conservatives (vs. 17 percent of self-identified liberals) opposed any legal recognition for gay and lesbian couples; 71 percent of self-identified conservatives (vs. 29 percent of self-identified liberals) felt that the government was trying to do too many things; 76 percent of self-identified conservatives (vs. 15 percent of self-identified liberals) believed that the war with Iraq had improved the long-term security of the United States; and 84 percent of self-identified conservatives (vs. 26 percent of self-identified liberals) considered the war in Iraq part of the war on terrorism. On average, 73 percent of self-identified conservatives took the conservative side and 74 percent of self-identified liberals took the liberal side on these five issues. These results, along with similar results from recent NES surveys, indicate that liberal-conservative identification is strongly related to positions on a wide range of specific policy issues.

Interestingly, in their response to Gary C. Jacobson, Fiorina and Levendusky acknowledge that the American electorate has become more ideological: "Strong partisans now make up a larger share of the active electorate and weak partisans and independents a smaller share. The result is an actual electorate (as opposed to an eligible electorate) that is considerably more ideological than a generation ago." Fiorina and Levendusky seem to be suggesting that the electorate has become more ideological because it has decreased in size, but this is not so. The rate of turnout of eligible voters in the 2004 presidential election was, in fact, comparable to the rate of turnout of eligible voters during the 1950s and 1960s.

Sorting vs. Polarization

Over the past three decades, differences between rank-and-file Democrats and Republicans have increased dramatically across a wide range of issues. According to NES data, between 1972 and 2004, the correlation (Pearson's r) of the party identification scale with the liberal-conservative scale increased from .32 to .63, the correlation with the abortion scale increased from −.06 to .20, the correlation with the jobs-and-living-standards scale increased from .20 to .41, and the correlation with the government-aid-to-blacks scale increased from .14 to .38.

The stronger correlations between the party-identification scale and a variety of issue scales indicate that the distance between Democratic and Republican voters on these issues has been growing. Democratic voters have been moving to the left while Republican voters have been moving to the right. By referring to this trend as "sorting," Fiorina and Levendusky appear to be downplaying its significance. However, the fact that the electoral base of the Democratic Party has become more liberal while the electoral base of the Republican Party has become more conservative is one of the most significant developments in American politics of the past thirty years. This trend has important implications for candidates and officeholders at every level in the United States. As a result of this ideological realignment, it has become more difficult for a conservative or a moderate to win a Democratic primary, and it has become more difficult for a liberal or a moderate to win a Republican primary. Increasing partisan polarization among elites reflects increasing partisan polarization in the electorate.

References

Abramowitz, Alan I. 1994. "Issue Evolution Reconsidered: Racial Attitudes and Partisanship in the U.S. Electorate." *American Journal of Political Science* 38 (1): 1–24.

Abramowitz, Alan I., and Kyle Saunders. 1998. "Ideological Realignment in the U.S. Electorate." *Journal of Politics* 60 (3): 634–52.

Adams, Greg D. 1997. "Abortion: Evidence of an Issue Evolution." *American Journal of Political Science* 41 (3): 718–37.

Aldrich, John. 1995. *Why Parties?* University of Chicago Press.

Ansolabehere, Stephen, Jonathan Rodden, and James M. Snyder Jr. 2006. "Purple America." *Journal of Economic Perspectives* 20 (2): 97–118.

Baker, Wayne. 2005a. *America's Crisis of Values: Reality and Perception.* Princeton University Press.

———. 2005b. "Social Science in the Public Interest: To What Extent Did the Media Cover 'Culture War? The Myth of a Polarized America'?" *The Forum* 3 (2): Article 4.

Bartels, Larry M. 2002. "Beyond the Running Tally: Partisan Bias in Political Perceptions." *Political Behavior* 24 (2): 117–50.

———. 2006. "What's the Matter with *What's the Matter with Kansas?*" *Quarterly Journal of Political Science* 1 (2): 201–26.

Brady, David W., Hahrie Han, and Jeremy C. Pope. Forthcoming 2007. "Primary Elections and Candidate Ideology: Out of Step with the Primary Electorate?" *Legislative Studies Quarterly.*

Carmines, Edward G., and Geoffrey C. Layman. 1997. "Issue Evolution in Postwar American Politics: Old Certainties and Fresh Tensions." In *Present Discontents: American Politics in the Very Late Twentieth Century,* edited by Byron E. Shafer, pp. 89–134. Chatham, N.J.: Chatham House.

Carmines, Edward G., and James A. Stimson. 1989. *Issue Evolution: Race and the Transformation of American Politics.* Princeton University Press.

Converse, Philip E. 1964. "The Nature of Belief Systems in Mass Publics." In *Ideology and Discontent,* edited by David E. Apter, pp. 206–61. New York: Free Press.

Delli Carpini, Michael X., and Scott Keeter. 1996. *What Americans Know about Politics and Why It Matters.* Yale University Press.

DiMaggio, Paul, John Evans, and Bethany Bryson. 1996. "Have Americans' Social Attitudes Become More Polarized?" *American Journal of Sociology* 102 (3): 690–755.

Downs, Anthony. 1957. *An Economic Theory of Democracy.* New York: Harper & Brothers.

Duverger, Maurice. 1954. *Political Parties: Their Organization and Activity in the Modern State.* Translated by Barbara North and Robert North. New York: John Wiley & Sons.

Dworkin, Ronald. 1996. *The Rise of the Imperial Self: America's Culture Wars in Augustinian Perspective.* Lanham, Md.: Rowman & Littlefield.

Edsall, Thomas Byrne, and Mary D. Edsall. 1991. *Chain Reaction: The Impact of Race, Rights, and Taxes on American Politics.* New York: W. W. Norton.

Eills, Christopher, and James A. Stimson. 1999. "Operational and Symbolic Ideology in the American Electorate: The 'Paradox' Revisited." Paper prepared for the annual meeting of the Midwest Political Science Association, Chicago, April 7–10.

Evans, John H. 2003. "Have Americans' Attitudes Become More Polarized? An Update." *Social Science Quarterly* 84 (1): 71–90.

Fiorina, Morris. 1999. "Whatever Happened to the Median Voter?" Paper prepared for the MIT Conference on Parties and Congress, Cambridge, Mass., October 2.

————. 2001. "Keystone Reconsidered." In *Congress Reconsidered,* 7th ed., edited by Lawrence Dodd and Bruce I. Oppenheimer, pp. 141–63. Washington: CQ Press.

————. 2002. "Parties, Participation, and Representation in America: Old Theories Face New Realities." In *Political Science: The State of the Discipline,* edited by Ira Katznelson and Helen Milner, pp. 536–38. New York: W. W. Norton.

Fiorina, Morris P., Samuel J. Abrams, and Jeremy C. Pope. 2006. *Culture War? The Myth of a Polarized America.* New York: Longman.

Frank, Thomas. 2004. *What's the Matter with Kansas? How Conservatives Won the Heart of America.* New York: Metropolitan Books.

Galston, William A., and Elaine C. Kamarck. 2005. *The Politics of Polarization.* Washington: ThirdWay.

Gelman, Andrew, and others. 2005. "Rich State, Poor State, Red State, Blue State: What's the Matter with Connecticut?" Columbia University, Department of Political Science.

Guth, James L., and others. 2005. "Religious Mobilization in the 2004 Presidential Election." Paper prepared for the annual meeting of the American Political Science Association, Washington, September 1–4.

Hillygus, D. Sunshine, and Todd Shields. 2005. "Reassessing Issue Polarization in the American Electorate: Partisan Incongruities and Presidential Voting." Harvard University, Department of Government.

Hunter, James Davison. 1991. *Culture Wars: The Struggle to Define America.* New York: Basic Books.

Jacobson, Gary C. 2000. "Party Polarization in National Politics: The Electoral Connection." In *Polarized Politics: Congress and the President in a Partisan Era,* edited by Jon R. Bond and Richard Fleisher, pp. 9–30. Washington: CQ Press.

————. 2006. "Polarized Opinion in the States: Partisan Differences in Approval Ratings of Governors, Senators, and George W. Bush." Paper prepared for the annual meeting of the Midwest Political Science Association, Chicago, April 20–23.

————. 2007. *A Divider, Not a Uniter: George W. Bush and the American People.* New York: Longman.

————. Forthcoming 2007. "Explaining the Ideological Polarization of the Congressional Parties since the 1970s." In *Process, Party, and Policy Making: Further New Perspectives on the History of Congress,* edited by David W. Brady and Mathew D. McCubbins. Stanford University Press.

Klinkner, Philip A. 2006. "Mr. Bush's War: Foreign Policy in the 2004 Election." *Presidential Studies Quarterly* 36 (2): 281–96.

Kristol, Irving. 1995. *Neoconservatism: The Autobiography of an Idea.* New York: Free Press.

Krosnick, Jon A., and Matthew K. Berent. 1993. "Comparisons of Party Identification and Policy Preferences: The Impact of Survey Question Format." *American Journal of Political Science* 37 (3): 941–64.

Layman, Geoffrey C. 2001. *The Great Divide: Religious and Cultural Conflict in American Party Politics.* Columbia University Press.

Layman, Geoffrey C., and Thomas M. Carsey. 2002. "Party Polarization and 'Conflict Extension' in the American Electorate." *American Journal of Political Science* 46 (4): 786–802.

Levendusky, Matthew S. 2006. "Sorting: Explaining Change in the American Electorate." Ph.D. dissertation, Stanford University.

McCloskey, Herbert, Paul Hoffman, and Rosemary O'Hara. 1960. "Issue Conflict and Consensus among Party Leaders and Followers." *American Political Science Review* 54 (2): 406–27.

Nie, Norman N., Sidney Verba, and John R. Petrocik. 1979. *The Changing American Voter.* Harvard University Press.

Prior, Markus. Forthcoming 2007. *Post-Broadcast Democracy: How Media Choice Increases Inequality in Political Involvement and Polarizes Elections.* Cambridge University Press.

Roberts, Jason M., and Steven S. Smith. 2003. "Procedural Contexts, Party Strategy, and Conditional Party Voting in the U.S. House of Representatives, 1971–2000." *American Journal of Political Science* 47 (2): 305–17.

Sanbonmatsu, Kira. 2002. *Democrats, Republicans, and the Politics of Women's Place.* University of Michigan Press.

Wattenberg, Martin P. 2006. *Is Voting for Young People?* New York: Longman.

Wolfe, Alan. 1998. *One Nation, After All.* New York: Viking.

3

Polarization Then and Now: A Historical Perspective

David W. Brady
Hahrie C. Han

I n political media, in academic journals, and at cocktail parties across the country, members of the political infotainment community have been debating how polarized the country really is. Pundits and scholars alike assert the polarization of contemporary politics, portraying an ever widening chasm between Democrats and Republicans:

> When George W. Bush took office half the country cheered and the other half seethed.

> The red states get redder, the blue states get bluer, and the political map of the United States takes on the coloration of the Civil War.

> Politics in the United States can now be characterized as an ideologically polarized party system.[1]

The authors would like to thank Joseph Cooper, Charles Jones, Pietro Nivola, and Jeremy C. Pope for their very helpful comments.

1. Quotes, respectively, from Jill Lawrence, "Behind Its United Front, Nation as Divided as Ever," *USA Today,* February 18 2002; E. J. Dionne, "One Nation Deeply Divided," *Washington Post,* November 7, 2003; McCarty, Poole, and Rosenthal (2006, p. 1).

Yet interpreting the meaning of polarization is problematic without having some benchmarks with which to assess it. There is a certain irony underlying all of the debate about polarization because the primary function of political parties is, by definition, to organize differences between factions in the political system. The *Oxford English Dictionary* offers three related definitions of a political party:

(a) A group of people on one side in a contest, battle, etc., or united in maintaining a cause, policy, or opinion in opposition to others; a faction; (b) *spec.* a formally constituted political group, usually organized on a national basis, which contests elections and aims to form or take part in a government; (c) the policy or system of taking sides on public questions; attachment to or support for a particular party; party feeling or spirit; partisanship, esp. in political matters.

In some sense, political parties exist in order to be polarized. So what is all the fuss? When we say parties are polarized, what does that really mean?

In this chapter we draw on history to provide benchmarks that can be used to better understand and interpret polarization in the present era. The analysis is based on the presumption that any discussion of polarization is inherently a comparative discussion. To say simply that parties are polarized is to define what parties are. Likewise, when we say American politics today are polarized, we are making an implicit comparison with another place, another type of government, or another time period. An attempt to establish the level of polarization—whether the difference between parties is high, medium, or low—implies some comparative metric that establishes what "high" levels of polarization are relative to "low" levels of polarization. The two-party system in American history is a natural metric to use in establishing benchmarks for evaluating polarization today. By examining historical patterns of polarization, we can assess how polarization today compares with polarization in the past, but also identify consistencies and inconsistencies with the past.

At the broadest level, perhaps the first key point to make is that polarization in American politics is nothing new. For many years, our political institutions and policymaking processes have withstood sharp divisions between the parties. In fact, the early history of the two-party political system in the United States exhibited much more colorful anecdotes about polarization. Party leaders during the founding era sought to settle debates with lethal duels, and Representative Preston Brooks famously caned Senator Charles Sumner in the antebellum Congress. In the late nineteenth century, the aptly named sergeant at arms busily disarmed members on the House floor, and the two parties used their platforms to exchange slurs. In their 1880 platform, Republicans charged Democrats with exhibiting "sacrifice of patriotism and justice to supreme and insatiable lust for office." In 1884, Democrats countered by claiming that Republicans have "steadily decayed in moral character and political capacity."[2] For much of American history, the two parties have been distant from each other in the policy positions they took, and the party coalitions have been relatively cohesive in acting out their party platforms.[3]

Yet beneath this broad characterization there are historical differences in how—and how much—politics have been polarized. To better understand these nuances, we examine two key dimensions of polarization. The first dimension is the breadth and depth of polarization, or the degree to which parties are both distant from each other and cohesive in their actions, and the extent to which polarization pervades the political system. How large are the ideological disparities between parties and how cohesive are parties in their behavior? Are both elites and masses polarized, or is polarization limited to certain segments of the population? In examining the breadth and depth of polarization, we thus ask what characterizes a polarized party system and who should reflect those characteristics. The second dimension is the character and intensity of issue divisions between the parties. Because parties are usually differentiated by their stances on key questions of public policy or government philosophy, we examine the kinds of issues that divide the parties and the fervor surrounding politics on each issue.

The historical analysis focuses on two major periods of polarization: the transition from an essentially agricultural economy to a modern industrialized economy at the turn of the twentieth century, and the class-based debate over responses to the Great Depression. We chose these periods because historians and political scientists generally agree that these were two major political "crises" that divided Republicans and Democrats.[4] At the turn of the twentieth century, American society was shifting from a rural to an industrial economy, and from a parochialized society to a more national community.[5] Managers and businessmen benefiting from the rise of industrialization battled disaffected groups of laborers, agrarians, and immigrants uncertain of their place in a changing society. Parties

2. Quoted in Gould (1996, p. 215).

3. Our understanding of polarization in the past is not limited to these anecdotes. A number of studies find quantifiable evidence substantiating the idea that polarization has long been a norm in American politics. For example, see Jacobson (2003); Schickler (2000); Han and Brady (forthcoming); Poole and Rosenthal (1991); Brady, Cooper, and Hurley (1979); Ansolabehere, Snyder, and Stewart (2001); Ansolabehere and Snyder (2002); McCarty, Poole, and Rosenthal (2006).

4. See Kennedy (1971, 1999); Silbey (1991); Keller (1990).

5. See Wiebe (1967); Silbey (1991); Keller (1979, 1990).

divided over questions about the role of government in growing and expanding the national economy (particularly the debate over tariffs and monetary standards), and the appropriate role of the United States in world affairs. Similarly, after the stock market collapse in 1929, Democrats painted President Herbert Hoover and the Republicans as woefully ineffective on the issue of economic recovery and swept themselves into office in 1932.[6] As historian David Kennedy has written, Franklin D. Roosevelt's New Deal for economic recovery led to a period in which Americans were made "free from fear."[7]

To examine the breadth and depth of polarization during these historical time periods, we have to be creative in our search for data. Reliable public opinion data are not available for the entire historical period, so instead we rely on electoral data and the historical record to develop a richer understanding of polarization in elections and in the electorate. These data sources have their limitations. Because the best available data are not as good as we might hope, we seek to substantiate our findings (wherever possible) by comparing several different indicators (see footnotes throughout the chapter). Overall, we find the patterns in the data to be consistent. Thus, even without perfect data, we can examine these historical eras to develop benchmarks for polarization and better understand polarization in American politics today.

We begin by more thoroughly defining what a polarized party system is in terms of the breadth and depth of polarization and the character and intensity of the issues involved. The Civil War era provides a framework for this discussion, since it is the only period in American history when existing political institutions were unable to accommodate the polarized divide between parties. An examination of the Civil War era thus allows us to delineate more clearly the criteria we are using to define what a polarized party system is. We then examine the economic and political transitions of 1890–1910 and the New Deal era relative to the present period of polarization. A close look at polarization during these three periods reveals nuanced similarities and differences that are difficult to summarize neatly. However, we do find that the present period is more similar to the 1890s than it is to the New Deal era. The final section of the chapter draws on this analysis to speculate about how polarization today will be resolved. We compare the way issues were resolved in the 1890s and during the New Deal era and argue that, as in the 1890s, resolution of polarized issues today will happen in more incremental fashion than during the New Deal.

6. See Leuchtenburg (1963); Key (1955, 1958).
7. Kennedy (1999).

Establishing Benchmarks for Polarization

The Civil War era was the only period in American history when polarization rendered political institutions unable to achieve compromise and adapt to shifting preferences. An examination of politics during this era reveals what it means to have a truly polarized political system. During the Civil War era, party coalitions differed clearly in their ideological views and displayed high levels of party unity around those views. In addition, polarization was present not only in elite politics, but also among the masses who expressed their views in elections. Polarization during this era, in other words, was broad and deep. Moreover, the issue divisions of the Civil War era were characterized by intense moral fervor, as partisans divided bitterly over issues of slavery, secession, and civil rights.

A simple definition of a polarized party system is one in which one party is very liberal and the other party is very conservative. The further apart the two parties are on a liberal-conservative spectrum, the more polarized they are. By this definition, we could measure polarization by identifying the median Democrat and the median Republican and simply seeing how far apart they are from each other. But this definition would be too simple.

First, polarization is not only a matter of how far apart the parties are from each other in their views, but also how cohesive the party coalitions are. Consider, for instance, the two hypothetical situations depicted in figure 3-1. In both situations the party medians are approximately the same and are relatively distant from each other. The parties in the top figure are also relatively cohesive, such that all the members of one party are relatively close to the median member. In other words, Republicans are relatively similar to each other and distinct from Democrats, while Democrats are similar to other Democrats and very different from Republicans. In the bottom figure, the parties are much more dispersed, such that some Democrats and some Republicans are indistinguishable from each other in their views. The more conservative Democrats are hard to distinguish from some Republicans, and the more liberal Republicans vote like many Democrats. Even if the median members of each party are relatively distant from each other in their views, it is still possible that a considerable number of Democrats and Republicans are not polarized. Thus, it is important to examine not only the distance between the parties, but also the cohesiveness of the party coalitions.

Second, in examining the disparity and strength of party coalitions, how do we define who constitutes the party? Like leaders in most organizations, party leaders are usually the most visible indicators of their party's stance on a given issue.

Figure 3-1. *Party Cohesion and Ideological Distance between Political Parties*

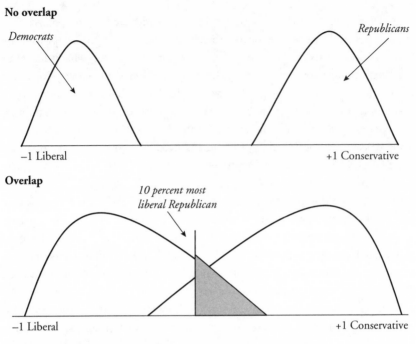

Source: Compiled by the authors.

The rhetoric and actions of elected officials and party activists usually outweigh the behavior of voters in determining public perceptions of the party. Yet as the political scientist V. O. Key Jr. argued in *Politics, Parties, and Pressure Groups,* parties should be understood at three different levels: party-in-government, party-as-organization, and party-in-the-electorate.[8] Mass partisans are as important to defining the party as party elites. In large part, this is because mass party voters either enable party elites to behave in a polarized fashion or constrain them from doing so. Low levels of polarization in the electorate constrain the ability of party elites to legislate in a polarized fashion. When the electorate is not very polarized, legislators are not necessarily rewarded electorally for polarized behavior. On the contrary, when the electorate is very polarized—in the sense that disparities

8. Key (1956).

Table 3-1. *Breadth and Depth of Political Polarization in the Civil War Era and Today*

	Ideological disparity between the parties	Cohesiveness of party coalitions
Civil War era		
Elite party politics	High	High
Mass party politics	High	High
Today		
Elite party politics	High	Party discipline is high, but more bipartisan action
Mass party politics	Ongoing debate, but much evidence shows sorting rather than disparity	Increasing

between the parties are large and party voters are cohesive—legislators will seek to satisfy their party base through more polarized behavior.[9] In other words, the breadth and depth of polarization depends not only on the disparity and strength of party coalitions, but also on the extent to which this is realized in both elite and mass party politics.

During the Civil War era, both party elites and party masses were ideologically distant from each other and relatively cohesive in their voting behavior (see table 3-1). Using roll-call voting scores, scholars have examined the ideological distance between the median Democrat and the median Republican in Congress over time, showing that congressional parties during the Civil War era had clear ideological disparities between them that were relatively high in comparison with other periods in American history.[10]

A similar pattern emerges in an examination of the cohesiveness of party coalitions. A relatively common way to examine the cohesiveness of party coalitions is to study the level of party voting, or the percentage of votes on which a

9. Note that this depends on the disparity *and* the cohesiveness of party coalitions in the electorate. For example, when the average Democrat and the average Republican are very distant from each other in their ideology but the party coalitions in the electorate are relatively weak, then there is still a considerable amount of overlap among voters in the middle of the ideological distribution. (This is depicted in the bottom half of figure 3-1.) In a situation like this, legislators seeking to win swing voters will be more constrained in their ability to vote in a polarized fashion.

10. See, for example, Schickler (2000); Poole and Rosenthal (1984).

majority of Democrats opposed a majority of Republicans.[11] In more polarized times, the sharp distinctions between parties should create greater cohesion as fewer members of Congress are able to straddle a middle line. An examination of historical voting patterns in Congress around the Civil War demonstrates relatively high levels of party voting and cohesion, as expected. Before the Republican takeover of Congress in 1857, 68 percent of all votes were party votes. From 1857 to 1873, the number rose to 75 percent—almost 10 percentage points higher than the subsequent period from the 1870s to the 1890s.[12]

It is more difficult to demonstrate the disparity and cohesiveness of party coalitions among mass partisans during the Civil War era. Historical data on voter preferences during this period are obviously very limited. Nonetheless, we can examine elements of the historical record, which reveal evidence of deep and heartfelt divisions among voters. Nothing evinces how deeply the divisions over slavery penetrated mass party politics better than the electoral reaction to the passage of the Kansas-Nebraska Act in 1854. This act was particularly significant in the lead-up to the Civil War because it fundamentally changed the nature of both politics and policy. The act represented a strategic move by political leaders to broaden the slavery issue to encompass not only the moral cause of abolition, but also economic freedom and prosperity.[13]

The strategy was successful—voters were highly activated. Voter turnout in House elections in 1854 shows how the act generated intense voter interest. In general, turnout in off-year elections is much lower than turnout in presidential election years. In 1858, for example, turnout in northeastern and midwestern states dropped about 18 percent from 1856, only to increase again in 1860. In the off-year elections of 1854, however, voter turnout actually *increased* in the midwestern states over the turnout for the 1852 presidential elections. As a comparison point, we can examine turnout in the northern states that held elections in 1853 before the passage of the Kansas-Nebraska Act, and we find that turnout follows the normal pattern of decline. This exceedingly unusual increase in voter turnout in a midterm election year demonstrates the extreme impact of the Kansas-Nebraska Act on voters. Both of the dominant parties at the time—Democrats

11. See, for example, Hurley and Wilson (1989); Cooper and Young (2002).

12. The results are the same even if we adopt a more stringent criterion and examine only the votes where at least 90 percent of Democrats opposed at least 90 percent of Republicans. For instance, before 1857, only 8.9 percent of all votes met the 90-90 criteria, but after 1857, 20.9 percent of votes did. For more detailed depictions of the data, see Hurley and Wilson (1989); Cooper and Young (2002); Brady (1988).

13. Foner (1970).

and Whigs—felt the impact. The increase in turnout yielded a strong pro-Republican Party vote, which persisted through the Civil War era. As a result, Republicans went from virtual nonexistence in 1852 to become a large minority party in the House of Representatives by 1855—and the majority party by 1860.

The unprecedented intensity of public reaction to the Kansas-Nebraska Act demonstrates the degree to which the fight over slavery and economic freedom penetrated all levels of politics—not just political elites. When party elites pursued a policy antebellum voters disliked, they reacted strongly at the polls, leading to the creation of a new majority party. Once these voters were able to carry the Republican Party to victory in the presidential election of 1860, southern voters reacted equally strongly, leading to the rapid secession of southern states from the union. Mass party politics, in other words, appears to have been as bitterly divided as elite politics during the Civil War era. Importantly, the fact that mass party politics was as polarized as elite party politics enabled the creation of a new majority party—the Republican Party—which took a clear, polarizing stance on slavery. The behavior of mass partisans in elections enabled greater polarization among elites. The key linking mechanisms were elections, which reflected the passion of voters on key national issues.

The second dimension of polarization that we examine is the character and intensity of the issue divisions between the parties. The Civil War era was unique not only for the breadth and depth of its polarization, but also because the polarization of the era resulted from a fundamentally moral issue. We distinguish moral issues from economic issues on the basis of whether an agreement exists about what the "right" outcome is. In some cases, the parties may agree on the goal they are trying to achieve, but disagree on how to achieve it. For example, during the New Deal era, the shared goal of the parties was to pull the nation out of economic depression, but the parties polarized over how best to do it. In other cases—on moral issues, as we define them—parties do not even agree on what the goal is. Should the country abolish slavery or keep it? This distinction between moral and economic issues is important, since moral issues are more difficult to resolve. When parties agree on the goal they are seeking to achieve, it is easier to compromise on questions of how to achieve the goal. When parties do not even agree on the goal they are seeking to achieve, it is more difficult to achieve collective action around a compromise.

Consider, for instance, the search for a compromise on abolition. Was there a centrist solution to slavery among the general antebellum public? One prominent proposed compromise was popular sovereignty, giving each state the right to decide whether to allow slavery. Yet this compromise offered no resolution to the fundamental question of whether slavery should be abolished. As such, it was untenable over time, since both pro- and anti-slavery factions continued to disagree passionately over that fundamental question. When issues such as how to handle fugitive slaves emerged, the weaknesses of popular sovereignty as a long-term solution became evident. Because they did not agree on the fundamental goals they were trying to achieve, pro- and anti-slavery camps could not achieve widespread collective action around fugitive slaves to preserve popular sovereignty. On moral issues, each side thus sees its own goals as the "moral" or "right" alternative, while the other side supports the "wrong" alternative. When defined in these terms, it is very difficult to achieve collective action around a compromise, and, ultimately, one side has to resoundingly defeat the other.

Although political leaders recast the issue in different ways over time, the root of the divisions in the antebellum period was a moral fight over slavery.[14] Scholars examining the polarization of issues during this period have shown that from the first publication of William Lloyd Garrison's abolitionist newsletter *The Liberator,* in 1831, to Reconstruction in the 1870s, issues of slavery, then secession, and finally civil rights divided the country along a unidimensional axis.[15] During the antebellum period, these issues were largely defined in binary terms—one camp was pro-slavery, while the other was anti-slavery—and a strong moral element defined the debate. The battle over slavery was not merely a political battle for power; it was a values-based battle for a moral view of the world.

The centrality of moral issues to polarization in the Civil War era is also reflected in the effect of the Panic of 1857 on Civil War politics. Usually, as with the Panic of 1893 and the stock market collapse of 1929, an economic downturn severely hurts the incumbent party. While the Panic of 1857 did not help Democratic president James Buchanan and incumbent Democrats, its effect was not as strong as the effect of other economic crises. This is because concern over economic depression was embedded in the broader debate over slavery. The Panic of 1857 initiated a dialogue between free traders and protectionists over the fate of the workingman, but positions in this debate were defined by views on slavery, not trade. Even after the economic downturn of 1857, southerners objected to high tariffs and free land in the West because neither economic policy would serve the slave economy. This stance married economic issues created by the panic to the slavery issues, thus providing additional support

14. Foner (1970).
15. See Clausen (1973); Silbey (1991); Sundquist (1983); Brady (1988).

for the Free Men, Free Soil, and Free Labor movement that eventually won a majority in the North for Republicans.[16] Slavery issues, in other words, dominated the debate over economic crises.[17]

The Civil War era thus provides clear benchmarks to use in examining polarization in later periods. Polarization is most acute when party divisions evince clear ideological disparities and party coalitions behave cohesively around those views—as they did during the Civil War. In addition, both party elites and mass partisans should demonstrate high levels of polarization, so that elections act as linking mechanisms between elite politics and mass politics. Finally, polarization around moral issues in which parties disagree about the fundamental outcome to achieve is more potent than polarization around economic issues in which parties agree on economic or other policy goals.

Examining the Breadth and Depth of Polarization

These benchmarks provide a framework for better understanding polarization today in light of the past. During the 1890s and the early twentieth century, American political parties struggled with the transition from an agrarian to an industrial economy and with the role of government in a changing international order. During the New Deal era, a hot debate about the appropriate role of government in the economy characterized party politics. In both periods, we can examine the degree to which party coalitions were distinct and cohesive in both elite and mass party politics. Thus, we can compare today's struggle for partisan definition in a changing nation to similar struggles in our historical past.

In terms of the ideological disparity between party elites, the present period of polarization is more similar to the period at the turn of the twentieth century than to the New Deal era. As noted earlier, a simple way to examine ideological

16. Gienapp (1987); Huston (1987).

17. In a recent work, historian Michael F. Holt argues that the coming of the Civil War was not inevitable. He claims that compromise was possible since majority opinion in both the North and the South was that slavery could never flourish in western expansion states. This implicitly contrasts with our argument that the Civil War period seems to be the one most deeply polarized, where parties from top to bottom are morally divided over issues of slavery. Without historical public opinion data, it is difficult to know where the public really was on this issue. It seems limiting to claim, however, that election-minded politicians were solely to blame for an avoidable war. Holt himself tempers this argument at certain points. In short, we hold to our view that with such deep divisions over a moral issue defined in absolutist terms, it seems that compromise was unlikely, and the ultimate recourse to war was almost unavoidable. See Holt (2004).

differences between party elites is to examine the distance between the median Democrat and the median Republican in Congress.[18]An examination of the difference in party medians from 1867 to 2003 shows that since the Civil War and the advent of the modern two-party system, political parties in Congress have been polarized for much of the time.[19]

Coming out of the Civil War, parties were highly polarized in 1867, and the distance between them grew slightly and peaked around the turn of the century in response to the battle over industrialization in the 1890s. After the turn of the century, the ideological distance between the parties began to decline slightly until the mid-1930s, when it leveled off until approximately the late 1950s. It then began to rise slowly through the 1960s and started to grow sharply in the mid-1970s. In the present era, the distance between the median Democrat and the median Republican has been steadily increasing since the 1970s. The difference between the parties today is less than the difference between parties in the 1890s, but greater than it was during the New Deal era.

The New Deal era stands out as unique in terms of the ideological disparity between party elites. Relative to the turn of the twentieth century and the present period of polarization, the ideological differences between parties in the 1930s were less prevalent. In large part, this is because our measure of ideological distance takes all issues into account, but polarization during this period focused solely on economic issues. After the stock market collapse of 1929 and its attendant ills, the parties divided over the appropriate role of government in the economy. The sweeping political success of the Democratic New Deal plan ousted anti–New Deal Republicans from office in 1932, and both congressional parties largely accepted the outlines of the New Deal after the 1930s. This was possible only because the parties sidelined any real discussion of race and civil rights. The tenuous regional compromises within the Democratic Party, which were essential to pass New Deal legislation, depended on ignoring any issue having to do with race. Thus, although polarization around economic issues was quite high, polarization on other issues was much lower.

If we examine the cohesiveness of party elites, however, polarization in the New Deal era and other periods of American history were similar, and the current period presents more anomalies. For example, in the 107th Congress

18. A commonly used measure relies on DW-nominate scores, a measure of legislator ideology based on roll-call voting behavior. The measures are scaled to make them comparable over time and range from approximately −1 to 1, with −1 indicating an extremely liberal member.

19. For the data, see Jacobson (2003); Schickler (2000).

(2001–02), a majority of Democrats opposed a majority of Republicans on only 51 percent of votes in the Senate and 42 percent of votes in the House.[20] This is much lower than the 1890s, when the 55th Congress (elected in 1896) had party votes 76 percent of the time in the Senate and 79 percent of the time in the House. Similarly, the 73rd Congress (elected in 1932) had party votes 69 percent of the time in the Senate and 73 percent of the time in the House. In other words, during the New Deal era and the 1890s, parties voted cohesively in Congress much more than they do in today's Congress.

Looking at the opposite side of the coin, however, we see that the level of bipartisan unity is much higher today than it was in previous periods of history.[21] Bipartisan unity indicates the percentage of partisans who vote with the majority of their party when it is not a party vote.[22] In other words, in instances when a majority of Democrats vote with a majority of Republicans, how large are the majorities in each party voting with the opposite party? These data are displayed in figure 3-2. In the Senate, the bipartisan unity score is higher now than it has ever been. Among the three periods, the New Deal era has the lowest bipartisan unity score in the Senate, and the 1890s score is between the present period and the New Deal era. Similarly, the bipartisan unity score in the House is lowest during the New Deal, and also extremely low after the 1896 elections. It had risen by the early twentieth century, but today's level of bipartisan unity is close to as high as it has ever been.[23]

These patterns of party voting and bipartisan unity tell an interesting story about party cohesion in Congress over time. In both the 1890s and during the New Deal era, party voting scores during intense periods of partisan struggle are higher than in the periods immediately preceding or following them. Overall, party cohesion appears to have been strongest in the period from 1890 to 1910, since the level of party voting was relatively high and party discipline was high even on bipartisan votes. During the New Deal era, however, there was a rela-

20. We thank Joseph Cooper of the University of Maryland for the data on this point.

21. On this point we are indebted to Joseph Cooper and work in Cooper and Young (2002).

22. These votes can cover a wide variety of issues, but pork barrel issues (such as federal spending on local rivers and harbors and road improvements) are prominent across all eras.

23. Obviously, it is possible that the rate of bipartisan unity has increased simply because Congress is publicly recording more votes on noncontroversial issues now than it did in the past. Analyses of the increase in the number of roll-call votes by Smith (1989) and Evans (2005, p. 509), however, show that procedural reforms in the early 1970s prompted an increase in the number of roll-call votes—but that parties used these votes as a way of forcing each other to take positions on controversial issues. Thus, it seems unlikely that the number of noncontroversial roll-call votes is much higher than in the past.

Figure 3-2. *Bipartisan Unity in the House of Representatives and in the Senate,*
1867–2001

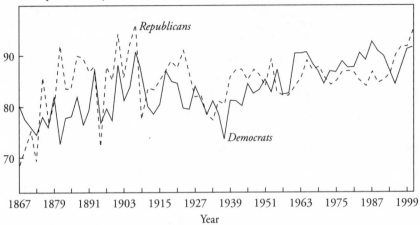

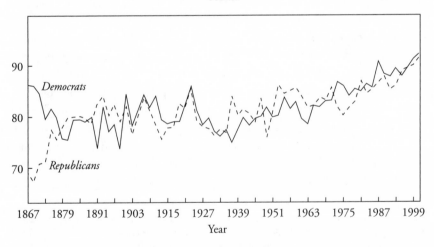

Source: Cooper and Young (1997, 2002).
Data compiled by Joseph Cooper and Garry Young and available at
http://home.gwu.edu/~youngg/research/index.html.

tively high number of partisan votes, but on bipartisan votes the level of party unity was much lower. This mainly reflects an internally divided Democratic Party on the question of race. Although party cohesion was high around issues concerning the New Deal, it was much lower on issues that tapped into the regional divides within the parties. The present era is distinct from both previous periods, however. The level of party voting is relatively low, indicating that there are not as many votes in which the two parties oppose each other. The level of bipartisan unity, however, is relatively high. That is, parties are cohesive, but they are using their cohesiveness toward more bipartisan and cross-partisan ends.

Thus, at the elite level, parties today are relatively distinct ideologically and cohesive, but they are applying their cohesiveness toward bipartisan votes more often than before. How do we interpret this? Historically, this pattern is an anomaly, and identifying its precise causes is a complex undertaking. We believe, however, that part of it can be understood to be a function of the patterns of polarization in the electorate. Examining partisan disparities and cohesion in the electorate is naturally more difficult than at the elite level. Systematic public opinion data did not become available until the birth of modern polling systems in the early to mid-twentieth century. To understand the depth of polarization within the electorate, we must rely primarily on the historical record, from which we can paint a picture of the nature of the divide between voters in each period. In addition, electoral data, while not perfect, allow us to make comparisons about change over time.[24] In general, this evidence shows that polarization in the electorate today is more similar to mass polarization in the 1890s than in the New Deal era.

To start with a broad overview, we examine the degree to which one party dominated the vote in each congressional district over time. By examining a distribution of presidential vote in congressional districts, we can understand one aspect of polarization in the electorate: interdistrict polarization, or how much polarization exists between congressional districts. The distribution of presidential vote shows the number of districts in which voters were closely divided—choosing a presidential candidate with narrow majorities around 50 percent—and the number of districts in which a large majority of voters

24. Although they are not perfect indicators of voter preferences, electoral data give us some sense of the patterns in voter behavior and the changes over time. As such, scholars have previously used the data (particularly presidential vote data) in a range of different ways as measures of electorate preferences. See, for example, Ansolabehere, Snyder, and Stewart (2000); Canes-Wrone, Brady, and Cogan (2002); Erikson and Wright (1993, 1997, 2005); Jacobson (2001); Levendusky, Pope, and Jackman (2005).

supported either the Democratic or the Republican candidate. Imagine the difference between red and blue states such as Massachusetts and Texas, which were solidly in favor of one party in the 2004 election, and centrist (or "purple") states such as Ohio or Florida, where one party won with only a narrow majority. In more polarized times, we should see more states—or, in this case, congressional districts—that support one party with large percentages of the vote and fewer districts split around 50 percent. If interdistrict polarization is high, then we expect to see more districts at the extremes of the distribution during polarized periods, and more districts in the middle during periods of lower polarization.[25] Figure 3-3 displays the distribution of presidential vote across congressional districts for the periods 1892 to 1900, 1928 to 1936, and 1996 to 2004.

Today's period appears to be similar to the 1890s in that a relatively small shift of voters could swing elections from one party to another. Roughly speaking, the data show that the New Deal era had the highest number of solidly red or blue districts. In 1928 a large number of districts voted strongly Republican for Herbert Hoover, while the data after 1932 show a large shift toward Franklin D. Roosevelt and the Democrats. In the 1890s, on the other hand, a solid number of districts voted at the extremes, but there were also a large number of purple districts. This means that in the 1920s a massive shift of voters across congressional districts was necessary to move an election from Republicans to Democrats; likewise in the 1930s, a massive shift from Democrats to Republicans was necessary to shift partisan control. In contrast, a relatively small number of voter shifts within districts could swing an election from one party to the other in the 1890s, reflecting the relatively close divisions between voters. Similarly, the majority of congressional districts today are still purple in that sweeping majorities do not support one party or the other. Although the number of red and blue districts has increased since the 1960s, the distribution

25. This measure has the advantage of providing a comparable measure of polarization in the electorate over time, but unfortunately does not extend back to the Civil War. In examining the distribution of presidential vote over time, it is important to note the institutional changes in electoral procedures that have occurred between 1876 and the present era. Some key changes include the introduction of the Australian ballot, the growing prevalence of primary elections, and the growth of "incumbency protection" in redistricting. See Cox and Katz (2002). Although these changes limit our ability to make strong comparisons over time, we can use the data to get some sense of how electoral patterns in House elections have been changing and to better understand the contours of each historical era relative to the others.

Figure 3-3. *Distribution of Presidential Vote across Congressional Districts, 1892–1900, 1928–36, 1996–2004*

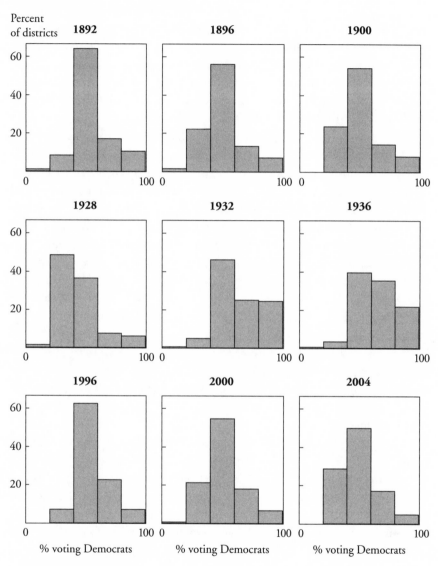

Source: Compiled by authors.

of districts is still a bell-shaped curve in which the largest number of districts is still in the purple middle.

The electoral data thus give us a good sense of interdistrict polarization, but what about intradistrict polarization, or polarization within congressional districts? Here we turn to the historical record for a more thorough understanding of the differences between mass partisans. We find that polarization within the electorate in the 1890s was characterized by high levels of partisan cohesion and that polarization among voters in the New Deal era was characterized more by ideological disparities.

In the 1890s, when mass media and sports did not dominate popular attention, people turned to politics as a form of recreation and used party identification as means of forming group attachments.[26] Historian Robert H. Wiebe argued that by the 1890s people of all ages and backgrounds had joined the movement of community protests and "generated their own nationwide crisis." Living in a time of high economic, social, and political uncertainty, people felt they had no alternative but to "select an enemy and fight."[27] Local communities and neighborhoods formed the basis of partisanship, and individuals were often highly attuned to political happenings. As such, partisanship was not isolated to party-in-government and party-as-organization; instead, individuals joined local party organizations all over the nation in an effort to bring order and definition to their rapidly changing lives.[28]

Partisanship in the 1890s thus seems to be as much a social as an ideological phenomenon.[29] There was, however, important overlap between these social groupings and their political attitudes. While people may have joined the groups to find meaning in a changing society, these groups often became vehicles for distinct political views on the key issues of the day. In this way, the ideological disparities between parties in the electorate seem to have been rooted in a strong sense of partisan cohesion.[30]

In contrast to voters at the turn of the twentieth century, New Deal voters had strong policy-based reasons for selecting their party. The redefinition of political parties based on their views about the role of government in the welfare state was reflected in the class-based divisions of the party bases. From 1930 to the

26. See Kleppner (1982); Wiebe (1967); Gould (1996).
27. Wiebe (1967, p. 76).
28. Wiebe (1967); Gould (1996).
29. For example, factory workers in the 1896 election voted for McKinley, as did northern farmers.
30. Kleppner (1982).

mid-1940s, voters from different socioeconomic classes selected different parties. In *The People's Choice,* a study of voters in Erie County, Ohio, in 1940, sociologists Paul F. Lazarsfeld, Bernard Berelson, and Hazel Gaudet found that "the poor, urban residents, and the Catholics are more likely to vote the Democratic ticket, while the well-to-do, the Protestants, and the rural dwellers are more frequently found in the Republican camp."[31] Robert R. Alford used Michigan Survey Research Center data and Gallup and Roper polls to analyze class voting from 1936 to 1960.[32] His findings showed that, from 1936 to the 1950s, voting differences between classes were consistently high. Berelson, Lazarsfeld, and William N. McPhee found in their study of Elmira, New York, that the swing to Harry Truman, which won him the 1948 election over Thomas E. Dewey, came from those to whom class issues were salient.[33] Political scientist Judson L. James concluded that "this fifth party system [1932–68] not only reversed the majority/minority party roles of the Republicans and Democrats, but also more nearly than any previous two-party system, it had a basis in class conflict."[34]

The New Deal system that characterized parties before and through World War II was thus undoubtedly defined in the electorate along class lines. There were, in other words, clear distinctions between voters that translated into partisan choices and defined the distance between Democratic and Republican voters. In addition, insofar as the New Deal dominated national politics (and ignored issues of race), the class-based divisions made each party's base relatively cohesive around protecting their economic interests.

Although scholars continue to debate the degree of mass party polarization in the present era, we believe that it is more similar to the 1890s than to the New Deal era. This is particularly true since the level of ideological disparity between mass parties remains more ambiguous than levels of partisan cohesion, which seem to be rising. Measures of partisanship in the electorate indicate that it has been increasing since the 1970s. By some demographic measures, for instance, Republicans today are more like other Republicans and unlike Democrats, and some measures of party affiliation show an increase over time.[35]

---

31. Lazarsfeld, Berelson, and Gaudet (1948, pp. xv–xvi).

32. Alford (1964).

33. Berelson, Lazarsfeld, and McPhee (1954).

34. James (1969, p. 45).

35. See the essays in this volume by William A. Galston and Pietro S. Nivola, Alan I. Abramowitz, and James E. Campbell. While there do appear to be slight increases in measures of partisan identification since the 1970s, we cannot compare the level of identification to the previous historical periods because such survey data are unavailable.

The debate about the ideological disparity between voters is less clear. Many studies indicate that most voters are still ideologically moderate.[36] These studies find that despite all the rhetoric today about red states and blue states, a close examination of public opinion demonstrates that voters are not nearly as polarized as some academics and journalists might believe. They argue that while party leaders are seemingly constantly at loggerheads on issues ranging from abortion to the war in Iraq to Social Security reform, Democratic and Republican voters are better sorted, but not nearly as divided.[37] Although the question of how much polarization exists in the electorate is still a matter of contention, our view is that the evidence favors an interpretation that the present era is much more similar to the 1890s than to the New Deal era.[38] As in the 1890s, high levels of partisan cohesion dominate polarization in the electorate.

Putting all the pieces together, when we examine the breadth and depth of polarization in today's politics relative to the past, we find an interesting pattern of behavior. While elite party politics can be characterized by relatively high levels of ideological disparity between the parties and high levels of cohesion, parties in Congress direct that cohesion toward more bipartisan behavior than in the past. Levels of party discipline are high in the sense that the parties often vote together, but there are fewer votes in which a majority of Democrats oppose a majority of Republicans relative to the historical past. In addition, on the votes in which majorities from both parties vote together, the majorities tend to be much larger than ever before.

When we examine mass party politics, however, we find different trends. Levels of partisanship, or party cohesion, appear to be increasing even though we cannot say precisely how high they are relative to the past. The levels of ideological disparity, however, remain ambiguous, although there is much evidence showing that they are not as high as people may think. This analysis is summa-

---

36. See Fiorina, Abrams, and Pope (2006); DiMaggio, Evans, and Bryson (1996); Gelman and others (2005); Collie and Mason (2000); Evans (2003).

37. Fiorina, Abrams, and Pope (2006); Evans (2003).

38. The discussion in this volume among Fiorina and Levendusky, Abramowitz, and Jacobson reflects the ongoing debate about the level of polarization in the electorate. Our reading of this debate is that the most thorough studies of public opinion data find that much of the apparent polarization in the electorate is the product of better partisan sorting, rather than large increases in ideological distance between mass partisans. Although there may be some increased polarization among small groups of partisans, it appears to us that much of the differentiation in public opinion is the product of sorting.

rized in table 3-1. This pattern of results resembles the politics of the 1890s more closely than it does the New Deal. But it is also historically unique, particularly in the pattern of bipartisan unity in elite politics, as well as seemingly low levels of ideological disparity between mass partisans. So how did these unique patterns of polarization emerge? Examining these patterns in their historical context, we discern a distinctive feature of today's politics: it follows on the heels of one of the most bipartisan eras in American political history. This has important implications for today's polarization, particularly in the way that mass party politics is linked to elite party politics. Elections are the primary mechanism that knits voters to elected officials. In the Civil War, the intensity of polarization among mass partisans was expressed through elections, in which party elites were rewarded and punished in a polarized manner.

But what is going on in today's elections? Unlike in previous eras of polarization, congressional elections today are not as nationalized as they were in the past. In the lead-up to the Civil War, the Republican takeover in the 1890s, and the implementation of the New Deal in the 1930s, elections became national affairs. The fate of candidates across congressional districts was determined by common national factors. Current congressional elections are slightly more complicated, however. Although congressional elections today are becoming more nationalized, nationalization comes much later than the increase in polarization. Electoral dynamics emerging from the bipartisan period immediately after World War II created a set of conditions that constrained the ability of elections to link mass polarization to elite polarization more closely.

The unique features of the immediate postwar era become particularly clear if we examine the partisan overlap among elites, or how many Democrats in Congress voted with Republicans, and vice versa. This measure captures both the ideological distance between the parties and the level of party cohesion. The overlapping region is shaded in the bottom of figure 3-1. There we depict the hypothetical placement of the 10 percent most liberal Republican member of Congress. To the left of that hypothetical Republican is the most liberal 10 percent of the Republican Party. To determine the degree of overlap, we simply count the number of Democrats who were more *conservative* than—or to the right of—the 10 percent most liberal Republican. After identifying the 10 percent, 25 percent, and 50 percent most liberal Republicans, we can count the number of Democrats who are more conservative than the Republicans at each of those points. To determine the number of Republicans in the overlapping region, we identify the 10 percent, 25 percent, and 50 percent most conservative

Democrats and count the number of Republicans who are more liberal than they are. Figure 3-4 shows how many members of each party were in the overlap region in each Congress from 1867 to 2003.[39]

Throughout the nineteenth and early twentieth centuries, there was no overlap between congressional parties. The parties were both distant from each other and cohesive in their voting patterns. This was not true in the mid-twentieth century, however. In the Senate, a slight rise in overlapping voting occurred with the rise of the bipartisan farm movement in the 1920s—but it dropped to zero again after the New Deal in the 1930s. Both the House and the Senate witnessed an unprecedented rise in overlapping voting in the 1940s that persisted until the 1970s, when it began to decline. In the House in 1967, for instance, 13 percent of House Democrats were more conservative than the 10 percent most liberal House Republican, and 15 percent of Republicans were more liberal than the 10 percent most conservative Democrat. In the Senate in 1969, 19 percent of Democrats were more conservative than the 10 percent most liberal Republican, and 19 percent of Republicans were more liberal than the 10 percent most conservative Democrat.[40] Historically, this was an unprecedented level of bipartisanship in elite American politics.

The bipartisanship of the 1950s eventually gave way to the social movements of the 1960s, however, once it became impossible for the parties to continue ignoring issues of race and civil rights. Right after World War II, the distinctions between parties on key national issues such as race, national defense, and the role of government were not very clear. Republicans had largely accepted the outlines

39. We created these overlap graphs using DW-nominate and standardized Americans for Democratic Action (ADA) (available from 1947 to the present) measures of legislator ideology. ADA scores rate the liberalism (and conservatism) of elected officials based on their roll-call voting records. DW-nominate scores do the same thing, using a larger number of roll-call votes. The DW-nominate scale runs roughly from −1 to 1, with more negative numbers indicating a more liberal member of Congress and more positive numbers indicating a more conservative member of Congress. We use these scores to identify how liberal or conservative members were relative to other members of their party. As an example, in 1947 the most conservative 10 percent of Democrats had DW-nominate scores higher than 0.10. To identify the degree of overlap with Republicans, we count the number of Republicans who had DW-nominate scores lower than 0.10. For purposes of brevity, we only show the distribution using DW-nominate scores here. Our findings do not change in any measurable way using ADA scores.

40. We perform the same analysis looking only at non-southern states to see if the partisan overlap was merely an artifact of one-party politics dominant in the South before the 1970s. We find that although the degree of overlap decreases among Democrats, the mid-twentieth century still emerges as a unique period of high partisan overlap. Among Republicans, we find that high levels of partisan overlap persist because there were few Republicans in the South.

Figure 3-4. *Partisan Overlap in the House of Representatives, 1867–2003*

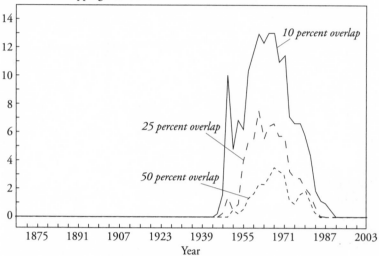

House Democrats

Percent of overlapping members

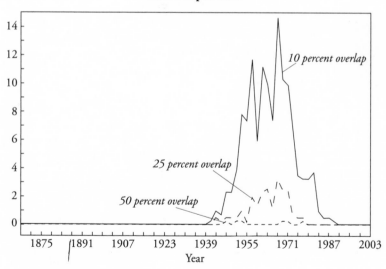

House Republicans

Source: Compiled by authors.

Figure 3-4. *Partisan Overlap in the Senate, 1867–2003 (continued)*

Senate Democrats

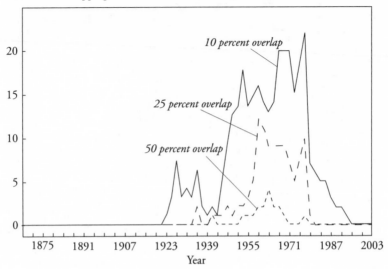

Senate Republicans

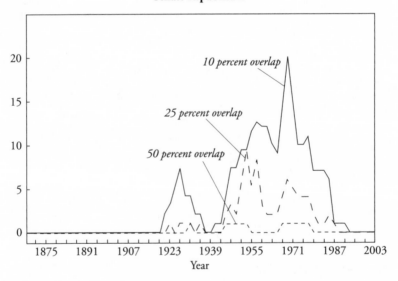

Source: Compiled by authors.

of the New Deal, and class-based voting declined after the war.[41] Similarly, Kennedy Democrats took the same hard line as Republicans on the cold war. Until the early 1960s, it was not clear whether Republicans or Democrats would be more supportive of civil rights.[42] With the passage of the Civil Rights Act in 1964, however, southerners divorced themselves from the Democratic Party, and a redefinition of partisan politics at the national level reemerged. The transformation of the political South was one of the most striking changes in twentieth-century politics, and it undoubtedly played a significant role in redefining—and thus repolarizing—the parties at the national level.[43]

Importantly, however, as national party politics repolarized after 1964, congressional party politics did not. Polarization in Congress did not reemerge until the late 1970s because congressional elections had become insulated from national partisan tides. The bipartisanship of the immediate postwar era gave rise to the personal incumbency advantage and the development of structures that supported the domination of congressional elections by local electoral forces. These factors were rooted in high levels of cross-party voting in elections. Without clear distinctions between the parties on key national issues, people with liberal or conservative views on the issues could vote for either party. Between the end of World War II and the 1964 contest between Barry Goldwater and Lyndon Johnson, a large number of voters with relatively liberal views voted for Republican presidential and congressional candidates, while many voters with conservative views voted for Democratic candidates.[44] The national parties, in other words, were no longer the sole—or even the major—determinant of election results. As a result, candidates learned to win reelection independent of the national parties as they became more responsible for their own electoral fate.

Thus we see the rise of the "personal vote" in the 1950s.[45] As the personal vote and the incumbency advantage increased, the impact of partisanship in determining electoral outcomes declined.[46] This was also reflected in the percentage

41. See Campbell and others (1960); Key (1959); Alford (1964).
42. Black and Black (2002); Carmines and Stimson (1981).
43. Rohde (1991); Shafer and Johnston (2006); Black and Black (2002).
44. For empirical evidence on this point, see Han and Brady (forthcoming).
45. The rise of the "personal vote" is well documented in political science scholarship through studies of the incumbency advantage. See Erikson (1972); Ansolabehere, Snyder, and Stewart (2000); Gelman and King (1990); Alford and Brady (1993); Jacobson (1987); Cain, Ferejohn, and Fiorina (1987).
46. Ansolabehere and Snyder (2002).

of districts with split partisan results at the presidential and congressional levels, which was zero at the start of the twentieth century and rose dramatically between 1948 and 1972.[47] The personal vote and localized factors became so important in congressional elections that even in the 1960s—as issues like civil rights, the Vietnam War, and the environment emerged as polarizing factors in national politics—voters continued to exhibit high levels of cross-party voting in congressional elections.[48] National forces did not become potent in congressional elections again until the 1990s.[49]

The disparities between elite and mass party polarization in the present era become somewhat clearer in light of this delinking of congressional elections and national party politics. The blurring of party lines in the immediate post–World War II era and the subsequent localization of congressional elections created a kind of "unsorting" of voters and elite partisans that was symbiotically "resorted" after the 1960s. In other words, the murkiness of party lines caused a number of congressional seats to be improperly sorted into parties—with some conservative districts represented by Democratic members and some liberal districts represented by Republican members. Small bands of activists forced the redefinition of elite parties in the 1960s, creating more polarization between the national parties. Slowly, this redefinition prompted voters to become less willing (or less able) to vote for congressional candidates of the opposite party, and congressional districts and representatives came back into partisan alignment.[50] This naturally led to a redefinition of congressional parties and to the high levels of ideological disparity and party cohesiveness that we see today. The sources of this elite polarization, however, depend in large part on sorting districts (or states) and their representatives into the appropriate parties, after they had become "unsorted" during previous periods.

The sorting of legislators and constituencies into the appropriate party, when combined with institutional forces that magnify partisan effects in elite politics, enables the historically anomalous levels of polarization in today's politics. The ideological distance between mass partisans remains ambiguous, but partisanship appears to be increasing as partisans sort themselves into the appropriate

47. Burden and Kimball (2002).

48. For data on this point, see Gary C. Jacobson's comment on Thomas E. Mann's chapter in this volume, as well as Han and Brady (forthcoming).

49. Brady, D'Onofrio, and Fiorina (2000).

50. For empirical evidence on this point, see Han and Brady (forthcoming).

parties. In Congress, however, sorting creates ideologically distant party coalitions, since the dynamics of partisan forces within our political institutions pulls legislators toward ideological extremes.[51] In addition, reforms in Congress in the 1970s strengthened the power of party leaders, making it easier (and more profitable) for parties to act as cohesive voting blocs.[52] Thus, although levels of party cohesion are high, there is simultaneously more bipartisan unity, since legislators are constrained by the lack of clarity around levels of ideological disparity in the electorate. In other words, there is a constant give and take between elite and mass party politics that shapes the contours of the polarization we witness today. The outcomes of this give and take, however, become clear only in light of a historical look at the present period of polarization.

Examining the Character of Issue Divisions

Finally, we turn to an examination of the second dimension of polarization: the character of issue divisions. Do moral or economic issues determine the partisan divide? When the parties disagree about what the "right" outcome on a set of moral issues is, it is more difficult to achieve compromise. Thus, the strong moral debate about slavery that characterized the Civil War era was ultimately resolved by war. Alternatively, when the parties agree about the ultimate goal, but disagree about how to achieve that goal, collective action around a set of compromises is more likely. The nature of the issues dividing the parties is crucial because it determines, in part, the extent to which political compromise is possible. We argue that while the New Deal era focused more on economic issues, polarization in the 1890s—as in the present era—represented a blend of both moral and economic issues.

Polarization in the New Deal era focused solely on whether the government should ameliorate economic woes created by the Great Depression. Other issues (such as race) were ignored. Both parties agreed that the economic depression was "bad" and that the primary objective of government should be to lift the

---

51. There is a broad literature discussing why the Median Voter Theorem does not always hold. This literature shows how institutional forces can magnify small shifts in the electorate to create greater polarization in elite politics than in mass politics. See Fiorina (1999) for an excellent summary. The literature also shows that party elites generally tend to be more polarized than party masses, and even among elites, party leaders are more polarized than rank-and-file members. See Ansolabehere, Snyder, and Stewart (2000); Coleman (1971).

52. See Rohde (1991); Van Houweling (2003); Jacobson (forthcoming 2007); Roberts and Smith (2003).

country into greater prosperity. The questions defining the polarization of this era were about how best to achieve that prosperity—not whether prosperity was the appropriate outcome. Thus, the parties debated how much social welfare, agricultural assistance, and governmental management there should be.

The difference between the defining issues of the Civil War era and this period becomes clear through an examination of the effect of the economy on the elections. Models of retrospective voting contend that election results follow the economic fortunes of the country—a good economy means that the president's party gets reelected, while a bad economy results in a switch in party governance. Studies of economic voting show that the New Deal era clearly fits a retrospective voting model.[53] As a comparison point, consider the Civil War era. Although we could not precisely replicate standard economic voting models for the Civil War period because the data are unavailable that far back, we could look broadly at the relationship between economic conditions and voting over the entire period by drawing on the number of business failures as an indicator of economic conditions. These data are consistently available from 1840 to the present. The results show that economic conditions are a relatively accurate gauge of presidential voting during the New Deal era, but not during the Civil War era. The New Deal era, in sum, turned more on economic issues than on moral issues.

Although economic issues such as the tariff and the gold standard were central to the 1890s, polarization in this period also focused on a set of moral issues. Questions about the appropriate role of government in a changing economy manifested themselves in battles over the tariff and the gold standard. Models of retrospective voting show that economic issues were the primary determinants of vote choice in the 1890s. But they were by no means the only determinants. The late nineteenth century was also a period of enormous social and international change, and parties were not able to relegate burgeoning moral issues to the sideline as they would in the New Deal era. Questions about U.S. expansionism abroad, Progressivism, Darwinism, and urbanization also played a major role in politics of the time. The debate over the appropriate role of the United States in the world often focused on questions of the country's moral responsibility, and Progressives in the early twentieth century were driven by a desire to make government more ethical and responsible. The debates between the parties on these issues were moralistic in the sense that the parties were not in agreement about what responsibility the United States had for protecting human rights abroad, or whether Darwinism should be accepted. Debates over the tariff and the gold

53. See Fiorina (1981); Fair (2002).

standard thus melded with debates about social questions to create a politics torn between moral and economic questions.

In that regard, the present era appears more similar to the 1890s than to the New Deal era. The combination of prospective and retrospective issues the country faces at the turn of the twenty-first century are similar, in many ways, to the issues faced at the turn of the twentieth century. Without the benefit of hindsight, it is more difficult to identify the key issues that define partisan differences in the present day. However, it is clear that, as in the 1890s (and in the New Deal era), broad economic changes characterize this period, and the national government is redefining its role in a changing global economy and a new global order.

Questions today about how aggressive the United States should be in promoting democracy in places like Iraq, or what responsibility the nation has in situations like the Rwandan genocide in 1994, are not unlike questions about the Spanish-American War and the "New Imperialism" in American foreign policy in the late 1890s. Questions about how government should respond to changes in the flow of labor and capital, economic outsourcing, and the displacement of manufacturing sector workers in the new information economy parallel questions at the turn of the twentieth century about how to confront the loss of a primarily agrarian economy and the shift to a more industrialized system.[54] All of these questions, like the questions at the turn of the twentieth century, are prospective and retrospective reflections on American national identity. As the economy and the international order change, what kind of country is America?

In today's politics, as in the late nineteenth century, economic questions occur alongside moral debates. In fact, perhaps even more than in the 1890s, a strong faction of each party today defines the debate moralistically. The rise of the Christian right as a powerful force within the Republican Party, and the rise of single-issue interest groups after the social movements of the 1960s, forced a range of new social issues—including abortion, women's rights, gay marriage, and school prayer—to the forefront of the political agenda. Despite the prevalence of these issues in the media, however, each party's stance on these issues has not always been clear. (Consider President Bill Clinton's "don't ask, don't tell" policy on gays in the military, or President George W. Bush's compromise on stem-cell research.) In this sense, moralistic undertones pervade politics at the turn of the twenty-first century as they did at the turn of the twentieth

54. See Frieden (2006); Friedman (2006).

century—but the parties still find ways to sidestep or compromise on the issues before them.

Yet because these are moral issues, compromises do not resolve them. Questions about the sanctity of life and whether government should protect the right of same-sex partners to marry continues to plague current politics. As in the 1890s, it is not clear today if economic or moral questions divide the two parties. While it seems that moral issues are often at the forefront of politics, some research shows that class voting is on the rise, and subsets of each party continue to define their partisan commitments through economic issues.[55]

The character of issue divisions between parties in the present era therefore remains somewhat more ambiguous. It is clear that historically resonant battles between labor and capital are present, but there are also strong debates about values.[56] These values-laden debates arise naturally from a changing society and economic order. As such, the parties themselves are still struggling to define their stances on many of these issues. Thus, in terms of both the breadth and depth of polarization and the character of issue divisions, the present period combines a historically unique complex of characteristics.

Resolving Polarization

How do polarizing issues get resolved? The processes by which political issues and disputes move on and off the national agenda are complex and multifaceted—and too complicated for a full treatment here. However, one commonality that does seem to exist in democratic politics is that the resolution of polarizing issues usually involves electoral change and, subsequently, shifts within parties. As a polarizing issue comes to dominate the political agenda and the two parties take opposing sides, one party usually experiences dramatic electoral loss, or the party loses a series of elections over time by increasing margins. The losing party often experiences a period of factionalism, in which different voices within the party battle for control. Continued electoral loss can prompt a faction within the party willing to shift its opinion on crucial issues in order to emerge victorious.

This phenomenon seems to occur across democratic systems; it is not limited to the United States. For instance, the fractured and conflicted history of Ireland's Sinn Fein party demonstrates the way factionalism over issues within a party can result in changing definitions of the party itself. Eamon de Valera, after a series

55. McCarty, Poole, and Rosenthal (2006).
56. Frieden (2006).

of consecutively greater electoral losses, eliminated Sinn Fein as the party for a united Ireland to lead Fianna Fail to dominance in Irish politics. In essence, the united-Ireland issue was resolved when the major parties implicitly accepted the division and fought elections over domestic and social issues in the lower twenty-six counties.[57] Similarly, throughout twentieth-century British politics, parties have shifted policies as different internal factions gained control as a result of electoral fortunes. Margaret Thatcher purged the "wets" from the Conservative Party before she and the Conservatives regained control of government in the late 1970s. Similarly, Tony Blair moved the Labour Party away from its traditional views so that it could win again. Although these are very broad characterizations of complicated political periods, they demonstrate how disputes between parties—and subsequent electoral shifts—can prompt in-fighting within the losing party to minimize the effect of a previously polarizing issue, or change the debate on a set of issues.

In the case of the United States at the turn of the twentieth century, a series of incremental electoral shifts ended the debate between parties about key domestic and international policy issues. Would the United States join the European economic and global trade systems? Would it accept an economic system largely financed by British banks and adopt the gold standard as its monetary system? Drawing on popular unrest created by economic changes, Populists slowly gained momentum within the Democratic Party by taking an anti-gold, anti-tariff stance that opposed U.S. involvement in the global economy. In 1892 the Populist Party received 9 percent of the three-party vote and finally gained a majority within the Democratic Party in 1896. Party elites polarized sharply around economic issues in 1896, with pro-gold Democrats (including President Grover Cleveland) getting booed at the Democratic convention and pro-silver Republicans literally being chased from the Republican convention. Once the parties took clear stances on these issues, voters had clearer choices to make. In 1896 the Democrats' presidential candidate, William Jennings Bryan, narrowly lost, and Republicans took control of a unified government. Republicans continued winning election after election, even as Democrats nominated Bryan two more times for president. Finally, after Bryan lost a third time (to William Howard Taft in 1908), the Populist faction within the Democratic Party died away, and the party shifted its policy on the new economic order.

In the New Deal era, the tables turned as Republicans became the minority party. The fundamental polarizing issue of the 1930s concerned government's

57. For more on this point, see Brady, Bullock, and Maisel (1988).

reaction to the Great Depression. Franklin D. Roosevelt and the Democrats swept to victory in 1932 on the idea that "the federal government had not merely a role, but a major responsibility, in ensuring the health of the economy and the welfare of citizens. That simple but momentous shift in perception was the newest thing in all the New Deal, and the most consequential too."[58] The Republicans first responded by arguing that Roosevelt's policies were imperiling the country by killing free enterprise, disregarding the Constitution, and destroying the morale of the people by making them dependent on government.

Despite this opposition, Democrats continued to win, prompting Republicans to nominate the moderate Wendell Willkie for president in 1940, who lost. After a third consecutive loss to Roosevelt, the moderate wing of the Republican Party gained full control of the party in 1944 and nominated Thomas E. Dewey on the first ballot. For the first time, the 1944 Republican platform accepted the broad outlines of the New Deal. It pledged support for "extension of the existing old-age insurance systems to all employees not already covered" and "a careful study of Federal-State programs for maternal and child health, dependent children, and assistance to the blind, with a view to strengthening these programs."[59] In the face of continued electoral loss, Republicans eventually shifted policy on the New Deal.

Thus, both the New Deal era and the turn of the twentieth century "resolved" polarization through a series of electoral shifts. Electoral change during the New Deal era was much more abrupt, however, given that the clarity of a single issue defined the divide between the parties. Change in the 1890s was more incremental since more complicated issues were on the partisan agenda.

So what does this imply for the present era? Although the breadth and depth of polarization in the present period is unique, we view it as more similar to the 1890s than to the New Deal era. Both eras are characterized by a melding of moral and economic issues on the partisan agenda. The key difference between the New Deal era and the global transformations at the turn of the twentieth and twenty-first centuries is that everyone could agree that the Depression was a "bad" thing. In contrast, there continues to be disagreement over the normative implications of the global changes occurring now and in the past, and the ongoing battle between labor and capital.[60] As economic transitions alter traditional life patterns, accompanying social and cultural changes raise questions about our most fundamental

58. Kennedy (1999, p. 377).
59. Schlesinger (1971, p. 3,044).
60. Friedman (2006).

values. Thus, the present era (like the 1890s) has witnessed a resurgence in religious activity, and debates between the parties are laden with moral overtones.

In terms of the breadth and depth of polarization, party elites in the present era have clear ideological differences, and parties themselves are more cohesive than parties in the 1890s and the New Deal era. Interestingly, however, there is more bipartisan action in Congress now than in the past—possibly because of the ambiguity of polarization in the mass electorate. The blurring of party lines after World War II created a disjuncture between congressional elections and national party politics that led to heterogeneous party coalitions. The sorting of voters and elites into parties after the 1960s, however, created increasing cohesion among partisans as party coalitions became more homogeneous. At the elite level, institutional forces magnified these partisan effects, creating more polarization. At the mass level, however, the extent of ideological disparity remains unclear.

This is likely to make the resolution of polarization in the current era more incremental than in the New Deal era and more similar to the slow shift around the turn of the twentieth century. The disparity between mass partisans is more ambiguous than disparities between elites, and party elites engage in far more bipartisan action than in the past. Given the low cost of information and improvements in polling technology, elites are much more likely now than in the past to have an accurate sense of public opinion.[61] In the 1890s and the New Deal era, parties were forced to take a stand on the issues without having much information about where voters were. Small shifts in opinion can thus spark more polarizing shifts in elite behavior today, but the difficulty of interpreting polarization in the electorate ultimately constrains elites. The lines between the parties on key issues of polarization therefore remain somewhat murky, and the responses of the electorate are challenging to interpret. Nonetheless, examining the present day in light of the past sheds some light on the ways in which today's politics is unique, and the ways in which it is a mirror of the past.

61. We thank David Plotz of Slate.com on this point.

Polarization Runs Deep, Even by Yesterday's Standards

COMMENT

James E. Campbell

Is America politically polarized? As David W. Brady and Hahrie C. Han remind us, politics is about differences over what government should do and who should do it. Political parties are organized around those differences, so there will always be some degree of polarization in a democracy. The real question is, how much? American politics are neither entirely and viciously polarized, nor blandly and homogeneously moderate. So where do we stand between harmony and vitriol? Is the polarization glass half empty or half full? Or more precisely, is it one-quarter full or three-quarters full? It is certainly not completely empty.

To get a sense of the current level of polarization in American politics, some historical perspective is useful. In reviewing three periods of intense partisan realignment in U.S. history (the Civil War, the 1890s, and the New Deal era of the 1930s), Brady and Han attempt to provide us with some much-needed benchmarks for comparison. Though observing "a historically unique complex of characteristics" in the present era, they conclude that polarization is now more limited in its breadth and depth than in the past.

Brady and Han find similarities between politics in the current era and the era from 1890 to 1910 (particularly in regard to the moral, as opposed to economic, issues). However, they also suggest that current politics may not be as polarized as in the 1890s, observing a "pattern of bipartisan unity in elite politics, as well as seemingly low levels of ideological disparity between mass partisans." And while current politics may seem especially contentious against the backdrop of the post–World War II era (when there were unusual numbers of liberal Republicans and conservative Democrats), Brady and Han believe that, put in perspective, polarization today is no big deal and that most voters are still ideologically moderate.

Undoubtedly, political polarization is not at its upper bounds today. (The nation is nowhere near the brink of another civil war.) And it is true that, all other things equal, political leaders and activists will always be more ideologically polarized than the general public.[1] But Brady and Han significantly under-

1. McCloskey, Hoffman, and O'Hara (1960).

state the current level of polarization. American politics are highly polarized—and that is true not just for political leaders and party elites, but for the public and the electorate as well.

The public has been significantly polarized for some time and in recent years has become more so. The unusual heterogeneity of the political parties in the mid- to late twentieth century masked the extent of this polarization. It was difficult to see the real extent of liberal and conservative differences when the political parties represented mixtures of the two. But as the Republican Party became more clearly the party of conservatives and the Democratic Party the party of liberals, the polarization of the electorate was revealed. In addition to this party sorting or realignment (and perhaps partly as a result of it), there has been some real growth in the polarization of the electorate—mostly in the number of conservatives, but a small increase in the number of liberals as well. Contrary to Brady and Han's assertion, moderates are now a political minority among American voters.

Conceptual and Measurement Concerns

If political leadership and the public are highly polarized, why do Brady and Han reach the opposite conclusion? Part of the problem is conceptual. Brady and Han implicitly equate polarization, whether at the mass or elite level, with polarization between the political parties—and the polarization measurements in their analysis are all party measurements.

While Brady and Han's concentration of party measures may reflect unavoidable data limitations of examining the politics of the mid-nineteenth and early twentieth centuries, it must be recognized that polarization may not always be well represented by the parties. During the 1950s and 1960s, for instance, many conservative voters in the South voted for Democrats, while many liberal voters in states outside the South voted for Republicans. In such eras, the parties may fail to reflect much of the nation's political conflict. Because the parties were heterogeneous in the mid-twentieth century does not necessarily mean that the public was less politically divided, only that the divisions that were present did not line up neatly along national partisan lines.

A second conceptual concern is the distinction that Brady and Han draw between moral and economic issues. They claim that moral issues are more polarizing than economic issues because compromise is more difficult on moral issues. Lacking a workable midway position to move to, both sides dig in for a bitter fight. The pre–Civil War issue of slavery is an example.

The idea that moral issues are particularly polarizing appears reasonable, but there may be less to it than meets the eye. Take Brady and Han's suggestion that there was no workable centrist position on the issue of slavery. Rather than staking out the extremes, both major parties of the day framed the debate in compromised or centrist positions. Democrats advocated "popular sovereignty," a policy that would permit the expansion of slavery if states voted to allow it. Even future Republican president Abraham Lincoln, the "Great Emancipator," took a middle-ground position in 1860 by opposing the extension of slavery in new territories—a position well short of abolition. Moreover, the post–Civil War resolution of the issue was effectively a compromised position. For several generations after the Civil War, African Americans were neither slaves nor accorded the full rights of citizenship. A reasonable reading of this history is that the nation reached a de facto middle position on the slavery issue, a position that survived until the civil rights era of the 1950s and 1960s.

It could be argued that virtually every issue involves moral values—and that all issues are subject to compromise, if there is enough support for it. Morris P. Fiorina, with coauthors Samuel J. Abrams and Jeremy C. Pope, argues that on the abortion issue, one of the most heated moral issues of our day, there is considerable middle ground and that a majority of Americans occupy a centrist position on the issue.[2] Looking at the economic side of the dichotomy, it is easy to think of appropriations bills or tax bills in which a compromise can be achieved by shifting a few percentage points one way or the other. But it should be recalled that for much of the twentieth century some of the most intense polarization in nations around the world centered on the economic and political philosophy of Marxism. The extent to which an issue is polarizing, then, depends on how intensely people feel about their positions—and no particular subject matter is off limits to strong feelings.

In addition to these conceptual issues, Brady and Han's conclusion that the electorate and Congress are not very polarized in comparison with the past is based on faulty measures of polarization. There is abundant evidence that the parties in Congress have become quite polarized since the 1970s. Average party unity scores (the percentage of members voting with a majority of their party on votes in which a majority of Democrats opposed a majority of Republicans) for both parties in both chambers hovered in the low 70 percent region in the 1970s. In more recent years, these party unity scores have been in the vicin-

2. Fiorina, Abrams, and Pope (2006). They refer to this centrist position as "pro-choice, but."

ity of 90 percent.[3] This is corroborated by Brady and Han's examination of DW-nominate scores (ideological roll-call scores). Although Brady and Han emphasize the lack of party polarization in Congress until the late 1970s (though this largely reflected a lag in the realignment due to the slow growth of a Republican Party in the solidly Democratic South), their data also reveal the absence of ideological overlap between the congressional parties since 1994, when the Republicans took control of the U.S. House after forty years of Democratic Party dominance. In short, the parties in congressional politics have been about as polarized as ever for at least a decade now.

Despite this evidence, Brady and Han's examination of bipartisan unity roll-call scores leads them to conclude that polarization in Congress is mild. They define bipartisan unity as the "percentage of partisans who vote with the majority of their party when it is not a party vote" (that is, when majorities in both parties join together to pass legislation). They find that "today's level of bipartisan unity is close to as high as it has ever been." But how can this high level of bipartisan unity be reconciled with the strong polarization witnessed on roll-call party votes?

The problem lies in the bipartisan unity measure. To get a sense of what this measure entails, I examined a number of bipartisan roll-call votes in the House of Representatives from the 109th Congress, second session (2006). Of the sixty-six roll calls on nonprocedural matters that passed the House through May 11, 2006, fifty-three passed with bipartisan majorities. With very few exceptions (for example, HR 4954, Security and Accountability for Every Port Act), these roll calls were either noncontroversial (such as reprimanding Iran for its threatening behavior, designating the birthplace of former President Bill Clinton a National Historic Site, extending a normal trade agreement with Ukraine, and reauthorizing the Office of National Drug Policy Control) or congratulatory (such as celebrating the Pittsburgh Steelers for winning the Super Bowl, honoring the contributions of Catholic schools, recognizing the anniversary of Israel's independence, and "supporting the goals and ideals of World Water Day").

Is Congress any less polarized if there is greater unity on these types of votes or if there are more of these types of votes? Of course not. Bipartisanship on important issues is meaningful, but bipartisanship on noncontroversial issues is not. Extreme liberals and extreme conservatives can agree on many noncontroversial matters (for example, celebrating World Water Day), but this does

---

3. See Stanley and Niemi (2005); Fleisher and Bond (2000a, 2000b).

not mean that they are any less fiercely opposed on a wide range of important issues.[4]

Brady and Han's conclusion that the electorate is not now highly polarized is also based on a problematic measurement: the distribution of the presidential vote at the congressional district level.[5] They assert that "in more polarized times, we should see more states—or, in this case, congressional districts—that support one party with large percentages of the vote and fewer districts split around 50 percent. If interdistrict polarization is high, then, we expect to see more districts at the extremes of the distribution during polarized periods, and more districts in the middle during periods of lower polarization."

Their analysis suggests that in recent years a large number of congressional districts have been competitive in presidential elections, which they interpret as a sign of tempered or modest polarization.[6] Unfortunately, this measure bears no necessary relationship to mass polarization. Whether presidential votes are evenly or lopsidedly divided in congressional districts reflects the organization of the votes (the sorting of votes into districts, in Fiorina's terms), not the polarization of the views motivating these votes. Equally polarized or unpolarized districts can have all 50–50 or all 100–0 vote divisions. The implication is that presidential candidates can win lopsidedly or narrowly in districts with either polarized or moderate electorates. Fiorina, Abrams, and Pope's observation about national vote divisions thus applies to district vote divisions: "By themselves, close election outcomes cannot tell us whether half the electorate hates the other half or whether everyone is flipping coins."[7] Competition (or the lack of it) does not indicate polarization.

4. Brady and Han's examination of the percentage of party votes is subject to a similar criticism. They observe that in 2001–02 a majority of Republicans opposed a majority of Democrats in the House on only 51 percent of the roll-call votes. But this is less meaningful if the percentages of party roll-call votes are lowered by a lot of votes on congratulatory and noncontroversial issues.

5. Brady and Han also observe a "delinking of congressional elections and national party politics" and that "national forces did not become potent in congressional elections again until the 1990s." This apparent delinking is often overstated and is attributable to the huge campaign financing advantage of incumbents, which dampens all other influences on the congressional vote. See Campbell (2003); Campbell and Jurek (2003).

6. In fact, it does not appear that the majority of districts have been competitive in presidential voting. Only 26 percent of districts in 2000 and 23 percent in 2004 were decided in the 55 percent to 45 percent range. Bare majorities of districts were competitive if the definition is extended to the 60 percent to 40 percent range, but this margin is generally designated as a landslide when applied to the national vote. In addition, one would expect more competitive districts if the parties are competitive nationally, as they are today and as they were not after 1896 or 1932. The 1896 and 1932 eras may have had fewer competitive districts not because they were more polarized, but because they were less competitive nationally.

7. Fiorina, Abrams, and Pope (2006, p. 15).

Evidence of a Polarized Public

There is an abundance of direct and indirect evidence to support the conclusion that the American public is substantially polarized and has become more so in recent years. The direct evidence of polarization comes from the National Election Studies (NES) data on self-described ideological orientations.

Since 1972, the NES has asked a national sample of Americans to classify their ideological perspectives on a seven-point scale (extremely liberal, liberal, slightly liberal, moderate, slightly conservative, conservative, and extremely conservative).[8] Respondents could also indicate that they had not thought much about their ideology or that they did not know how to classify their political views. To simplify matters for presentation, this scale has been collapsed to those with or without an ideological orientation so that we are left with two groups: moderates and nonmoderates.[9] Those who said that they did not know how to classify themselves ideologically are included along with the nonideologicals in the moderate group.[10] Tracking the level and change in the percentage of moderates over time allows us to assess directly whether the public is polarized and whether polarization has increased.

Figure 3-5 displays the percentage of self-declared moderates (plus "don't knows") since 1972 among all NES respondents and among reported voters.

8. Some may prefer to examine specific issue positions of respondents rather than general ideological perspectives. On any given issue, however, some ideologues may depart from those with whom they are generally like-minded. Moreover, issues can be thought of by voters in many ways other than as asked on surveys. As Fiorina and Levendusky observe in this volume, "individual issue items vary in question format and (therefore) reliability." While conservatives and liberals may differ among themselves as to the precise meaning of their labels, their reactions to the labels (the NES thermometer questions, for example) are consistent, and ideological dispositions have strong general effects on the positions taken on a variety of issues and on the presidential vote. The General Social Survey (GSS) has also asked the ideology question over this period. The trends observed in NES ideology data are corroborated by the GSS ideology data. Because of space limitations, only the NES data are presented here.

9. It can be argued that "slightly liberal" and "slightly conservative" respondents should be counted as moderates. My analysis of the thermometer scales, various issues, and the presidential vote indicates that the slightly ideological behave differently than either moderates or the outright ideological. Including them with the declared liberals and conservatives may inflate these categories, but including the "don't knows" with the moderates probably inflates that category even more. In any case, using either treatment, the share of moderates declined over time.

10. Grouping the "don't knows," who represent anywhere from 20 to 36 percent of the sample, with self-professed nonideologicals produces a very generous count of moderates. Certainly some of the "don't knows" had ideological leanings but did not know what label appropriately described them. Still, the lack of awareness of their ideological label suggests a lack of its salience to these respondents.

Figure 3-5. *The Shrinking Political Middle, 1972–2004*[a]

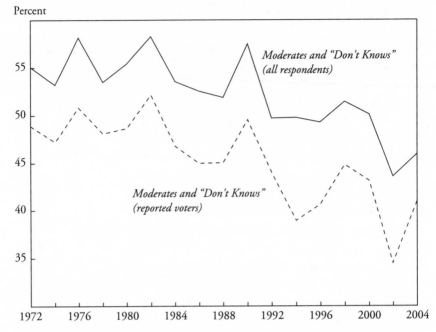

Percent

Moderates and "Don't Knows" (all respondents)

Moderates and "Don't Knows" (reported voters)

Source: Calculated from variable VCF0803 in the National Election Studies cumulative data file dataset. Weight variable VCF0009A was used.

a. The percentages are of respondents (or reported voters) either placing themselves in the moderate category on the NES seven-point ideological scale or responding that they did not know how to classify themselves ideologically on this scale.

Examining the entire public first, the evidence indicates that moderates were a majority in the 1970s and 1980s, barely a majority in the 1990s, and a minority in 2002 and 2004.[11] Even in the 1970s, at least 40 percent of respondents were either conservatives or liberals. This represents, by any standard, a good deal of polarization. But in more recent times, liberals and conservatives matched or outnumbered the nonideologicals. In short, there has been a fair degree of polarization among the public for some time, and it has increased in recent years.

11. As the nonideological moderates and "don't knows" lost ground in the 1990s, conservatives gained. Conservatives had been in the mid to high 20 percent range in the 1970s and 1980s. They have been at least 30 percent of respondents since 1992. Liberals also may have gained some ground in the last couple of years, but this is not as clear.

The evidence indicates somewhat greater polarization among reported voters. During the 1970s and 1980s, about half of reported voters were in some sense moderates; half were not. Since then, however, the moderates' share of the vote has declined—and the percentage of voters with an ideological perspective has increased. Before 1992, moderates had not dipped below 45 percent of voters. Since 1992, they have not reached 45 percent. There is no mistaking the conclusion: moderates are now a minority of voters.[12]

There is also compelling indirect or circumstantial evidence that the American electorate was substantially polarized and has become more so. This evidence is drawn from how the public has reacted to the polarization of the political parties. Numerous studies, including Brady and Han's analysis of DW-nominate scores, have documented the increased polarization of the political parties in recent years.[13] Political scientists Nolan McCarty, Keith T. Poole, and Howard Rosenthal's analysis of ideological roll-call voting indicates that, after a decline to unusually low levels for much of the twentieth century, party polarization in Congress has increased steadily since the late 1970s and in recent years is about as great as it was in the late nineteenth century.[14]

The public's reaction to greater polarization in the political parties should depend on whether the public itself is moderate and relatively unpolarized or quite ideological and highly polarized. If the political parties became more polarized but the public remained moderate, we should be able to detect three measurable responses among the public. First, the percentage of strong party identifiers should decline. If the parties adopted strong ideological positions that were out of step with a moderate electorate, the electorate should have less reason to identify strongly with these parties. Second, turnout should decline because of greater public indifference and alienation from the extreme candidate choices. The American public should turn away from political leadership that misrepresents them. Third, more voters should split their tickets. As Fiorina's policy-balancing theory claims, moderates should split their tickets to counterbalance a too liberal Democratic Party against a too conservative Republican

12. The finding that moderates have declined is robust and both statistically and substantively significant. Besides being corroborated by General Social Survey data, the decline is evident and statistically significant regardless of whether more or less inclusive classifications of moderates are examined. The decline is also substantively significant. The median percentage of moderates dropped 7 percentage points (48 percent to 41 percent) in the 1990s. This would be of realignment proportions if we were examining partisan identification rather than ideology.

13. See Fiorina, Abrams, and Pope (2006, figure 2.2).

14. McCarty, Poole, and Rosenthal (2006).

Party.[15] As the parties move further away from the center, this logic should become more persuasive with a larger number of centrist voters.

We should expect exactly the opposite reactions if the electorate is highly polarized. Party polarization should strengthen party identifications in a polarized electorate. A conservative might be lukewarm about a wishy-washy Republican Party, but might have real enthusiasm for a staunchly conservative Republican Party. Similarly, a liberal might not care too much about a center-left Democratic Party, but could become strongly committed to an unabashedly liberal Democratic Party. Polarized voters should also be more likely to turn out to vote for (and against) candidates of polarized parties. Fewer potential voters should be indifferent to the parties' candidates. Finally, if both voters and the political parties are polarized, split-ticket voting should decline. To the extent that voters are liberals or conservatives and the candidates of the parties are the same, there should be less reason to split their votes between parties.[16]

What do these indirect tests indicate? In each instance, the indirect evidence is unambiguously consistent with a polarized American electorate and unambiguously inconsistent with a moderate, relatively unpolarized American electorate. First, there has been an increase in strong party identifiers in recent years.[17] The percentage of NES respondents who were strong party identifiers increased from an average of 25 percent between 1972 and 1980 to 31 percent between 1994 and 2004. In 2004, strong party identifiers were fully a third of respondents, more than in any election since 1964. Second, turnout in recent elections has increased.[18] As a percentage of the voting-eligible population in the 1970s, turnout was in the mid-50 percent range. In 2004 it exceeded 60 percent. Third, ticket splitting is on the decline. According to NES data, among those who cast votes for candidates of the major parties, split-ticket voting for presidential and U.S. House

---

15. Fiorina (1996).

16. There are several virtues to these indirect tests of polarization. First, they offer quite clear expectations. Whether a polarized public feels better represented by polarized parties or whether a moderate public feels disconnected from polarized parties produces precisely the opposite expectations about partisanship, turnout, and ticket splitting. Multiple tests also provide greater reliability. Forces other than polarization may cause turnout to rise or fall, partisanship to strengthen or weaken, and ticket splitting to increase or decrease. But for all three to move in an expected direction is less easily explained away. Finally, the reliability of the measurements of partisanship, turnout, and ticket splitting is a virtue. There is little question about these increasing or decreasing in recent years.

17. See Abramowitz and Saunders (1998); Hetherington (2001).

18. McDonald (2004).

candidates dropped from an average of 26 percent between 1972 and 1992 to 18 percent since 1992. There is just too much that does not fit the idea of a moderate public and polarized parties.

The indirect evidence also suggests that, in accord with the direct evidence, Americans have been fairly polarized for some time. Consider what politics would look like if the public were fairly polarized while the parties failed to reflect this polarization. The public would be expected to turn away from unresponsive politics, party identification would weaken, voters would be more inclined to split their tickets, and turnout would remain low or decline further. Once the parties better reflected the long-standing polarization of the public, party identification would pick up, turnout would rise, and split-ticket voting would decline. This is exactly what has happened in the post–World War II years, during which the parties lagged behind the public in polarization.

The reason why polarization of the public preceded polarization of the parties is that the New Deal party system overlaid two sets of issues (racial issues and economic issues), and this caused a good deal of ideological heterogeneity within the parties. As political scientists Edward G. Carmines and James A. Stimson observed, in contrast to the parties' relative positions on New Deal economic issues, Democrats were the more conservative party on racial issues (because of their large southern conservative contingent) as late as the 1960s.[19] Between 1958 and 1964, a number of liberal Democrats defeated a number of liberal Republicans in northern states, shifting the balance of power within the Democratic Party to the liberals. The sorting process, however, was staggered over many years in congressional voting, in part because of the campaign finance advantages of incumbents but also because of the absence of a viable Republican Party across the South.[20] Southern conservatives began voting right away for Republican presidential candidates (a sign of their polarization), but the absence of strong Republican congressional candidates in the South delayed the completion of the realignment. The delay ended with the Republican breakthrough election of 1994, allowing the polarization of the parties to catch up with the polarization of the electorate. Party polarization, in turn, fueled additional polarization in the electorate.

19. Carmines and Stimson (1989).
20. Campbell (2006).

Back to Benchmarks

Based on this reanalysis, how does the current level of polarization compare with that in past eras? The only relevant hard data to turn to are the ideological scores of congressional roll-call voting, which indicate that the congressional parties are more polarized in the current era than they were during the New Deal era. This makes sense, given Carmines and Stimson's insight that the race issue complicated politics through the early 1960s by cutting across the economic issues of the New Deal era.

As James Madison suggested in *The Federalist No. 10,* multiple cross-cutting cleavages complicate and dampen conflict, while single or multiple reinforcing cleavages simplify and intensify conflict. The politics of both the 1890s and the New Deal era were complicated by the racial issues cutting across or at odds with economic issues. This is not the case in current politics. The Democratic Party is on the liberal side and the Republican Party is on the conservative side of all political issues. This should intensify polarization.

The intensity of polarization may also be affected by the competitive balance between the two sides. Polarized politics with an even division should be quite a bit different than polarized politics with a clearly dominant side. In both the 1890s and during the New Deal era, one side of the conflict clearly dominated the political landscape—the Republicans after 1896 and the Democrats after 1932. Decisive numbers may draw some of the heat out of polarization. The minority side may be resigned to opposition and the majority side may be less threatened by the opposition.

But when politics are polarized and the divisions are nearly even, as they were at the time of the Civil War and as they are today, polarization may have quite different consequences. With an increase in the need for bipartisanship and a decrease in its likelihood, the prospects for major policy change through normal political processes may diminish and frustrations grow. Political conflict should heat up.

Although the paucity of data makes historical assessments of polarization difficult, some impressionistic comparisons are possible. On the one hand, current levels of polarization, though substantial among both the parties and in the electorate, fall well short of what they were at the time of the Civil War. On the other hand, because of the relatively simple cleavage lines of current politics and the closeness of the political divisions, it seems plausible to suspect that our politics will be far more heated than those at the turn of the last century or in the New Deal era. Future political historians may look back at our political era as the era of bad feelings.

COMMENT

Carl M. Cannon

In his May 1956 mea culpa for his early writings romanticizing the South's agrarian history, poet Robert Penn Warren observed that "the past is always a rebuke to the present."[21] Fifty years later almost to the day, political scientists David W. Brady and Hahrie C. Han, after analyzing the patterns of long-forgotten U.S. voting records, have produced a lengthy essay to remind us fretting good-government types that the fictional turn-of-the-century bartender Martin J. Dooley had it right when he quipped that in America "politics ain't beanbag"— and never has been.[22]

While a degree in statistics would be helpful to fully comprehend Brady and Han's research, the gist of their argument is not complicated: "For many years, our political institutions and policymaking processes have withstood sharp divisions between the parties. . . . For much of American history, the two parties have been distant from each other in the policy positions they took, and the party coalitions have been relatively cohesive in acting out their party platforms."

I have left it to my co-respondent, James E. Campbell of the University of Buffalo, to get into the weeds with Brady and Han on their social science. But this card-carrying member of the "political infotainment community" (Brady and Han's phrase) does have some thoughts regarding their broader contention. The essence of their argument is not that things are going swimmingly in American politics today; it is that we have seen such days before—and the Republic survived. Because we have gotten through such times before, the authors imply, we can do so again.

I have no doubt about that. But I would like to raise some questions that might chip away at their sanguinity. In doing so, I am reminded of another, lesser known, observation made by Mr. Dooley's creator, Finley Peter Dunne: "The past always looks better than it was: it's only pleasant because it isn't here."

Well, the past is upon us again—in the form of political polarization. My question is whether there is any escaping it.

---

21. Purdy (1959, p. 210).

22. Dooley was a creation of legendary Chicago columnist Finley Peter Dunne. According to William Safire's *New Political Dictionary*, Dooley's "beanbag" quip first appeared in the *Chicago Evening Post* on October 5, 1895.

Why Now?

In recent years, political polarization has been the subject of countless journalistic articles, numerous academic papers, and several academic conferences. And one remarkable feature of these discussions is how fungible the phrase "political polarization" has become. Many social scientists use the term technically to characterize the self-sorting of the two major parties along strict ideological lines. Others use it to describe the intense partisanship in Congress these days and the lousy personal relations among its members. Still others employ more poetic terms, taking aim at "the politics of personal destruction," or the ad hominem attacks, personal invective, and generally low level of discourse found in modern political campaigns. Some look with a wider lens at the culture as a whole, focusing on the self-segregation going on in everything from military enlistment and higher education enrollment to where Americans choose to live, worship, and get their news.

Actually, all these phenomena are evidence of polarization, just as they are all interlocking—and reinforcing. Brady and Han are not interested in these kinds of nuance. They focus instead on two quantifiable indicators: the disparities over time between the political parties and the cohesiveness of party coalitions—measuring both party elites and mass voters. Their conclusion is *not* that today's America is not politically polarized. By their criteria we are indeed polarized. What they prove is that the country has been there at least twice before, first in the years around the turn of the twentieth century, and again in the years at the beginning of the Great Depression. (They discuss but do not compare the present era to the Civil War, a period in which political polarization grew to an entirely different magnitude.) "These benchmarks provide a framework for better understanding polarization today in light of the past," the authors assert. "During the 1890s and the early twentieth century, American political parties struggled with the transition from an agrarian to an industrial economy, and with the role of the government in a changing international order. During the New Deal era, a hot debate about the appropriate role of government in the economy characterized party politics." But once this has been established, a series of other questions arise. I'll pose three of them. First, what is the source of the social upheaval today that generates the same level of political ill-will and ideological segregation that characterized the Great Depression? How did previous periods of polarization resolve themselves? And if the conditions that existed at the turn of the century and in the 1930s do not exist now, is there any kind of roadmap available to reformers who want to fix the broken politics of today?

When the United States entered World War II, Franklin Roosevelt presided over a nation in which 25 percent of able-bodied adults could not find employment (when most households had just one breadwinner), and where crops rotted in the fields because it cost more to harvest them than they would fetch at market. Half a million homeowners, many of them family farmers, defaulted on their mortgages, thousands of banks failed, the stock market lost 75 percent of its value, and the gross national product was cut in half. In the 1930s the United States realized negative immigration for the first time in its history. The nation's marriage rate declined, as did its birthrate.[23] The question on the table in those years—at least on some tables—was as basic as whether capitalism itself should survive.

The very fact that the United States would be as politically polarized today as it was in times such as those suggests that politics itself is what is broken in America, and that our national discourse is what is sick. Certainly the economy isn't; nor are our government or social institutions.

As of May 2006, with President Bush's job approval numbers hovering just above 30 percent and historians asserting with straight faces that he is the worst president in U.S. history, the unemployment rate was just 4.7 percent. Inflation was a modest 3.5 percent, and the Dow Jones Industrial Average had climbed back to 11,000. Crime rates had continued their decade-long drop, homeownership was at record levels, and the infant mortality rate was at an all-time low. Oh yes, and one more thing: The political parties were barely speaking to each other, and those approval ratings of President Bush were lower than of any occupant of the White House since Jimmy Carter—when the economic numbers were really a horror show.

Something is wrong with this picture.

In Franklin Roosevelt's era, certain country-club Republicans felt a class betrayal by the economic policies of the high-born president—so much so that they could barely bring themselves to utter the name of "that man in the White House." But that kind of implacable (and dare I say irrational) hatred of FDR was, until recently, viewed as an aberration—and hardly the fault of Roosevelt himself.

Today President Bush and his predecessor, Bill Clinton, are routinely described in the press and academia as "polarizing" presidents, as if this is entirely their fault. But what war did Bill Clinton start? And why is Hillary Clinton, a prospective 2008 presidential candidate, routinely derided (within

23. Distilled from Kennedy (1999).

her own party!) as "the most polarizing" Democrat in the country? An alternate explanation suggests itself: that the last two presidents inhabited a polarized political environment—and that instead of being its architects, they were its victims.

The Factors—Some Old, Some New

This response to Brady and Han's study is not the place to examine all of the conditions that brought about America's current state of polarization. But a short list of culprits would include the following:

—The sorting out of liberals into the national Democratic Party and conservatives into the GOP.

—The wane of southern Democrats, who constituted a de facto (and temporizing) third party in American political life.

—The decline of regionalism as a source of political identity, which has resulted in there being few conservative Democrats from Dixie left in Congress and an ever dwindling band of liberal Republicans from the East.

—Social issues such as abortion and gay marriage that elude compromise (especially when the courts get involved) because they essentially pit two incompatible theologies against each other.

—Gerrymandered districts that squeeze centrists out of the House of Representatives.

—Incivility by members of Congress, who no longer socialize (or even converse) across party aisles.

—The 1994 Republican takeover of Congress, which by dramatically ending forty years of Democratic control made every election seem potentially cataclysmic.

—The impeachment of President Clinton on charges of perjury and obstruction of justice relating to the Monica Lewinsky affair, an issue most voters considered trivial.

—The 2000 presidential election and Florida recount controversy, which for the first time in more than a hundred years put a president in the White House who lost the nationwide popular vote.

—The shout-fest journalism of cable television and talk radio, which helps fragment audiences along ideological lines.

—The Internet, which has democratized political communication and made it easier to raise political money, but also created an echo chamber of intolerant and often ill-informed partisan commentary.

"The Internet fosters community, but also fragmentation," says futurist Esther Dyson. "You are far more likely to find people who share your passion for Hungarian folk music on the 'Net, but that leaves you less time to speak with your neighbors, who might have different perspectives on a lot of things. Like everything else, there's a good side and a bad side."[24] This fragmentation is part of a larger national phenomenon that Georgetown University linguist Deborah Tannen has called "the argument culture."[25]

To be sure, not all of this is new. As Brady and Han note in passing, politics—especially presidential politics—has always had a bruising quality to it. Of the forty-two men who have held the office of president of the United States, two (Andrew Johnson and Bill Clinton) were impeached, and a third (Richard Nixon) resigned one step ahead of the posse. Four U.S. presidents (Abraham Lincoln, James A. Garfield, William McKinley, and John F. Kennedy) were assassinated in office, and six others (Andrew Jackson, Theodore and Franklin Roosevelt, Harry Truman, Gerald Ford, and Ronald Reagan) were shot at—it happened to Ford twice. Teddy Roosevelt and Reagan were hit.

In such a milieu, verbal assaults seem mild. But even the best of presidents can feel their sting. Thomas Jefferson was christened "Mad Tom" by his political opponents, and Lincoln was routinely characterized by Democratic Party newspapers as an ape. During the Vietnam War, Lyndon Johnson's daughter Luci recalled hearing demonstrators chant "LBJ, LBJ, how many boys have you killed today?" from her bedroom in the White House.

Wartime Partisanship

But the Vietnam era, which included the civil rights struggle, has nothing on our own when it comes to polarization—and this is disquieting. Vietnam was a far larger undertaking than Iraq, with much greater carnage, heartbreak, expense, and loss of American military lives. Yet the war in Iraq has engendered a partisan antipathy to President Bush so pervasive that pollsters know the answers to most questions about the president and his policies by the time they ask the first survey question—the one in which respondents identify their political party affiliation.

24. Quoted in Carl M. Cannon, "Taking Stock of America," *National Journal,* January 16, 1999, p. 91.
25. Tannen (1998).

Consider these sobering numbers from a February 2006 CBS News poll:[26]

"Looking back, do you think the United States did the right thing in taking military action in Iraq or should the U.S. have stayed out?"

	Democrat	Republican
Right thing	19 percent	71 percent
Stayed out	76 percent	25 percent

Contrast those findings with polls taken by the Gallup Organization during the Vietnam and Korean wars.[27]

"Was the Vietnam War a mistake?"

	Democrat	Republican
Not a mistake	37 percent	34 percent
Mistake	51 percent	56 percent

"Was the Korean War a mistake?"

	Democrat	Republican
Not a mistake	45 percent	37 percent
Mistake	43 percent	55 percent

These are not isolated findings. Questions seeking to ascertain Americans' feelings about the wisdom, efficacy, and likely success of the U.S. invasion of Iraq suggest that Republicans and Democrats are talking about different wars.

Asked by CBS News in February 2006 whether Iraq was "worth the loss of American life and other costs," 58 percent of Republicans answered yes while 82 percent of Democrats said no. Asked if things were going "very well" or "somewhat well" in Iraq, 65 percent of Republicans said yes, while 81 percent of Democrats said no—including an eye-opening 48 percent who said the war was going "very badly."

No gaps like these even remotely existed during the supposedly cataclysmic Vietnam era. At its most partisan divide (in the presidential election year

26. CBS News Poll, "President Bush, the Ports, and Iraq," February 27, 2006 (www.cbsnews.com/htdocs/pdf/poll_bush_022706.pdf).

27. Results of the Gallup polls are cited in Carl M. Cannon, "A New Era of Partisan War," *National Journal*, March 18, 2006.

of 1952), the gap between Democrats and Republicans on the Korean War was 17 percentage points (61 percent of Republicans and 44 percent of Democrats considered Korea a mistake). A year earlier, the gap was only 12 points.

That this is a potentially ominous development seems obvious, even though it has generated little public discussion. If support for the Iraq war is partisan, does that make Iraq a Republican Party war? How do the troops feel about that? The taxpayers? "We have reached a situation that, were the partisan composition of the White House and Congress reversed, spokesmen for both parties would change positions on a dime," said Al Felzenberg, a former Reagan administration official who served on the staff of the 9/11 Commission.[28]

This dichotomy is not limited to views on Iraq, however. It exists on nearly every issue, ranging from right-track/wrong-track polls to the state of the economy and views on immigration policy, race relations, and Social Security reform. Some of that is understandable, as the two parties have differing ideologies. But the closer one looks at polling data on attitudes and perceptions of American life, the more it becomes apparent that partisanship is interfering with Americans' ability to process factual information.

A National Election Studies survey conducted by the University of Michigan in 1988 sought to determine how voters thought the country had progressed during the Reagan administration. Party affiliation had a lot to do with it—far too much, an objective person would say. Asked, for example, whether inflation had increased or decreased during Reagan's two-term presidency, Democrats could not even bring themselves to acknowledge basic facts. When Reagan took office in 1981, inflation was running at almost 14 percent. By the time he flew back home to California in retirement, it was less than 4 percent. But less than a quarter of self-described Democrats allowed that there had been an improvement in inflation under Reagan. Half of all Democrats said inflation had *worsened.*[29]

Larry Bartels of Princeton University drew attention to these findings at a December 2004 polarization conference he cohosted at his university. "So that's the way in which partisanship operates both to maintain and to exacerbate differences in people's political views," he said, "by presenting a kind of partisan filter on all sorts of events."[30]

28. Quoted in Carl M. Cannon, "A New Era of Partisan War," *National Journal,* March 18, 2006, p. 44.

29. Data from the National Election Studies survey cited in Bartels (2002).

30. From a transcript of a panel discussion, "The Polarization of American Politics: Myth or Reality?" at the Center for the Study of Democratic Politics, Princeton University, December 3, 2004 (www.princeton.edu/~csdp/events/pdfs/Panel1.pdf).

Let's put it more bluntly: excess partisanship literally inhibits Americans from processing information that challenges their biases. This is no small matter. This nation must soon come to some kind of judgment about the war effort in Iraq. It is an issue that is simply too important for political leanings.

At a recent reception of the Scoop Jackson Foundation honoring Senators John McCain and Joe Lieberman (it was a very small reception), American Enterprise Institute scholar Norman Ornstein put it this way: "We've gotten so polarized that you can take the president's job approval rating, by party, and simply move it to an opinion over something as profound as war and get the same numbers. Whoa, there's nothing good about that."[31]

Partisanship has always played some role in how Americans view foreign wars, just nothing like it does today. "This is totally unprecedented," said Ohio State University political scientist John Mueller, who has studied how public opinion shifted on Korea, Vietnam, and Iraq. "It's so extreme, it's really off the charts. We're in a new era."[32]

31. Norman Ornstein, interview with author, Washington, D.C., March 14, 2006.
32. John Mueller, telephone interview with author, March 2006.

References

Abramowitz, Alan I., and Kyle L. Saunders. 1998. "Ideological Realignment in the U.S. Electorate." *Journal of Politics* 60 (3): 634–52.

Alford, Robert R. 1964. *Party and Society: The Anglo-American Democracies.* Chicago: Rand-McNally.

Alford, John R., and David W. Brady. 1993. "Personal and Partisan Advantage in U.S. Congressional Elections, 1846–1990." In *Congress Reconsidered,* 5th ed., edited by Lawrence C. Dodd and Bruce I. Oppenheimer, pp. 141–57. Washington: CQ Press.

Ansolabehere, Stephen, and James M. Snyder Jr. 2002. "The Incumbency Advantage in U.S. Elections: An Analysis of State and Federal Offices, 1942–2000." *Election Law Journal* 1 (3): 315–38.

Ansolabehere, Stephen, James M. Snyder Jr., and Charles Stewart III. 2000. "Old Voters, New Voters, and the Personal Vote: Using Redistricting to Measure the Incumbency Advantage." *American Journal of Political Science* 44 (1): 17–34.

———. 2001. "Candidate Positioning in U.S. House Elections." *American Journal of Political Science* 45 (1): 136–59.

Bartels, Larry M. 2002. "Beyond the Running Tally: Partisan Bias in Political Perceptions." *Political Behavior* 24 (2): 117–50.

Berelson, Bernard R., Paul F. Lazarsfeld, and William N. McPhee. 1954. *Voting: A Study of Opinion Formation in a Presidential Campaign.* University of Chicago Press.

Black, Earl, and Merle Black. 2002. *The Rise of Southern Republicans.* Harvard University Press.

Brady, David W. 1988. *Critical Elections and Congressional Policy Making.* Stanford University Press.

Brady, David W., Charles S. Bullock III, and L. Sandy Maisel. 1988. "The Electoral Antecedents of Policy Innovations—A Comparative Analysis." *Comparative Political Studies* 20 (4): 395–422.

Brady, David W, Joseph Cooper, and Patricia A. Hurley. 1979. "The Decline of Party in the U.S. House of Representatives, 1887–1968." *Legislative Studies Quarterly* 4 (3): 381–407.

Brady, David W., Robert D'Onofrio, and Morris P. Fiorina. 2000. "The Nationalization of Electoral Forces Revisited." In *Continuity and Change in House Elections,* edited by David W Brady, John F. Cogan, and Morris P. Fiorina, pp. 130–48. Stanford University Press.

Burden, Barry C., and David C. Kimball. 2002. *Why Americans Split Their Tickets: Campaigns, Competition, and Divided Government.* University of Michigan Press.

Cain, Bruce, John Ferejohn, and Morris Fiorina. 1987. *The Personal Vote: Constituency Service and Electoral Independence.* Harvard University Press.

Campbell, Angus, and others. 1960. *The American Voter.* New York: Wiley.

Campbell, James E. 2003. "The Stagnation of Congressional Elections." In *Life after Reform: When the Bipartisan Campaign Reform Act Meets Politics,* edited by Michael J. Malbin, pp. 141–58. Lanham, Md.: Rowman & Littlefield.

———. 2006. "Party Systems and Realignments in the United States, 1868–2004." *Social Science History* 30 (3): 359–86.

Campbell, James E., and Steve J. Jurek. 2003. "The Decline of Competition and Change in Congressional Elections." In *Congress Responds to the Twentieth Century,* edited by Sunil Ahuja and Robert Dewhirst, pp. 43–72. Ohio State University Press.

Canes-Wrone, Brandice, David W. Brady, and John F. Cogan. 2002. "Out of Step, Out of Office: Electoral Accountability and House Members' Voting." *American Political Science Review* 96 (1): 127–40.

Carmines, Edward G., and James A. Stimson. 1981. "Issue Evolution, Population Replacement, and Normal Partisan Change." *American Political Science Review* 75 (1): 107–18.

———. 1989. *Issue Evolution: Race and the Transformation of American Politics.* Princeton University Press.

Clausen, Aage. 1973. *How Congressmen Decide: A Policy Focus.* New York: St. Martin's Press.

Coleman, James S. 1971. "Internal Processes Governing Party Positions in Elections." *Public Choice* 11 (Fall): 35–60.

Collie, Melissa P., and John Lyman Mason. 2000. "The Electoral Connection between Party and Constituency Reconsidered: Evidence from the U.S. House of Representatives, 1972–1994." In *Continuity and Change in U.S. House Elections,* edited by David W. Brady, John F. Cogan, and Morris P. Fiorina, pp. 211–34. Stanford University Press, Hoover Institution Press.

Cooper, Joseph, and Garry Young. 1997. "Partisanship, Bipartisanship, and Crosspartisanship in Congress since the New Deal. In *Congress Reconsidered,* 6th ed., edited by Lawrence C. Dodd and Bruce I. Oppenheimer. Washington: CQ Press.

———. 2002. "Party and Preference in Congressional Decision Making: Roll Call Voting in the U.S. House of Representatives, 1889–1997." In *Party, Process, and Political Change in Congress: New Perspectives on the History of Congress,* edited by David W. Brady and Mathew D. McCubbins, pp. 64–106. Stanford University Press.

Cox, Gary W., and Jonathan N. Katz. 2002. *Elbridge Gerry's Salamander: The Electoral Consequences of the Reapportionment Revolution.* Cambridge University Press.

DiMaggio, Paul, John Evans, and Bethany Bryson. 1996. "Have Americans' Social Attitudes Become More Polarized?" *American Journal of Sociology* 102 (3): 690–755.

Erikson, Robert S. 1972. "Malapportionment, Gerrymandering, and Party Fortunes in Congressional Elections." *American Political Science Review* 66 (4): 1234–45.

Erikson, Robert S., and Gerald C. Wright. 1993. "Voters, Candidates and Issues in Congressional Elections." In *Congress Reconsidered,* 5th ed., edited by Lawrence C. Dodd and Bruce I. Oppenheimer, pp. 91–114. Washington: CQ Press.

———. 1997. "Voters, Candidates, and Issues in Congressional Elections." In *Congress Reconsidered,* 6th ed., edited by Lawrence C. Dodd and Bruce I. Oppenheimer, pp. 132–61. Washington: CQ Press.

———. 2005. "Voters, Candidates, and Issues in Congressional Elections." In *Congress Reconsidered,* 8th ed., edited by Lawrence C. Dodd and Bruce I. Oppenheimer, pp. 77–106. Washington: CQ Press.

Evans, C. Lawrence. 2005. "Politics of Congressional Reform." In *Institutions of American Democracy: The Legislative Branch,* edited by Paul J. Quirk and Sarah A. Binder, pp. 490–524. Oxford University Press.

Evans, John H. 2003. "Have Americans' Attitudes Become More Polarized? An Update." *Social Science Quarterly* 84 (1): pp. 71–90.

Fair, Ray C. 2002. *Predicting Presidential Elections and Other Things.* Stanford University Press.

Fiorina, Morris P. 1981. *Retrospective Voting in American National Elections.* Yale University Press.

———. 1996. *Divided Government,* 2d ed. Boston: Allyn & Bacon.

———. 1999. "Whatever Happened to the Median Voter?" Paper prepared for the MIT Conference on Parties and Congress, Cambridge, Mass., October 2.

Fiorina, Morris P., Samuel J. Abrams, and Jeremy C. Pope. 2006. *Culture War? The Myth of a Polarized America.* New York: Longman.

Fleisher, Richard, and Jon R. Bond. 2000a. "Congress and the President in a Partisan Era." In *Polarized Politics: Congress and the President in a Partisan Era,* edited by Jon R. Bond and Richard Fleisher, pp. 1–8. Washington: CQ Press.

———. 2000b. "Partisanship and the President's Quest for Votes on the Floor of Congress." In *Polarized Politics: Congress and the President in a Partisan Era,* edited by Jon R. Bond and Richard Fleisher, pp. 154–85. Washington: CQ Press.

Foner, Eric. 1970. *Free Soil, Free Labor, Free Men: The Ideology of the Republican Party before the Civil War.* Oxford University Press.

Frieden, Jeffrey. 2006. *Global Capitalism: Its Fall and Rise in the Twentieth Century.* New York: W. W. Norton.

Friedman, Benjamin M. 2006. *The Moral Consequences of Economic Growth.* New York: Vintage.

Gelman, Andrew, and Gary King. 1990. "Estimating Incumbency Advantage without Bias." *American Journal of Political Science* 34 (4): 1142–64.

Gelman, Andrew, and others. 2005. "Rich State, Poor State, Red State, Blue State: What's the Matter with Connecticut?" Paper prepared for the annual meeting of the Midwest Political Science Association, Chicago, April 7–10.

Gienapp, William E. 1987. *Origins of the Republican Party, 1852–1856.* Oxford University Press.

Gould, Lewis L. 1996. "Party Conflict: Republicans versus Democrats, 1877–1901." In *The Gilded Age, Essays on the Origins of Modern America,* edited by Charles W. Calhoun, pp. 215–34. Lanham, Md.: Rowman & Littlefield.

Han, Hahrie, and David W. Brady. Forthcoming. "A Delayed Return to Historical Norms: Congressional Party Polarization after the Second World War." *British Journal of Political Science.*

Hetherington, Marc J. 2001. "Resurgent Mass Partisanship: The Role of Elite Polarization." *American Political Science Review* 95 (3): 619–31.

Holt, Michael F. 2004. *The Fate of Their Country: Politicians, Slavery Extension, and the Coming of the Civil War.* New York: Hill and Wang.

Hurley, Patricia A., and Rick K. Wilson. 1989. "Partisan Voting Patterns in the U.S. Senate, 1877–1986." *Legislative Studies Quarterly* 14 (2): 225–50.

Huston, James. 1987. *The Panic of 1857 and the Coming of the Civil War.* Louisiana State University Press.

Jacobson, Gary C. 1987. "The Marginals Never Vanished: Incumbency and Competition in Elections to the U.S. House of Representatives, 1952–82." *American Journal of Political Science* 31 (1): 126–41.

———. 2001. *The Politics of Congressional Elections.* 5th ed. New York: Longman.

———. 2003. "Explaining the Ideological Polarization of the Congressional Parties." Paper prepared for the Conference on the History of Congress at the University of California, San Diego, December 5–6.

———. Forthcoming 2007. "Explaining the Ideological Polarization of the Congressional Parties since the 1970s." In *Process, Party, and Policy Making: Further New Perspectives on the History of Congress,* edited by David W. Brady and Mathew D. McCubbins. Stanford University Press.

James, Judson L. 1969. *American Political Parties: Potential and Performance.* New York: Pegasus.

Keller, Morton. 1979. *Affairs of State: Public Life in Late Nineteenth Century America.* Cambridge, Mass.: Belknap Press.

———. 1990. *Regulating a New Economy: Economic Change and Public Policy in America, 1900–1933.* Harvard University Press.

Kennedy, David M. 1971. *Progressivism: The Critical Issues.* Boston: Little, Brown.

———. 1999. *Freedom from Fear: The American People in Depression and War, 1929–1945.* Oxford University Press.

Key, V. O., Jr. 1955. "A Theory of Critical Elections." *Journal of Politics* 17 (1): 3–18.

———. 1956. *Politics, Parties, and Pressure Groups.* 3d ed. New York: Thomas Crowell.

———. 1958. *A Theory of Critical Elections.* New York: Irvington Publishers.

———. 1959. "Secular Realignment and the Party System." *Journal of Politics* 21 (2): 198–210.

Kleppner, Paul. 1982. *Who Voted? The Dynamics of Electoral Turnout, 1870–1980.* New York: Praeger.

Lazarsfeld, Paul F., Bernard Berelson, and Hazel Gaudet. 1948. *The People's Choice: How the Voter Makes Up His Mind in a Presidential Campaign.* Columbia University Press.

Leuchtenburg, William E. 1963. *Franklin Delano Roosevelt and the New Deal.* New York: Harper Perennial.

Levendusky, Matthew S., Jeremy C. Pope, and Simon Jackman. 2005. "Measuring District Level Preferences with Implications for Analysis of U.S. Elections." Paper presented at the annual meeting of the Society for Political Methodology, Tallahassee, Fla., July 21–23.

McCarty, Nolan, Keith T. Poole, and Howard Rosenthal. 2006. *Polarized America: The Dance of Ideology and Unequal Riches.* MIT Press.

McCloskey, Herbert, Paul J. Hoffman, and Rosemary O'Hara. 1960. "Issue Conflict and Consensus among Party Leaders and Followers." *American Political Science Review* 54 (June): 406–27.

McDonald, Michael P. 2004. "Up, Up and Away! Voter Participation in the 2004 Presidential Election." *The Forum* 2 (4): Article 4.

Poole, Keith T., and Howard Rosenthal. 1984. "The Polarization of American Politics." *Journal of Politics* 46 (4): 1061–79.

———. 1991. "Patterns of Congressional Voting." *American Journal of Political Science* 35 (1): 228–78.

Purdy, Rob Roy, ed. 1959. *Fugitives' Reunion: Conversations at Vanderbilt, May 3–5, 1956.* Vanderbilt University Press.

Roberts, Jason M., and Steven S. Smith. 2003. "Procedural Contexts, Party Strategy, and Conditional Party Voting in the U.S. House of Representatives, 1971–2000." *American Journal of Political Science* 47 (2): 305–17.

Rohde, David. 1991. *Parties and Leaders in the Postreform House.* University of Chicago Press.

Schickler, Eric. 2000. "Institutional Change in the House of Representatives, 1867–1998: A Test of Partisan and Ideological Power Balance Models." *American Political Science Review* 94 (2): 269–88.

Schlesinger, Arthur M., ed. 1971. *History of American Presidential Elections, 1789–1968*, Vol. 4. New York: Chelsea House.

Shafer, Byron E., and Richard Johnston. 2006. *The End of Southern Exceptionalism: Class, Race, and Partisan Change in the Postwar South.* Harvard University Press.

Silbey, Joel H. 1991. *The American Political Nation, 1838–1893.* Stanford University Press.

Smith, Steven S. 1989. *Call to Order: Floor Politics in the House and Senate.* Brookings.

Stanley, Harold W., and Richard G. Niemi, eds. 2005. *Vital Statistics on American Politics 2005–2006.* Washington: CQ Press.

Sundquist, James L. 1983. *Dynamics of the Party System: Alignment and Realignment of Political Parties in the United States.* Brookings.

Tannen, Deborah. 1998. *The Argument Culture: Moving from Debate to Dialogue.* New York: Random House.

Van Houweling, Robert. 2003. "Legislators' Personal Policy Preferences and Partisan Legislative Organization." Ph.D. dissertation, Harvard University.

Wiebe, Robert H. 1967. *The Search for Order, 1877–1920.* New York: Hill and Wang.

4

Polarized by God? American Politics and the Religious Divide

E.J. Dionne Jr.

Has religious commitment become the most important factor in determining the outcome of American elections? Can the bitter polarization so evident in so many aspects of our politics be explained by Pat Buchanan's famous claim in his 1992 speech at the Republican National Convention that we are in the middle of both "a cultural war" and "a religious war"?

If that's true, politics is inevitably bitter because it becomes a battle over the most fundamental questions between individuals and groups who do not understand each other and, often, can't stand each other. Have the traditional drivers of political choice—class, race, region, economic circumstances, and views on foreign policy and on government's role at home—withered in their explanatory power when faced with the power of faith? The short answer is no. Race, especially, but also class and region, still matter greatly in our elections. One would not know that, however, from the current obsession with the role of religion and "moral values" in American politics.

Yet there is good reason to focus on religion's role in our political life. Religion has always been influential in American elections, and there is a new

The author would like to thank Claudia Deane, assistant polling director at the *Washington Post,* for her enormous help in analyzing the 2004 exit polls.

saliency to religious concerns, as William Galston and Pietro Nivola point out in their introduction to this volume. The new religious divide is not between Protestants, Catholics, and Jews, but between traditionalists on the one hand and moderates and modernists on the other. It is between those who are highly observant and those who are not.

The attention religion is now receiving is entirely healthy if it reminds us that politics is about more than who gets what, when, and how. Those questions, raised seventy years ago by Harold Lasswell, are perennially relevant, but they are not the only questions.[1] Voters are motivated by material concerns, but also by moral and, yes, spiritual concerns. There is considerable truth to the suggestion of Michael Barone, the author of the biennial *Almanac of American Politics,* that religion has become "the great divider" in American elections.[2] If not all of the polarization in American politics can be explained by attitudes toward religious faith, a significant part of it certainly can be.

The paradox of the rise of religious conservatism is that it became an important factor in American politics primarily because of liberal victories—on abortion, school prayer, the rising power of feminism, the sexual revolution of the 1960s. Jerry Falwell, who had once condemned the role of preachers in politics ("Preachers are not called upon to be politicians but to be soul winners," he declared in 1965), wrote in his autobiography that he began changing his mind on the question of evangelical involvement in politics on January 23, 1973, the day the Supreme Court issued the *Roe* v. *Wade* decision.[3]

We also forget that the past eight decades have seen the steady erosion of Protestant dominance in American politics and culture. Al Smith's presidential candidacy was rejected in 1928 in part because Protestant America decided it could not accept the election of a Catholic president. But Smith's losing coalition presaged Franklin Roosevelt's winning coalition that kept the Protestant South in the Democratic camp while bringing in millions of urban Catholics and Jews who had no sympathy for Prohibition and much suspicion of the old Protestant order. John F. Kennedy's election in 1960 signaled the arrival of Catholics as an accepted group in American public life—and also signaled the end of white Protestant hegemony. This hegemony was further undermined by the end of prescribed prayer in public schools (the prayers had been "nondenominational" but Protestant in spirit) and by the growing role of new immigrant groups in

1. Lasswell (1936).
2. Barone (1993, p. xxvii).
3. Falwell (1987, p. 337).

American politics. The reemergence of religion (and in particular white evangelical Protestantism) as an organizing and polarizing force in American politics
can be seen, in part at least, as a reaction against the marginalization of a once-
dominant Protestantism in the American public square.[4]

The Causes of Religious Polarization

The 1960s and early 1970s saw the rise of cultural politics—or what political
scientist Ronald Inglehart called "post-materialist" politics—at both ends of the
political spectrum.[5] The cultural battles of the 1960s redefined not only the
right, but also the left. As Peter Steinfels has said, "American political liberalism
has shifted its passion from issues of economic deprivation and concentration of
power to issues of gender, sexuality, and personal choice. . . . Once trade union-
ism, regulation of the market, and various welfare measures were the litmus tests
of secular liberalism. Later, desegregation and racial justice were the litmus tests.
Today the litmus test is abortion."[6] And, one might add, stem-cell research, gay
marriage, and Hollywood culture.

The religious and cultural politics of our time are clearly rooted in the rebel-
lions of the 1960s against 1950s "conformity." The academy and the mass media
mostly noticed what was happening on the New Left. But a New Right shared in
the New Left's reaction against "the liberal establishment" (or, as the New Left
preferred, "establishment liberalism"). And the new conservative religious movements shared roots with the New Age and countercultural reactions against the
religious establishment. Peter Clecak has argued that the resurgence of the old-
time religion was part of a broader revolt against modernism and scientific
rationality that can be traced to the counterculture.[7] Leonard Sweet, an evangelical church historian, saw both the new religions of the 1960s and 1970s and the
new turn to the old ones as part of a "subjectivist search for authority."[8]

The political parties understood the power of cultural and religious issues and
used them to mobilize—and polarize—the electorate. Falwell and the Moral
Majority were called into being by long-time Republican organizers and leaders

4. Dionne (2000, pp. 115–20).
5. Inglehart (1997).
6. Peter Steinfels, "Reinventing Liberal Catholicism: Between Powerful Enemies and Dubious
Allies," *Commonweal*, November 19, 1999.
7. Clecak (1983).
8. Sweet (1984, esp. pp. 37–43).

who realized that they could bulk up the conservative vote by appealing to the cultural concerns of whites with moderate incomes and socially conservative views. Democrats realized that wealthier voters, who had traditionally been Republican, had no use for restrictions on abortion. If Republicans were going to gain ground among social conservatives in the middle class, Democrats would gain ground among social liberals in the upper middle class. In politics, it is usually the case that every action encourages an opposite if not always equal reaction.

And the polarization was deepened by the fact that the contours of the religious and cultural battles were defined in significant part by region. Social conservatives loomed especially large in the South and in many (though not all) of the Rocky Mountain and Plains states. Social liberals were important in the Northeast, on the West Coast, and in many states of the Midwest. The shift to the Republicans in the South was thus counterbalanced by a shift toward the Democrats elsewhere. The realignment of the traditionally Democratic South toward the Republican Party—rooted initially in racial politics—did not call forth a sudden counter-realignment in Republican parts of the Northeast, the Midwest, and the West Coast. But the counter-realignment developed gradually and came to dramatic fruition in the 1996 election.

The *Washington Post*'s political reporter Dan Balz was one of the first to notice that large suburban counties—places that had been faithfully Republican for decades and had voted Republican as recently as 1992—turned to Clinton four years later.[9] These included Oakland County outside of Detroit, Bergen and Monmouth Counties in New Jersey, and Lake County east of Cleveland. The one-time Republican bastions of Nassau and Westchester Counties in New York drifted Democratic. So did once Republican counties in California and coastal Oregon, as well as suburban counties outside of Philadelphia. The 1992 and 1996 elections marked the first time that all six New England states voted Democratic two elections in a row, a sign of the new regional polarization. (They all went that way again in 2004, after New Hampshire's brief excursion, albeit by a very narrow margin, into Republican territory in 2000.)

As Seymour Martin Lipset and William Schneider have argued, battles over religion, culture, and values are necessarily more polarizing than fights over the distribution of money and resources.[10] Lipset described the New Deal and post–World War II eras in American politics as entailing a "democratic class

---

9. Dan Balz, "Clinton Broke Republican Grip on Some Suburban County Strongholds," *Washington Post,* November 10, 1996.

10. Lipset and Schneider (1987).

struggle" in which less-privileged groups used electoral politics to enhance their living standards and incomes.[11] In battles over money, differences can be split with mathematical certainty if not precision. But in battles over faith and values, the differences cannot be split so easily because the struggle is over fundamentals. This was true at moments in the nineteenth century no less than in the late twentieth and early twenty-first centuries. As James Q. Wilson argued in *The Moral Sense,* "Once the issues were slavery, temperance, religion and prostitution; today the issues are divorce, illegitimacy, crime and entertainment."[12]

Religion's role as a polarizing force in contemporary politics might be seen to have gone through three stages. The first big shift occurred between 1976 and 1980 with the rise of the Moral Majority, the disillusionment of conservative evangelical Christians with their fellow evangelical Jimmy Carter, and Ronald Reagan's conversion into a strong foe of abortion. (As governor of California, Reagan had signed one of the most liberal abortion laws in the country.) In 1976 Carter ran strongly among evangelicals and seemed to restore the Democratic Party's standing among social conservatives, particularly in the South. His loss to Reagan in the 1980 campaign ended that.

In 1992 Bill Clinton seemed poised to play Jimmy Carter's role by winning back a share of the conservative religious vote. Clinton often used the language of faith. He spoke of covenants, personal responsibility, and community. He appeared often in pulpits, carrying a well-thumbed Bible. He sang the old hymns without forgetting a word and quoted the Scriptures with the authority of a preacher. His administration brokered agreements among a broad range of religious and secular civil liberties groups to protect the rights of religious students in public schools and the religious rights of public employees. Toward the end of Clinton's second term, Adam Meyerson, then a vice president of the conservative Heritage Foundation (and no friend of Clinton's politics), said that "Clinton's greatest legacy may well be his leadership in reducing the bigotry against religion that has been expressed in recent decades by much of the Democratic Party and American liberalism."[13]

That might have been a powerful Clinton legacy absent the Monica Lewinsky sex scandal. The reaction to the scandal among religious conservatives (not to mention other even moderately traditional Americans) wiped out the gains

11. Lipset (1960, p. 220).
12. Wilson (1997, p. xi).
13. E. J. Dionne Jr., "A Welcome Peace in Our Religious Wars," *Washington Post,* August 19, 1997.

Clinton might have secured for Democrats among the religiously committed and repolarized the electorate along religious lines.

In the 2000 election, George W. Bush took full advantage of the opening. Without dwelling on the Lewinsky scandal, he simply promised to restore "honor and dignity" to the White House. Everyone knew what he was talking about. He let voters know, without sounding the least bit judgmental, that he was a committed evangelical Christian and that his faith was important to him. (Even his political enemies in Texas said this was an authentic assertion.) He signed up the religious right early in his campaign. Ralph Reed, the political consultant who had once been executive director of the Christian Coalition, became a well-paid campaign lieutenant.

Bush had learned the tempos and sensibilities of the Christian conservative movement when he represented his father's campaigns in church after church after church. In 2000 his experience showed. He told a national audience during an early Republican debate in Iowa that Jesus Christ was his favorite political philosopher. And when Bush ran into trouble after losing the 2000 New Hampshire primary to John McCain, the religious conservatives came to W's rescue eighteen days later in the South Carolina primary.

Over the course of his administration, Bush's "God talk" gave secular voters (and not a few religious ones) the willies, even though Bush did not, in fact, invoke the Almighty all that differently from his predecessors (including, notably, the theologically fluent Clinton). The notion of Bush as a wild-eyed religious fanatic undertaking a new Crusade in the Middle East became a widely held view on the left over time. Bush did not help his cause when he told the *Washington Post*'s Bob Woodward that he had not consulted his father about going into Iraq, but did consult "a higher Father."[14] (Many who had nothing against prayer wished he had called his dad.) And Karl Rove's open and successful effort to increase the turnout of evangelical Christians in the 2004 election only deepened the ties that bound them to Bush—and the mistrust and hostility of more secular Americans, along with religious liberals.

Thus was the scene set for what can be seen as one of the three most religiously charged elections in American history. (The other two, 1928 and 1960, involved the first and second Catholic candidates for president.) The returns of 2004 told the story. Yet the recent shifts in American politics cannot be understood in cultural and religious terms alone. If it is foolish to underestimate reli-

14. Woodward (2004, p. 421).

gion's obvious and important role in recent elections, it is also wrong to see religion wiping out or overwhelming other factors in politics. The central theme of this essay might thus be seen as "Yes, but." Yes, religion is important, but there is a temptation on both the religious right and the secular left to exaggerate its influence. Yes, religious observance affects voting, but many conservatives who happen to be believers would likely be conservative even if they never went to church. Yes, secular voters tend to be more liberal than others, but their liberalism shares important roots with the philosophy of their fellow citizens who are practicing believers.

The Significance of "But"

The "but" side of the argument is important because so much of the analysis immediately after the 2004 election was framed by a view that George W. Bush owed his reelection to religious and moral issues. But John Kerry was not defeated by the religious right. He was beaten by moderates who voted—reluctantly in many cases—for President Bush. This was hard for many Democrats to take. It was easier to salve their wounds by demonizing religious conservatives. In the 2004 election, Democrats left moderate votes on the table that could have created a Kerry majority.

Consider these findings from network exit polls: about 38 percent of those who thought abortion should be legal in most cases voted for Bush. Bush got 22 percent from voters who favored gay marriage and 52 percent from those who favored same-sex civil unions. Bush even managed 16 percent among voters who thought the president paid more attention to the interests of large corporations than to those of "ordinary Americans." A third of the voters who favored a government more active in solving problems went for Bush. True, 22 percent said that "moral values" were decisive in their choices. But 71 percent picked some other issue. (The remainder exercised their constitutional right to decline to answer pollsters' questions.)

All this means that Bush won *not* because religious conservatives were on the march, and not because there is a right-wing majority in the United States, but because the president persuaded just enough of the nonconservative majority to go his way. Even with their increased numbers, conservatives still constituted only 34 percent of the electorate in 2004. The largest share of the American electorate (45 percent) calls itself moderate. The moderates went 54 to 45 percent for Kerry—good, but not enough. And 21 percent of the voters in 2004 called themselves liberal, which means that liberals can win only in alliance with a large share of moderate voters. This suggests that polarized politics may be of more help to conservatives than to liberals, unless liberals can turn a reaction to polarization into a reason for rejecting the currently dominant political forces.

The numbers of 2004 do not lend themselves to a facile ideological analysis of what happened. The populist left can fairly ask why so many pro-government, anti-corporate voters backed Bush. The social liberals can ask why so many socially moderate and progressive voters stuck with the president. The centrist crowd can muse over the power of the terrorism issue. When Karl Rove went after the red-hot right-wing vote, he did so largely through person-to-person contact, mailings, and conservative talk-meisters. Bush always spoke in code to this group—he talked of a "culture of life" far more than he did about abortion, to reduce the risk of turning off the middle.

Democrats have an unlimited capacity to declare that their party suffers from some deep intellectual dysfunction. The insistence that Democrats need "new ideas" is especially popular among think-tankers and columnists, a band I have a personal interest in keeping employed. But Rove and Bush won the 2004 election on decidedly old strategies that had nothing to do with ideas. These included attacks on Kerry for being weak and the claim, subscribed to by a majority, that Bush would be tougher on the bad guys. That's familiar, cold war era stuff. To get a sense of how the war on terror and other factors may have played a larger role than religious affiliation in the 2004 outcome, consider where Bush made gains over his 2000 vote. The exit polls found that perhaps 10 percent of Al Gore voters in 2000 switched to Bush in 2004, and that of those more than eight in ten thought the war in Iraq was part of the war on terror. According to the 2004 exit polls, Bush increased his vote by only 1 percentage point among voters who attended religious services at least once a week. But he gained 4 points among monthly attenders, 3 points among those who attend a few times a year, and 4 points among those who never attend religious services. Put simply, the swing to Bush was higher among the less religiously observant than among the more religious.

Polarization around moral issues in the electorate is also not a simple story. Consider that even among the most vexed there is a broad middle ground in the electorate. Asked about abortion in the 2004 exit poll, 21 percent of voters said that it should always be legal, 34 percent that it should be legal in most cases, 26 percent that it should be illegal in most cases, and 16 percent that it should always be illegal. Viewed one way, respondents were "pro-choice," 55 to 42 percent. Viewed another way, 60 percent of them gravitated to a "middle" position on abortion. There is most certainly a conflict akin to a culture war among the

37 percent of Americans—21 percent consistently pro-choice, 16 percent consistently pro-life—who were absolutely certain about where they stood on abortion. And that is a very large group. But a majority of the population, while having leanings on the issue, does not have anything like the degree of engagement or commitment of the true warriors.

On the question of gay marriage, the exit polls found that 25 percent of voters thought homosexuals should be able to marry legally, 35 percent favored civil unions, and 37 percent opposed any legal recognition for gay relationships. These findings could be used mischievously by either side in the argument. It can truthfully be said that 72 percent of voters opposed gay marriage. With equal truthfulness it can be said that 60 percent favored either gay marriage or civil unions.

What the numbers on both abortion and gay marriage suggest is that there is great strength in the moderate middle of American politics—just as there is great strength among the passionate believers at the far reaches of the political spectrum who confront each other every day on blogs, in newspaper columns, and on argumentative radio and television shows. None of this disproves the importance of religious commitment in influencing voter decisions. But it does suggest that even in the polarized climate of 2004 religion was by no means the only important factor, and may have been less important to the final outcome than other factors.

Religion Still Matters—A Lot

For some years, the media-financed exit polls on election day have asked voters how often they attend religious services, and those who said they attend often have tended to be far more Republican in their sympathies than those who attend less frequently or not at all. In 2004, exit polls found that Americans who attend services more than once a week voted for George W. Bush over John Kerry, 64 to 35 percent. By contrast, those who said they never go to religious services backed Kerry, 62 to 36 percent. Case on religiosity closed?

Taken together, these two groups account for only about three voters in ten—the 16 percent of Americans who attend religious services more than once a week and the 15 percent who never do. What of the rest? Again, there is a definite relationship between Republican leanings and religious attendance, but it is not as strong as one would assume, looking only at the most and least religious. Weekly attendees backed Bush, 58 to 41 percent. Those who attend once a month split evenly, 50 percent for Bush, 49 percent for

Kerry. Those who attend religious services a few times a year backed Kerry, 54 to 45 percent.

Consolidating the categories of those who participated at least some of the time in organized religion, the four voters in ten who said they attend religious services at least once a week gave Bush 61 percent of their ballots; the four voters in ten who participate only occasionally gave Bush 47 percent, a difference of 14 percentage points. Without question, these numbers are important, and they explain why Democratic strategists have spent so much time since 2004 pondering God, faith, and the attitudes of religious believers. There is good reason to think that some of the passion underlying the nation's current political polarization is religious passion. It reflects a clash between ardent believers and those who are less devout or highly skeptical.

But this is not the whole story. There are factors that matter even more than religious commitment in American politics, most notably race. And there are factors that compete with religious commitment in explaining the allegiances of voters, most notably class. There are local and regional factors that scramble class and religious differences. And in 2004, as we have seen, there was an issue that mattered more to the electoral outcome than any of the issues related to faith: the war on terror.

To put the findings on religion in perspective, it is important to review the exit poll data on these other factors. Race has always played a role in American politics, and since the 1964 election, fought in part around civil rights, the African American vote has been overwhelmingly Democratic. Despite small gains for Bush, that was again the case in 2004. Where white voters backed Bush 58 to 41 percent, black voters supported Kerry, 88 to 11 percent. The gap between black and white supporters of Bush was 47 percentage points, a far larger difference than the divide between the most religious and the most secular voters. Indeed, the impact of church attendance on voting decisions, while very strong among whites and important among Latinos, was minimal among African American voters (see table 4-1).

African American loyalty to the Democratic Party in 2004 remained strong across the board. But the numbers do suggest some openings for Republicans in the future. Republican strategists believe they can make inroads into the black and the Latino vote among the most religious members of both communities. There is at least some evidence that religious attendance modestly boosted Bush's share of the black vote. This may have been especially important in the battleground state of Ohio. There, Bush's share of the African American vote—16 percent, according to the exit polls—was above his national average. The Bush

Table 4-1. *Religious Attendance and Vote by Race, 2004 Presidential Election*
Percent

| | Frequency of | Voted for | |
Race	church attendance	Bush	Kerry
White	Weekly	71	29
	Occasionally	54	46
	Never	38	60
Black	Weekly	15	85
	Occasionally	7	93
	Never	9	90
Latino	Weekly	52	46
	Occasionally	37	60
	Never	31	65

Source: 2004 National Election Pool exit poll.

campaign reportedly invested considerable resources in appealing to Ohio's African American voters, particularly around the issue of gay marriage, which was strongly opposed in the black churches.

Religion also played an important role in Bush's gains in the Latino community, with Bush narrowly carrying frequent churchgoers but losing among the less observant. A 2004 exit poll by the William C. Velasquez Institute found that Bush won 53 percent of the Latino Protestant vote, but only 31 percent of the Latino Catholic vote.[15] The 2004 National Annenberg Election Survey produced similar results: 57 percent of Latino Protestants for Bush, compared with 33 percent of Latino Catholics.[16]

The degree to which religion affected the behavior of voters also varied greatly by region. As table 4-2 suggests, the South is more religiously observant than the rest of the United States. The West is considerably less observant. And religious observance among voters varies sharply from state to state (see table 4-3). It is worth paying attention to the extreme ends of the scale. Over half of the voters in Georgia and Louisiana attend religious services at least weekly—and a quarter to a fifth more than once a week. Only 7 and 8 percent of voters in these states, respectively, claimed never to attend religious services. By contrast, in California

15. William C. Velasquez Institute, "2004 WCVI National Exit Poll of Latino Voters," March 8, 2005 (www.wcvi.org/latino_voter_research/polls/exit_poll_results_030805.htm).

16. Annenberg Public Policy Center, "Bush 2004 Gains among Hispanics Strongest with Men, and in South and Northeast, Annenberg Data Show," December 21, 2004 (www.annenbergpublic policycenter.org/naes/2004_03_zhispanic-data-12_21_pr.pdf).

Table 4-2. *Religious Attendance by Region, 2004 Presidential Election*
Percent

Region	More than weekly	Weekly	Monthly	A few times a year	Never
East	10	25	14	34	15
Midwest	13	29	14	29	13
South	24	27	15	21	11
West	13	21	11	30	23

Source: 2004 National Election Pool exit poll.

and Washington over half the voters attend religious services occasionally or never—including a fifth to a quarter who never attend. The contrast between the religious patterns in the Deep South and on the Pacific Coast offers important clues as to the different political cultures of these regions.

But an analysis of the data on religion, region, and race presents a classic chicken-and-egg problem. Southern whites are, all at once, more religious, more conservative, and more Republican than the rest of the country. This means that the pool of frequent churchgoers includes a moderately disproportionate

Table 4-3. *Religious Attendance in Selected States, 2004 Presidential Election*
Percent

State	More than weekly	Weekly	Monthly	A few times a year	Never
Georgia	25	26	18	23	7
Louisiana	21	31	16	21	8
Virginia	19	27	14	25	12
Michigan	15	27	13	29	13
Ohio	14	26	15	28	14
New Mexico	13	29	15	22	18
Pennsylvania	12	27	15	29	13
Iowa	12	31	16	26	12
Florida	12	23	16	29	17
Minnesota	10	30	16	29	15
Wisconsin	9	27	15	31	15
California	12	20	14	30	22
Washington	13	22	11	27	26

Source: 2004 National Election Pool exit poll.

share of southerners. The Pacific Coast states are considerably less religiously observant than the rest of the country. It is thus important to disentangle the effects of region and race on religious observance and voting.

White southerners began to turn to the Republican Party long before the rise of the religious right, in reaction to the Democratic Party's support for civil rights laws. The conversion began with Barry Goldwater's campaign in 1964, continued with George C. Wallace's run as an independent conservative in 1968, and culminated in 1972, when Richard Nixon pursued his "southern strategy" appealing to white voters below the Mason-Dixon line. Many of the conservative whites who switched sides were evangelical or fundamentalist Protestants, but their new voting behavior was driven more by race than by religion.

The overlap between race and religion was underscored by the findings of Albert J. Menendez, a careful student of religious voting. He estimated that, in 1972, Richard Nixon defeated George McGovern by a margin of 10 million votes (13 million to 3 million) among fundamentalists and evangelicals. Menendez also found that in the nation's ninety-six most heavily Baptist counties Nixon secured 75 percent of the vote. In 1976 Jimmy Carter won back a good share of that vote for the Democrats, then lost it to Reagan in 1980. (Menendez estimated that in 1980 Carter ran 18 percentage points behind his 1976 showing in the nation's most heavily Baptist counties; in the nation as a whole, Carter ran only 10 points behind his showing four years earlier.)[17]

But it is significant that in 1980, *after* the rise of the Moral Majority and the organized religious right, Reagan's share of the Baptist vote was still 15 percentage points smaller than Nixon's. In other words, the movement of white evangelical southerners into the Republican ranks was fueled initially by civil rights and a reaction to liberalism, not by religious fervor. This factor must be taken into account in any analysis of the religion factor in subsequent elections.

Table 4-4 underscores the important partisan difference between southern whites and whites in the rest of the country. The gap between black and white voters is large across the country. But it is especially marked in the South— 24 points larger in the South than in the East, 15 points larger than in the Midwest or West. Southern particularism explains part of the religion gap—but only part.

Table 4-5 underscores this. On the one hand, there was a "religion gap" in 2004 in every region of the country. On the whole, frequent churchgoers were

17. Menendez's findings are summarized in Phillips (1982, pp. 187–88).

Table 4-4. *Vote for Bush by Race and Region, 2004 Presidential Election*
Percent

Region	Whites	African Americans	Latinos	Percentage point gap between black and white voters
East	50	13	28	37
Midwest	56	10	32	46
South	70	9	64	61
West	54	18	39	36

Source: 2004 National Election Pool exit poll.

more likely to vote Republican, and those who never attend religious services were decidedly more likely to vote Democratic. But those who attended religious services regularly in the East were considerably less likely to support Bush than those in the South. This is the flip side of the finding at the other end of the chart: southerners who never attend services are considerably more Republican than easterners who stay away from church services altogether. Figures in the West and Midwest fall roughly in the middle range between the other two regions.

Table 4-6 provides a closer look at these patterns in states where exit poll data are available. While it is possible to make too much of these differences, it is worth noting that the "religion gap" is much larger in some states than in others. The gap barely exists in Louisiana, but is enormous in Minnesota and Washington State. California is the only state on the list in which Bush failed to secure a majority among weekly worshippers. In all these cases, racial and ethnic factors explain at least some of the differences. In Louisiana, the Demo-

Table 4-5. *Vote for Bush by Religious Attendance and Region, 2004 Presidential Election*
Percent

Region	More than weekly	Weekly	Monthly	A few times a year	Never
East	51	52	49	39	24
Midwest	66	58	51	44	37
South	65	64	54	55	46
West	69	57	44	43	36

Source: 2004 National Election Pool exit poll.

Table 4-6. *Vote for Bush by Religious Attendance in Selected States,*
2004 Presidential Election
Percent

State	More than weekly	Weekly	Monthly	A few times a year	Never
Georgia	66	64	51	55	43
Louisiana	60	61	51	57	52
Virginia	62	56	47	54	40
Michigan	58	55	47	42	32
New Mexico	75	54	49	46	31
Ohio	69	64	50	40	35
Pennsylvania	62	55	52	43	31
Iowa	69	54	50	45	33
Florida	65	63	51	47	37
Minnesota	74	58	48	40	19
Wisconsin	66	59	54	44	31
California	60	47	42	43	34
Washington	72	60	46	39	27

Source: 2004 National Election Pool exit poll.

cratic share among regular churchgoers was boosted by African Americans and, to some degree, Cajun Catholics. Minnesota and Washington have relatively small African American populations—and African Americans are the most Democratic group among loyal churchgoers. In California, the Democratic share among those who attend religious services once a week was boosted by a large Latino vote—and by the fact that California's Latinos are, on the whole, more Democratic than their counterparts elsewhere.

Table 4-7 summarizes the interaction among race, religion, and region. It demonstrates that despite southern particularism, there was a definite religion gap among whites across the country.[18] It's worth noting that the religion gap among whites was slightly higher in the East, perhaps because regular worship is, as we have seen, less of a norm: voters in the East who do attend religious services frequently may thus be more distinctive (and more conservative) in their views than the rest of the region's voters. The gap is smallest in the Midwest, where the proportions of the most and the least observant are roughly equal.

18. I have consolidated some of the categories on religious attendance to ensure that there were enough data to support the analysis.

Table 4-7. *Vote for Bush by Region and Religious Attendance, 2004 Presidential Election*
Percent

Race	Frequency of church attendance	East	Midwest	South	West
White	Weekly	63	66	80	69
	Occasionally	47	52	65	49
	Never	27	39	49	37
Black	Weekly	17	13	13	n.a.
	Occasionally	9	6	5	n.a.
	Never	n.a.	n.a.	n.a.	n.a.
Latino	Weekly	30	n.a.	63	36
	Occasionally	16	15	52	27
	Never	n.a.	n.a.	n.a.	n.a.

Source: 2004 National Election Pool exit poll.
n.a. = not available (too few data to permit analysis)

Table 4-7 is a commentary on how difficult it is to generalize about Latinos without taking into account sharp regional and ethnic differences. While Bush carried a substantial majority of frequent church attendees among Hispanics in the South, Kerry carried a substantial majority of Latino churchgoers in the East and the West.[19] This difference reflected the presence in the southern sample of a large number of Cuban Americans, a Republican-leaning group, and the fact that Mexican Americans in California are more staunchly Democratic than Mexican Americans in Texas. These findings suggest the need for caution in generalizing about the religious factor among Latinos—and the need for more research designed to disentangle regional, ethnic, and religious factors in Latino voting patterns.

In sum: the religion gap exists—but it varies by region and by state. Republican strength in the South is enhanced by the region's religious commitment. Democratic strength in the West, particularly on the Pacific Coast, is enhanced by the region's relatively low levels of formal religious participation. Religious commitment and region interact. The polarization in American politics is partly a religious phenomenon, partly a regional phenomenon. And race remains a more decisive factor in American politics than religion.

19. Kerry also appeared to have had a significant majority among Latino church attendees in the Midwest, but the sample size was too small to say this with confidence.

The Significance of Class: The Push and the Pull

But what of social and economic class, which lay at the heart of the New Deal political alignment that dominated American politics from 1932 to 1968? The debate over the role of religion is intimately linked to the debate over the extent to which class has been in decline as an organizing force in American elections. In recent years, this decline has been attributed to the rise of issues related to culture, religion, and "moral values" since the 1980s. But it is important to see that the decline of class politics began much earlier, connected both to the politics of race and to a reaction against the counterculture in the late 1960s and early 1970s. It is impossible to understand the current polarization in American politics unless it is seen *not* as a sudden development—the product of a new religiosity or a simple reaction to the presidencies of Bill Clinton and George W. Bush—but as a phenomenon that has been a long time in the making.

In a thoughtful 1998 article, political writer David Brooks summarized one important version of the argument that, as he put it, "all around us, American life offers evidence of the declining significance of class." Brooks insisted that "the working class (whatever that means these days) is no longer the most influential group in society." That distinction, he said, belongs to the "educated upper-middle class." He continued:

> There are now 7 million households in America with incomes over $100,000 a year, and their influence on the marketplace, the culture, the media, and the categories of thought is enormous. This mass upper class—even its many liberals—does not think in terms of class conflict. Its members think in bohemian-versus-bourgeois terms (if they think in terms of conflict at all).
>
> Maybe it was possible to build class consciousness at a time when reporters, broadcasters, movie producers, and teachers came from working-class backgrounds. But now these people are college graduates, the children of college graduates even, and they are reading Scott Turow, not John Steinbeck. Maybe you could build a class movement when the Democratic Party was staffed by proletarian ethnics organized into urban machines. But now the Democratic Party is staffed by lawyers and media consultants.
>
> The upper-middle class has taken over progressive opinion just as it has taken over everything else, and its causes are affirmative action, a tobacco ban, campaign-finance reform, gay rights, global warming, the balanced budget, and multicultural recognition, not class war or trade restrictions. That's why liberal groups like Greenpeace collapse when they try to move beyond their

upper-middle-class base and gin up working-class support. That's why the politically astute Bill Clinton has decided that race and affirmative action are more salient issues than the class struggle.[20]

This is one version of the argument, particularly popular among conservatives: that the decline of class politics was driven by the rise of the educated upper middle class and its tastes, preferences, and values. A corollary to this argument is that the move of working-class and lower-middle-class voters away from the Democratic Party was the result of an effort by this educated class to impose its more permissive and less religious worldview on a more traditional and more religious "middle America." The idea here is that such voters were *pushed* out of the Democratic Party.

An alternative view, popular on the left, is that the corporate allies of the wealthy understood that they could never win the support of a majority of the electorate for an economic program that tilted government policies toward their own interests and away from those of the majority. These groups therefore formed alliances with social and religious conservatives in an effort to encourage working-class and middle-class voters to cast ballots on the basis of "values" issues and against their own economic interests. This is a simplified version of the argument made in Tom Frank's important book *What's the Matter with Kansas?*[21] This view suggests that white voters at the lower end of the income structure were *pulled* (or, in the eyes of some, manipulated) into a new conservative political coalition.

Frank was building on years of scholarship and reporting on the decline of class politics in the United States, including such works as Thomas Byrne Edsall and Mary D. Edsall's *Chain Reaction: The Impact of Race, Rights, and Taxes on American Politics,* and Jonathan Reider's *Canarsie: The Jews and Italians of Brooklyn against Liberalism.*[22] The Edsalls and Reider are especially shrewd on the importance of racial politics in cutting the Democratic Party's traditional advantage in the white working class. They, like Frank, showed how cultural issues, often linked to religion, broke the New Deal coalition by creating a new group of working-class conservatives, later known as "Reagan Democrats," who often found themselves reacting against upper-middle-class social liberalism. This,

---

20. David Brooks, "The Democratic Party Gets a Brain—and Loses Its Mind," *Weekly Standard,* January 26, 1998.

21. Frank (2004).

22. Edsall and Edsall (1991); Reider (1985).

therefore, is not a new phenomenon. It was, after all, Richard Nixon's 1972 campaign that cast George McGovern's liberalism as being devoted to the causes of "acid [as in LSD], amnesty [for draft resisters], and abortion."

Kevin Phillips's seminal 1969 work, *The Emerging Republican Majority,* made a powerful and—judging by subsequent electoral results—successful case for a new conservative and Republican politics of class among whites.[23] It was based, Phillips wrote, on "public anger over busing, welfare spending, environmental extremism, soft criminology, media bias and power, warped education, twisted textbooks, racial quotas, various guidelines and an ever expanding bureaucracy."[24] Note here the mix of racial issues ("busing, welfare spending") and values issues ("warped education, twisted textbooks"). At the heart of the Phillips view was a critique of limousine liberalism, a concept introduced into American politics by conservative Democrat Mario Procaccino when he ran for mayor of New York City in 1966, and a defense of "middle America," a clarion call to Nixon-era conservatives. It was the precursor politics to the religious right, a reaction to the "modernist liberation" movements among the well off, well educated, and college young. Phillips's class analysis was so hard-edged that the conservative *National Review*—to Phillips's pleasure—accused him of "country and western Marxism."[25] The charge was more prophetic than the magazine may have realized, given the use to which conservative politicians (even wealthy Yale-educated presidents) would later put country music and NASCAR races in casting theirs as a movement of "real people" as opposed to upper-class snobs.

The argument received a certain intellectual heft when Irving Kristol and other neoconservatives introduced the idea of the "new class," borrowed from Milovan Djilas, a dissident Yugoslav Marxist. It was an elastic term that could refer to reform-minded intellectuals and bureaucrats generally as well as to specific groups ranging from Marxist professors and do-gooder social workers to activist lawyers and psychologists who defended more permissive sexual norms. Thus was born the idea of the "elitist liberal" that was to haunt Democratic candidates from George McGovern to John Kerry.

Again, it is important to put today's arguments in historical perspective: the declining significance of class among whites was first noticed more than three decades ago. This idea is substantiated in table 4-8, which is drawn from the 1975 work by Everett Carll Ladd Jr. and Charles D. Hadley, *Transformations of*

---

23. Phillips (1969).
24. Quoted in Judis (1988, p. 378).
25. Williamson (1978).

Table 4-8. *Democratic Percentage of Vote among Whites, 1948 and 1972 Presidential Elections*
Percent

Voter class	1948	1972	Percentage point change
High socioeconomic status	30	32	+2
Middle socioeconomic status	43	26	−17
Low socioeconomic status	57	32	−25

Source: Ladd and Hadley (1975).

the American Party System. Notice the stark differences between Harry S. Truman's support among lower-status whites in 1948 and George McGovern's in 1972. Also note that while McGovern suffered an overwhelming defeat, he actually made marginal gains among upper-status white voters. The times they were a-changin', though not in the direction many who sang the song hoped.

All this was a prelude to the rise of the religious right in the late 1970s and early 1980s. Religious conservatives, ignited by court decisions on school prayer and abortion and reacting against what they saw as the depredations of trashy magazines, movies, and television programs, decried the growing "secularization" of America and engaged in what sociologist Nathan Glazer has called a "defensive offensive." It was meant to restore the consensus on values that existed—or at least seemed to exist—before the 1960s.[26] The Christian conservatives cast themselves as a beleaguered minority suffering under the oppression of both Washington and Hollywood. This movement did not change the cultural direction in politics set in the late 1960s and early 1970s, but rather reinforced it. And again, the appeal of this movement was not to traditionally well-off Republicans, but to middle-class and working-class whites.

In light of this history, the remarkable fact is that, in the 2004 election, class (measured by income) had not disappeared as a key determinant of voting decisions. Nearly four decades of conservative mobilization around the issues of race, culture, and religion have certainly dented Democrats' appeal to middle-income and lower-income whites. But the facts suggest that claims about the death of class have been exaggerated.

At the most extreme ends of the income structure, for instance, Bush received 63 percent from voters in households with annual incomes of $200,000 or more,

26. Glazer (1987, pp. 245–58).

but only 36 percent from those with households incomes of less than $15,000. Bush also won 57 percent from voters in the $100,000 to $200,000 annual income range, but only 42 percent among those in the $15,000 to $30,000 range. Consolidating these income groups, Bush won 56 percent of the vote among those who earned more than $50,000, but only 44 percent among voters with incomes of less than $50,000 a year. This 12 point gap is certainly not as robust as the class divide that was so important in the Democratic victories of the 1930s and 1940s. But the divide does persist.

The income split is reinforced by the rift between Americans who belonged to unions and those who did not. Bush received 38 percent of the votes of union members, but 54 percent among nonmembers. It is, of course, a problem for Democrats that union membership has been in a long-term decline—a phenomenon that, along with the steady drop in manufacturing employment, has reinforced the decline in class politics. But despite being more muted than in the past, the persistence of class politics remains the story.

It is commonplace to suggest that the Democratic Party is now, in some way, the "elite" party because of its strength among voters with high levels of education. And it is indeed true that Kerry defeated Bush, 55 to 44 percent, among voters—16 percent of the total—with postgraduate educations. It was Kerry's strongest showing in any educational grouping. If ever a datum supported the existence of a "new class" of liberals, this would seem to be it. But it is worth noting that Kerry ran strongest among voters with postgraduate education and household incomes of less than $100,000—a group he carried with 59 percent to Bush's 40 percent. Voters with postgraduate educations and household incomes of more than $100,000 voted narrowly for Bush, 51 percent to 48 percent (interestingly, an almost perfect mirror of the overall result). Of the highest-income earners, Bush did better among those who lacked postgraduate educations than he did among those who had done at least some graduate work. There is clearly a "postgrad effect" that helps the Democrats.

But Kerry's relative strength among the highly educated earning less than $100,000 is important because it suggests that many of the Democrats in that category may be part of a "new class" by certain definitions, but are not necessarily part of an "elite" group. The exit polls found that fully a quarter of Kerry's supporters with postgraduate educations earned less than $50,000 a year and that half earned less than $75,000. These are the incomes of teachers, social workers, nurses, and skilled technicians, not of Hollywood stars, bestselling authors, or television producers, let alone corporate executives.

Table 4-9. *Vote by Income and Race, 2004 Presidential Election*
Percent

Household income	White voters		Black voters		Latino voters	
	Bush	Kerry	Bush	Kerry	Bush	Kerry
Less than $15,000	43	57	14	86	42	58
$15,000 to $29,999	51	48	8	91	37	61
$30,000 to $49,999	58	41	8	91	43	57
$50,000 to $74,999	63	37	13	86	46	51
$75,000 to $99,999	59	40	8	92	55	43
$100,000 to $149,999	62	38	25	75	57	37
$150,000 to $199,999	62	38	n.a.	n.a.	n.a.	n.a.
$200,000 or more	63	35	n.a.	n.a.	n.a.	n.a.
Under $50,000	53	46	9	90	59	40
$50,000 or more	62	37	14	86	49	47
Under $100,000	57	42	10	90	44	55
$100,000 or more	63	36	21	79	43	50

Source: 2004 National Election Pool exit poll.
n.a. = not available (too few data to permit analysis).

But, as we have seen, the "southern strategy," the appeals to "middle America," and—until recently—the mobilization of conservative Christians have always been aimed primarily at *white* voters, designed by shrewd conservative political strategists to cut traditional Democratic advantages among middle-class, lower-middle-class, and working-class whites. Table 4-9 shows that this strategy continues to bear fruit.

Among whites, Kerry carried only the group whose annual household income was less than $15,000. That Bush carried a majority of all white voters in households earning less than $50,000 a year suggests an ongoing Democratic problem. Yet the extent to which American politics has realigned around social issues is underscored by this fact: despite their weak showings among low-income whites, Democrats have managed to stay at near parity with the Republicans. This suggests not only the importance of African American and Hispanic voters to the Democratic coalition, but also offsetting gains for Democrats among social and religious moderates. The closely divided electorate suggests that for all the attention given by the media and academics to religious conservatives, they are only one force in a complicated political landscape.

Table 4-10. *Vote among White Voters by Income and Religious Attendance, 2004 Presidential Election*
Percent

| Household income | Voted for | Frequency of church attendance | | |
		Weekly or more	Occasionally	Never
Less than $15,000	Bush	55	33	25
	Kerry	44	65	74
$15,000 to $29,999	Bush	62	49	35
	Kerry	36	50	63
$30,000 to $49,999	Bush	69	55	39
	Kerry	29	43	59
$50,000 to $74,999	Bush	74	57	38
	Kerry	24	42	60
$75,000 to $99,999	Bush	72	53	35
	Kerry	27	45	63
$100,000 to $149,999	Bush	74	54	47
	Kerry	23	45	50
$150,000 or more	Bush	76	59	42
	Kerry	23	39	56

Source: 2004 National Election Pool exit poll.

But for all the qualifications I have tried to introduce here about the role of religious commitment in influencing voting patterns in 2004, there is simply no doubt about its importance—and no doubt that the Republican leanings of religiously committed voters are cutting what had once been a substantial Democratic advantage among white voters with low to moderate incomes. Table 4-10 makes this abundantly clear.

Several aspects of these findings are worth underscoring. Even among white voters with household incomes of less than $30,000 a year, those who said they attended religious services at least once a week voted for Bush over Kerry by a substantial margin. Even among white voters who earned more than $150,000 a year, those who said they never attended religious services voted for Kerry over Bush by a substantial margin. In other words, class did not disappear as a factor in how people voted in 2004. Lower-income white churchgoers were more pro-Kerry than white churchgoers with higher incomes, for example. And among non-churchgoers Bush did better on the whole among those with higher incomes.

In sum: religious commitment has joined race, class, and region as a key driver of voting decisions, and its influence seems to have increased over the past three elections. But religious commitment is not as powerful an influence on voting decisions as race, and has so far had very little impact on the voting patterns of African Americans. Religion has not obliterated class politics, and its effect varies by region and state. Indeed, as Morris P. Fiorina and others have shown, there is evidence that class (as measured by income) has become a more important factor in explaining voting patterns over the past several elections.[27] Be that as it may, the power of church attendance in driving voting decisions is undeniable.

The Varieties of Religious Politics

It was a common enough event in American political life: a Baptist minister in a southern state complaining about a media "smear." Only the "smear" in question was not typical—or, perhaps more accurately, stereotypical. "There is widespread disenchantment with the media within the Christian community," declared the Reverend Robert E. Seymour, pastor emeritus of Brinkley Memorial Baptist Church in Chapel Hill, North Carolina, "for constantly implying that if you are a Christian, you are conservative." Writing in the *Chapel Hill Herald* in 2005, Rev. Seymour declared:

> Moderate mainstream Christians and believers on the left have become vic-tims of a stereotype for which the press must bear large responsibility. Many in the public now accept as truth that if you go to church you are Republican and that Democrats are secular. The press has failed to give a fair and accu-rate picture of political diversity in the congregations. Nearly all mainline Protestant groups are aware of the smear. . . . I hesitate to identify myself as a Baptist clergyman for fear I will be prejudged as right wing, homophobic or anti-intellectual. . . . Baptists are widely regarded as backward and bigoted.[28]

Understanding polarization in American political life requires understanding that the electorate is *not* polarized simply between the religious and the nonreligious. The Reverend Seymour is quite right that many who are religious are not conser-vative. Religious people are not all religious in the same way.

This is not just about the obvious: that Catholics are different from Baptists, who are different from Muslims, who are different from Mormons, who are dif-ferent from Jews, who are different from Hindus, who are different from

27. Fiorina, Abrams, and Pope (2006, pp. 134–37); Gelman and others (2005).
28. Robert Seymour, "Not All Believers Are Conservative," *Chapel Hill Herald,* September 9, 2005.

Methodists. It is also about the differences within traditions. Catholics are divided between those who emphasize the "life issues," such as abortion and stem-cell research, as central to their voting decisions, and those who vote on the basis of social justice concerns or the death penalty. (There are also Catholics who worry about *all* of these, which the Church formally teaches *should* all be weighed.) Mainline Protestants include those who are theologically and politically very liberal and those who are theologically and politically conservative. One can see this in the battles within the mainline congregations over gay marriage—or, as a friend once pointed out, in the fact that the cars in the parking lots of many Episcopal, Methodist, and Presbyterian churches often sported roughly equal numbers of Bush and Kerry stickers. Jews as a group voted overwhelmingly for Kerry. But Orthodox Jews were significantly more sympathetic to Bush than Reform, Conservative, or Reconstructionist Jews. Muslim voters—who are difficult to analyze because they do not yet bulk large enough in national surveys—appeared to swing sharply from Bush in 2000 to Kerry in 2004.

And believers believe in different ways. Some Christians believe in the literal truth of the Scriptures; others do not. Some speak of Jesus Christ as "my personal Lord and Savior," while others are uncomfortable with this language. Some believers place a great emphasis on public liturgy, others on personal piety (and some, of course, value both). Some believers see faith as therapeutic, others as a challenge, still others as a mystery.

These differences aggravate political polarization in certain ways and moderate it in others. The struggle over gay issues within the mainline Protestant denominations bring the political battles of the broader culture into the heart of the Church. Roman Catholics found themselves sharply divided by politics in 2004. Leaflets from a group called "Catholic Answers" arguing that questions such as abortion and gay marriage were "nonnegotiable" for Catholics appeared in the literature racks of many churches. These messages comforted (and may have motivated) more conservative Catholics and enraged liberal Catholics who voted on other issues. Yet, as Allen Hertzke of the University of Oklahoma has argued, believers often found themselves rallying across political and theological lines on behalf of human and religious rights around the world, in support of help for victims of AIDS, in defense of those facing slaughter in Darfur, and in support of debt relief for poor nations.[29]

The religious landscape is also changing. In the past, Catholics were a predominantly Democratic group and mainline Protestants were predominantly

---

29. See Hertzke (2005, pp. 16–22).

Republican. Now both are swing groups. Catholics are less reliably Democratic than they used to be, mainline Protestants less reliably Republican. Catholics and mainliners are, roughly speaking, "40-40-20" groups: each party can count on roughly 40 percent of the ballots cast by each, with the remaining 20 percent in their ranks up for grabs from election to election.

But even as old divisions have disappeared, new ones have taken their place. In the past, evangelical Protestants battled Catholics ("Papists") over such issues as government aid to parochial schools. When Protestantism was publicly dominant, public schools were infused with the Protestant faith, leading Catholics to start their own schools. Now, traditionalist Protestants and Catholics alike see public schools as essentially secular, and both groups favor aid to religious schools (as do many Orthodox Jews).

Splits between denominations have now been replaced by splits within denominations—liberal Catholics, Protestants, and Jews ally against conservative Catholics, Protestants, and Jews. "One of the most remarkable changes of the twentieth century is the virtual evaporation of hostility between Protestants and Catholics," notes Grant Wacker, a professor of religious history at Duke University Divinity School; "I don't think it's because Baptists have come to have a great respect for Tridentine theology. It's because they see Catholics as allies against graver problems. There's a large reconfiguration going on now."[30] One kind of polarization (political) has replaced another (theological). It is another example of how the polarization in the political world is invading other sectors of American life.

No one has been more thoughtful in mapping America's diverse political and religious terrain than John C. Green of the University of Akron. In a series of studies, Green has shown how oversimplifications diminish our political knowledge while also stereotyping people of faith. His survey of the role of religion in the 2004 election is especially revealing.

To capture the differences among the religiously affiliated in their theology, their behavior, and their attitudes toward divisive cultural questions, Green created a scale that divides members of different religious communities into "traditionalists," "centrists," and "modernists." Green explains that traditionalists exhibit "strongly orthodox belief" and "a high level of religious engagement," centrists exhibit "moderate belief and engagement," and modernists exhibit "heterodox belief and lower levels of engagement."[31] These

30. Quoted in Dionne (2000, p. 118).
31. Green (2004, p. 1).

social science categories are broadly consistent with the philosophical definitions offered by James Davison Hunter, a sociologist at the University of Virginia who introduced the culture-war concept to a wide audience. Hunter defines the orthodox or traditionalist view as "the commitment on the part of adherents to an external, definable, and transcendent authority." Those Green calls "modernist," Hunter called "progressivist." In progressivism, Hunter argues, "moral authority tends to be defined by the spirit of the modern age, a spirit of rationalism and subjectivism."[32]

Green's categories turn out to have a great deal of explanatory power. Table 4-11 summarizes what might be seen as his 2004 "census" of American religion. Green identifies four large, primarily white groups in the electorate: evangelical Protestants, mainline Protestants, Catholics, and the "unaffiliated." His most surprising finding, in light of the conventional wisdom, is that evangelical Protestants—who constitute just over a quarter of all Americans—are by no means a monolithic group. Just under half of the evangelicals are traditionalists, and this subgroup accounts for just 12.6 percent of the population. The traditionalists are, indeed, a solid part of the Republican coalition: 70 percent of them identify with the Republican Party, only 20 percent with the Democrats. Centrist evangelicals are more Republican than the country as a whole, but are much more closely split: 47 percent Republican, 31 percent Democratic. A small group of modernist evangelicals leans Democratic, 44 to 30 percent.

According to Green, Catholics account for 17.5 percent of the population, and his figures underscore why they have become a swing vote. Overall, 44 percent of Catholics are Democrats, 41 percent are Republicans. But there are deep splits among Catholics. Traditionalist Catholics pick the Republicans over the Democrats, 57 to 30 percent, while modernist Catholics favor the Democrats, 51 to 38 percent. But the largest group of Catholics, the centrists, leans Democratic, 47 to 34 percent. Mainline Protestants (16 percent of the population) are also a swing group. Traditionalist mainliners pick the Republicans over the Democrats, 59 to 31 percent. But modernists are the reverse: 54 percent Democratic, 26 percent Republican. Centrist mainliners split for the Republicans, 46 percent to 33 percent. It is worth noting that centrist Catholics and centrist mainliners reflect the tug of the older traditions within their groups: Catholics have historically leaned Democratic, and so do today's centrist Catholics. Mainliners have historically leaned Republican, and so do today's centrist mainliners.

32. Hunter (1991, p. 44).

Table 4-11. *Religious Affiliation and Self-Identified Partisanship, Spring 2004*
Percent

Religious affiliation	Percent of U.S. population	Partisanship[a]		
		Republican	Independent	Democratic
White evangelical Protestant	26.3	56	17	27
Traditionalist evangelical	12.6	70	10	20
Centrist evangelical	10.8	47	22	31
Modernist evangelical	2.9	30	26	44
White mainline Protestant	16.0	44	18	38
Traditionalist mainline	4.3	59	10	31
Centrist mainline	7.0	46	21	33
Modernist mainline	4.7	26	20	54
Latino Protestant	2.8	37	20	43
Black Protestant	9.6	11	18	71
Catholic	17.5	41	15	44
Traditionalist Catholic	4.4	57	13	30
Centrist Catholic	8.1	34	19	47
Modernist Catholic	5.0	38	11	51
Latino Catholic	4.5	15	24	61
Other Christian	2.7	42	36	22
Other faiths	2.7	12	33	55
Jewish	1.9	21	11	68
Unaffiliated	16.0	27	30	43
Unaffiliated believers	5.3	28	37	35
Secular	7.5	29	27	44
Atheist or agnostic	3.2	19	27	54
Total		38	20	42

Source: Green (2004, table 1). Note, in his study, Green explains that Latino Protestants and Catholics and Black Protestants were placed in separate categories because of their religious and political distinctiveness.

a. Independents who "lean" toward a party are included with Republicans or Democrats. Minor-party affiliation (for example, Green Party) is included with independents.

The "unaffiliated" category (16 percent of the population) is a fascinating group. It mixes believers who do not affiliate with a specific faith but have traditional religious beliefs, secular voters who have no religious affiliations or traditional beliefs, and self-identified agnostics and atheists. Not surprisingly, political independents constitute the largest group among unaffiliated believers, with the rest leaning slightly Democratic. Seculars also include a large share of independents, but lean more strongly to the Democrats. Self-identified atheists and agnostics are more Democratic still—54 percent identify with the party—and, interestingly, political independents outnumber Republicans in this group, 27 to 19 percent.

Table 4-12. *Vote and Turnout by Religious Group, 2004 Presidential Election*
Percent

Religious affiliation	Bush	Kerry	Turnout
White evangelical Protestant	78	22	63
Traditionalist evangelical	88	12	69
Centrist evangelical	64	36	52
Modernist evangelical	48	52	65
White mainline Protestant	50	50	69
Traditionalist mainline	68	32	78
Centrist mainline	58	42	68
Modernist mainline	22	78	71
Latino Protestant	63	37	49
Black Protestant	17	83	50
White Catholic	53	47	67
Traditionalist Catholic	72	28	77
Centrist Catholic	55	45	58
Modernist Catholic	31	69	70
Latino Catholic	31	69	43
Other Christian	80	20	60
Other faiths	23	77	62
Jewish	27	73	87
Unaffiliated	28	72	52
Unaffiliated believers	37	63	39
Secular	30	70	55
Atheist or agnostic	18	82	61
Total	51	49	60.8

Source: Green and others (2004, table 1).

Nearly as large as these four groups are Black Protestants, 9.6 percent of the population. They are overwhelmingly (71 percent) Democratic. Latinos are split between Catholics (4.5 percent of the population) and Protestants (2.8 percent). Latino Catholics are strongly Democratic; Latino Protestants are closely split between the parties. Jews are overwhelmingly Democratic (68 percent). Green's category "other Christians" includes Mormons, Eastern Orthodox, and smaller churches. This group leans Republican. Those who profess "other faiths," a category that includes Muslims, Hindus, New Age practitioners, and other groups, lean Democratic. The impact of these groups on the election of 2004 is summarized in table 4-12.

To summarize: Bush won his strongest majorities among traditionalist groups: traditionalist evangelical and mainline Protestants, "other Christians," and traditionalist Catholics. He also did very well among centrist evangelical and mainline Protestants and Latino Protestants, while carrying 55 percent of the centrist Catholic vote. Kerry's strongest groups were black Protestants, atheists and agnostics, modernist mainline Protestants, members of "other faiths," and Jews. He also did very well among seculars, modernist and Latino Catholics, and unaffiliated believers. Modernist evangelicals (a small group) split 52 to 48 percent for Kerry.[33]

Green's analysis of the 2004 presidential election reveals several interesting patterns. Of the Bush voters, 65 percent were Protestant, 59 percent were white Protestant, and 43 percent were traditionalists, including evangelicals, mainliners, and Catholics. Traditionalist evangelicals were by far the largest group in the Bush coalition, constituting 27 percent of his supporters, and evangelical Protestants taken together accounted for 40 percent of his voters. These figures help explain the many gestures (both substantive and symbolic) that the president has made toward evangelicals, and conservative evangelicals in particular.

Of the Kerry voters, 49 percent were Protestants and only 35 percent were white Protestants. The contrast between Bush's dependence on white Protestant votes and the relatively small role this group played in the Kerry coalition is striking—and another sign of polarization in the electorate. It is also worth noting that whereas unaffiliated believers, seculars, atheists, and agnostics constituted 20 percent of the Kerry vote, they constituted only 7 percent of the Bush vote. And it is quite clear from Green's survey (see table 4-12) that the electorate is polarized, in part because those at the ends of the religious spectrum are more likely to participate than those in the middle. Among both evangelicals and Catholics, traditionalists and modernists were far more likely to vote than centrists. Centrist mainline Protestants participated almost as much as modernists, but at a somewhat lower rate than traditionalists. Jews had the highest turnout of any group, unaffiliated believers the lowest.

Judging from the contrast between party affiliation and voting in 2004, there is considerable potential for movement among centrist Christians (particularly Catholics and mainline Protestants, but also evangelicals). The current balance in American politics could be shifted substantially just by modestly higher rates of participation among blacks, Latinos (particularly Latino Catholics), and centrist white evangelicals. One could also imagine a decline in polarization if Democrats found a way to reduce the exceptionally large Republican advantage among traditionalist evangelicals, Catholics, and mainliners—or, alternatively,

33. Green and others (2004).

if Republicans could cut their deep deficits among the religiously unaffiliated. But this would require a substantial change in the way in which cultural and religious issues are debated in American politics. Is that possible? As Green's analysis suggests, it is a mistake to see the American religious landscape as black or white, religious or secular. It is similarly mistaken to view America's cultural argument as involving only permissive cultural radicals on the one side and cultural traditionalists or reactionaries on the other.

Most Americans are social moderates of one sort or another. The largest number probably falls into a group that William Galston has labeled "tolerant traditionalists." Many Americans long for freedom but understand freedom's limits. Many long for orthodoxy yet want it to be flexible on something that matters to their own sense of freedom. Thus does a rabbi from Montana teach David Brooks the wonderfully useful term "flexidoxy."[34] The bourgeois bohemians Brooks has introduced us to in his writing are resolutely flexidox.

A Return to Moderation?

Opponents of abortion often cannot find it in themselves to condemn a woman they know who has had an abortion for a reason they understand. Some supporters of abortion rights find the issue morally troubling nonetheless, and might never choose to have an abortion themselves. Liberals desperately do not want to be bluenosed or judgmental, yet they are uneasy with a consumerist, individualistic culture that often violates their sense of community, decency, and mutual obligation. Conservatives who dread economic regulation and defend capitalism at every turn often find the cultural fruits of capitalism bitter and distasteful. Liberals and conservatives may battle over gay marriage or abortion and yet agree wholeheartedly on what television programs their children should not watch, what websites they should not visit, and what video games they should not play. And liberals and conservatives might well disagree over exactly what the First Amendment means, what role religion should play in public policy debates, and how presidents should talk about God and still admire the charitable work of our religious institutions and the compassionate instincts of many of their fellow citizens.

A reaction to the culture wars of the 1960s helped create our current religious divide. A reaction to today's sharp polarization may well lead to a rendezvous with moderation and a healing of the religious breach.

34. Brooks (2000, p. 224–28).

Myths and Realities of Religion in Politics

COMMENT
Alan Wolfe

I may be the wrong person to comment on E. J. Dionne's essay on the role of religion in American political life, if only because I agree with so much of it. The main point behind his perceptive analysis can be summarized in just a few words: religion is important, but it is not everything. He is right. When evangelicals began to flex their political muscle in the 1970s, almost no political scientists—and very few journalists—paid them much attention. That we could ignore something so important was, in my opinion, one of the biggest mistakes our fields could have made. The question now is whether we will compound this mistake with another. We all know the vital role played by religion in American democracy, but now I worry that we will see faith everywhere—even where it does not belong. Fortunately, Dionne avoids this—and by doing so, he reminds us that other things matter, too.

For all my agreement with Dionne, there is something that a sympathetically critical commentator can offer. Like so much other work in this area, Dionne's approach relies substantially upon quantitative data. It is vitally important that we examine voting behavior and survey data and other empirical material in order to understand the role religion plays in American politics. But there are other kinds of valuable social scientific data—the kind that comes from field-work, participant observation, and other studies that rely on qualitative forms of data. Since much of my work relies on this kind of data, I will try to supplement Dionne's observations on religion and polarization by focusing more on how people actually practice their religion in the concrete conditions of their lives.[1]

So let me start with a thought experiment. Suppose we were to go and spend a year in Alpharetta, Georgia; Sugar Land, Texas; or some other place that appears to represent the heartland of the new evangelical voters in the United States. What would we find there?

We would certainly find that religion is enormously important. We would find megachurches sprouting up where the interstate highways connect with

---

1. See also Wolfe (1998, 2001, 2003).

one another. Although these churches can hold enormous numbers of worshipers (sometimes in the range of 15,000), they would be full—and not just on Sundays. In fact, most of the activity takes place during the week, when small groups meet to discuss the Bible or their spiritual needs. Our first impression would be that while Americans may be "bowling alone," they are certainly not praying alone.

As we spent more time in these exurbs, we would begin to learn more about our new neighbors. We would find out, for example, that many of them were born in the North and moved to the South in search of economic opportunity. (None of them are actually from Alpharetta or Sugar Land because when they were growing up those places were farms.) We would also notice that they have been upwardly mobile in the course of their lives. Once residents of small towns or economically depressed cities, many of them are now professionals working in the corporate world for solid middle-class incomes. Whether or not they went to college, they want their kids to go—and they have hopes that they will get into the top colleges in the region or even the nation. For that purpose, high schools run by churches and denominations may not be the best bet, but even among those who choose religious schools for their kids, there is an emphasis on learning the skills necessary for success. Some of the smartest students among the megachurch attendees will aim for schools such as Wheaton College, an evangelical Protestant school in Illinois, where the average SAT score for entering freshmen is not too different from those at the top secular institutions.

In other words, we would discover in the heartland of conservative America— in the places that have voted into Congress such leaders of the Republican Party as Newt Gingrich and Tom DeLay—a world of increasingly prosperous and increasingly mobile Americans for whom religion is a very important aspect of their lives. This is decidedly not Dayton, Tennessee, which hosted the Scopes trial in the 1920s, or anything like the growing urban centers that gave birth to the movements led by Billy Sunday in Chicago or the Pentecostals in Los Angeles. Whatever the religion to be found in exurban America is, it is not the old-time religion that, according to the hymn sung in "Inherit the Wind," was "good for the Hebrew children and is good enough for me." In this sense, our ethnographic study of exurban America would find that the United States remains one of the most religious countries in the world.

However, our findings would also challenge the way social scientists talk about religion and its role in American politics. That way of talking has been strongly influenced by University of Akron political scientist John C. Green, upon whose work Dionne relies.[2] Green seeks to differentiate religions, and tendencies within religions, on the basis of how conservative they are. He is right to do this; clearly some conservative Protestants, for example, lean more to the fundamentalist camp and others in a more evangelical direction, and the differences between them are important. (I would say that fundamentalists reject the culture as corrupt, whereas evangelicals engage the culture in order to save it.)

The problem is what we call these various degrees of conservatism in religion. Using relatively familiar language, Green calls more conservative believers "traditionalists" and the less conservative ones "modernists." And from these familiar terms there emerges a problem. Terms such as "traditional" and "modern" do not, I believe, get at the heart of what is happening among religious believers in this country, especially in places such as Alpharetta and Sugar Land.

In my work I have tried to show how Americans are a combination of both traditionalist instincts and modernist lifestyles. This is as true of liberals in Massachusetts who, no matter how progressive they are in politics, value—and refuse ever to destroy—historic homes that date from the eighteenth century. It is just as true of religious believers in Texas who insist on the literal truth of the Bible and yet work for companies engaged in advanced software design. There are no pure traditionalists, and there are no pure modernists, in the United States.

This observation certainly applies to the evangelicals who typically vote Republican. If I were looking for a phrase in the English language to describe the exact opposite of a traditionalist person, I would choose the one that evangelical Protestants use to describe themselves: born again. A traditionalist, after all, is someone who is born into a situation, inherits certain values from his or her parents, and feels a strong obligation to pass those values on unchanged to the next generation. But this is not what evangelicals believe or do. Born-again Christians discover, through an authentic experience in which they develop a personal relationship with their savior, Jesus Christ, that everything their parents taught them was wrong, that the religion they inherited did not give them the sense of personal efficacy they get from knowing that Jesus is a living presence in their lives. Their faith is about authenticity, not tradition. They believe that living right is more important than living the way others did in the past.

Consider the case of Pentecostals. This fast-growing, largely evangelical religion is usually thought of as conservative. And in politics and theology it is. But

2. Green (2004).

as Grant Wacker of the Duke University Divinity School has pointed out, Pentecostals are really "mavericks at heart."[3] For all their conservatism, they are rebels, people in constant search of ways to express their devotion, even if doing so means rejecting long-established liturgies, creeds, and ways of worshiping. Pentecostals bring to their faith a dynamism and entrepreneurialism that attracts people looking for belonging and spiritual meaning. Their culture is as radical as its biblical literalism is conservative.

Once we appreciate the anything-but-traditional cultural styles of conservative Protestantism, we can begin to make sense of the sociology of conservative Protestant America. States that vote Republican are often states with high divorce rates and with large numbers of children born of out of wedlock. At the same time, in the bastions of liberal America (states such as Connecticut and Massachusetts, for example), divorce rates are low, families are stable, and out-of-wedlock births are rare. When I interview an evangelical in Oklahoma, I often find stepchildren and ex-spouses. Among my friends in Brookline and Cambridge, people seem to have been married forever.

To some degree, this contrast is explained by economics: divorce is higher where people are poorer. But the ongoing search for the right partner is not unlike the constant quest for the right faith. In both cases there is a culture of starting over, as innovative as it is frustrating. If you want to go to a place in the United States where people live postmodern lives, constantly transforming their lifestyles to keep up with the latest cultural trends, go to the red states, not the blue states.

If we ought to be cautious when using the distinction between traditionalists and modernists, we ought to be especially careful before accepting an analysis built upon that distinction. There is one such analysis in particular that, however rich it may appear at first, ought to be treated with at least some skepticism. Following the work of sociologist James Davison Hunter, a fascinating hypothesis has emerged that in many ways serves as the definition of the culture war in which a presumably polarized America is deeply engaged.[4] This hypothesis posits that at one time religions were polarized against each other, but that now the polarization takes place within each religion.

Traditional Catholics, traditional Jews, and traditional Protestants, we are told, now have more in common with each other than they do with the liberals or modernists within their respective religions. Once, Protestants were

3. Wacker (2001, p. 28).
4. Hunter (1991).

anti-Catholic and antisemitic. Now, conservative Protestants form alliances with conservative Jews and support conservative Catholic nominees for the Supreme Court. At the same time, Episcopalians are divided into liberal and conservative camps because of their radically different views on the ordination of gay priests— a division so deep that it may split their church. But despite the abundance of anecdotal evidence supporting this hypothesis (and because Dionne's analysis depends so much on it), I again want to raise some concerns.

My first concern with this thesis is that it downplays the significance of the very phenomenon being used to explain what is happening in the United States: religion itself. It may be true that some people attach so much importance to their views on abortion, capital punishment, or gay marriage that they seek allies in other religious traditions. But if so, it is their political views— their take on public policy—that they are putting first, while their theology or religious practice comes second. At earlier periods in American history, people have argued over which Bible should be read in schools and how it should be interpreted. Those were debates that put theology first. The people who fight today's culture war, by contrast, put politics first. It is not their stance on what God wants that determines the party for which they vote. They know what they believe on political matters, and they pick a party just as they pick a denomination.

In 1991 Dionne published an important book called *Why Americans Hate Politics.*[5] But if Americans hate politics (as they seem to do) and love God (as they certainly do), why would they want to mix one with the other? At some point, people who line up this way and begin to put their political convictions ahead of their theological beliefs will have to scratch their heads and ask, "Is this what we are really about? We came to religion to express our spirituality and find out about the nature of the divinity, yet here we are being urged by our pastors to vote for tax cuts and the war in Iraq?" Such a shift in priorities cannot be all that satisfying to a genuine religious believer.

As an example of how politics has replaced religion for many conservatives in the United States, I would point to the Southern Baptist Convention's endorsement of *Roe* v. *Wade,* the Supreme Court's landmark abortion decision, in 1973. This is a fact that has been all but forgotten. To be sure, part of the reason for the Baptists' endorsement was their distrust of Catholics. (If Catholics were going to be against a woman's right to choose, Baptists were going to be for it.)

5. Dionne (1991).

But the more serious and important reason was that Baptists—as firm believers in religious liberty—traditionally distrusted government. If the state could tell a woman what to do with her body, it could tell a believer what to do with his mind. In 1973 the libertarian strain in the Baptist tradition, its fear of political theology, won out.

But all that has since changed. In the 1980s the Southern Baptist Convention repudiated its earlier support for a woman's right to choose. In doing so, it also repudiated Baptists' historic fear of government and politics. By becoming directly involved in political issues (sometimes to the point of seeming to be an adjunct arm of the Republican Party), Baptists moved closer to the position of Catholics. Baptists today have little in common with the tradition of strict separationism and religious liberty that inspired Roger Williams, John Leland, and other great Baptist figures in history.

Given this shift, there is reason to ask whether ordinary Baptists in the pews have any memory of that old tradition of separationism. I am frequently told that they do not—and that one of the reasons why is that many Baptists today were something else when they were children or young adults. A significant number of Americans are religious switchers. They are people who were raised in one tradition but when the spirit moves them, go to another. (That too is part of the experience of what it means to be born again.) It is how faith appeals to them now, and not what faith stood for in the past, that moves them. For this reason, specific denominations and their long-established creeds and statements are not all that important to them. But even if they do not necessarily appreciate the fact that their church has long distrusted overt political involvement, the very things that attracted them to evangelical religion in the first place—a sense of the sacred and a distrust of the profane—will lead them to tire of explicit partisan engagement.

A second reason, therefore, why it may make less sense to view Americans as divided between traditionalists and modernists between faiths rather than within them grows out of recent indications that Americans are growing tired of the culture war and of the politicization of religion that accompanies it. There is, in a sense, a new form of switching emerging in America. It is not from one politicized denomination to another, however, but instead reflects a growing feeling that people of faith may be in search of a spiritual sense that does not change as parties and politics change. After all, if the Southern Baptist Convention can have one position on abortion in the 1970s and another in the 1980s, its positions can hardly be the word of God. (He rarely changes His mind that quickly.) People who want truths that are set on solid ground and are less subject to political fashion may be better off associating with a church that does not take positions on stem-cell research or gay marriage.

There is evidence that this has already begun to happen. In the Baptist world today, for instance, the most important figure is not Jerry Falwell, the founder of the Moral Majority. It is Rick Warren, the California-based pastor whose book of spiritual advice, *The Purpose-Driven Life,* has sold about 25 million copies since 2002 and helped make Warren the most widely read and admired Baptist preacher in America. Warren is best known, however, not for his position on abortion, but for his trips to Africa to combat AIDS and fight poverty. From my meetings with him, I would guess that Warren is most likely a Republican who voted for George W. Bush. But he has also made it fairly clear that he is deliberately trying to occupy a new space in the American political landscape, one in which it is understood that the harsh fundamentalist rhetoric of a Jerry Falwell or a Pat Robertson is a dead end. And Warren is not alone. The decision of the National Association of Evangelicals in 2004 to endorse a program calling for respect for the natural environment reflects the same kind of movement away from partisan politics toward more permanent things.[6]

A similar move away from politics is observable among Catholics. There is no doubt that more Catholics are voting for Republican candidates than in the past. (Many fewer Catholics voted for John Kerry than voted for John F. Kennedy, for instance.)[7] But no evidence exists, at least not yet, that this was for religious reasons. It makes far more sense to assume instead that the extraordinary economic success and suburbanization of the American Catholic community in recent years lies behind the shift from Democratic to Republican voting. Once urban and working class, non-Latino American Catholics have joined the ranks of the upwardly mobile. Their changing voting behavior has more to do with these socioeconomic changes than it does with the view of the Vatican about issues involving human sexuality. Indeed, large numbers of Catholics resolutely disagree with the Vatican on birth control and abortion.[8]

And just because Catholics vote for both parties, it does not mean they are losing what is distinctively Catholic about them. The university where I teach, Boston College, is a Catholic university whose students come from extraordi-

---

6. National Association of Evangelicals, "The Sandy Cove Covenant and Invitation," June 2004 (www.nae.net/index.cfm?FUSEACTION=editor.page&pageID=121&IDCategory=9).

7. For an examination of the "Catholic vote" in the 2004 presidential election, see Gray, Perl, and Bendyna (2006).

8. See, for instance, McNamara (1992).

narily prosperous families. They are fully modern and suburban. I am actually surprised that there are not more Republican voters among them. The reason why has a great deal to do with Catholic teachings about social justice. When I ask my students what makes them Catholic, I do not hear about mass or the real presence. Social justice is what makes them Catholic—and because it does, even the Republicans among them rarely think of themselves as deeply conservative Republicans. They are not as liberal as Jews, to be sure, but in many ways their voting behavior and attitudes are closer to those of Jews than of evangelical Protestants.

But none of this means that my liberal Catholic students have more in common with liberal Jews and mainline Protestants than they do with conservative Catholics. Nor does it mean that my Republican Catholic students agree with Jerry Falwell. On the contrary, both have a distinctly Catholic sensibility—one that shapes how they think about economic *and* moral issues. Hence, the liberal students—enthusiastic Democrats—have serious reservations about abortion and questions about stem-cell research. And much the same is true of my Republican Catholic students, if in reverse: they like Bush and his programs, but they also worry that aggressive tax cutting will begin to tear at America's social fabric. They are, in short, the compassionate conservatives to whom Bush once appealed.

In conclusion, I would suggest that an emphasis on qualitative research methods yields a slightly different picture of the role religion plays in political polarization than quantitative methods do. There is a debate over what the quantitative data show, but if Stanford political scientist Morris P. Fiorina is correct, a good proportion of those data suggest that Americans are less polarized than is commonly thought.[9] Adding qualitative findings to their quantitative analysis suggests that the extent of the polarization may be even less.

If so, it strikes me that the approach taken by Dionne is the correct one. In a society like ours, one would be foolish ever to ignore religion; Americans speak about God more than people in other societies do, and people who go to church frequently are likely to vote differently than people who do not. At the same time, American culture plays just as important a role in shaping politics as American religion does. Indeed, it may shape religion itself. Whatever their religious differences, Americans are struggling to hold on to traditional teachings while living under modern circumstances. No wonder their commonalities sometimes outweigh their differences.

9. Fiorina, Abrams, and Pope (2006).

COMMENT
Andrew Kohut

E. J. Dionne adds some much needed perspective to the debate over the impact of religion on American politics and public opinion. He carefully maps out where and how religious beliefs matter, and he shrewdly highlights the "yes, but" factor—yes, religion matters, but "there is a temptation on both the religious right and the secular left to exaggerate its influence." Religion and moral values were important to voters in 2004, and they continue to be important today. But, as Dionne notes, many observers have overemphasized hot-button social issues in determining how people voted. And, I would add, they have overlooked other key factors, such as the importance of strong leadership and the weight voters assign to presidential performance in office.

Much of the recent obsession with the political impact of religion stems from misinterpretations of the 2004 National Election Pool exit poll. A great deal of attention was paid to a flawed question on the exit poll that asked respondents to choose the one issue that was most important in determining their vote for president. From a list of seven issues (taxes, education, Iraq, terrorism, economy/jobs, health care, and moral values), a small plurality of 22 percent named moral values. In the days following the election, many political analysts seized on this finding and concluded that religious voters had been the key to the President Bush's reelection.

However, a close examination of the exit poll results suggests that moral values were *not* the election's dominant issue. After all, as Dionne points out, while roughly one in five voters named moral issues, 71 percent chose something else. If you combine terrorism (19 percent) and Iraq (15 percent), about one-third of voters cited foreign policy concerns as their top priority. And, as Dionne astutely observes, elsewhere in the exit poll data there is evidence that President Bush's biggest gains between 2000 and 2004 occurred among the least religious voters.

Moreover, a poll of voters conducted just after the election by the Pew Research Center found that the relative importance of moral values varied considerably depending on how the question was framed. Half of the respondents in the Pew survey were asked the same question that was on the exit poll (with the same "fixed list" of seven answer options). The results, as shown in table 4-13, were very similar to the exit poll responses: 27 percent mentioned moral values. However, when Pew asked the other half to name, in their own words, the issue that mattered most to them when deciding how to vote, only 14 percent cited

Table 4-13. *What Mattered Most to Voters in the 2004 Presidential Election?*
Percent

Respondents' answers	Answer from fixed list[a]	Open-ended answer[b]
Moral values (total)	27	14
Moral values	. . .	9
Social issues[c]	. . .	3
Candidate's morals	. . .	2
Iraq	22	25
Economy/jobs	21	12
Terrorism	14	9
Health care	4	2
Education	4	1
Taxes	3	1
Other	4	31
Honesty/integrity	. . .	5
Like/dislike Bush	. . .	5
Like/dislike Kerry	. . .	3
Direction of country	. . .	2
Leadership	. . .	2
Foreign policy	. . .	2
Don't know	1	5

Source: 2004 National Election Pool exit poll.

a. Respondents selected from a "fixed list" of seven options. Items not included among the fixed-list options are marked ". . .".

b. Percentage of voters citing issue in an unprompted verbatim response to open-ended question.

c. Abortion, gay marriage, stem-cell research, etc.

a moral values issue. In this "open-ended" version of the question, Iraq—at 25 percent—was the most commonly mentioned issue.[10]

The Pew poll also found that voters defined moral issues in a variety of ways. When asked "what comes to mind" when they think about moral values, less than half (44 percent) of the respondents who selected moral values in the fixed-list question mentioned gay marriage, abortion, or stem-cell research. About one in four (23 percent) said they associated moral values with candidate qualities such as honesty or integrity, while 18 percent explicitly referred to religion.

10. Pew Research Center for the People and the Press, "Voters Liked Campaign 2004, but Too Much 'Mud-Slinging,' " November 11, 2004 (people-press.org/reports/display.php3?ReportID =233).

Table 4-14. *Most Important Candidate Qualities to Voters in the 2004 Presidential Election*
Percent

Quality	Bush voters	Kerry voters
Strong leader	29	4
Clear stand on issues	27	7
Honest and trustworthy	16	7
Strong religious faith	14	1
Cares about people like me	4	14
Intelligent	1	13
Bring about needed change	2	47
Don't know	7	7
Total	100	100

Source: 2004 National Election Pool exit poll.

Another 17 percent described general traditional values, using language such as "right and wrong" or "the way people live their lives." Thus, even among people who cast their votes based on moral issues, there was no consensus on what those issues are.

In addition to the ways in which religion may influence how voters think about key issues, political analysts have emphasized the supposed importance voters attach to the personal religious faith of candidates. President Bush's well-documented religious commitment was undoubtedly an appealing quality to many Americans—a fact underscored by the 14 percent of Bush voters who, responding to a 2004 exit poll question, said a "strong religious faith" was the most important personal quality a candidate could have. But the response was quite different among supporters of John Kerry: only 1 percent of those voters said a strong religious faith was a candidate's most important quality (see table 4-14).

Even among Bush supporters, however, religious conviction trailed behind other personal characteristics. Notably, 29 percent of Bush voters cited strong leadership, compared with only 4 percent of those who voted for Kerry. (At 47 percent, the desire to bring about change was the most important trait to Kerry voters.) Clearly, the Bush campaign's strategy to contrast a strong, steadfast president with a waffling, indecisive challenger proved effective among many voters. And the exit poll data suggest that perceptions of Bush as a strong leader were more important than perceptions of him as a man of faith.

Dionne makes a strong case that religion has yet to supplant the "traditional drivers of political choice," including the most important ones, class and race. He perceptively describes the "push-pull" dynamics of class and religion—with the secular worldview of upper-middle-class Democrats pushing working and lower-middle-class voters away from the Democratic Party, while conservatives' focus on social issues pulls them toward the Republicans. Meanwhile, despite the much publicized efforts by Republican leaders to bring African Americans and Latinos into the GOP, minority voters remain largely Democratic. Their resistance, Dionne observes, has allowed Democrats to stay at near parity with Republicans, despite the strong movement of religious conservatives toward the GOP in recent years.

However, Dionne does not mention another key factor that has helped keep Democrats in the game: the rise of secular voters. With all the attention given to the effects of white evangelical Protestants on the political landscape, too little attention has been paid to the sizable—and growing—bloc of seculars in the electorate. The General Social Survey, which has measured the attitudes and values of Americans on a range of social issues since 1972, has documented a solid rise in the number of people saying they have no religious preference, up from 7 percent in the 1970s to 14 percent in the current decade. At the same time, the group has become more solidly Democratic, with John Kerry making significant gains in the 2004 election. (According to the exit polls, Kerry received 67 percent of the secular vote in 2004, compared with Al Gore's 61 percent in 2000.) Nonreligious voters are thus becoming a core constituency for the Democratic Party.

There is one other important influence not covered by Dionne. Although he analyzes several of the sometimes conflicting structural factors shaping public opinion (including religion, race, class, and regional differences), one nonstructural factor cannot be overlooked: the performance of the incumbent president. Performance can make as strong an impression on public opinion as any of the structural variables, to the benefit or detriment of the incumbent. Good performance can often act as a mitigating power to bring about political consensus or even a political cease-fire, but poor performance can turn even your most solid supporters against you.

In the year and a half following his reelection in 2004, President Bush's overall job approval rating dropped 15 percentage points, from 50 percent to 35 percent (see table 4-15). And even though the president's core supporters—white evangelicals (55 percent), weekly church attendees (44 percent), and people in higher income brackets (42 percent)—were still more likely than the

Table 4-15. *President Bush's Approval Ratings*
Percent

Respondent characteristics	January 2005	April 2006	Percentage point change
Total	50	35	−15
Total Protestant	55	40	−15
White evangelical	72	55	−17
White nonevangelical	54	37	−17
Black Protestant	19	10	−9
Total Catholic	52	31	−21
White non-Hispanic	55	32	−23
Seculars	31	24	−7
Frequency of church attendance			
Weekly or more	60	44	−16
Monthly or less	47	31	−16
Seldom/never	41	28	−13
Household income level			
$75,000+	56	42	−14
$50,000–74,999	51	38	−13
$30,000–49,999	55	33	−22
$20,000–29,999	48	28	−20
<$20,000	37	30	−7

Source: National polls conducted by the Pew Research Center for the People and the Press.

general public to give the president positive marks, they were considerably less enthusiastic about the Bush administration than they were after the election, proving that the performance of the president matters at least as much as the structural influences of religion and class.[11]

Nevertheless, the commitment of white evangelical Protestants to the Republican Party in general has so far weathered the storm. Scott Keeter, director of survey research at the Pew Research Center, observed in May 2006:

There is little indication, as of now, that evangelicals are likely to abandon the Republican Party electorally. Pew's polling finds that the percentage of white evangelicals identifying as Republicans has actually increased slightly

11. The numbers in this paragraph are based on polls conducted by the Pew Research Center for the People and the Press in January 2005 and April 2006. They are available at http://people-press.org/reports/.

in 2006, and the number of these who say they intend to vote for Republican candidates [in November 2006] is no lower now than it was at a comparable point in 2002, the last midterm election.[12]

Whether these religiously conservative voters provide significant shelter for Republican candidates in the 2006 midterm elections will be an important measure of their political influence—not just now, but for the years to come.

12. Scott Keeter, "Will White Evangelicals Desert the GOP?" Pew Research Center for the People and the Press, May 2, 2006 (people-press.org/commentary/display.php3?AnalysisID=133).

References

Barone, Michael. 1993. "Postwar Politics." In *The Almanac of American Politics, 1994*, edited by Michael Barone. Washington: National Journal Group.

Brooks, David. 2000. *Bobos in Paradise: The New Upper Class and How They Got There*. New York: Simon & Schuster.

Clecak, Peter. 1983. *America's Quest for the Ideal Self: Dissent and Fulfillment in the 60s and 70s*. Oxford University Press.

Dionne, E. J., Jr. 1991. *Why Americans Hate Politics*. New York: Simon & Schuster.

———. 2000. "The Third Stage: New Frontiers of Religious Liberty." In *What's God Got to Do with the American Experiment?*, edited by E. J. Dionne Jr. and John J. DiIulio Jr., pp. 115–20. Brookings.

Edsall, Thomas Byrne, and Mary D. Edsall. 1991. *Chain Reaction: The Impact of Race, Rights, and Taxes on American Politics*. New York: W. W. Norton.

Falwell, Jerry. 1987. *Strength for the Journey: An Autobiography*. New York: Simon & Schuster.

Fiorina, Morris P., Samuel J. Abrams, and Jeremy C. Pope. 2006. *Culture War? The Myth of a Polarized America*. New York: Longman.

Frank, Thomas. 2004. *What's the Matter with Kansas? How Conservatives Won the Heart of America*. New York: Metropolitan Books.

Gelman, Andrew, and others. 2005. "Rich State, Poor State, Red State, Blue State: What's the Matter with Connecticut?" Paper prepared for the annual meeting of the Midwest Political Science Association, Chicago, April 7–10.

Glazer, Nathan. 1987. "Fundamentalists: A Defensive Offensive." In *Piety and Politics: Evangelicals and Fundamentalists Confront the World*, edited by Michael Cromartie and Richard John Neuhaus, pp. 245–58. Washington: Ethics and Public Policy Center.

Gray, Mark M., Paul Perl, and Mary E. Bendyna. 2006. "Camelot Only Comes but Once? John F. Kerry and the Catholic Vote." *Presidential Studies Quarterly* 36 (2): 203–22.

Green, John C. 2004. "The American Religious Landscape and Political Attitudes: A Baseline for 2004." Ray C. Bliss Institute of Applied Politics, University of Akron (www.uakron.edu/bliss/docs/Religious_Landscape_2004.pdf).

Green, John C., and others. 2004. "The American Religious Landscape and the 2004 Presidential Vote: Increased Polarization." Ray C. Bliss Institute of Applied Politics, University of Akron (www.uakron.edu/bliss/docs/TheAmericanReligiousLand.pdf).

Hertzke, Allen D. 2005. "The Shame of Darfur." *First Things* 156 (October): 16–22.

Hunter, James Davison. 1991. *Culture Wars: The Struggle to Define America*. New York: Basic Books.

Inglehart, Ronald. 1997. *Modernization and Postmodernization: Cultural, Economic and Political Change in 43 Societies*. Princeton University Press.

Judis, John B. 1988. *William F. Buckley, Jr.: Patron Saint of the Conservatives*. New York: Simon & Schuster.

Ladd, Everett Carll, and Charles D. Hadley. 1975. *Transformations of the American Party System: Political Coalitions from the New Deal to the 1970s*. New York: W. W. Norton.

Lasswell, Harold D. 1936. *Politics: Who Gets What, When, How*. New York: McGraw-Hill.

Lipset, Seymour Martin. 1960. *Political Man*. (London: Heinemann Education Books).

Lipset, Seymour Martin, and William Schneider. 1987. *The Confidence Gap: Business, Labor and Government in the Public Mind*. John Hopkins University Press.

McNamara, Patrick H. 1992. *Conscience First, Tradition Second: A Study of Young American Catholics*. State University of New York Press.

Phillips, Kevin P. 1969. *The Emerging Republican Majority.* New Rochelle, N.Y.: Arlington House.

———. 1982. *Post-Conservative America: People, Politics and Ideology in a Time of Crisis.* New York: Random House.

Reider, Jonathan. 1985. *Canarsie: The Jews and Italians of Brooklyn against Liberalism.* Harvard University Press.

Sweet, Leonard I. 1984. "The 1960s: The Crises of Liberal Christianity and the Public Emergence of Evangelicalism." In *Evangelicalism in Modern America,* edited by George Marsden, pp. 29–45. Grand Rapids, Mich.: W. B. Eerdmans.

Wacker, Grant. 2001. *Heaven Below: Early Pentecostals and American Culture.* Harvard University Press.

Williamson, Chilton, Jr. 1978. "Country & Western Marxism: To the Nashville Station." *National Review* 30 (23): 711–17.

Wilson, James Q. 1997. *The Moral Sense.* New York: Free Press.

Woodward, Bob. 2004. *Plan of Attack.* New York: Simon & Schuster.

Wolfe, Alan. 1998. *One Nation, After All.* New York: Viking.

———. 2001. *Moral Freedom: The Search for Virtue in a World of Choice.* New York: W. W. Norton.

———. 2003. *The Transformation of American Religion: How We Actually Live Our Faith.* New York: Free Press.

5

How the Mass Media Divide Us

Diana C. Mutz

The chapters in this book suggest that scholars are nowhere near a consensus on whether the mass public is more polarized than it has been in the past and, if it is, relative to precisely when. Nonetheless, among those who believe the mass public has, indeed, become increasingly polarized in its views, mass media are very likely to be invoked as a cause. Perhaps this should come as no surprise—throughout American history, mass media have been blamed for just about every social ill that has befallen the country.

But in the midst of so much disagreement about when and whether and among whom this phenomenon has occurred, why is there so much agreement that media must somehow be to blame? A consensus on this point exists not so much because the empirical evidence is overwhelming, but because there are multiple theories that predict and explain how media might logically influence levels of mass polarization. Furthermore, it is possible to view mass media as engines of polarization even if one believes the public in general has not become polarized to any significant degree. Mass media are, after all, only one influence in a much larger system of institutions and influences.

For purposes of this chapter, I set aside the question of whether and to what extent mass polarization has occurred, in favor of an exploration of ways in which media have been implicated in polarizing processes. How might mass media be contributing to this widely decried state of affairs? And even if the public has not polarized, how might mass media nonetheless be encouraging mass opinion in more extreme directions?

More from Which to Choose

One obvious and unmistakable characteristic of the current media landscape is choice. No one questions the idea that there is more choice, that there are more media outlets now than thirty or forty years ago. As political scientist Markus Prior notes in a forthcoming book, television provided a mere seven channels to the average household in 1970, and the three broadcast networks captured 80 percent of all viewing. By 2005, over 85 percent of households had cable or satellite access, and the average viewer had a choice of about a hundred channels. There are now more broadcast networks than in 1970, but they collectively capture only 40 percent of viewing.[1] When one adds to this the choices offered by "new media"—the Internet, cell phones, iPods, and the like—then it seems indisputable that Americans have more media choice than ever before.

There are two different theories that tie increased media choice to higher levels of political polarization. One argument points to the increased number of choices people have in sources of political *news* as a cause of polarization. An altogether different theory suggests that it is the expansion of choices of nonpolitical *entertainment* media content that is most consequential for mass polarization.

Choosing Sources of Political News

Greater choice in sources of political news is relevant to political polarization because it means that people must decide on some basis which sources to use and which not to use. More optimistic scholars have suggested that perhaps this will lead the United States toward a better approximation of a true "marketplace" of ideas, one in which people are exposed to many different perspectives and can weigh a broader range of views in formulating their opinions than was once the case. This idealistic vision is appealing, but for the most part scholars have focused on the other side of this double-edged sword: more choice also means that people can more easily limit their exposure based on their own predispositions.

To the extent that the many sources of political news have identifiable political complexions, some people may end up choosing news sources that reinforce and intensify their preexisting views. In academic jargon, this phenomenon goes by

1. Prior (forthcoming 2007).

the name of "selectivity" or "biased assimilation of information." Selectivity can take place at several junctures with respect to mass media, including *exposure* to a particular source of political news, *attention* to what the source says, and biased *interpretation* when processing the content of political news. Because exposure to a source of political news is a prerequisite for any of the subsequent kinds of selection to become relevant, selective exposure has been the target of the greatest research attention.

Concerns about selective exposure date back to the very earliest selection studies conducted in the 1940s by Paul Lazarsfeld and his colleagues at Columbia University.[2] These early studies became closely linked with psychologist Leon Festinger's theory of cognitive dissonance.[3] Festinger suggested that people want to avoid information that conflicts with their preexisting beliefs, and that they seek out information—through activities such as selective exposure—that confirms their current beliefs. Although a trickle of studies of selective exposure to partisan information continued over the past five decades, a renewed interest in the topic has been spawned by the relatively recent proliferation of news outlets. Moreover, as a result of television programs that now appear more unabashedly partisan, more scholars are finding this hypothesis and its potential polarizing influence worthy of study.

What do these recent studies suggest about whether selective exposure to like-minded political content occurs and thus contributes to a more extreme public? Do people select media content that is compatible with their own views and avoid exposure to alternative opinions? There is, for better or worse, no simple answer to these questions, in part because the internal context of these studies varies, but also because the external context—that is, the media environment—has changed so tremendously since the 1940s, when the hypothesis was formulated.

Studies of the real-world context in which media choices are made tend to support the selective exposure hypothesis, but with important limitations. If one compares the political views promoted by any given medium with the political views held by that medium's audience, investigators regularly find significant relationships. For example, conservatives are more likely to read conservative newspapers, and liberals are more likely to read liberal ones.

Unfortunately, such correlations are very limited in what they tell us about the public's propensity to selectively expose itself to political information. Most obviously, it is possible that the partisan leanings of the media sources influenced

2. Lazarsfeld, Berelson, and Gaudet (1948).
3. Festinger (1957).

the readers, viewers, or listeners, so that they ended up holding similar political perspectives. In this case, a relationship between the partisanship of a news source and the partisanship of its audience cannot necessarily be attributed to selective exposure. For example, in David Barker's panel study of Rush Limbaugh listeners, he finds that regular listeners developed an antipathy toward Rush Limbaugh's favorite targets, thus suggesting that influence as well as selective exposure was occurring.[4]

Yet another prominent reason that these kinds of relationships are often dismissed is because of the lack of direct evidence that people are actually making choices motivated by a desire to avoid dissimilar perspectives. In their influential review of the literature on both political and nonpolitical forms of selective exposure, David O. Sears and Jonathan L. Freedman suggested that the similarity between audiences' opinions and the opinions of their media sources was because of "de facto selective exposure."[5] According to this line of thought, a correlation exists between the opinions of an information source and its audience, but not because the audience is motivated to avoid disagreeable views, or because it is influenced by the media. Instead, the correlation arises because media environments tend to supply more like-minded sources of information to the bulk of the populations they reach than they supply dissonant sources. Red states tend to have more conservative newspapers than blue states, but according to the de facto interpretation it is not because Republicans have chosen not to read more liberal newspapers—thus driving them out of business. Instead, they read conservative newspapers because, in conservative regions, they are more widely available than liberal ones.

Of course, a consideration of market forces turns this argument into a bit of a chicken-and-egg debate. For instance, does Provo, Utah, not have any liberal-leaning media because no one there would choose to consume it, or can no one choose it because it is not available there? In their review of the evidence in the 1960s, Sears and Freedman emphasized the latter, suggesting that much of what had been deemed as evidence that audiences were motivated to avoid oppositional political perspectives was really evidence of de facto selective exposure.

However, the preponderance of evidence cited in recent studies confirms that partisan audiences do select media that lean in the direction of their own views. And the evidence of such a relationship is common across virtually all forms of media. Talk-radio listeners are likely to have views similar to those of the host

4. Barker (2002).
5. Sears and Freedman (1967).

whose program they listen to, Republicans are more likely to be viewers of the right-leaning Fox News Channel, and political films such as *Fahrenheit 9/11* are attended primarily by those who are already sympathetic to the films' political perspectives. Likewise, visitors to a candidate's website will predominantly already be the candidate's supporters.[6] Even when political differences in media are fairly muted, such as when there are two competing daily newspapers in the same city, there is evidence that people systematically choose to read the newspaper with an editorial slant closer to their own politics.[7] In this case, availability is held constant (making the de facto interpretation moot), providing clear evidence of politically motivated selective exposure.[8]

Although it seems logical to conclude from this that partisans on both sides would, as a result, polarize further in the direction of their original views, this consequence is not yet well documented. Studies of small group interactions have suggested that like-minded company leads to greater attitude extremity, but there is little evidence to date that documents that same process of influence with like-minded mass media.[9] Moreover, if this process of reinforcement has been taking place all along, why have scholars only begun to suspect selective exposure as a cause of greater polarization in recent years?

Heightened concern about mass media's role in polarization stems from an increase in partisan differences across the many news sources now available to citizens. Selective exposure requires that people associate particular news sources with particular brands of politics. So although it is unlikely that people today are any more selective than they ever were, the media environment itself has made being selective easier than it was in the past, just by offering more diverse sources. Just how much easier selectivity is now remains unclear. Few mainstream news sources bill themselves explicitly as Republican or Democratic in orientation, though increasingly some use terms such as "progressive" and "traditional" to cue their audiences as to what they can expect.

The way in which openly partisan media facilitate selective exposure is abundantly clear when one compares audience patterns in the United States with

6. See Cappella, Turow, and Jamieson (1996); Annenberg Public Policy Center, "Fahrenheit 9/11 Viewers and Limbaugh Listeners about Equal in Size Even Though They Perceive Two Different Nations, Annenberg Data Show," August 3, 2004; Bimber and Davis (2003).

7. Mutz and Martin (2001).

8. Ironically, having a choice of daily newspapers means that readers will be exposed to *fewer* oppositional viewpoints since few people bother to read multiple papers. More voices means more choice, but having choice means that people will pick and choose content that comports with their own viewpoints and thus makes it less likely that they will hear the other side.

9. For a review of the evidence of small group interactions, see Sunstein (2002).

Figure 5-1. *Exposure to Like-minded Media Content by Partisanship and Medium, 1996*[a]

Extent of exposure to like-minded content

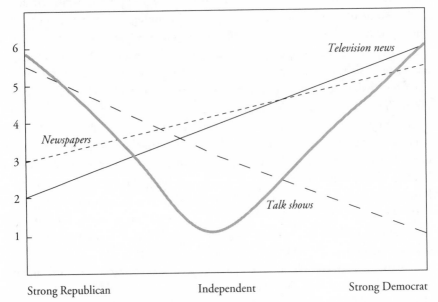

Source: Based on the data shown in Mutz and Martin (2001, figure 4A).
a. Respondents were asked about their most frequently used source in each category.

those in a country such as Great Britain, where newspapers openly carry partisan labels. In Great Britain, newspaper readers perceive political agreement in their media in roughly the U-shaped pattern shown in figure 5-1. The pattern of newspaper readership in Great Britain demonstrates classic evidence of partisan-based selective exposure (with Conservative and Labour parties replacing Republican and Democrat, respectively). Strong partisans are the most motivated to selectively expose, but weaker partisans also do so to a lesser extent. Partisans can self-select like-minded content at either end of the political spectrum, and thus strong partisans on both sides are exposed primarily to like-minded political perspectives in their newspapers.

In the 1990s, there was limited partisan choice among mainstream daily newspapers in the United States. At least at that time, as shown in figure 5-1, Republicans found their daily newspapers significantly less compatible with their political views than Democrats did. Relative to newspaper readers in Great Britain,

Americans were not as successful at selective exposure. Most Republicans found less to like about the partisanship in television news broadcasts than did Democrats. Not surprisingly, Republicans found talk shows to be highly compatible, whereas Democrats found little to comport with their views on talk shows.[10]

Perhaps Americans exercised selective exposure by gravitating to different media (Republicans to talk shows, Democrats to television) rather than finding something politically compatible within each medium. But one wonders how different these patterns would look if the same data were available for 2006. Since the 1990s, Fox News has provided Republicans with a politically compatible television network, and the number of news sources on television and the Internet has proliferated. In addition, the availability of openly partisan television programs, radio shows, and websites may mean that the pattern of U.S. news consumption will more closely approximate that of British newspapers in the not-so-distant future. To the extent that the media environment in the United States continues to develop along the lines of a niche market based on partisanship, this new news environment should facilitate selective exposure by making it easier for people to find the most compatible source of news.

Be that as it may, data demonstrating that selective exposure to media is responsible for mass polarization do not yet exist. Nonetheless, a recent experimental study of Internet news attempted to mimic the kinds of choices people make in today's media environment. Shanto Iyengar and Richard Morin attempted to document evidence of partisan-based selective exposure by randomly assigning a set of news stories to four news sources: Fox News, National Public Radio (NPR), CNN, and the BBC.[11] Participants were shown four news story headlines, one under each news organization's logo. Participants were then asked which of the reports they would like to read. This scenario was repeated for articles in six news categories, including American politics, the war in Iraq, race in America, crime, travel, and sports. Some respondents were randomly assigned to a control condition without logos of any kind attached to the stories.

The results suggest that selective exposure is alive and well—even among relatively mainstream news sources. Republicans overwhelmingly preferred stories from Fox News, whereas Democrats divided between NPR and CNN. Democrats systematically avoided Fox News, whereas independents demonstrated no particular pattern of preferences. And while the difference between Republicans

10. Mutz and Martin (2001, pp. 105–07).

11. Shanto Iyengar and Richard Morin, "Red Media, Blue Media: Evidence for a Political Litmus Test in Online News Readership," *Washington Post*, May 3, 2006.

and Democrats was most pronounced when the stories involved hard news (such as national politics and the war in Iraq), it did not disappear entirely even when the story was about possible vacation destinations.

A comparison of how many partisans chose certain stories with news organization labels versus the same stories without labels provides a clear picture of how news sources may serve as a guide to selective exposure. Republicans were three times as likely to choose a news story accompanied by the Fox News logo as without it, and less likely to choose it if it was labeled a CNN or NPR story. Among Democrats the pattern was less pronounced; they were somewhat more likely to choose a story if it was labeled from CNN or NPR and significantly less likely to choose the same story labeled as being from Fox News. As news consumers increasingly have the ability to customize their news environments to their own tastes, the likelihood that news will simply reinforce existing views and produce a subsequent polarization of partisan groups seems all the more plausible.

Relative to much of the twentieth century, the current direction of political news seems to portend greater division rather than greater consensus. But in the midst of considerable alarmism about the impact of modern media, it is worth remembering that during the days of the openly partisan press of the nineteenth century, selective exposure was even easier to accomplish. Newspapers of that era openly aligned themselves with political parties and endorsed candidates on every page, not just in their editorial content.

But even though the question of whether selective exposure exists seems to have been resolved affirmatively, the consequences of selective exposure for public attitudes have not yet been well studied. It is common to assume that if Democrats, Republicans, and independents all exposed themselves to exactly the same information, the public would be less polarized. Perhaps, but some evidence suggests that this would not happen. Macro-level research on selectivity in the processing of political information suggests that even if audiences did experience identical exposure to political information, it might not diminish polarization much because of the selective way in which partisans *interpret* new information.

Imagine a situation in which new information becomes available to all three groups—for example, news that the economy has improved. Assume also that there is a Republican president in office, so that the president's job approval starts out higher among Republicans than among independents, who in turn give the president more favorable job approval ratings than Democrats do. Nonetheless, all three partisan groups in a situation such as this generally increase their levels of presidential approval. In other words, they respond to new information in a reasonable manner. Likewise, downturns due to bad news such as declining economic indicators would generally cause all three groups' approval levels to fall. According to aggregate data compiled over time, Republicans, Democrats, and independents do indeed respond by changing their views in the same direction—and to roughly the same extent—in response to new information.[12] But this kind of parallel change is not particularly helpful in reducing polarization. If each group moves up or down to roughly the same extent, the gap between Republicans and Democrats remains the same. The two groups are as polarized as before they received new information.

The underlying assumption of much work on information processing is that if people were truly unbiased processors of the same political information, they should ultimately *converge* in their judgments. As new information becomes available (perhaps news that the economy has worsened), partisans update their presidential approval ratings in light of their initial views. The extent of decreased presidential approval due to negative information should not be even across all groups, but should be more pronounced in groups that begin with higher levels of approval. New information matters more when it contradicts initial expectations. In this scenario, new information should logically result, over time, in a convergence of opinion. Whether the news is positive or negative, the three groups' opinions should move closer and closer together.

Empirical data suggest, however, that convergence is not usually what happens. Instead, patterns of aggregate opinion suggest that partisanship is a driving force in how people perceive, interpret, and respond to the political world.[13] This means that even if selective exposure to information were not a problem, it is doubtful that information from mass media would decrease the gap between the perspectives of Republicans and Democrats. Biased processing is prevalent in the American public, and partisanship is its driving force.

Biased processing models underscore a skepticism prevalent in contemporary political psychology that information is the cure-all for what ails the quality of political decisions. If people are not passive recipients of information, but rather active choosers, interpreters, and rationalizers, then mass media are severely limited in what they can do about political polarization. Even if citizens were still limited to the choice between three indistinguishable network news broadcasts, biased assimilation models would predict that differences would persist because of the ways in which people process the information they receive.

12. Gerber and Green (1999).
13. Bartels (2002).

The Internet has become a particular target of concern with respect to selectivity. Law professor Cass Sunstein, author of *Republic.com,* has suggested that the cacophony of online political voices, including some very extreme ones, raises the possibility that extreme political views will be reinforced and encouraged.[14] Selectivity is made easier on the Internet by search engines and links between websites that espouse similar views. The voices represented on the Internet include those of fringe groups whose extremist ideas would never be covered by more traditional mainstream media. For many, that alone is cause for concern. While it is possible (even likely) that these groups have always been out there, they are more visible and better organized now as a result of the Internet. And even if their numbers have not increased as a result of the Internet, better organization means that they could be more likely to pose a threat by taking violent action of some kind. Still others worry that their mere presence on the Internet encourages those with similar political leanings by reinforcing and exacerbating the extremity of their views, and by convincing them that they are not alone and thus need not abandon their unpopular positions. In all of these scenarios, Internet-based selective exposure is cause for alarm.

Nonetheless, the irony of all of this hand-wringing about the Internet and the expansion in the number of political voices on television should not go without notice. For years, scholars who studied mass media voiced concerns about the near monopolistic media and the paucity of non-mainstream political voices on the air or in print. Today, the marketplace is more—and less—ideal. The proliferation of voices on the Internet means there is a larger marketplace of political ideas than in the past, but that does not necessarily lead citizens to freely sample all of its products.

Choosing Whether to Watch Political News

Partisan-driven selectivity is only one mechanism by which increasing media choice has been tied to increasing polarization. In a more novel argument linking choice and polarization, Markus Prior suggests that greater media choice in the form of *entertainment* content, combined with the availability of twenty-four-hour news channels, has widened the gap between the politically informed and those without interest and information.[15] The rise of cable television has clearly changed contemporary presidents' ability to commandeer the national airwaves, as political scientists Matthew Baum and Samuel Kernell

14. Sunstein (2001).
15. Prior (forthcoming 2007).

have shown.[16] The average size of the audience watching prime-time presidential addresses and news conferences decreased steadily in the late twentieth century— a trend that appears to be primarily a function of the availability of cable television. Likewise, debate watching fell, particularly among cable viewers. People without cable are essentially a captive audience, and their debate watching is less a function of political interest than it is for those with cable, for whom watching the president on television is clearly a choice.

Many of today's television viewers no longer need to suffer through a State of the Union address if they would rather watch a sitcom. In the era of hundreds of channels from which to choose, viewers need not watch the political debates or presidential press conferences that dominated all three networks not so long ago. There is always another—and often far more entertaining—choice for the less politically interested American, from cooking shows to crime dramas to feature films.

The lack of largely involuntary exposure to political content among the less politically involved, according to Prior, makes this group even less likely to turn out to vote. (On the other hand, there is a steady diet of political media for political junkies, thus further energizing and reinforcing their proclivities to be politically active.) Thus, changes in the media environment lead to less involuntary exposure to political information and less incidental learning about the political world. This "byproduct learning," it is argued, is what motivates the less politically interested to turn out to vote. Without it, the increasing gap in political knowledge between the politically interested and uninterested translates into an increasing turnout gap at the polls. Less politically involved, more moderate voters are *less* likely to turn out than before, while the more politically involved are even *more* likely to vote than usual. The electorate is thus robbed of its middle, with the result that the electorate that does go to the polls is more polarized in its views.[17]

In light of this long chain of proposed causal influences, Prior's evidence in support of this theory consists of tests of the many links that make up this larger process. Using an experiment embedded in a national survey, he randomly assigned respondents different amounts of choice, asking the hypothetical question, "If you had free time at 6 o'clock at night and the following programs were available, which one would you watch, or would you not watch television then?" Respondents in the low-choice condition were given only five options: the three

16. Baum and Kernell (1999).

17. Notably, this process results in no individual-level shifts in extremity of views, and thus in no polarization at the level of individuals or the mass public. But it produces a compositional shift in the electorate such that the extremes are well represented in voting booths, but the middle, less extreme segments of the population are less likely to be heard.

network news programs, *The NewsHour with Jim Lehrer,* and not watching at all. Respondents in the high-choice condition had those five options, plus several cable news programs and several entertainment options described as "a comedy or sitcom program like *Friends* or *The Simpsons,*" "a drama program like *ER* or *Law and Order,*" and similar examples from other genres including science fiction, reality TV, and sports.

The results of Prior's tests suggest that in the high-choice condition the news audience is half of what it is in the low-choice condition. To the extent that this hypothetical situation generalizes to real-world changes in U.S. media, this is a striking result. But it also raises the question of why so many people watched the news in the past when it was not what they ideally would have selected. Media economists suggest that they did so out of habit, as well as a tendency to decide to watch television before knowing precisely what the viewing options were. This process no longer rings true for many Americans today. As the ability to "time shift" the viewing of preferred programs becomes more popular, and the degree of choice at any one time becomes still more expansive, it seems unlikely that habitual viewing times will result in much incidental exposure to political content.

A related—and important—matter is whether the politically unenthused really picked up political knowledge from their incidental viewing in the days of less choice. And what about the pre-television era, when the literacy levels of the less educated segments of the population limited their direct access to political information? Prior suggests that during the pre-television era, when media options were largely limited to newspapers and radio, a similar gap existed between the political haves and have-nots, but that television exerted a democratizing influence on the public, making it less effortful for even the less educated to receive political news. The less interested still remained less knowledgeable than in the days before television, but the gap was smaller.

Using National Election Studies data from the 1950s and 1960s, Prior documents how the number of television stations to which an individual had access predicts political knowledge, particularly among the less educated segments of the population. His models suggest that access to television has increased political interest and turnout among the less educated segments of the population.

With the more recent advent of cable television and the Internet, the gap between the politically informed and uninformed should be widening again in the contemporary population. To measure this, Prior develops the concept of "relative entertainment preference"—that is, the extent to which a given respondent prefers entertainment over news. One measure involves directly asking people what genre they like best from a list of ten categories, then having them select a second, third, and fourth favorite. Of the remaining options, they are allowed to indicate those that they "really dislike." The respondents who claim to actively dislike news are at the high end of the "relative entertainment preference" scale, while those who indicate neither a like nor a dislike are next highest, and those who rank news among their four favorite types of programs are at the lower end of the scale.

Central to Prior's thesis is the group he dubs "switchers," people who will switch from news viewing to entertainment viewing when given the choice. This is the segment of the population whose level of political knowledge (and level of turnout at the polls) should be most affected by greater choice. Because switchers abandon news once they have a choice of entertainment content, they reduce their incidental exposure to political content, which in turn limits their accidental political learning.

Prior's thesis presents a conundrum for a society that is addicted to choice. Some segments of the population will expose themselves to political news voluntarily and turn out to vote regularly regardless of the shape of the current news environment. Others will not watch political news regardless of how little choice they have, and they are unlikely to bother voting in any case. But for those on the margins of these groups—those who are not political activists, yet not totally disengaged—incidental exposure to the political world is an important way in which they are drawn into the political process. Without involuntary exposure to political media, these more moderate voters will drop out of the electoral process, and the voting public will be increasingly extreme in its composition.

Losers' Consent in an Age of Illegitimacy

Yet another way in which media may contribute to political polarization stems from the nature of contemporary media content during elections. It has been often observed, extensively documented, and widely lamented that election coverage tends to emphasize the "behind-the-scenes" insider perspective on what drives election outcomes. Rather than emphasize the substantive reasons why voters might have selected one candidate over another, media coverage tends to emphasize the role of political consultants, advertising campaigns, and other factors that have less to do with the quality of the candidate or the extent to which aspects of his agenda resonate with voters, and more to do with strategic aspects of how campaigns are waged.

In his book *Out of Order,* Thomas E. Patterson documented the stark increase in this type of coverage from the 1960s through the 1990s.[18] Patterson's analysis

18. Patterson (1993).

shows that it is not simply that horse-race coverage—that is, coverage of who is ahead and who is falling behind—remains popular among journalists. (Indeed, many argue that horse-race coverage is a time-honored journalistic tradition that predates both polls and television.)[19] But in comparison with forty or fifty years ago, there is now far more of what Patterson calls "game-centered" coverage of elections, in which journalists focus on the suspense and speculation about likely winners and losers and the behind-the-scenes machinations of candidates and their staffs. As Patterson notes:

> The game schema dominates the journalist's outlook in part because it conforms to the conventions of the news process. . . . The conventions of news reporting include an emphasis on the more dramatic and controversial aspects of politics. . . . The game is always moving: candidates are continually adjusting to the dynamics of the race and their position in it. Since it can almost always be assumed that the candidates are driven by a desire to win, their actions can hence be interpreted as an effort to acquire votes. The game is thus a perpetually reliable source of new material.[20]

Patterson's analysis of *New York Times* coverage between 1960 and 1992 demonstrates that in 1960 the majority of election stories were framed as stories about candidates' policy positions. By 1992, election stories were six times more likely to be framed in the context of campaign strategy than as policy stories. Over the course of several decades, stories about candidates' policy positions were replaced by an increasing number of articles about the campaigns themselves.

In what comes across as an effort to give ordinary people a behind-the-scenes perspective on how elections are run, today's election coverage is replete with analyses of the strategic decisions involved in campaigning for office. When a presidential candidate gives a speech about health care in Atlanta, campaign journalists are likely to frame the event not in terms of a discussion of health care policy or the candidate's platform, but as an effort to woo southern voters. For reporters—and perhaps for their audiences as well—the text is not nearly as interesting as the subtext.

Some speculate that journalists highlight the strategic aspects of campaigns as a means of insulating their readers and viewers from the more manipulative aspects of campaigns; if audiences are aware of candidates' real intentions and the reasons for their actions, then surely they will not be duped by them. In his book *Seducing America,* Roderick P. Hart has suggested that strategic coverage is

19. Sigelman and Bullock (1991).
20. Patterson (1993, pp. 60–61).

popular with the public because it gives them the illusion of being informed and knowing what is *really* happening in the campaign.[21]

The problem with constant reporting on the campaign is that it suggests to news media audiences that being persuaded by a politician is a bad thing, a sign of weakness, gullibility, or stupidity. For the same reason that no one admits to having his or her mind changed by a political ad, few Americans see open-mindedness to campaign propaganda as a good thing. Another problem with game-centric coverage is that it shifts the audience's attention away from what is being said (on health care, for example) toward the journalist's perspective on the strategic reason *why* it is being said.

From the perspective of polarization, why is the rise in this kind of coverage a concern? The link to polarization comes later in the election process, after the winners and losers have already been decided. To the extent that citizens are convinced by game-centric coverage that elections are won or lost by the right choice of advertisements, a new haircut, the best speechwriters, or the cleverest consultants, one could understand why voters on the losing side in any given contest might feel they have been robbed. The best advertisements do not necessarily mean the best presidents, and a good haircut seldom leads to good governance. Moreover, a good campaign can be waged by a weak candidate, and a bad campaign by a strong candidate.

It is a much more polarizing experience to think that one's candidate lost an election because of a minor misstatement, a failure to look good on television, or a failure to hire the right advertising agency than to think that he lost because his policy ideas were less popular than his opponent's. If electoral victories are, according to the press, about the candidate's ability to play the game, then electoral losses also are about the candidate's failure to play the game well.

Empirical evidence backs up this broad argument, though scholars have yet to test the multiple steps in this process within a single study. For example, there is considerable empirical evidence of the media's increased emphasis on the strategic aspects of campaigns. A separate body of evidence suggests that the explanations the mass media put forth for how an election was won or lost are widely adopted by the public. Today's media coverage is more likely to suggest apolitical, illegitimate explanations for a candidate's electoral victory, and the public on the losing side is likely to believe them.[22] A belief that one's side has experienced an illegitimate loss, in turn, prompts the losing partisans to become increasingly angry

21. Hart (1999, pp. 77–100).
22. See Mutz (1993); Hershey (1992).

and frustrated. If one believes the other side won by running deceitful ads, then it is easy to villainize the opposition and thus create more extreme perceptions of the consequences of one political choice over another. At this point, it is no longer about differing political philosophies; it is about right versus wrong, truth versus deceit, good versus evil.

The link in this chain of events that has not been well documented is the extent to which delegitimizing explanations lead to more polarized views, particularly in the form of an intensified dislike for the "other side." In a 2005 book, *Losers' Consent,* Christopher J. Anderson and his coauthors examine the role that elections play in legitimizing their own outcomes. For citizens who end up on the winning side in a given contest, accepting the outcome is not particularly difficult. But what produces consent from the losers? Not surprisingly, those who participate in an election but end up on the losing side are significantly more negative about their system of government. Losing naturally leads to anger, particularly if the loss is seen as illegitimate—and evaluations of the legitimacy of elections and democracy are significantly less positive among losers than among winners.[23]

Although it has yet to be tested, one would likewise expect that those exposed to media coverage that emphasizes delegitimizing explanations of an election outcome—such as the idea that the election was won primarily by ads containing lies or half-truths—should come away from the experience of loss more polarized in their views. Nobody wants to end up on the losing side, but losing to an opponent who won for the wrong reasons would be expected to create much more negative feeling toward the opposition.

By suggesting this, I do not mean to refer specifically to the unusual, extremely close election outcomes that occurred in the 2000 and 2004 presidential elections, though they obviously come to mind. The more general point is that regardless of how lopsided an outcome might be, media coverage plays an important role in structuring explanations for why one side was victorious and the other side failed. Once the people have spoken, it is the mass media that decide what they have said. To the extent that delegitimizing explanations are encouraged by the press and adopted by the losing side, a more polarized electorate is likely to be the result.

Media Bracketing of Acceptable Opinion

Yet another explanation linking the media to political polarization originates in two studies of the role of the news media as a political institution. In a 1984

---

23. Anderson and others (2005).

study, political scientist Dan Hallin examined the oft-repeated assertion that during the war in Vietnam the American news media (television in particular) became more oppositional toward government and thus helped lead public opinion away from support for the war. In Hallin's study of political elites, media coverage, and mass opinion, he found little support for this thesis of an oppositional media. Although media coverage of the war did become increasingly critical after the Tet Offensive in 1967, Hallin demonstrated that this was because elite opinion became more divided on the war at that time. By relying on elite sources, reporters mirrored the division of elite opinion—and subsequently their coverage influenced the range of opinions held by the mainstream public as well.[24]

Hallin's study pointed to the importance of the mass media in "bracketing" the range of acceptable opinion for the public. By defining the boundaries of acceptable controversy, the media define the range of legitimate opinions that the public may adopt. An issue such as Vietnam may shift over time from the sphere of consensus to the sphere of legitimate controversy, but this is a top-down phenomenon originating with elites rather than with the media. Others have similarly noted that media coverage tends to be "indexed" to the range of elite opinion rather than more broadly to the range of mass opinion.[25]

When members of Congress represent some of the more extreme positions (as they do now), it follows then, as a result of journalists' tendency to rely on official sources, that those more extreme viewpoints are also more likely to be covered by the press. Although the views that are covered originate with elites (such as members of Congress), the media play an important role in conferring legitimacy on a given range of views simply by covering those perspectives regularly, but not others. What this process suggests is that by covering what is essentially a more polarized group of political elites, journalists may be offering a wider range of acceptable views to the public and thus discouraging consensus. If the smorgasbord of views offered in today's media represents greater extremes than in the past, then it is perhaps not surprising that more of the public now endorses more extreme views.

This "indexing" or "bracketing" hypothesis has been relatively well documented in terms of the effects that political elites have on the range of views reported in mainstream media. But the impact of indexing on the mass public within those media audiences is less well studied. By simply broadening the range of views

24. Hallin (1984).
25. The use of "indexing" in this context was coined by Bennett (1990).

they present, does media coverage also produce a public with more diverse views? The jury is still out with respect to the impact on the public.

To the extent that this mechanism of polarization holds true, it suggests that perhaps the media critics of the previous generation should have been more careful about what they wished for. In a paradoxical way, longtime critics of the lack of diversity in media and the lack of representation for more extreme voices have seen the change they desired: there is no question that today's media carry a broader range of political perspectives than they did a generation ago. But the very diversity of those same voices may encourage the public to adopt more polar positions—an unforeseen and less desirable consequence of a more vibrant marketplace of political ideas.

In-Your-Face Politics: Gut Reactions to Televised Incivility

"Shout-show" television has been the target of a tremendous amount of criticism from many quarters, academic and otherwise. The world of political disagreement as witnessed through the lens of political talk shows is quite polarized. Increased competition for audiences has led many programs on political topics to liven themselves up in order to increase audience size.[26] Thus, political talk shows such as *The McLaughlin Group, The O'Reilly Factor, Meet the Press, Capital Gang, Hardball,* and many others tend to involve particularly intense and heated exchanges.

The issue of contentiousness and incivility in political discourse was brought to a head in October 2004, when *Daily Show* host Jon Stewart appeared on *Crossfire* and openly criticized this program (and others like it) for its "partisan hackery," which Stewart said was "hurting America." Is there any truth to Stewart's claim? Aside from the obvious distastefulness some find in watching politicians scream, yell, and interrupt one another for thirty minutes or more, how is this kind of in-your-face politics implicated as a potential cause of mass polarization?

The tendency on television is to highlight more emotionally extreme and less polite expressions of opinion, and research suggests that these expressions of incivility may have important consequences for attitudes toward the opposition. These consequences flow from the fact that politeness and civility are more than mere social norms; they are means of demonstrating mutual respect.[27] In other words, uncivil discourse increases polarization by helping partisans think even less of their opponents than they already did.

26. Fallows (1996).
27. This is a point made in Kingwell (1995).

And yet market forces seem to favor the kind of television that encourages polarization. Polarized political discourse and an angry opposition makes for compelling television. Viewers may claim that they find it disgusting, but they cannot help watching—just as passing motorists cannot help "rubbernecking" when there is an accident alongside the highway. It is not that people actually *enjoy* what they are seeing, but there is something about information of this kind—information about life and death, about conflict and warring tribes in a dispute—that makes it difficult to ignore. Evolutionary psychologists have pointed to the adaptive advantage of having brains that automatically pay attention to conflict as a means of staying alive in an earlier era. At a cognitive level, of course, no one really expects to be caught in the "crossfire" of a televised partisan shout-fest. But even when it is "only television," and thus poses no real threat of bodily harm, people cannot help but watch and react to incivility.

My own research suggests that psychologists are correct about the demands of incivility on human attentional processes. To examine the difference that incivility makes independent of political content, I produced a mock political talk show—on a professional television set using professional actors as congressional candidates. The candidates espoused the same issue positions and made exactly the same arguments for and against various issue positions in two different versions of the program. In one discussion, however, they raised their voices, rolled their eyes, and engaged in an impolite, uncivil exchange. In the civil version of the program, they spoke calmly, refrained from interrupting one another, and showed mutual respect simply by obeying the social norms for polite discourse.[28]

The differences in viewer reactions to the two programs were startling. The group randomly assigned to the uncivil version of the political discussion came away with roughly the same feelings toward their preferred candidate as those in the civil group. But attitudes toward the "other side" became much more intensely negative when the two exchanged views in an uncivil manner. The more dramatic, uncivil exchanges encouraged a more black-and-white view of the world: their candidate was not just the best; the alternative was downright evil.

This effect was evident for partisans on both sides of the political spectrum and regardless of which candidate they liked best. Interestingly, watching the uncivil version led to greater polarization in perceptions of "us" versus "them," relative to a control group, but watching the civil version of the exchange led to *decreased* levels of polarization. This pattern of findings suggests that political television has the potential to *improve* as well as to exacerbate the divide among

28. Mutz and Reeves (2005).

partisans of opposing views; it simply depends upon how those differences of opinion are aired. When differences of opinion are conveyed in a manner that suggests mutual respect, viewers are able to understand and process the rationales on the other side and are less likely to see the opposition in starkly negative terms. Differences of opinion are perceived as having some legitimate and reasonable basis. But when those same views and rationales are expressed in an uncivil manner, people respond with an emotional, gut-level reaction, rejecting the opposition as unfairly and viciously attacking one's cherished views.

Using indicators of physiological response, my studies also demonstrate that televised incivility causes viewers' levels of emotional arousal to increase, just as they do when people encounter face-to-face incivility. In the face of real-world conflict, this reaction supposedly serves a functional purpose—participants are given the rush of adrenaline they may need to flee the situation. But with televised incivility, this kind of reaction serves no purpose; it is simply a remnant of brains that have not adapted to twentieth-century representational technology.[29]

Even though viewers are just third-party observers of other people's conflicts on television, they show heightened levels of emotional arousal, just as people do when encountering face-to-face disagreement. This is not so surprising if one considers how it feels to be a third-party observer of a couple's argument at a dinner party. The same discomfort, awkwardness, and tension exist, even for those not directly involved in the conflict. Likewise, when political commentator Robert Novak stormed off the set of a live broadcast of CNN's *Inside Politics* in August 2004, viewers were uncomfortable—and they paid attention. The tension was palpable to viewers, even though few may be able to remember what the substance of the conflict was.

The heightened arousal produced by incivility can make it difficult to process the substance of the exchange. Some arousal helps to call attention to what otherwise might be considered bland and uninteresting. But at extremely high levels of arousal, people will remember only the emotional content of the program (who screamed at whom, who stomped off in a pique) and recall little of the substance of the disagreement. As anyone who has ever had an argument knows, there is a point at which the emotional content of the exchange overwhelms any potential for rational discourse. As a result, viewers gain little understanding of the other side. They perceive their own side of the debate as unfairly attacked, and thus the incivility their own candidate displays is simply an appropriate level of righteous indignation in reaction to an unprovoked attack. The incivility

---

29. Reeves and Nass (1996).

demonstrated by the opponent demonstrates that he is a raving lunatic, wholly unfit for office.

In addition to this disdain for the opposing side, incivility produces a second important reaction—heightened attention. As Bill O'Reilly, host of *The O'Reilly Factor,* suggests, "If a radio producer can find someone who eggs on conservative listeners to spout off and prods liberals into shouting back, he's got a hit show. The best host is the guy or gal who can get the most listeners extremely annoyed—over and over and over again."[30] Evidently, these sorts of shows have hooked Senator Hillary Rodham Clinton (D-N.Y.), who indicated that she and her husband Bill now have TiVo, a technology that allows a viewer to record and replay television programs. And for what purpose do the senator and the former president use TiVo? According to Senator Clinton, they use it to record the most outrageous statements made by their political opponents so they can play them over and over and yell back at the television.[31] An optimist might regard this vignette as an example of how viewers are *not* necessarily selectively exposing themselves to politically compatible media. But the pessimist would undoubtedly point out that yet another media mechanism of polarization has kicked in to take its place. Uncivil political discourse that produces such strong emotional reactions is unlikely to further the cause of political moderation.

Controlled laboratory studies suggest, for better or worse, that O'Reilly is correct: incivility is extremely entertaining and people like to watch it, even if it is just to scream back. Despite the fact that many viewers claim to be repulsed by it, the respondents who viewed the identical but uncivil version of the same program always rated it as more entertaining, found it more exciting to watch, and indicated a greater desire to see the uncivil program again than the civil version.[32] Polite conversation is boring, and the deliberative ideal for political discourse makes for dull television. "I acknowledge there are some good points on my opponent's side" will probably never make good television, whereas "These evil people must be stopped!" always will.

With these findings in mind, it is important to consider the extent to which the rise of televised political incivility can help explain mass polarization. Is political discourse truly any more uncivil now than in the past? Some have suggested that the United States is in the midst of a "civility crisis" in its public life.

30. O'Reilly (2000, p. 52).
31. Senator Hillary Rodham Clinton, speech at the Doherty-Granoff Forum on Women Leaders, Brown University, April 8, 2006.
32. Mutz and Reeves (2005).

As then University of Pennsylvania president Judith Rodin argued in 1996, "Across America and increasingly around the world, from campuses to the halls of Congress, to talk radio and network TV, social and political life seem dominated today by incivility. . . . No one seems to question the premise that political debate has become too extreme, too confrontational, too coarse."[33] Similar calls for greater civility in political discourse have come from a wide array of scholars, as well as from philanthropic organizations.

Some scholars concur that incivility is on the rise. Political scientist Eric M. Uslaner, for example, has suggested that members of Congress are increasingly likely to violate norms of politeness in their discourse.[34] Linguist Deborah Tannen has characterized the United States as having "a culture of argument" that encourages "a pervasive warlike atmosphere" for resolving differences of opinion.[35] Even journalists concur that "hyperbole and venomous invective have become the order of the day" in American politics.[36]

Clearly, there is a widespread perception that political discourse is much more uncivil now than in the past, but there is little historical evidence to confirm such a trend. As then senator Zell Miller (D-Ga.) implied when he wistfully said he would like to challenge *Hardball* host Chris Matthews to a duel, violence among political opponents was once far more common than it is now. Senator Miller's statement was made during an uncivil exchange between himself and a journalist during the 2004 Republican National Convention. It made headlines, precisely because the idea of using weapons to resolve political differences seemed absurd. We have not had a duel to the death among politicians for many years, and thus one could easily characterize today's political talk shows as mild by comparison.

So is it fair to say that incivility is on the rise in political discourse? There is no definitive answer to this question, but the increased *visibility* of uncivil conflicts on television seems indisputable. Although politicians of past eras may frequently have exchanged harsh words, without television cameras there to record these events and to replay them for a mass audience their impact on public perceptions was probably substantially lower. The dominance of television as a source of exposure to politics suggests that public exposure to uncivil political discourse has

33. Judith Rodin, speech at the Penn National Commission on Society, Culture, and Community, December 9, 1996 (www.upenn.edu/pnc/pubkeynote.html).

34. Uslaner (1993).

35. Tannen (1998).

36. Michiko Kakutani, "Polarization of National Dialogue Mirrors Extremists of Left and Right," *New York Times,* November 26, 2000.

increased. Moreover, it is one thing to read about political pundits' or candidates' contrary views in the press, and quite another to witness them directly engaged in vituperative argument. The sensory realism of television conveys a sense of intimacy with political actors that people were unlikely to encounter in the past, even among the few lucky enough to have face-to-face meetings.

Television provides a uniquely intimate perspective on conflict. In the literature on human proxemics, the distance deemed appropriate for face-to-face interactions with public figures in American culture is more than twelve feet.[37] Yet exposure to politicians on television gives the appearance of being much closer. When people are arguing, the tendency is to back off and put greater space between those who disagree. Instead, when political conflicts flare up on television, cameras tend to go in for tighter and tighter close-ups. This creates an intense experience for the viewers, one in which they view conflict from an unusually intimate perspective. Political scientist Jane J. Mansbridge has noted that when open political conflict occurs in real life, bringing people together in one another's presence can intensify their anger and aggression.[38] To the extent that a television presence has similar effects, incivility is likely to encourage polarization.

What Are the Prospects?

In thinking about the prospects for the future, it is useful to consider separately and collectively the four mechanisms by which the media may be involved in the polarization of the mass public. Two of these mechanisms, discouraging losers' consent and bracketing the range of acceptable opinion, are driven by the content of news media. In one case, journalists' game-centric coverage of campaigns is implicated, and in the other, the diversity of political voices affects the range of mass opinion. The other two mechanisms are driven more or less by technological change. Because of the proliferation of channels on cable television, along with the development of the Internet, most Americans have access to more partisan political voices than they ever did before. Whether through partisan-based selective exposure, or through selective avoidance of political content altogether, the distribution of opinion in the electorate has changed. Finally, the ability of television to present an unnatural "in-your-face" perspective on politicians may have further increased levels of vitriol directed toward the opposition.

37. Aiello (1987).
38. Mansbridge (1983).

How likely is it that these processes will change? Theoretically, the mechanisms based on media content could become less tenable if journalistic norms were to change. For example, if not only *Crossfire* were taken off the air, but also every other uncivil shout-fest show that involves politics, then one could see how this polarizing mechanism might abate in significance. Likewise, if campaign coverage were to shift away from its predominantly strategic angle and focus instead on taking political statements at face value, one could imagine losers who would be less angry about the opposition's victory, particularly if it were deemed to result from legitimate differences of opinion. There are several problems with such proposed changes, of course. Even if they were possible to implement (which they are not), it seems unlikely that they would offer tenable solutions or even modest improvements on the current situation.

News is commerce, to be sure. What all four of the mechanisms described in this chapter share is a tension between drawing viewers, readers, and listeners to political media, and producing media content that does not encourage polarized political perspectives. The goal of niche marketing and the extent of choice is to give viewers more of what they want, but not necessarily more of what they need. Likewise, the game-centric, campaign-oriented journalism that is so common today exists because viewers and readers find such discussions of interest. The greater publicity that extreme views now receive probably also helps draw larger audiences. It is far more dramatic to show starkly opposed foes engaged in battle than to illustrate the political world with two moderates calmly discussing their small differences. If it were not for the need to make politics more interesting for marginally politically involved viewers, then it is doubtful that there would be a need for confrontational shout shows to exist either.

Moreover, any changes to media content designed to alleviate the impact of one of these mechanisms are likely to replace one mechanism of media polarization with another. Take, for example, the incivility that is so prevalent in political talk shows. What would happen if producers were to tone down these programs so that levels of civility approached the norms of everyday people in their social interactions? On the one hand, viewers would not have the chance to intensify their dislike for the opposition by viewing uncivil repartee. But on the other hand, in-your-face incivility is precisely what people like about these shows. In study after study, even those who responded negatively to incivility reported that the uncivil shows were more interesting and exciting to watch. Those exposed to the civil versions of the same show were far less likely to indicate any interest in seeing it again or in watching it regularly. As a result, in a hypothetical era of civil political television, those viewers would be unlikely to watch at all.

They would fall into the category of viewers that Prior refers to as "switchers"—people who would switch to entertainment when given a choice—and thus fall out of the reach of political information altogether.

Three general approaches to improving this situation are possible. The first is to push for less commercial pressure. In *Breaking the News,* James Fallows excoriates his fellow journalists for turning news coverage into more of an effort to entertain than to edify. He faults the focus of media companies on their bottom lines as the source of the corruption of news.[39] From a broader perspective, however, it seems too facile to claim that the commercial interests of U.S. media companies are to blame. What Fallows misses is that even if all political content were government-funded, the lack of commercial pressures would not alleviate the need to attract audiences to political content. In order to do good or harm, political news must have large audiences; high-minded programs with small audiences are hardly better than no programs at all.

A second, equally fruitless, approach has been to wag fingers accusingly at the civically bankrupt American public. Why is it, many ask, that Americans do not take their civic duty more seriously and educate themselves on political issues?

A third option is to change the shape of political media so that they can draw audiences without inadvertently polarizing the public. Traditional television news programs are in a state of turmoil these days over which direction to take. Do they reinvent themselves to become more like entertainment programs and vie for audiences on the edge of political interest? Or do they take the so-called high road and remain serious and hard-hitting? The problem with the high road is that even if it leads to critical acclaim and journalistic respect, it is unlikely to draw in the politically marginal audiences who prefer to watch entertainment. By many normative accounts, doing the "right thing" would result in precisely the wrong effect—further chipping away at the proportion of Americans who expose themselves to politically relevant television content.

In a 2005 interview, CBS chairman Leslie Moonves indicated just how drastically he thinks traditional news broadcasts must be revamped in order to increase audiences and survive. "We have to break the mold," he stated. The alternatives Moonves has considered include mold-breaking formats ranging from the comedy of Jon Stewart's mock news program, *The Daily Show,* to the zany humor of England's *The Big Breakfast,* to Canada's *Naked News,* during which anchors present a newscast while doing a striptease.[40]

39. Fallows (1996).
40. Lynn Hirschberg, "Giving Them What They Want," *New York Times Magazine,* September 4, 2005.

These solutions—comedy and sex—are only two of many possible alternative attention-generating mechanisms. But those pursuing the solution need to move away from the premise that commercial pressures alone are responsible and realize that this is a problem that has been faced before, albeit in very different contexts. Children's television, for example, was once widely bemoaned as antisocial in its consequences. Kids were particularly drawn to highly arousing, violent programs—precisely the kind of content most feared by parents. Yet through collaborations with researchers, organizations such as the Children's Television Workshop were able to draw on knowledge of human behavior to come up with alternative means of grabbing children's attention. The early evidence on entertainment-oriented news programs is promising in demonstrating that audiences do learn something about politics from their content.[41] While it is not unreasonable to be optimistic that answers will be found, it seems foolhardy at this point to try to predict the future of political media.

The underlying question that still needs to be confronted—by scholars as well as those in the media business—is how to make a topic that is not inherently interesting to many Americans nonetheless exciting to watch. And if the answer is not behind-the-scenes coverage of election strategy, or mudslinging on political talk shows, or partisan extremists rallying the troops, then what will keep those politically marginal citizens from watching movies on cable instead?

41. Baum (2003).

Two Alternative Perspectives

COMMENT

Thomas Rosenstiel

How much do the news media contribute to political polarization? The question might be restated in more basic terms this way: to what extent do the media reflect the political culture versus shape it? In her cogent essay, Diana C. Mutz thoughtfully outlines four major contemporary theories about the influence of mass media in political polarization. In what follows, I will note where I think some of these theoretical arguments are stronger or weaker, and where changes in media usage not captured yet by academic research might suggest further study.

The four primary theories Mutz outlines do not require long repetition here. The first deals with the impact of increased media fragmentation or consumer choice. The second deals with the impact of having opposing views vilified. The third concerns the role of the media in amplifying the increasingly polarized views of political elites. The fourth, from Mutz's own research, focuses on the impact of people's reactions to the more polarized style of presentation on television. Mutz takes a measured view in assessing each theory, not swallowing any of it whole. But without dismissing the effect of the media on increasing polarization out of hand, I would argue that the impact may be more muted, or at least contradictory, than even she would suggest.

The first theory deals with the idea that media fragmentation may intensify polarization. If consumers have more choice about which media to choose, they will spend greater amounts of time with more ideological media (Rush Limbaugh or Al Franken), and also devote more time to infotainment and diversion (the pop-culture news of E! Entertainment Television). That much is hard to differ with. People have finite amounts of time—and the more time they devote to offerings such as these, the less they will have to devote to more moderated traditional mainstream media, where citizens may be more likely to be exposed to the best arguments from both sides of major political issues.

The theory of cognitive dissonance—that people want to avoid information that challenges or confuses their preexisting beliefs—also applies well. When information is in oversupply, knowledge becomes harder to create. One has to sift through more material to know how to feel and think about issues. The polarized media create shortcuts that allow people to do that. Mutz deals nicely with the limits of these pressures, but she also suggests that the momentum will increase and perhaps even topple the dominant American model of an independent press: "The availability of openly partisan television programs, radio shows, and websites," Mutz writes, "may mean that the pattern of U.S. news consumption will more closely approximate that of British newspapers in the not-so-distant future . . . along the lines of a niche market based on partisanship."

Here, I think, things can be taken too far. It is fashionable among media watchers trying to spot trends and draw lines into the future to imagine the end of the nonpartisan press model that has dominated—but never exclusively defined—American media since the mid-nineteenth century. (The country's first nonpartisan newspaper, the *New York Sun,* was founded by Benjamin Day in the 1830s.) Several factors mitigate against the partisan model gaining force or dominating in the United States. The first is that advertising is a far more important part of the revenue of American media than of European. As an example, roughly 80 percent of the revenue of American newspapers is from advertising, and only 20 percent from circulation.[1] The reverse is generally true in England.

Even in the age of targeted media, major advertisers (such as car manufacturers and other mass consumer product manufacturers) want the largest and most credible platform they can find. In the age of fragmentation, these advertisers are willing to pay a premium for those few remaining media malls where they can efficiently reach large groups. The vast majority of media outlets in the United States garnering the largest audiences remain nonpartisan and nonideological for just that reason. Even Rupert Murdoch, who owns Fox News on cable, does not pursue an ideological approach with his local TV stations. It would not be good for business.

A second factor working against the ideological fragmentation of U.S. media is geography. The European press model involves a handful of national newspapers and media outlets competing for audiences large enough that they can carve them up into ideological slices. In the United States, all but three of the country's 1,450 newspapers are local or metropolitan.[2] There is no sensible economic rationale for them to divide their audience by pursuing an ideological approach and becoming more polarized. The same is true even for the roughly 600 local TV stations that produce some news and public affairs programming—at least while their revenue base is major advertisers such as General Motors and Wal-Mart, companies that want to reach everyone.

---

1. Project for Excellence in Journalism (2006).
2. The three newspapers are the *New York Times,* the *Wall Street Journal,* and *USA Today.*

The third factor arguing against complete polarization is political. The European press model tends to flourish more in parliamentary multiparty settings. The American model flourishes in a more amalgamated two-party presidential system, in which people reside uneasily in large political parties and may cross party lines when voting. If anything, this has increased in the past three decades. Today, voters are divided roughly equally: a third independent, a third Democrat, and a third Republican.[3] Where do those independents or uneasy partisans go for media representation?

Finally, the data suggest that consumers no longer rely on single sources for their primary media consumption. They dine each day at a diverse media buffet, one that includes a little talk radio, a little cable news, some local TV, and perhaps some print news, websites, and other sources. The menu changes from day to day. This can be easily seen in polling data, which show that "regular" consumers of media overlap by sector—newspapers, network, local, cable, etc.[4] But it is also apparent in virtually every public talk I give when I ask people where they get their news throughout the day. It has been years since someone said he or she got it from only one source. Mainstream nonideological media remain a part of virtually everyone's diet. It may be the radio news summary from CBS that comes on before *The Rush Limbaugh Show*. It may be the rip-and-read headlines on Fox before *The O'Reilly Factor*. It may be the Associated Press and Reuters stories that appear on thousands of websites, from aggregators such as Google and Yahoo! to the many commercial websites on which news and headlines have become standard features. It may be the news headlines people receive on their phones and PDAs.

The news—that is, the reporting of original information about new and breaking events—still rests solidly on the old independent press model, only now it coexists alongside an emerging partisan media. For now and the foreseeable future, however, those emerging ideological media remain limited to a few platforms. Cable news has two channels that are now, in audience profile, broken down along ideological lines. (CNN's audience is dominated by Democrats, while Fox News is more Republican.) Talk radio as a medium has a heavily conservative audience. But the audience for local TV news is ideologically balanced. The same is true for network news and newspapers. Even on the Internet, the dominant websites for news (MSNBC, CNN, AOL, and Yahoo!) are

3. Pew Research Center for the People and the Press, "2004 Political Landscape: Evenly Divided and Increasingly Polarized," November 5, 2003 (people-press.org/reports/display.php3? ReportID=196).

4. See Project for Excellence in Journalism (2006).

nonideological. Blogs are a much more fragmented, and supplemental, part of that environment. Despite what is fashionable to imagine, the independent press is alive and well.

This smorgasbord style of information consumption also works against the idea that the incidental acquisition of knowledge is going to precipitously decline, and with it the participation and engagement of those only casually political. While the studies are inconclusive, the most persuasive case is that, with the arrival of e-mail and the Internet, incidental knowledge is on the rise. Nor can we establish that moderates are not turning out to vote. Recent elections suggest that, with more polarized turnout, more people are voting. We do not really know whether that is because moderates stayed home while more polarized voters turned out in greater numbers, or whether moderates themselves have become more polarized. And if moderates did become more polarized, was that attributable to the media or was it the reality of political events, particularly the leadership style of President Bush and the events on the ground in Iraq?

The second theory of media polarization is that the game-theory approach of so much political coverage today makes the losers in elections feel their defeat is illegitimate because it was not their ideas that lost, but inferior political technique that cost them the election. There is little doubt that this critique of campaign coverage is correct. And liberals' anger over the losses to Ronald Reagan and George W. Bush certainly explains their slowness to accept the argument that the country has moved to the right. But it is hardly a proven fact that voter anger or the perceived illegitimacy of political leaders is greater today than at other times in the past. We cannot establish whether this is any different in character from how quickly conservatives came to acknowledge that the country had shifted to the left from 1932 to 1968, or how they accepted the presidency of "That Man Roosevelt" in four elections. Andrew Jackson was certainly more bitter about winning the popular vote and losing the presidency in the early nineteenth century than Al Gore was in the early twenty-first.

But there is one thing on the other side of this ledger we can say with greater confidence. The influence of the mainstream media in framing campaigns as horse races or clashes of political technicians—a phenomenon that Harvard's Thomas E. Patterson found with increasing prevalence from the 1960s to the early 1990s—has been diminishing. If people have more sources of information, the framing of the mainstream media becomes less consequential as people add other sources to their mix and spend less time with the mainstream media.

The third theory Mutz outlines is that the media might further polarize politics through their role in framing the range of legitimate or acceptable opinions the public may adopt. There are doubts here, however, worth considering. First, the same issue of waning influence of mainstream media that undermines the impact of horse-race coverage applies here, as well. If Americans are getting information from many other sources beyond the mainstream press, fragmentation should be expanding the spectrum. Indeed, the arguments that fragmentation is increasing polarization appear to contradict the arguments about the influence of the press in polarizing the public by legitimizing the more extreme views of political leaders.

This brings us to the last theory Mutz outlines—about the appeal of staging political debate on television in an extreme style. Much of this is based on Mutz's own research examining audience reactions to in-your-face TV talk shows. Her findings—that people are more likely to be stimulated by the entertainment value of these shows, but less likely to absorb the ideas of politics from them—seems persuasive and intuitively correct. Those who appear on these programs often complain that people, even their friends, never seem to recall what was said.

There are reasons, however, to believe that this style of TV presentation may be beginning to wane. I believe that what linguist Deborah Tannen dubbed the "argument culture" of the 1990s is subtly giving way to what we might call the "opinion culture" of the new century. In opinion culture media, there is no longer an argument; the host or moderator is offering answers, not staging an unruly debate. It is the difference, say, between *Crossfire,* which staged debates from both sides, and *The O'Reilly Factor,* in which host Bill O'Reilly tells viewers how to think about matters. On *O'Reilly,* the other side of the argument is a straw man, not something given equal weight. Even some of the talk shows of the new age that do offer arguments are less of a balanced battle than *Crossfire* or *The McLaughlin Group* might have seemed in their heydays. Fox's *Hannity & Colmes* is a talk show in that more classic sense. But the two hosts do not bring on two combatants to have at it. Instead, they tend to interview one guest from one side of the political spectrum or the other. And Fox's viewers, who skew conservative, are probably more likely to think that the handsome and hulky Sean Hannity is more persuasive than his liberal cohost, the less physically imposing or intellectually decisive Alan Colmes.

What is going on here? I believe that the appeal of the new opinion culture is that it is helping people make order of things. In the minds of their audiences, Limbaugh, O'Reilly, Franken, and even, in a less direct way, comedians Jon Stewart and Stephen Colbert, are offering knowledge creation. They are helping people put things in place. They are helping people know how to feel and think about issues. People have, or think they have, enough information. What they want is for someone to help them clarify matters, to feel more sure of things.

The O'Reilly or Limbaugh style of presentation itself is less polarizing (in the direct sense of staging an argument) than it is analytical or interpretative. It is less about game theory and more about ideas. Some may dismiss those ideas as mere talking points from one side or the other. They may even long for the more evenhanded, if hyperventilated, style of *Crossfire*. But therein lies the problem. Are we better off as a society with Bill O'Reilly and Keith Olbermann denouncing each other and carrying on a feud across their own programs on different channels? Or would it be better if they were on the same program screaming at each other face to face?

That, in other words, is the modern way of asking whether the new media culture is becoming more polarizing than what it replaced. But in the end that is probably the wrong question. Most likely, as is the case with most media effects, the impact of this shift will cut in different directions. Are the media adding to polarization or merely reflecting it? Or are the new media in some cases even offering a mitigating reaction to it? The answer to each of these questions is yes. It's a big country, with lots of different kinds of people using each of these media outlets in different ways for different kinds of news. All three things are likely occurring at the same time.

The one shift that seems clearest is that the changes in the media culture are shifting power. Influence is moving from the media producers as mediators and gatekeepers to citizens functioning as their own editors. And citizens are having to change from merely passive consumers of media to pro-active assemblers of their own media diet each day. In the hands of some citizens, this may mean becoming more informed, and going deeper into subjects, than they ever could before. In other cases, it may mean making new connections across interdisciplinary or traditional intellectual lines, and forging new intellectual and ideological alliances beyond anything that would have been set up by party or activist elites.

In the new media environment (or perhaps better understood as the new media options), one can imagine the emergence of, say, family-values-oriented green conservatives—a group interested in home schooling and environmental activism, religious politics, and bigger government. That is something that would not happen if communication were still coming down from elite structures. In the hands of other citizens, the new media environment may mean a further slide into diversion and infotainment. For still others, it may mean a hardening of political isolation and aggrievement. The new media environment will enable all three. Culture and human nature will dictate which way different people will go.

Do the media reflect political culture or shape it? The answer: You bet.

COMMENT

Gregg Easterbrook

"If the smorgasbord of views offered in today's media represents greater extremes than in the past, then it is perhaps not surprising that more of the public now endorses more extreme views," writes communications scholar Diana C. Mutz. To which my reaction is: if the media are encouraging polarization, then we should expect polarization to decline! I would like to believe the public reliably does the reverse of whatever the mainstream media try to push the public to do. If only it were that simple, of course.

Mutz's chapter provides many statistically solid—and culturally discouraging—reasons to think that media polarization is harming the body politic. Her demonstration that extremists are increasingly likely to vote while centrists are less likely to do so, partly because centrism is ignored by the media, is disturbing. So is her demonstration that, as television viewing habits shift away from news programs toward entertainment and sports, people who were already less politically engaged become even less likely to vote.

Here is how I think it would go if Professor Mutz attempted to explain her conclusions on one of the "shout-fest" political shows she deplores. Let's call it *The Decibel Factor:*

HOST: Today we have Professor Diana Mutz, who says she can scientifically prove that media polarization is bad for America. Also in the studio is Ann Cutthroat, author of the new bestseller *Bring Back Lynching,* and filmmaker Michael Blimp, whose fabricated docudrama *Heil Cheney!* opens everywhere this weekend. Professor Mutz, please explain your thesis.

DIANA MUTZ: Well, my research shows . . .

ANN CUTTHROAT: Your research comes from Moscow! I hope your pal Kim Jung-il fires his next missile at traitors like you and your gay lover Howard Dean.

MUTZ: If you'd let me explain . . .

MICHAEL BLIMP: Bush apologist! There's nothing to "explain." Everybody knows this is a war for oil. Admit it, this is a war for oil!

MUTZ: My study says nothing about . . .

HOST: We interrupt for breaking news. We're taking you to New York, where we have exclusive video of Angelina Jolie hailing a cab.

Mutz makes many important points, and they should be of keen interest to readers because she ranks among the best and most original scholars on media analysis. Still, there are reasons to be skeptical of the polarization hypothesis—and not just because "'twas ever thus." I will outline a few points of skepticism, and then suggest why, even if it is true that the media cause polarization, we must learn to live with it.

First, my suspicion is that a lot of what looks like rising polarization is actually society becoming more opinionated. A generation ago, it was considered by many to be good manners to avoid expressing strong opinions, especially regarding politics and religion, while the media restricted opinion to quotations from experts and to clearly labeled editorial pages. In recent decades, such restraints have been weakened—or even reversed. A generation ago, schoolteachers would have discouraged pupils from expressing opinions. Now they hector them if they do not. Spin and slant have spread from the editorial pages to most arenas of journalism, print and electronic. We not only expect talking heads on television to have instant opinions on anything and everything, we also expect the man on the street to have strongly felt opinions on any topic raised. This opinionization of America may be good or bad—but I see it mainly as a fad. Try thinking of it in economic terms: as opinions get ever cheaper, we produce more of them!

Next, though high-level political and media discourse in the United States has become more divisive (as Mutz points out), this has not translated into social discord. Quite the contrary, in fact. Today, discrimination based on race, gender, religion, or ethnicity is the lowest it has ever been. It is considered shameful to discriminate in the United States today—and this is a broadly shared view, held even by most traditionalists and conservatives. Americans may be denouncing each other in the electronic square, but in the real public square they are getting along better than ever before, at least as measured by rising tolerance and declining discrimination. In the United States of 1950, the media were highly restrained and unfailingly polite, while ugly prejudice permeated the social interaction of Americans. Compared with that alternative, today's polarized media but tolerant society are a pretty good bargain.

Third, it may be not far off the mark to guess that there is a relationship between rising tolerance in daily life coupled to expressions of intolerance in politics and media. Negative feelings require outlets. Better that Americans should be considerate of each other in their personal dealings and then rant on impersonal blogs or talk shows than the many possible alternatives.

Even considering these factors, the intensity of the anger level in American politics is puzzling given that we live in a time when nearly all national trends are positive, resources are plentiful, real-dollar prices are falling, unemployment is low, tolerance is rising, the necessities of life are in oversupply, and the country's future seems bright. Be that as it may, what can be done about polarization in the American media? Practically nothing.

The primary reason why we have no choice but to live with media polarization is the First Amendment. The First Amendment is absolute and was designed to be absolute: the views, slants, and story choices presented on television and radio and in newspapers and magazines are not subject to regulation. If television networks want to air a steady diet of red-faced partisans wagging their fingers, and if newspapers want to bury serious public policy stories while giving front-page play to extremists hurling accusations, the Constitution forbids government to interfere. The First Amendment bargain was always that law must shield stupid speech in order to safeguard significant speech. The polarized coverage many news organizations now present is the price we pay, in constitutional terms, for the assurance that the next Pentagon Papers will be published.

Even if the Constitution forbids formal government influence on news coverage, public officials can still jawbone editors and media executives about their reporting. This happens all the time—and it appears to have almost no effect. Elected officials frequently denounce the news media as biased, or call on editors and producers to become more responsible and civic-minded. (Of course, when politicians decry "media bias," what they often mean is "stop running articles about my fundraising violations.") During the 1990s there was a movement to encourage news organizations to practice "public journalism" or "civic journalism," loosely defined as more coverage of average people and less of celebrities and politicians, more coverage of reforms that succeed and programs that work and less fixation on gaffes and screw-ups. Public journalism sounded great, yet was embraced by few news organizations—partly because reporters enjoy covering celebrities, gaffes and screw-ups, while having little interest in average people or programs that work.

Consumers of news also seem to prefer the sort of stories the media present. The cliché that bad news sells is among the bulwarks of the communications business for good reason. To a point, bad news ought to sell: negative information (government corruption, crime, security threats) is often that which the public most urgently needs to hear. Beyond this, stories about sex, shocking outrages, and disgraceful scandals are simply more attention-grabbing than stories about ordinary people or smoothly run programs. When it comes to polarization, this dynamic clearly applies: a story about two angry opposing camps condemning each other is more likely to draw attention than a story about how some problem was solved after a meeting of the minds.

Consider this question: if there were a publication called *Consensus Today,* would anyone buy it? The current edition of *Consensus Today* might have page-one articles on how air pollution in Los Angeles has declined to a tiny fraction of its 1950s level, thanks to cooperation among activists, industry, and regulators; on reforms that allowed New York City to transform from a murder capital into one of the world's safest cities; and on volunteer work and charitable giving running at all-time highs. But if *Consensus Today* were sitting on the newsstand next to any mainstream newspaper with headlines about explosions, scandals, and Hollywood divorce, which one would the typical reader reach for? There is a real publication along the lines of my fictional one: *Positive News,* published in the United Kingdom. *Positive News* is not a Pollyanna sheet. Its reporting focuses on community-based reform initiatives that have been successful, and the lessons that can be learned from those successes. *Positive News* thus covers a news category utterly ignored by the mainstream media. And because it has so few subscribers, it is published only quarterly.

This alludes to another reason why polarization in the media may be unstoppable—market forces favor it. Back when most major cities had competing dailies, newspapers were more polarized than today. When hawkers rather than home delivery were the key to sales, dailies competed for the most eye-catching banner headlines. Exaggeration and wild charges were common on the front page. Today most cities have a single dominant daily, and the front pages of newspapers have calmed down and professionalized. The exception is New York, which is the last American city that still has hawker-based newspaper wars—and the *Daily News* and *Post* wage a daily competition for the most outrageous front page.

As newspapers have become a mature, contracting industry, there has been explosive growth in television, Internet, and radio communication. And what do we observe in all three categories? Polarization—because it is favored by market forces as a way to stand out from the crowd. CNN appeared to have the cable news market to itself until Fox News differentiated itself from CNN's liberal-establishment worldview with a conservative slant and polarizing figures such as Bill O'Reilly. In the Internet realm, polarization is equally essential to carving out an audience. Most of the popular blogs and commentary sites of the moment have strong ideological slants and are devoted to denouncing opponents, real or imagined, from DailyKos on the left to FreeRepublic on the right. Imagine a website about the things we can all agree on, and you have imagined a website that no venture capitalist will underwrite.

Market forces favor media polarization in still other ways, including technical ones. Increasingly, cable news and local news stations monitor each other's broadcasts and switch to the competitor's topic if it appears to be more racy or confrontational. Ubiquitous remote control makes it easier for users to push this process along. Once, viewers chose a channel and left it there; now they channel-surf, looking for something that catches the eye. If Fox News is showing helicopters above a burning building and MSNBC is broadcasting a speech to the United Nations, which will draw the surfers? If one news channel shows angry zealots enraged at each other's comments, while on another the anchor says, "Now two experts from the Brookings Institution will debate infrastructure renewal," who is going to get the audience?

Is seems likely that market forces will continue to exert pressure for media polarization. One of the reasons American media have grown more polarized is that we have developed ever better techniques that cause this result: polling, focus groups, zip code analysis. In the past three decades, technological advances, especially in inexpensive electronics, have tended to make it more practical for news organizations to tailor content to what they think readers and viewers want. Of course, market forces sometimes also pressure news organizations to improve. Market forces aided the professionalization of the newspaper business. The news pages of today's major dailies are widely perceived to be more accurate and thorough than a generation ago. This is so partly because readers have chosen high-quality newspapers over low-quality ones, but also because major advertisers have pressured newspapers to improve their accuracy. Thus, market forces do not always push news organizations in the direction of greater polarization. But if market forces decide to favor polarization, that is the market's choice to make.

Bear in mind that the same market forces and technical advances that promote polarization also foster variety, diversity, and democratization. Think back to forty years ago, a time some might characterize as a golden age for the media because per capita newspaper readership was higher and there was never any shouting on television news programs. Mutz notes that 80 percent of American families who watched the news then were watching the major networks, versus less than a third today. But in that golden age, if you wanted televised national news, the dinner hour was the only time to get it. There was no on-demand access to national and international news via twenty-four-hour news channels on cable, nor were there twenty-four-hour local news channels, as many major cities now have.

If you wanted newspaper news forty years ago, there were competing morning and afternoon dailies. But if you did not like the local dailies, you were out of luck. Your only option for getting an out-of-town newspaper was to take out a mail subscription, which was expensive and slow. Today, if you don't like the local paper you can read online—often at no cost—the *New York Times, Los Angeles Times, Chicago Tribune, The Guardian, Le Soir, Bangkok Post, Pakistan Times, Pravda,* and hundreds of others. Many are available in multiple languages— *Pravda* may be read in Russian or English, for example. Most days I check the *Buffalo News* for news about my hometown and the *Colorado Springs Gazette* for news about my college town. When Hurricane Katrina hit New Orleans in August 2005, I pointed my browser to the *New Orleans Times-Picayune*'s website to get unfiltered news directly from the scene. The price of Internet access is less than it would have cost to subscribe to a single mail-delivery daily a generation ago.

Forty years ago, the *Atlantic Monthly* and the *New Yorker,* plus other serious publications, would have come to the educated person's home. Serious magazines are much less prominent today. But on the other hand, most Americans do have access to the Internet, and this provides them with access to many of the serious and scholarly articles published worldwide. All Internet users also have access to the world's millions of blogs. Blogs may pull up considerably short of literature, but they allow typical readers far more access to a range of opinions and serious writing than typical readers of a generation ago.

We may not like any of this; we may wish to return to the era of the *Huntley-Brinkley Report;* but market forces and technical advances are two unguided missiles of a free society. But would you really trade the news media of 2006 for that of 1966? Maddening as today's shout shows may be, today's news readers, listeners, and viewers are significantly better served than their counterparts of generations past. The same technical innovations and market forces that increase polarization have also been central to the vast improvement of media service to the public.

References

Aiello, John R. 1987. "Human Spatial Behavior." In *Handbook of Environmental Psychology*, edited by Daniel Stokols and Irwin Altman, pp. 359–504. New York: John Wiley & Sons.

Anderson, Christopher J., and others. 2005. *Losers' Consent: Elections and Democratic Legitimacy*. New York: Oxford University Press.

Barker, David. 2002. *Rushed to Judgment: Talk Radio, Persuasion, and American Political Behavior*. Columbia University Press.

Bartels, Larry M. 2002. "Beyond the Running Tally: Partisan Bias in Political Perceptions." *Political Behavior* 24 (2): 117–50.

Baum, Matthew A. 2003. *Soft News Goes to War: Public Opinion and American Foreign Policy in the New Media Age*. Princeton University Press.

Baum, Matthew A., and Samuel Kernell. 1999. "Has Cable Ended the Golden Age of Presidential Television?" *American Political Science Review* 93 (1): 99–114.

Bennett, W. Lance. 1990. "Toward a Theory of Press-State Relations in the United States." *Journal of Communication* 40 (2): 103–27.

Bimber, Bruce, and Richard Davis. 2003. *Campaigning Online: The Internet in U.S. Elections*. Oxford University Press.

Cappella, Joseph N., Joseph Turow, and Kathleen Hall Jamieson. 1996. "Call-in Political Talk Radio: Background, Content, Audiences, Portrayal in Mainstream Media." Annenberg Public Policy Center, University of Pennsylvania.

Fallows, James. 1996. *Breaking the News: How the Media Undermine American Democracy*. New York: Pantheon.

Festinger, Leon. 1957. *Theory of Cognitive Dissonance*. Stanford University Press.

Gerber, Alan, and Donald Green. 1999. "Misperceptions about Perceptual Bias." In *Annual Review of Political Science*, Vol. 2, edited by Nelson W. Polsby, pp. 189–210. Palo Alto, Calif.: Annual Reviews.

Hallin, Daniel C. 1984. "The Media, the War in Vietnam, and Political Support: A Critique of the Thesis of an Oppositional Media." *Journal of Politics* 46 (1): 2–24.

Hart, Roderick. 1999. *Seducing America: How Television Charms the Modern Voter*. Thousand Oaks, Calif.: Sage.

Hershey, Marjorie Randon. 1992. "The Constructed Explanation: Interpreting Election Results in the 1984 Presidential Race." *Journal of Politics* 54: 943–76.

Kingwell, Mark. 1995. *A Civil Tongue: Justice, Dialogue and the Politics of Pluralism*. Pennsylvania State University Press.

Lazarsfeld, Paul, Bernard Berelson, and Hazel Gaudet. 1948. *The People's Choice: How the Voter Makes Up His Mind in a Presidential Campaign*. Columbia University Press.

Mansbridge, Jane J. 1983. *Beyond Adversary Democracy*. Chicago: University of Chicago Press.

Mutz, Diana C., 1993. "Deriving Meaning from Election Outcomes." Paper prepared for the annual meeting of the American Association for Public Opinion Research.

Mutz, Diana C., and Byron Reeves. 2005. "The New Videomalaise: Effects of Televised Incivility on Political Trust." *American Political Science Review* 99 (1): 1–15.

Mutz, Diana C., and Paul S. Martin. 2001. "Facilitating Communication across Lines of Political Difference: The Role of Mass Media." *American Political Science Review* 95 (1): 97–114.

O'Reilly, Bill. 2000. *The O'Reilly Factor: The Good, the Bad, and the Completely Ridiculous in American Life*. New York: Broadway Books.

Patterson, Thomas E. 1993. *Out of Order*. New York: Alfred A. Knopf.

Prior, Markus. Forthcoming 2007. *How Media Choice Changes Politics*. Cambridge University Press.

Project for Excellence in Journalism. 2006. *The State of the News Media 2006: An Annual Report on American Journalism.* Washington.

Reeves, Byron, and Clifford Nass. 1996. *The Media Equation: How People Treat Computers, Television, and New Media Like Real People and Places.* Cambridge University Press.

Sears, David O., and Jonathan L. Freedman. 1967. "Selective Exposure to Information: A Critical Review." *Public Opinion Quarterly* 31 (2): 194–213.

Sigelman, Lee, and David Bullock. 1991. "Candidates, Issues, Horse Races and Hoopla: Presidential Campaign Coverage, 1888–1988." *American Politics Quarterly* 19 (1): 5–32.

Sunstein, Cass. 2001. *Republic.com.* Princeton University Press.

———. 2002. "The Law of Group Polarization," *Journal of Political Philosophy* 10 (2): 175–95.

Tannen, Deborah. 1998. *The Argument Culture: Moving from Debate to Dialogue.* New York: Random House.

Uslaner, Eric M. 1993. *The Decline of Comity in Congress.* University of Michigan Press.

6

Polarizing the House of Representatives: How Much Does Gerrymandering Matter?

Thomas E. Mann

Whatever the disputes about its historical uniqueness, reach, causes, consequences, and correctives, partisan polarization is undeniably a central feature of contemporary American politics. Political parties today are more internally unified and ideologically distinctive than they have been in many decades, perhaps a century. This pattern is most evident in Congress, state legislatures, and other bastions of elite politics, where the ideological divide is wide and relations between the parties often descend into a form of tribalism. But it also reaches into the arena of mass politics, as voters increasingly sort themselves by ideology into either the Democratic or Republican Party, view politicians, public issues, and seemingly objective conditions (such as the state of the economy) through distinctly partisan lenses, and increasingly vote only for candidates of their own party.

There is a natural tendency to search for a single root cause of the partisan polarization that characterizes so much of today's politics. But almost any recounting of recent history will reveal that polarization has multiple roots, and that those roots are entwined and run deep. One such recounting begins with the fissures in the Democratic Party's New Deal coalition that were evident in the 1960s, with an initial weakening of the party's stronghold in the South, the rise of the counterculture, and opposition to the war in Vietnam. The 1964 presidential campaign of Barry Goldwater initiated a long-term struggle among Republican activists to develop a more distinctly conservative party agenda. The passage of the Voting Rights Act in 1965, along with the ongoing economic development of the South, broke up the uneasy coalition between blacks and conservative whites that had allowed the Democrats to dominate the region for many decades. The Supreme Court's 1973 abortion decision in *Roe v. Wade* prompted a pro-life movement that years later would form the core of the Republican Party's largest and most reliable constituency, the religious conservatives. California's tax-limiting Proposition 13 in 1978 and the emergence of Ronald Reagan on the national political scene gave the Republican Party a more distinctive economic platform. As president, Reagan's vigorous challenge to the Soviet Union added national security to the set of new issues dividing the parties.

Party realignment in the South—fueled by these developments associated with race, religious fundamentalism, economic development, and patriotism—led to a sharp decline in the number of conservative Democrats serving in Congress and an increase in the number of conservative Republicans and liberal Democrats (mostly minorities) elected from the region. That alone would appear to account for the lion's share of the increased ideological polarization between the parties in Congress.

As these developments played out over time, party platforms became more distinctive. The realigning process in the South was extended to the rest of the country by the increasingly distinctive positions taken by the national parties and their presidential candidates on a number of salient social and economic issues. Those recruited to Congress were more ideologically in tune with their fellow partisans, congressional leaders worked aggressively to promote their party's agenda and message, interest groups increasingly aligned themselves with one party or the other, network news lost audience share and was challenged by more partisan cable news and talk radio, and voters sorted themselves into the two parties based on their ideological views.

At the same time, voters were making residential decisions that reinforced the ideological sorting already under way. Citizens were drawn to neighborhoods, counties, states, and regions where others shared their values and interests. This ideological sorting, geographic mobility, and more consistent party-line voting produced many areas that were dominated by a single party at the municipal, county, and state levels, and in state legislative and congressional districts. In turn, the increasing partisan homogeneity of political jurisdictions, exacerbated in legislative districts by redistricting practices, diminished electoral competition and reinforced the polarizing dynamic between political elites and voters.

Near parity between the parties in Congress after the Republican sweep in the 1994 election raised the stakes of subsequent elections and intensified pressure on members not to defect from their party's position on key votes. The new Republican majority developed a formidable political machine to boost its electoral and legislative prospects. Party fundraising put a high priority on redistributing resources from the many safe districts to the few remaining competitive ones, effectively involving all members in the larger campaign to retain or achieve majority status. Regular order in the legislative process—the set of rules, practices, and norms designed to ensure a reasonable level of deliberation and fair play in committee, on the floor, and in conference—was often sacrificed for political expediency. The election in 2000 of the first unified Republican government since 1952 and governance by the most polarizing president in contemporary American history further hardened party divisions in Congress.[1]

This stylized account of the emergence of partisan polarization suggests that multiple forces operated on voters, activists, and elected officials to produce our distinctly partisan era. It contrasts strongly with the explanation that has gained currency among politicians, editorial writers, journalists, foundation officials, and political activists—namely, that gerrymandering is at the root of the polarization problem.

Gerrymandering—the political manipulation of legislative boundaries for partisan or incumbency-protection purposes—provides an almost irresistible account of how self-interested incumbent officeholders and political parties dominate the redistricting process to diminish competitiveness and build ever-safer partisan enclaves in legislative districts around the country. These skewed districts, in which the threat of competition in the primary election becomes more worrisome than the general election, turn into breeding grounds for politicians operating at their party's ideological pole. The shockingly low level of competitiveness in the two U.S. House elections following the post-2000 round of redistricting—as well as the colorful (and appalling) story of Tom DeLay's successful mid-decade re-redistricting in Texas—has reinforced the widespread view that gerrymandering is responsible for partisan polarization.

But is gerrymandering really at the crux of the polarization problem? And would reforming the practice actually make a substantial difference? The foregoing account of the historical evolution of partisan polarization raises doubts. And as we shall see, the weight of scholarly evidence comes down on the side of those who argue that redistricting is not the sole or even a primary cause of

1. Jacobson (forthcoming 2007).

polarization. But that does not mean it is irrelevant. Gerrymandering may contribute marginally to the decline in competitiveness (and, in turn, to the collapse
of the center), but most of the important developments in democratic politics are
shaped at the margin.

In addition, gerrymandering increasingly may be less of a cause and more of an
effect of polarization, providing a means for intensely competitive and ideologically polarized parties to maintain or achieve majority control. It may, in other
words, accelerate a dynamic that was set in motion by other forces. Finally, while
redistricting may not be a major source of partisan polarization, redistricting
reform could be part of the solution—especially when combined with other steps
designed to interrupt the polarizing dynamic between political elites and voters.

The Argument

The popular case for gerrymandering as a primary source of polarization in Congress is, at first glance, deceptively straightforward. It begins with a link between
redistricting and competition. In the vast majority of states, district boundaries for
U.S. House seats (and for state legislative seats) are redrawn after each decennial
census through the normal legislative process, with plans crafted and approved by
the legislature and signed into law by the governor. House incumbents and
national parties work long and hard to persuade elected officials at the state level
to draw lines in a manner that maximizes their electoral security or the potential
of the party to gain seats.

In states controlled by one party, the process favors a partisan gerrymander. In
states with divided party control, bipartisan incumbent-protection gerrymanders
are more likely to emerge. In either case, according to this argument, the lines are
drawn in a way that diminishes competition. Incumbents are afforded familiar
and compatible electoral terrain, thereby reducing the prospects of potential
challengers—and districts become more homogeneous in their partisan composition, making it less likely that a candidate representing the minority party can
ever succeed there.

The impact of redistricting on competition is thought to have been strengthened by the implementation of the Voting Rights Act of 1965 and the emergence
of new technologies. In the case of the Voting Rights Act, the imperative to maximize the number of "majority-minority" districts—in which a majority of residents are part of an ethnic minority—led to an increase in safe Democratic seats
represented by African Americans and Hispanics. But it also led to a jump in
safe Republican seats in surrounding districts that had been drained of minority

voters who might otherwise have formed the core of a competitive opposition. Meanwhile, computer technologies—including sophisticated mapping software and voter databases—have made it much easier for line drawers to generate plans that meet judicial requirements (such as equal population) and state standards (such as contiguity, civil boundaries, and communities of interest), while at the same time achieving their political objectives of creating districts immune to serious competition.

The second link in the causal chain is between competition and polarization. Safe incumbents are under little pressure to listen to—much less accommodate—the views of the political opposition in their districts. Districts with overwhelming partisan majorities among voters effectively remove any general election threat to the incumbent (or, in the case of open seats, the party successor) and lodge electoral accountability almost entirely with primary voters. In both cases, which are conceptually distinct but overlap empirically, politicians elected and reelected predictably and comfortably are likely to emerge from—or gravitate toward—the ideological pole of their party.

The Evidence

After this initial glance, however, the story becomes more complicated—and more problematic. Signs of a sharp increase in partisan polarization are by no means limited to legislative bodies whose districts are subject to regular redrawing of boundaries. The increasing ideological polarization between the parties in the House has been clearly mirrored in the Senate, whose constituency boundaries—states—are fixed. The decline of the political center, as measured by the percentage of members who are ideological moderates in their roll-call voting, has moved in lockstep over the past several decades in both chambers.[2] And while the Senate may have been indirectly affected by redistricting through the election of more partisan and ideologically extreme House members, this seems unlikely to account for the striking similarity in the timing and shape of the rise of polarization in the two bodies. State-level competitiveness in presidential elections has declined markedly over the past half-century—and most of that decline has been registered since 1976.[3] By several measures states have become redder or bluer, and fewer remain in the highly competitive range. Senate constituencies have become less competitive without the assistance of political gerrymandering.

2. Binder (2005, p. 155).
3. From figures compiled by William A. Galston of the Brookings Institution (on file with author); Jacobson (2005).

If one looks back at the last deeply partisan era in U.S. history at the turn of the twentieth century (well before the Supreme Court transformed the periodicity and politics of redistricting with its "one person, one vote" decisions), redistricting appears to have increased—not decreased—the competitiveness of congressional elections. The highly competitive structure of elections in that era proved fully compatible with the growing ideological polarization of the parties in the House.[4] And then there are the signs of elite partisan polarization outside of Congress altogether. For example, since 1980 the national party platforms have increasingly diverged on a host of economic, social, and national security policies, reflecting a broader transformation in each party's ideological center and aligned interest groups.[5]

Gerrymandering and Competition

Before examining the evidence of a causal link between gerrymandering and competition, it is important to acknowledge that the decline in competition in House elections is not just a recent phenomenon. Whether measured by the number of marginal seats (those decided within the range of 55 to 45 percent of the two-party district vote, as shown in figure 6-1) or the absolute number of seats gained or lost by the major parties from one election to the next (figure 6-2), competitiveness declined throughout the twentieth century.

The "vanishing marginals" of the late 1960s and early 1970s, noted by David Mayhew and others, were attributed largely to an increase in incumbency advantage.[6] But the growing advantage of incumbency was evident in redrawn and untouched districts, in states that gained or lost seats (and thus required substantial redistricting) and in those that did not.[7] The growth of candidate-centered campaigns and the accumulation of a "personal vote" dwarfed redistricting as a cause of declining competition during this period.[8] The strengthening of partisanship in the 1980s, which increasingly shaped campaigning and voting in House elections, enhanced the opportunity to achieve partisan and incumbent protection objectives through redistricting. Whether the opportunity could be seized depended on the suppleness of the redistricting tool.

No one examining any of the individual state redistricting plans renowned for achieving their partisan or bipartisan goals could fail to be impressed by the poten-

4. Carson, Engstrom, and Roberts (2006).
5. Hershey (forthcoming 2007).
6. See Mayhew (2004); Jacobson (2004b).
7. Ferejohn (1977).
8. See Mann (1978); Cain, Ferejohn, and Fiorina (1987).

Figure 6-1. *Number of Marginal House Seats, 1876–2004*[a]

Number of marginal seats

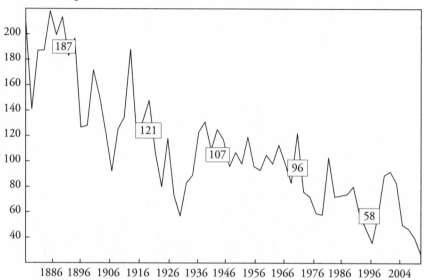

Source: Campbell, Hankinson, and Koch (2005)

a. Marginal seats are those decided within the range of 55 to 45 percent of the two-party district vote. The numbers in the boxes are the median values for each quarter of the century. (Elections since 2000 are included in the last quarter of the twentieth century.) Multimember districts are included. The numbers have been adjusted to a constant House size of 435 seats.

tial power of gerrymandering. Before Tom DeLay's 2003 masterpiece in Texas, Democratic representative Philip Burton's 1981 handiwork in California, reputedly sketched on the back of a paper placemat without the aid of computers and quantitative data, was perhaps the most infamous example of a successful partisan gerrymander. Two decades later, another Democratic-controlled California state legislature (working with a Democratic governor) defied expectations and produced a bipartisan plan that shielded the entire House delegation from competition. In the 1990s round of redistricting, the successful Republican strategy of coalescing with African Americans to pack minority residents into overwhelmingly majority-minority districts, thereby diluting Democratic strength in surrounding districts, contributed to the dramatic Republican gains in the 1994 election.

But whether these "successes" are routinely matched in other states, and whether they cumulate to produce net national partisan and incumbency gains, is another matter. Line drawers in state legislatures are constrained and often

Figure 6-2. *Number of House Seats Gained or Lost by the Major Parties,*
1900–2004[a]

Net absolute seat swing

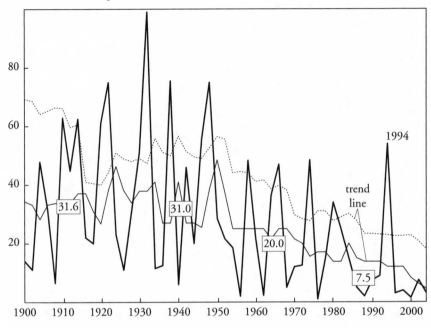

Source: Campbell (2003).

a. The solid lines show the absolute number of House seats gained or lost by the major parties from one election to the next. The numbers in the boxes are median values for each quarter of the century. For comparability, seats won by third-party and independent candidates are divided equally between the major parties. The numbers have been adjusted to a constant House size of 435 seats. The solid trend line is the median absolute seat change in the ten prior elections. The dashed trend line is the standard deviation of Democratic Party seat change for the previous ten elections.

replaced by the courts, which tend to favor the status quo. And state legislators often bring their own interests and ambitions, which may conflict with the interests of the national party or the House incumbent, to the redistricting process.

Rapid shifts in population can be unsettling to incumbents. The geographic clustering of like-minded citizens, which by most accounts has accelerated in recent decades, reduces the degrees of freedom available to those drawing the lines, but it contributes naturally and powerfully to more homogeneous districts and less competition. Aggressive pursuit of partisan gains, as argued by political scientist Bruce Cain—and seconded by Justice Sandra Day O'Connor in her opinion in *Davis* v. *Bandemer,* 478 U.S. 109 (1986)—is inherently self-limiting:

the greater a party's reach for additional seats, the higher the risk of losing some of its existing seats.[9] In other words, partisan gerrymanders can increase rather than decrease the level of competitiveness—or so it seemed before the post-2000 round of redistricting. As we will see, there is some evidence that partisan gains and less competitiveness may not be incompatible after all.

Additional questions can be raised about the impact of racial gerrymandering and redistricting technology on competition. While most districts in the House represented by minorities are overwhelmingly safe, this is as much a result of the social and political homogeneity of urban centers as it is of redistricting. The post-2000 round of redistricting reflected the Supreme Court's ruling in *Shaw* v. *Reno,* 509 U.S. 630 (1993), and subsequent cases that race could be considered—but not as the predominant factor—when states redraw district lines. It also reflected the growing receptivity among minority politicians and activists to the formation of coalitional districts (in which minority voters can form coalitions with other racial and ethnic groups to nominate and elect candidates of their choice) rather than majority-minority districts.

The power and affordability of computers and software now allows groups, individuals, and the courts—not just state legislatures and political parties—to draw new district lines and measure their likely impact on party strength, competition, and adherence to other state standards. As more transparency requirements are built into the law and state courts become more active in reviewing plans, the inside game of redistricting is weakened.

Finally, there is the example of Iowa. Iowa uses a uniquely nonpartisan redistricting process, one in which responsibility for drawing maps is delegated to a legislative support staff office, the Legislative Services Bureau, which operates under strict standards and is blind to incumbency and party. This neutral process has led to an unusually large proportion of competitive races in recent decades. Nevertheless, the Iowa state legislature retains the authority to override the plan generated by the Legislative Services Bureau and draw its own map. That it has never done so, even when the neutral process produced far-from-neutral results, probably reflects a unique set of factors that make the state such an outlier. Its relatively small size, its mix of social and geographic characteristics, and its close partisan balance naturally support more competitive legislative districts, and the low number of racial minorities removes all of the complicated considerations of the Voting Rights Act. Iowa's strong tradition of progressive nonpartisanship supports the unusual practice of delegating responsibility to professional staff and the legis-

9. Cain (1984).

lature's restraint from using its full authority to control redistricting. In states with more diverse populations and geography, such blind redistricting performed by nonpartisan bodies might well produce undesired outcomes relative to competition and partisan fairness.[10]

Calibrating the net national effects of redistricting on competition has been done in a variety of ways. Initially, scholars sought to detect a link between redistricting and the advantages of incumbency. Some found that the incumbency advantage (and decline of competitiveness) increased as much in districts unaffected by redistricting as in those that were.[11] Others noted a variable effect of redistricting on the "personal vote" of House members—increasing it for some, decreasing it for others.[12] Overall, there was a near consensus that the effects of redistricting were minimal. In their 2002 book, *Elbridge Gerry's Salamander,* political scientists Gary W. Cox and Jonathan N. Katz challenged this consensus, concluding that redistricting contributed to the jump in incumbency advantage. The effect, however, was not direct but through the prudential retirement of incumbents and the strategic entry by challengers.[13] Other scholars have refuted this conclusion, finding that such strategic behavior falls well short of explaining the magnitude and growth of the incumbency advantage.[14]

More recently, scholars have investigated the impact of redistricting on the underlying partisan composition of congressional districts. Working separately, Michael P. McDonald of the Brookings Institution and Alan I. Abramowitz of Emory University have examined the underlying change in district partisanship before and after redistricting.[15] Both use the normalized two-party presidential vote within a district (that is, one that measures each party's performance in House districts relative to its national performance) to assess changes in district competitiveness within and between rounds of redistricting over the preceding three decades. McDonald uses the most recent presidential election before redistricting, while Abramowitz and his colleagues use the most proximate presidential election. This difference leads to a divergence in data used to assess the post-1990 round of redistricting and to somewhat different results. Both, however, categorize a district as "competitive" if the percentage of the normalized vote (calculated by subtracting the national average of the Democratic and Republican

10. Mann (2005, p. 102).

11. This literature is summarized in Cox and Katz (2002, pp. 18–22).

12. Desposato and Petrocik (2003).

13. Cox and Katz (2002).

14. Ansolabehere and Snyder (2002).

15. Cain, Mac Donald, and McDonald (2005); Abramowitz, Alexander, and Gunning (2006a, 2006b, 2006c); McDonald (2006).

Table 6-1. *Competitive House Districts, 1970–2002*

Percent competitive	Number of competitive districts							
	1970	1972	1980	1982	1990	1992	2000	2002
According to McDonald								
45–55	147	150	169	171	150	146	122	111
48–52	52	67	69	79	61	58	53	38
According to Abramowitz								
45–55	...	...	174	165	151	154	123	116

Sources: Data from Cain, Mac Donald, and McDonald (2005); McDonald (2006); Abramowitz, Alexander, and Gunning (2006a, 2006b, 2006c).

vote from the proportion of the votes received by the Democrat out of the total number cast for the two parties in a particular district) falls within a certain range around the 50 percent mark. Their results are provided in table 6-1.

It is clear from the data that redistricting has not had a uniform net national effect on the competitiveness of House districts. In some rounds the number of competitive districts increased, while in others it decreased. The post-2000 redistricting was associated with a decline in the number of competitive districts, but most of the reduction in the 45 to 55 percent range between 1992 and 2002 occurred mid-decade. In other words, the decline in competitiveness was because of changes entirely unrelated to redistricting. Those changes are associated with both mobility and increased partisanship among voters.

The authors diverge on the impact of the 1980 and 1990 redistricting rounds: McDonald finds a slight increase in the number of competitive districts after the 1980 round and a decline after 1990. Abramowitz obtains the opposite result. Abramowitz sees the impact of redistricting on competitiveness as very modest or negligible—indeed, close to trivial. McDonald attaches more importance to redistricting, especially during the most recent round and when its impact is measured on a tighter range of competitiveness (48 to 52 percent). They also disagree on the efficacy of alternative redistricting processes, including independent commissions operating under various standards and guidelines.

So what can we safely conclude from these analyses of the impact of redistricting on district partisanship and the decline of competition in House elections? Abramowitz makes a powerful case that district partisanship has become more pronounced largely as a result of the ideological sorting of voters into the two parties and geographic mobility. Moreover, he persuasively demonstrates that the number of competitive House races is significantly smaller than the number of competitive House districts, a result largely because of campaign fundraising shortfalls by challengers in these districts. In other words, redistricting is clearly not the driving force in reducing the number of competitive House districts and contests.

But it would be a mistake to dismiss redistricting entirely as a factor in the declining competitiveness of congressional elections. Clearly observable effects within individual states may not always have a benign national impact. Gary C. Jacobson of the University of California, San Diego, finds that the latest round of redistricting had a significant partisan and competitive impact. Republicans, already enjoying a more efficient distribution of voters across congressional districts, saw their partisan advantage grow from 228 to 240 in the new districts, even though their presidential candidate lost the popular vote in the 2000 election. Moreover, both parties gained safer districts from redistricting: "Of the twenty-five districts Republicans had won in 2000 with less than 55 percent of the vote, nineteen were strengthened by increasing the proportion of Bush voters; of the nineteen similarly marginal Democratic districts, sixteen were given a larger share of Gore voters."[16] At least at a cumulative national level, line drawers seem to have defied the proposition widely accepted among redistricting scholars that partisan gerrymanders inevitably increase competitiveness.

A case study of how this can be done is provided by the mid-decade gerrymander in the state of Texas in 2003. Political scientist John R. Alford of Rice University in Houston submitted two affidavits that powerfully demonstrated how the Republican plan would produce both a likely gain of seven seats for the GOP and a sharp decline in competitiveness.[17] Now largely sanctioned by the Supreme Court, the new map (with a single exception) will likely freeze each party's current control of Texas districts throughout the decade. The lone exception is the 17th district—a strongly pro-Republican district currently held by Democratic representative Chet Edwards. As long as Edwards retains the seat, it will remain competitive. But if he loses, it is likely to become a safe Republican seat, producing the seventh pickup for the Republicans predicted by Alford's analysis.

Competition and Polarization

The commonsensical notion that higher levels of competition push politicians toward policy moderation, and lower levels of competition toward policy extremism, has not withstood empirical scrutiny over the years.[18] As far back as 1950,

16. Jacobson (2005, p. 112).

17. "Declaration of John A. Alford—*Session* v. *Perry*," Appendix K, in Jurisdictional Statement of Eddie Jackson (www.jenner.com/files/tbl_s69NewsDocumentOrder/FileUpload500/503/Jackson_v_Perry_JS_Appendix.pdf#page=222 [May 2006]).

18. This literature is summarized in Gulati (2004), from which the following discussion is drawn.

Harvard's Samuel P. Huntington found that marginal members were the most partisan of their colleagues in roll-call voting, while members representing safe seats were the least partisan. Among Democrats, that finding was surely shaped by safe southern Democrats regularly coalescing with Republicans in support of conservative policies.

Subsequent analysts refined the relationship to measure a member's policy moderation or extremism relative to constituency opinion, not to one's colleagues in the legislature. But here too marginal representatives were less likely than safe ones to be responsive to constituency opinion. The moderation hypothesis—that competitiveness induces responsiveness to the views of the median voter and therefore policy moderation—was supplanted by the mobilization hypothesis, which poses a negative relationship between competitiveness and responsiveness and policy moderation. In this theory, marginal incumbents are more likely to be responsive to their party's base supporters, while safe incumbents are more responsive to the center of public opinion.

The relationship between competitiveness and partisan polarization might depend upon the underlying basis of the level of competition. A personal incumbency advantage might induce different partisan and policy responses within Congress than an electoral advantage based primarily on the partisan composition of the district. Incumbents who build substantial margins of victory based largely on their personal appeal and efforts might not feel the same level of electoral security as those who represent districts in which their party is dominant in the electorate. Such incumbents might therefore be found less frequently at their parties' ideological poles than safe-district incumbents.

There is some evidentiary support for this proposition. Figure 6-3 displays the relationship between the margin of victory of winning House candidates in the 2002 election and their ideological scores on roll-call voting in the 108th Congress. Figure 6-4 substitutes the margin of victory of the 2000 presidential candidates in each 2002 House district as a measure of the districts' electoral competitiveness. This is a surrogate for the partisan composition of the district, independent of the congressional candidates and their campaigns.

The contrast between the two figures is striking. Electoral safety, as measured by the candidates' own margins of victory, appears to have no relationship to the ideological voting of the members—Democratic or Republican. Even uncontested candidates (those with the highest margin of victory) display a wide range of roll-call voting behavior. However, when the partisan composition of the district is used as a measure of competitiveness, an expected relationship emerges: competitive districts are represented by members with more moderate voting

Figure 6-3. *House Member Ideology by 2002 Congressional Election Margin, 108th Congress*

DW-nominate score (1st dimension)[a]

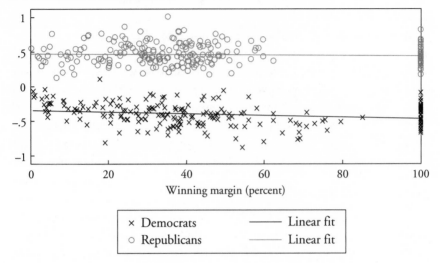

Winning margin (percent)

| × Democrats | —— Linear fit |
| ○ Republicans | —— Linear fit |

Source: Data provided by Gary C. Jacobson, Michael P. McDonald, and Keith T. Poole.

a. DW-nominate scores, developed by political scientists Keith T. Poole and Howard Rosenthal, use all the roll-call votes in each Congress to assign each member of the House and Senate a unique score on a liberal-to-conservative scale.

records than safe districts. Or, at the ends of the scale, Democrats representing safe Democratic districts have more liberal voting records, and Republicans in safe Republican districts more conservative ones.

Even more striking, however, is the gap in ideological voting between Democrats and Republicans across all levels of competitiveness. The ideological scores of Democratic members are closely grouped among other Democrats and are completely separate from Republican members. Indeed, the two parties in the House of Representatives seem to operate in distinct ideological worlds. Partisan polarization in the House clearly operates to a substantial extent independent of the competitiveness of congressional districts.

Figures 6-5 and 6-6 present comparable data for the 95th Congress, which immediately followed the 1976 presidential election. A quarter-century ago, the same relationship between competitiveness and ideological voting in Congress was present as today. When measured by the partisan composition of the district, rather than the electoral safety of the incumbent, competitiveness breeds mod-

Figure 6-4. *House Member Ideology by 2000 Presidential Election Margin, 108th Congress*

DW-nominate score (1st dimension)[a]

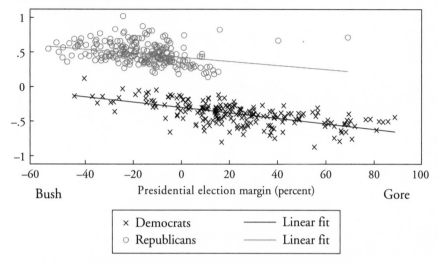

Bush — Presidential election margin (percent) — Gore

| × Democrats | —— Linear fit |
| ○ Republicans | —— Linear fit |

Source: Data provided by Gary C. Jacobson, Michael P. McDonald, and Keith T. Poole.

a. DW-nominate scores, developed by political scientists Keith T. Poole and Howard Rosenthal, use all the roll-call votes in each Congress to assign each member of the House and Senate a unique score on a liberal-to-conservative scale.

eration. It is a pattern that has persisted over time, as we can see by comparing figures 6-4 and 6-6. Also evident is the reduction in the number of competitive districts over time, which undoubtedly has contributed to the thinning of centrist ranks in the House. But more significant is the growing ideological gap between the parties independent of the level of district competitiveness.[19] Just as gerrymandering cannot account for much of the decline in district competitiveness, so too the decline in competitiveness cannot explain most of the growth in the partisan polarization of the House.

Gary Jacobson's analysis of the electoral sources of the increased partisan polarization in the House and Senate over the past three decades provides an even richer evidentiary base for this conclusion.[20] He has demonstrated how the growing differences between the two parties' electoral coalitions—mediated through selection (membership turnover and the changing regional and social composition

19. Ono (2005).
20. Jacobson (2004a).

Figure 6-5. *House Member Ideology by 1976 Congressional Election Margin,*
95th Congress

DW-nominate score (1st dimension)[a]

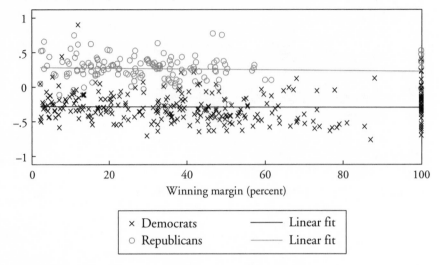

× Democrats   —— Linear fit
○ Republicans   ----- Linear fit

Source: Data provided by Gary C. Jacobson and Keith T. Poole.
a. DW-nominate scores, developed by political scientists Keith T. Poole and Howard Rosenthal, use
all the roll call votes in each Congress to assign each member of the House and Senate a unique score on
a liberal-to-conservative scale.

of the party caucuses) and adaptation (continuing members adjusting their roll-
call behavior in response to changes in their electoral constituencies)—account for
roughly half of the widening ideological gap between the congressional parties.
The decline of district (or state, in the case of the Senate) competitiveness is an
important part of the electoral story, but is by no means the only one. The party
realignment of the South clearly played a major role.

The other half of the ideological gap that is not explained by electoral forces is
attributed by Jacobson to a series of events and developments in Congress. These
endogenous forces driving polarization include the strengthened hand of party
leaders, more partisan use of the rules, the increasing role of parties in congressional campaign finance, the guerrilla war designed and led by then Speaker Newt
Gingrich to lift the Republicans out of their long-term minority status in the
House, heated disputes over electoral recounts and ethics charges, narrow majorities in both the House and Senate after the 1994 elections, and the return of unified party government in 2001 under a president whose style and substance of

Figure 6-6. *House Member Ideology by 1976 Presidential Election Margin, 95th Congress*

DW-nominate score (1st dimension)[a]

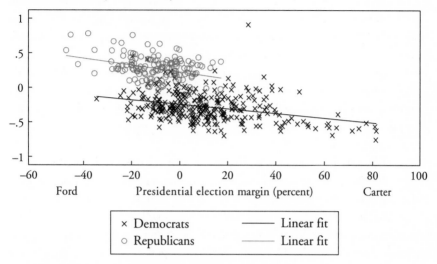

| × Democrats | —— Linear fit |
| ○ Republicans | —— Linear fit |

Source: Data provided by Gary C. Jacobson and Keith T. Poole.

a. DW-nominate scores, developed by political scientists Keith T. Poole and Howard Rosenthal, use all the roll call votes in each Congress to assign each member of the House and Senate a unique score on a liberal-to-conservative scale.

governing is extremely polarizing.[21] In sum, the growth in the number of safe Democratic and Republican districts has contributed to the growing ideological polarization of the parties in Congress, but it is only one of several forces.

Might the decline in competitiveness account for a greater share of the partisan polarization if the impact of primaries is taken into account? As a district becomes safe for one party or the other, the argument goes, the only serious electoral threat to the incumbent lies in a primary challenge. Since primary electorates are skewed toward each party's ideological pole, the appearance of a credible threat in the primary election will push the incumbent in the same direction. Stanford University's David W. Brady, with coauthors Hahrie Han and Jeremy C. Pope, has produced evidence in support of that proposition.[22] Democratic incumbents who lost primary elections were more conservative than those who were victorious, and

21. See Jacobson (2004a); Mann and Ornstein (2006).
22. Brady, Han, and Pope (2005).

losing Republicans were more liberal than those who won. Moreover, Democrats defeated in primaries were replaced by more liberal candidates, Republicans by more conservative candidates.

This pattern is persuasive, but the incidence of serious primary challenges and defeats raises questions about the credibility of the threat. Outside of redistricting years, when two incumbents are often forced to run against each other in a primary election, the number of incumbent House members defeated in a primary election in recent decades has usually been in the low single digits. Relatively few incumbents face anything resembling a serious primary challenge. Stephen Ansolabehere of the Massachusetts Institute of Technology has documented a sharp decline in primary competition, particularly in districts without a competitive general election.[23]

On the other hand, it may be that the lessons of the few are shared by the many. Politicians are demonstrably risk-averse, and they might adjust their behavior—by moving to their party's ideological pole—to ward off primary threats that have ended the careers of some of their colleagues in the House. This strategic response to a threat that materializes with low frequency seems unlikely to account for the striking increase in ideological polarization of the parties over the past couple of decades, but it could be a contributing factor.

The Implications

Gerrymandering cannot account for the sharp partisan polarization of the House, and diagnoses that place it at the center of the problem—as well as the prescriptions that invest entirely in redistricting reform—are clearly flawed. But there are several good reasons to keep it in our focus. Gerrymandering merits our continued attention if only because it reinforces developments set in motion by other forces, operates at the margin to decrease competitiveness, and fuels further polarization.

The story of partisan polarization, as we have seen, is a complicated one involving dynamic relationships between political elites and the mass public and the independent effects of electoral and institutional forces. Even if gerrymandering accounts directly or indirectly for only a small share of the decline of moderates and the sharpening of partisan tensions in the House, that share should not be dismissed as trivial. Tipping points for social change are not easily identifiable.

23. Ansolabehere and others (2006).

But if gerrymandering is not a major source of polarization, it appears increasingly to be a consequence. Partisan polarization and parity raise the stakes of electoral competition between the parties. Leaders in Washington have a strong incentive to manipulate the playing field and rules of the game to boost their party's prospects of holding or gaining majority control. James Madison, the architect of our pluralist, ambition-based democracy, nonetheless cautioned against incumbents having the power to determine the rules that perpetuate their control of government. The post-2000 round of redistricting reflected the intensity of the efforts by the national parties to gain partisan advantage and protect their vulnerable incumbents in the line-drawing process. And Tom DeLay's investment in the 2002 Texas state legislative elections and his 2003 redistricting plan could encourage a pattern of continuous redistricting (in those states without a prohibition on more than a single round of redistricting per decade) following changes in partisan control of state government. Increasing national party investments in the normal rounds of redistricting heighten partisan tensions and reinforce polarization.

Finding solutions that moderate the forces fueling partisan polarization will not be an easy task. Redistricting reform, in which authority is shifted from state legislatures to independent redistricting commissions that operate under standards and procedures to encourage competitiveness and partisan fairness, is one of the more promising responses available.[24] But since the current era of partisan polarization took decades to develop, involving a complex interaction between electoral and institutional forces, it should come as no surprise that efforts to ameliorate some of its more pernicious manifestations will take time—and will require more measures than redistricting reform. It is possible to identify a number of electoral and institutional developments and reforms that might dampen today's polarization and improve the functioning of Congress and American democracy.[25]

The starting point is the realization that major change within Congress is likely to originate outside. The last era of intense partisan polarization in American history—the late nineteenth and early twentieth centuries—was displaced largely by the rise of the Progressive movement, which divided the majority Republican Party and led to new political alignments. A Teddy Roosevelt–like figure today might sense a market opportunity and use his presidential campaign to build a more centrist coalition. The necessary strategy and style of leadership—one more inclusive, less partisan, and less divisive than we have seen in recent years—is more likely to emerge when an ideologically aggressive majority takes a pounding in the

24. Mann (2005).
25. See Mann and Ornstein (2006, chap. 7).

midterm election leading up to the presidential contest. Whether such a presidential candidate could navigate the rapids of our distinctive nominating and general election processes and then successfully implement such a governance strategy is uncertain at best.

Even more daunting is the adoption of major structural changes designed to increase the competitiveness of legislative districts and states and to diminish partisan polarization. Shifting presidential elections from a contest for electoral votes to a direct popular election would certainly increase the incentive for Democratic nominees to campaign seriously in red states and Republicans in blue states. But the cost-benefit tradeoffs of this constitutional change are complex, and its impact on partisan polarization is by no means certain.[26] Furthermore, it is difficult to see how the opposition of smaller states could be overcome—though one group has recently advanced a plan to implement a direct popular vote without requiring a constitutional amendment.[27]

Another possible structural change involves introducing some form of proportional representation.[28] There is no constitutional impediment to states' establishing multimember congressional districts, statewide party-list systems, or German-style hybrid single-member systems. But a congressional law that requires single-member congressional districts would have to be repealed. While a proportional representation-based legislature, one likely to facilitate the election of third-party candidates, may not be a good fit with the United States' separation-of-powers system in which the president is elected independent of Congress, it would at least expand the scope of competition and sharply lower the stakes of redistricting.

A third structural reform with potential for reducing partisan polarization is the reform of the primary process. Practices across states already vary greatly.[29] Some restrict participation in party primary elections to those who register as partisans. Others permit registered independents or all voters to participate in either party's primary. Yet other states have no registration by party and allow voters to choose their party primary at the polling place. "Blanket" primaries allow voters to select a candidate from either party for each office on the ballot.[30] An all-party

26. See Edwards (2004); Ross (2004).

27. Koza and others (2006).

28. Cox (1997).

29. See Cain and Gerber (2002).

30. See Ann E. Marimow, "Voters Appear to Favor Current Primary System," *San Jose Mercury News,* November 3, 2004; Steve Geissinger, "Props. 60, 62: Dynamic Changes to How We Vote," *Alameda Times-Star,* October 19, 2004.

system places all candidates for each office together and, if none garners at least 50 percent of the vote, uses a runoff election between the top two finishers, whatever their party. Champions of the latter two systems believe they encourage candidates to appeal to more moderate voters in both parties, thereby countering the current race to the ideological poles.

A final structural change that might reshape the electoral environment that breeds partisan polarization is to alter the way in which campaigns are financed. Outside of a few dozen competitive congressional districts, challengers face daunting obstacles to garner the resources needed to run credible and visible campaigns. Reforms designed to increase the resources available to challengers—more generous contribution limits for seed money, tax credits for small donors, free air time, and other forms of public subsidies—would increase the competitiveness of elections. Ironically, one of the recent developments in campaign finance—the more prominent role played by the political parties in raising, contributing, and spending campaign funds—has actually contributed to partisan polarization. The political machines developed by congressional party leaders—Tom DeLay's being the most notorious—are built around campaign money. It is one thing to recognize this new reality, but entirely another to recommend diminishing the role of political parties in congressional elections.

And while the major impetus for change is likely to come from outside of Congress, steps designed to reduce the intensely partisan operation of Congress could be helpful as well. The demise of regular order is both a consequence of polarization (and parity between the parties) and a cause of further bitter partisanship. Restoring an appreciation and respect for the rules and norms of the House and Senate cannot be achieved simply through the adoption of an internal reform package. A powerful belief that the ideological and partisan ends justify the legislative means can easily trump such a measure. But small steps taken to rebalance party and institutional interests and to reestablish meaningful lines of communication (if not bonds) across the partisan divide would certainly help.[31]

31. A number of such steps are suggested by Mann and Ornstein (2006).

Why Other Sources of Polarization Matter More

COMMENT

Gary C. Jacobson

Thomas Mann addresses the question of whether gerrymandering of U.S. House districts deserves a share of the blame for the increasing partisan polarization in America's national politics. He concludes that, contrary to the view common among pundits and editorial writers, gerrymandering has contributed only marginally to polarization. He observes that the trend of increasing polarization is the product of diverse and more fundamental political developments and that it would have occurred with or without any tinkering with district boundaries. But Mann does not entirely absolve gerrymandering, and he astutely notes that the causal arrow may also work in reverse—with polarized politics encouraging partisan gerrymandering. And just as he views redistricting itself as only part of the problem, Mann sees redistricting reform as only part of the solution.

In my view, Mann's analysis is largely on target. Members from lopsidedly partisan districts do tend to be more extreme in their roll-call ideologies. And House districts have clearly become more lopsidedly partisan (and, partly for this reason, less competitive). But this development is more a consequence of changes in the behavior of voters than of changes in the way congressional district boundaries have divided them up. Mann cites some of the evidence for this conclusion, but it is instructive to expand on his analysis.

Like others investigating this question, I approximate district partisanship using the district-level presidential vote, normalized around the national mean for each election year to remove the effects of particular presidential contests.[1] By this measure, the more balanced districts are those in which the presidential vote falls closer to the national mean. Figure 6-7 shows that, according to each of three alternative cutoff points (districts with the presidential vote falling within 2, 3, and 5 percentage points of the national average), the proportion of districts closely balanced between the two parties has fallen over the past couple of decades, reaching new lows in 2004.

How has redistricting contributed to this decline? As figure 6-7 indicates (and as Mann points out in his essay), most of the loss of closely balanced districts occurred

---

1. See McDonald (2006); Abramowitz, Alexander, and Gunning (2006a).

Figure 6-7. *Competitive Districts as Measured by the Adjusted Presidential Vote, 1952–2004*

Number of districts

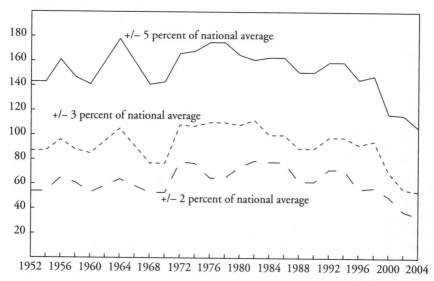

Source: Compiled by author.

between 1994 and 2000, a period during which only a small number of districts were redrawn (and none in a way that affected these data). Thus, most of the decrease had to be a consequence of changes in the behavior of district electorates.

The data in table 6-2 support this conclusion. When the contributions of redistricting and behavioral change are parsed out by counting changes following redistricting and between reapportionment years, it is clear that redistricting was a source of the loss of balanced districts, especially after 2000. But gerrymanders were not the most important sources of change; voters were. Redistricting made things worse, but most of the trend would have occurred without it. Only by the most stringent standard of party balance (within 2 percentage points of the national average) did redistricting make more than a very minor contribution to the overall change. Even by that standard, behavioral change was still nearly twice as consequential.

The consequences of the decline in the number of closely balanced House districts have been compounded by an even larger decline in the propensity of districts to elect representatives whose party does not match the district's presidential

Table 6-2. *Sources of Decrease in Number and Percentage of Closely Balanced House Districts*

Year	Deviation from average district (presidential vote)		
	+/–2 Percent	+/–3 Percent	+/–5 Percent
1980	74	108	165
1982 (1980 presidential vote)	79	112	161
Redistricting change (1980–82)	+5	+4	–4
1984	78	100	163
1988	62	89	151
Behavioral change (1982–88)	–17	–23	–10
1992 (1988 presidential vote)	58	97	145
Redistricting change (1988–92)	–4	+8	–6
1992	72	98	159
1996	56	92	145
2000	50	70	117
Behavioral change (1992–2000)	–8	–27	–28
2002 (2000 presidential vote)	38	56	116
Redistricting change (2000–02)	–12	–14	–1
2004	34	54	106
Behavioral change (2002–04)	–4	–2	–10
Net change since 1982 because of redistricting	–16	–6	–7
Net change since 1982 because of voter behavior	–29	–52	–48
Total change	–45	–58	–55

Source: Adapted from Jacobson (2006, table 1).

leanings. As Mann notes, this decline was largely—but not entirely—a consequence of the southern realignment, in which white southerners, who had voted Republican at the presidential level for decades, finally began voting with nearly the same regularity for Republicans at the congressional level in the 1990s.

Illustrative data appear in figure 6-8. For this figure, each congressional seat is classified as "unfavorable," "neutral" or "favorable" for the party holding it based on the district's underlying partisanship (as measured against the presidential vote in the most recent presidential election). A congressional district is classified as favorable to the incumbent party if the presidential candidate of that party received a vote that ran more than 2 percentage points greater than his national average. A district is neutral if the vote was within 2 percentage points of the national average, and is unfavorable if the presidential candidate's vote was 2 percentage points or more below his national average.

Figure 6-8. *Competitive Districts as Measured by the Adjusted Presidential Vote,* *1952–2004*[a]

Percent of House seats

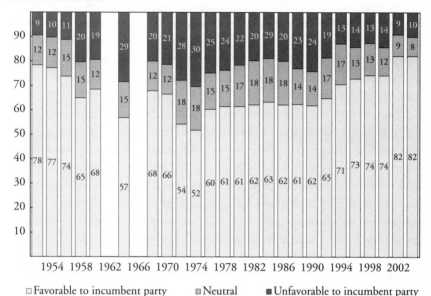

☐ Favorable to incumbent party   ▪ Neutral   ■ Unfavorable to incumbent party

Source: Compiled by author.

a. Entries for 1962 and 1966 are missing because the presidential vote is not available for redrawn districts in these years.

The data show a declining proportion of House seats that are either neutral or unfavorable to the incumbent party, as well as a complementary rise in the proportion of seats held by the locally favored party. These trends are sharply different for Democrats and Republicans, however. Eighty-two percent of the reduction in seats held by the "wrong" party since 1980, and 93 percent of the reduction since 1990, occurred among Democrats. Republicans accounted for 70 percent of the growth in seats held by the "right" party since 1980 and 90 percent of the growth since 1990. The two critical moments were the 1994 midterm elections, when Republicans took sixteen seats from Democrats in Republican-leaning districts (thereby switching the same number from "unfavorable" to "favorable" to the incumbent party), and the 2002 election which, with the help of Republican gerrymanders in key states, put an additional eighteen Republicans into "favorable" partisan districts.

It is obvious how this trend would contribute to partisan polarization. Members representing districts that lean toward the other party at the presidential level tend toward moderation in their voting patterns. (They have little choice if they want to keep their seats.) Moreover, members of the party opposite the president's are more inclined to support his policy initiatives if the president also won the vote in their districts.[2] With fewer seats won against the partisan grain, fewer members are subject to the cross-pressures of party and constituency that encourage moderate positions and participation in cross-party coalitions.[3] The consequence is greater polarization.

Mann points to another feature of the current electoral system that deserves additional attention: the structural advantage of Republicans in the distribution of their party's regular voters. Although successful Republican gerrymanders augmented this advantage after the 2000 census, the advantage itself is nothing new. For a long time, Democrats have won a disproportionate share of minority and other urban voters, who have tended to be concentrated in districts with lopsided Democratic majorities.[4] As figure 6-9 shows, except after the 1964 election, Republicans have consistently held more seats where their party enjoyed a partisan advantage than have Democrats.[5] In past decades, Democrats were able to win a substantial proportion of these Republican-leaning seats, but, as figure 6-10 shows, their ability to win them has dropped dramatically since the 1980s, a major reason why Democrats have been unable to retake the House since losing it in 1994. Republicans have never done particularly well in Democratic presidential territory, but this is not a problem for them at present because their structural advantage can deliver a Republican majority in the House even if they win only Republican-leaning seats.[6]

Taken together, the elements of Mann's analysis that I have amplified here suggest that redistricting reform may be even more problematic than he imagines. If

2. Jacobson (2003).

3. For example, between 1990 and 2002, the average DW-nominate score for Democrats in Republican-leaning seats, as defined for figure 6-8, was −.20, compared to −.45 for Democrats in Democratic-leaning seats. The score for Republicans in Democratic-leaning seats was .26, compared to .46 for Republicans in Republican-leaning seats. (DW-nominate scores take values of −1 to 1, with −1 most liberal and 1 most conservative.) See also Fleisher and Bond (2004).

4. For instance, a poll conducted by CBS News and the *New York Times* found that Democratic identifiers outnumbered Republicans nearly five to one in New York City. CBS News/*New York Times*, "New York City and the Republican Convention," August 20–25, 2004 (www.cbsnews.com/htdocs/CBSNews_polls/nyc.pdf).

5. The substantive point is unchanged even if the standard is 5 rather than 2 percentage points.

6. Jacobson (2006).

Figure 6-9. *District Partisan Advantage, 1952–2004*

Percent of House seats

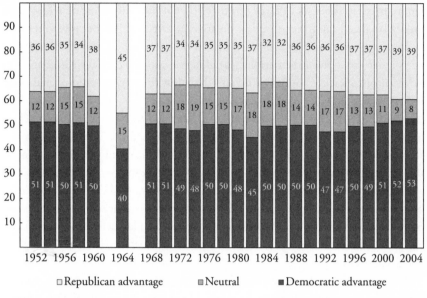

□ Republican advantage   ▪ Neutral   ▪ Democratic advantage

Source: Compiled by author.

Figure 6-10. *Winning against the Partisan Grain, by Decade*[a]

Percent

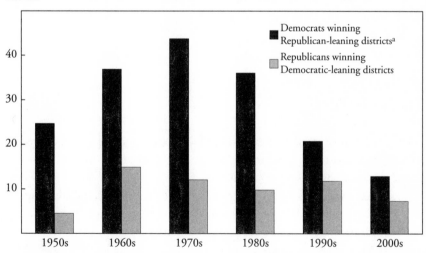

Source: Compiled by author.

a. Leaning districts are defined as those in which the district-level presidential vote was at least 2 percentage points higher than the national average for that election.

redistricting were taken from legislatures and given to neutral bodies enjoined to ignore partisan interests in favor of other criteria, they might create a few more evenly balanced (and therefore less polarizing) districts. But because voters are to blame for most of the recent diminution of such districts, the effect of redistricting reform—given the current spatial distribution of partisan voters and the levels of polarization and party loyalty they now display—would probably be modest at best.

More important, any effective scheme intended to increase the number of balanced—and therefore competitive—districts would inevitably threaten the Republicans' structural advantage and, thus, their control of the House. Unless they are considerably more public-spirited about such matters than we have reason to believe, Republicans will oppose any such reform. And Democrats ought to be wary of any "objective" or "neutral" system that, by ignoring party interests, might worsen their structural disadvantage. Arguably, Democrats now *need* partisan gerrymanders to win a share of seats that reflects their level of support among voters nationally.

Finally, it should be noted that the Republicans' structural advantage gives them a strong incentive to polarize politics along party lines. All the Republicans need to do to retain majority control of the House is to win the seats in districts that lean their way. A partisan standoff—with both sides highly motivated and loyal to their parties—virtually guarantees, at present, Republican control of Congress. And in that case, polarization may well be the status quo for the foreseeable future.

COMMENT

Thomas B. Edsall

Over the past forty years, political elites and ideological leaders have capitalized on a long list of issues that drive polarization. A prominent factor on this list—and one of the usual suspects in any discussion of political polarization—is gerrymandering, the drawing of congressional district boundaries for electoral advantage by one party or the other. But the importance of gerrymandering as a strategy that the political parties can exploit for partisan advantage is frequently overstated, a case that Mann and my codiscussant Gary Jacobson make in their essays. So if gerrymandering is not the primary force of political polarization, what is? I will attempt to describe some of the major social and cultural developments that have created a political environment ripe for the tactics of dividing the electorate into what have become known as red and blue camps, and some of the partisan advantages that the Republican Party has commandeered through the use of aggressive polarization strategies.

Almost all of these issues have their roots in six social upheavals: the civil rights, antiwar, women's rights, and anti-tax movements; the sexual revolution; and the rise of religious conservatism. All six are closely intertwined and reinforce each other in mobilizing and unifying the electorate into two separate camps—their supporters and their opponents. Increasingly, those on the liberal side of these moral-cultural and racial-ethnic issues have aligned themselves with the Democratic Party, while those on the conservative end of the spectrum have joined the ranks of the Republican Party.

"Throughout the electorate, there has been a fundamental change in the relationship between partisanship and social/cultural ideology. A generation ago, for most members of the mass electorate, party identification and social values were only weakly related. Now, for a sizable portion of the U.S. electorate, party and these kinds of ideologies are deeply intertwined," political scientist Matthew S. Levendusky has demonstrated. In addition, he says, "The national parties have drifted further from one another over the past thirty years, and became more ideologically distinct, which means that the parties now send a more unified and homogenous ideological signal. As voters see this purer signal from each party, they can more easily see what policy positions make someone a Democrat or a Republican. The parties come to function as political 'brand names.'"[7]

On the basis of their extensive examination of poll data, political scientists Thomas M. Carsey and Geoffrey C. Layman conclude that "party identification indeed serves as a perceptual screen that shapes attitudes toward policy issues."[8] In effect, voters are increasingly evaluating issues and debates by looking through Republican or Democratic lenses. The power of partisanship was clearly shown in "The Separate Realities of Bush and Kerry Supporters," a survey conducted by the Center on Policy Attitudes and the University of Maryland's Center for International and Security Studies in 2004. It found high levels of factual misinformation on the justifications for the war in Iraq, and that the misinformation was heavily concentrated among Bush partisans and supporters: "Despite the report of the 9/11 Commission saying there is no evidence Iraq was providing significant support to al Qaeda, 75 percent of Bush supporters believe Iraq was providing

7. Levendusky (2005).
8. Carsey and Layman (2006, p. 474).

substantial support to al Qaeda (compared to 30 percent of Kerry supporters), with 20 percent believing that Iraq was directly involved in 9/11." In fact, 56 percent of Bush supporters said the 9/11 Commission reported that Iraq was either directly involved in the attacks on the World Trade Center and Pentagon, or that Iraq gave substantial support to al Qaeda—a clear distortion of what the commission actually reported.[9]

The wedge issues used by campaigns, advocacy groups, candidates, and operatives fall into a variety of categories, but these categories have become less and less distinct and mutually exclusive. Instead, in a crucial development making more pervasive polarization possible, elites have increasingly developed ideologically consistent stands on all of these categories, and voters have been joining them in a process described by Morris P. Fiorina, Samuel J. Abrams, and Jeremy C. Pope as "sorting," and by Alan I. Abramowitz, Jacobson, and Layman and his coauthors as "polarization."[10]

The various constellations of wedge issues include:

—Controversies surrounding questions of sexual freedom, personal autonomy, and sexual privacy; abortion, including parental notification, *Roe* v. *Wade,* and the picketing of abortion clinics; contraception and the prevention of sexually transmitted diseases, including the distribution of condoms to public school children, sex education, and abstinence programs; the "morning-after pill" (Plan B); homosexuality, including legalization of sodomy, gays in the military, same-sex marriage, civil unions; rights to anonymity for those who test HIV-positive; and hate-crime laws.

—Issues of war and peace, including the broad area of the "use of force" and the right of the United States to wage preemptive war, military spending and weapons development, women in combat, what constitutes legitimate national defense, questions regarding torture, surveillance, and eavesdropping, as well as the open-ended detention of prisoners at Guantanamo and at other undisclosed locations.

—Issues of religion, including school prayer, government financing of faith-based social service programs, the teaching of evolution, the physical display of religious symbols in public places (such as the Ten Commandments and nativity scenes), and the tax-exempt status of politically active religious organizations—

9. Steven Kull, "The Separate Realities of Bush and Kerry Supporters," Program on International Policy Attitudes, University of Maryland, October 21, 2004 (www.pipa.org/OnlineReports/Pres_Election_04/Report10_21_04.pdf).

10. Fiorina, Abrams, and Pope (2006); Jacobson (forthcoming 2007); Abramowitz and Saunders (2005); Layman and others (2005).

from African American churches to Focus on the Family and the Family Research Council.

—The range of topics tied to race and ethnicity, including affirmative action, crime, welfare, equalization of school funding, cross-county busing, multiculturalism, and (increasingly) the costs associated with a non-marital birthrate, which now stands at approximately 34 percent for the entire U.S. population and at 69 percent for African Americans.[11]

—Issues relating to taxes and spending, including tax cuts skewed toward the affluent and the cutting of revenues to finance liberal social welfare services—especially services that redistribute resources toward racial and ethnic minority constituencies.

—Conflicts growing out of the women's movement, including the movement toward nontraditional sex roles, equal pay for equal work, gender preferences in hiring and promotion, sexual harassment, "hostile workplace" regulations, and court-ordered gender parity in admissions, the awarding of grants and fellowships, and student athletic opportunities.

A central achievement of legions of Republican political operatives—from Lee Atwater, chief adviser to George H. W. Bush in the 1980s, to Karl Rove today—has been to accelerate the fusion of these issues, linking them in order to assemble a larger, coherent, conservative vision. Taxes, for example, are portrayed as financing secularization, along with welfare and Great Society programs that shift public spending and regulatory decisions that encourage family dissolution. African Americans, Latino immigrants, and their children are deeply affected by such government policies, but in the Republican view, no family is immune.

The partisan-ideological consistency of voters has allowed the GOP to bundle seemingly disconnected issues. Support for the Iraq war and for traditional family values, for example, overlapped in some constituencies. Republican white evangelical Christians were, in June 2005, far more supportive of the war than any other Republican group. When asked, "All in all, considering the costs to the United States versus the benefits to the United States, do you think the war with Iraq was worth fighting, or not?" 88.5 percent of the Republican evangelicals said it was worth fighting, just over 17 percent more than all other Republicans,

11. Paul Offner, "Reducing Non-Marital Births," Brookings Institution, August 2001 (www. brookings.edu/es/research/projects/wrb/publications/pb/pb05.htm): "Between 1960 and 1999, the non-marital ratio went from 5.3 percent (low enough to please even the most committed conservative) to 33 percent. . . . The same pattern holds for African Americans, who are disproportionately represented on the welfare rolls, and whose non-marital ratio went from 23.3 percent in 1960 to an alarming 69.1 percent in 1999."

71.3 percent. Forty-six percent of all those surveyed said the benefits outweighed the costs. Asked about the number of U.S. casualties in the Iraq war, 63.7 percent of the evangelicals said the losses were "acceptable," compared with 47.8 percent of all other Republicans. For the entire sample, 29 percent described the casualties as acceptable.[12]

Partisan divisions over the various wedge issues reached new heights in 2001, shortly after George W. Bush was inaugurated. Bush-Cheney campaign pollster and strategist Matthew Dowd examined survey data collected from election day 2000 through the first month of 2001 and came to a crucial conclusion: polarization had become so intense and pervasive that "you can lose the swing voters and still win the election, if you make sure your base is bigger than theirs."[13] Instead of directing the main thrust toward the "swing" voter, it was much more important in the post-2000 election period to focus on registering, mobilizing, and turning out "your base," Dowd found. He was, in fact, proven correct. Bush won decisively in 2004 despite actually losing ground among the small fraction of "independent" and "apolitical" voters who had voted for him in 2000, when he did better among swing voters but lost the overall popular vote. Among independent, apolitical, and swing voters, Bush's percentage fell from 55 to 42 percent, while Gore received 45 percent and Kerry 58 percent, according to National Election Studies (NES) surveys.[14]

While polarization has worked exceptionally well for Republicans, the adoption of a parallel strategy—addressing the concerns of the partisan base rather than of the center—has not proven to be a dependable option for Democrats. Roughly 30 to 34 percent of the population describes itself as "conservative," while only 20 to 25 percent is made up of self-described "liberals."[15] A base strategy for the Republicans means investing heavily in getting conservative nonvoters and intermittent voters registered and to the polls. There are many more unreliable or nonvoting conservatives than liberals—almost twice as many—giving the GOP a much larger pool to draw upon.

Because the number of hard-core liberal adherents is smaller, Democrats are far more dependent on winning the votes of self-described moderates. Democratic election strategy thus depends on first winning a large percentage of reliably vot-

12. Jacobson (forthcoming 2007, pp. 234–35).

13. Matthew Dowd, interview with author, 2005.

14. National Election Studies data are available at www.umich.edu/~nes/nesguide/gd-index. htm#9.

15. In 2004 the National Election Studies survey found that 23 percent of voters were liberal and 33 percent were conservative.

ing centrists—who are alienated by hard-left appeals—and then building turnout among nonvoting moderates. In effect, the moderate voter is much more important to the Democratic Party than to the Republican Party. Political scientists William A. Galston of the Brookings Institution and Elaine C. Kamarck of the University of Maryland made this argument effectively in their 2005 study, *The Politics of Polarization*.[16]

Just as increasing partisan consistency on the issues growing out of the social upheavals of the 1960s and 1970s is driving polarization, so too are key technological developments. The huge advances and lowered costs of information technology have created the fields of data mining and micro-targeting, which allow the parties to segregate voters into highly detailed categories based on issues, partisanship, consumption patterns, or demographic factors. To date, the Republican Party has outdistanced the Democratic Party in the use of these technologies, employing them to identify with growing precision the "anger points" of current and prospective voters—whether their dominant concern is abortion, taxes, AIDS, "standards-based" education, the federal budget, gun rights, religious expression, welfare, sentencing guidelines, "family values," terrorism, or the war in the Mideast. Armed with this information, the Republican Party has been able to register citizens who hold views supportive of the GOP, to turn out those with weak records of going to the polls, and to build local networks of similarly minded voters (a twenty-first-century version of the precinct captain system). When elections are decided by margins of 1 or 2 percentage points, the value of such technology cannot be underestimated.

Since 2001 the Republican Party has invested heavily in the technology of micro-targeting, acquiring consumer databases, marketing studies, detailed census data, state motor vehicle registration reports, voting records of individuals and households, and membership lists of churches and social organizations (including even hunting and fishing clubs). Firms run by GOP operatives and consultants have surpassed Democrats in compiling not only unprecedented quantities of politically relevant data, but also the names of thousands of local volunteers, and have developed software and processes for combining and strategically deploying all of these lists. The GOP has then repeatedly tested the information and the technologies at its disposal to determine what has worked in identifying, contacting, and turning out Republican voters. Its goal has been to develop the capacity to locate individual voters it might have previously overlooked—including, for example, black churchgoers who are opposed

16. Galston and Kamarck (2005).

to abortion and gay marriage, conservative Latino business owners who are opposed to an increase in the minimum wage, the Rush Limbaugh listener who never registered to vote, or the union activist who owns guns and loves to hunt. "[In 2004] they were smart. They came into our neighborhoods. They came into Democratic areas with very specific targeted messages to take Democratic voters away from us," said former Democratic National Committee chairman Terence R. McAuliffe. "They were much more sophisticated in their message delivery."[17]

Finally, fundraising, working in tandem with the Internet and other technology, is helping to drive polarization. Web-based appeals and advertisements for contributions are conducted through left- and right-of-center blogs and via other ideologically segmented sites. In his failed bid for the Democratic nomination in 2004, Howard Dean pioneered web-based fundraising, tapping into a goldmine of very socially liberal and strongly antiwar donors.

A survey by the Pew Research Center in late 2004 found that these Dean activists were "much more liberal across a range of issues, more dissatisfied with President Bush and with the direction of the country. Their liberalism stands out even when compared with delegates to the 2004 Democratic convention, who themselves were significantly more liberal than rank-and-file Democrats." Dean's contributors were more likely to want the party to take more liberal or progressive positions than the party as a whole, and they were more likely to support gay marriage and less likely to support the use of military force than Democrats nationally.[18]

While polarization may be a dangerous strategy for Democrats in general election appeals to voters (especially swing voters), it has proven highly effective as a fundraising tool. The universe of small donors that Dean tapped into in his primary campaign provided a crucial foundation of donors both for John Kerry, once he became the de facto nominee in March 2004, and for the Democratic National Committee. For the first time in recent memory, Kerry and the DNC effectively matched their Republican counterparts, empowered by record-breaking levels of small contributions.

A postelection study of donors by George Washington University's Institute for Politics, Democracy, and the Internet and the Campaign Finance Institute provided this explanation for the record level of small contributions:

17. Quoted in Thomas Edsall and James Grimaldi, "On Nov. 2, GOP Got More Bang for Its Billion, Analysis Shows," *Washington Post,* December 30, 2004.
18. The Pew Research Center for the People and the Press, "The Dean Activists: Their Profile and Prospects," April 6, 2005 (people-press.org/reports/display.php3?ReportID=240).

Any consideration of the 2004 presidential election has to begin with the partisan divide in the electorate, the acrimony of the presidential campaigns and the polarized attitudes toward President Bush, especially framed in terms of the War in Iraq and national security. It was an extraordinary campaign in this respect. We certainly found some donors motivated by a dislike for John Kerry, but the hostility was more prevalent among those opposed to President Bush. This anger helps explain how the Democratic National Committee and John Kerry were essentially able to close the funding gap that has historically existed between the parties.[19]

How these polarizing strategies will affect future federal elections, especially presidential elections, depends on a number of factors. The most important, perhaps, is whether the Democratic presidential nominee is vulnerable to the Republican manipulation of wedge issues. From the start of his run for the presidency in 1992, Bill Clinton set out to defuse the impact of wedge issues by declaring his support for welfare reform, by stressing a "new covenant" based on "responsibilities" instead of on rights, by presenting himself and his wife as embodying family values, by supporting the death penalty (as governor of Arkansas, Clinton executed an Arkansas inmate during the campaign), and by pointedly breaking with African American leader Jesse Jackson. As a prospective Democratic nominee in 2008, Hillary Clinton—who used her years in the Senate to lay claim to a moderate centrism—would have to expect Republicans to capitalize on voters' highly polarized views of her.[20] The growing strength of the liberal blogosphere—both as a source of financing and as a conduit of information between newly active political participants and liberal political elites—will serve to intensify pressure on Democratic candidates to adopt more polarizing positions, especially on the Iraq war and on other foreign entanglements.

19. Institute for Politics, Democracy, and the Internet, "Small Donors and Online Giving: A Study of Donors to the 2004 Presidential Campaigns," March 6, 2006 (www.cfinst.org/studies/ IPDI_SmallDonors.pdf).

20. See, for example, the repeated finding of high unfavorability ratings in a series of polls listed on the *National Journal*'s PollTrack (nationaljournal.com/members/polltrack/2008/races/whitehouse/ 06wh2008.htm), and the Pew Research Center's determination that "Hillary Clinton and John Kerry remain highly polarizing figures. Democratic voters view Kerry favorably by roughly four-to-one, while Republicans view him unfavorably by the same margin and independents are divided (49% favorable, 51% unfavorable among those able to give a rating). Sen. Clinton receives similar ratings, though somewhat higher than Kerry among independents." Pew Research Center for the People and the Press, "Public Sours on Government and Business," October 25, 2005 (people-press.org/reports/ display.php3?ReportID=261).

On the Republican side, the likelihood of using these polarizing strategies will again depend, in part, on the nominee. In 2000 a major source of John McCain's early success in the fight for the nomination lay in his nonpolarizing appeal to independents and Democrats in states where voters were allowed to cross over and cast ballots in Republican primaries. This would suggest that McCain would prefer to duplicate his pointedly nonpolarizing strategies in order to maintain his viability in 2008. But as his anticipated presidential campaign gains momentum, McCain is already under strong pressure to move to the right—and he will be under much more pressure to do so as the Christian right and other conservative constituencies make demands on him.

Partisan gerrymandering may play only a modest role in polarizing the electorate, but the trends in redistricting have served to reinforce polarization. The Republican Party, as the home of successful businessmen and, in general, of those who are socially dominant, has had the skill and leverage to gain incremental but significant advantages in the competition to control gerrymandering and the mechanics of election-day operations. Observers such as Gary Jacobson in academia to the GOP's Matthew Dowd have noted that the increasing partisan differentiation of congressional districts reflects the changing residential and lifestyle patterns of voters, as those with conservative values and inclinations toward the GOP choose neighborhoods made up of people who share their views—a practice also common among those with more liberal and Democratic views.

The issues posed by the six upheavals described at the beginning of this paper—the civil rights, women's rights, and antiwar movements; the rise of the religious right; the sexual revolution; and the anti-tax movement—do not lend themselves to easy resolution. Conflicts over war and peace, abortion as a right or abortion as murder, women as subordinate to men or as their equals, homosexuality as a sin or as a universal epiphenomenon of human nature—issues such as these do not lend themselves to political compromise. As a result, ideological and culture war conflicts are almost certain to continue shaping politics and the political parties, and to reinforce the use of polarization as a key tool in the competition for political advantage.

References

Abramowitz, Alan I., and Kyle Saunders. 2005. "Why Can't We All Just Get Along? The Reality of a Polarized America." *The Forum* 3 (2): Article 1.

Abramowitz, Alan I., Brad Alexander, and Matthew Gunning. 2006a. "Incumbency, Redistricting, and the Decline of Competition in U.S. House Elections." *Journal of Politics* 68 (1): 75–88.

———. 2006b. "Don't Blame Redistricting for Uncompetitive Elections." *PS: Political Science & Politics* 39 (1): 87–90.

———. 2006c. "Drawing the Line on District Competition: A Rejoinder." *PS: Political Science & Politics* 39 (1): 95–98.

Ansolabehere, Stephen, and James M. Snyder Jr. 2002. "The Incumbency Advantage in U.S. Elections: An Analysis of State and Federal Offices, 1942–2000." *Election Law Journal* 1 (3): 315–38.

Ansolabehere, Stephen, and others. 2006. "The Decline of Competition in U.S. Primary Elections, 1908–2004." In *The Marketplace of Democracy: Electoral Competition and American Politics,* edited by Michael P. McDonald and John Samples, pp. 74–101. Brookings.

Binder, Sarah A. 2005. "Elections, Parties, and Governance." In *Institutions of American Democracy: The Legislative Branch,* edited by Paul J. Quirk and Sarah A. Binder, pp. 148–70. Oxford University Press.

Brady, David W., Hahrie Han, and Jeremy C. Pope. 2005. "Primary Elections and Candidate Ideology: Out of Step with the Primary Electorate?" Stanford University, Graduate School of Business.

Cain, Bruce E. 1984. *The Reapportionment Puzzle.* University of California Press.

Cain, Bruce E., and Elisabeth R. Gerber, eds. 2002. *Voting at the Political Fault Line: California's Experiment with the Blanket Primary.* University of California Press.

Cain, Bruce, John Ferejohn, and Morris Fiorina. 1987. *The Personal Vote: Constituency Service and Electoral Independence.* Harvard University Press.

Cain, Bruce E., Karin Mac Donald, and Michael P. McDonald. 2005. "From Equality to Fairness: The Path of Political Reform since Baker v. Carr." In *Party Lines: Competition, Partisanship, and Congressional Redistricting,* edited by Thomas E. Mann and Bruce E. Cain, pp. 6–30. Brookings.

Campbell, James E. 2003. "The 2002 Midterm Election: A Typical or an Atypical Midterm?" *PS: Political Science & Politics* 36 (2): 203–07.

Campbell, James E., Chad Hankinson and Walter Koch. 2005. "Re-evaluating the Theory of Surge and Decline: Seat Change Requires Competition." Paper prepared for the annual meeting of the New England Political Science Association, Portland, Maine, April 29–30.

Carsey, Thomas M., and Geoffrey C. Layman. 2006. "Changing Sides or Changing Minds? Party Identification and Policy Preferences in the American Electorate." *American Journal of Political Science* 50 (2): 464–77.

Carson, Jamie L., Erik J. Engstrom, and Jason M. Roberts. 2006. "Redistricting, Candidate Entry, and the Politics of Nineteenth-Century U.S. House Elections." *American Journal of Political Science* 50 (2): 283–93.

Cox, Gary W. 1997. *Making Votes Count: Strategic Coordination in the World's Electoral Systems.* Cambridge University Press.

Cox, Gary W., and Jonathan N. Katz. 2002. *Elbridge Gerry's Salamander: The Electoral Consequences of the Reapportionment Revolution.* Cambridge University Press.

Desposato, Scott W., and John R. Petrocik. 2003. "The Variable Incumbency Advantage: New Voters, Redistricting, and the Personal Vote." *American Journal of Political Science* 47 (1): 18–32.

Edwards, George C., III. 2004. *Why the Electoral College Is Bad for America.* Yale University Press.

Ferejohn, John. 1977. "On the Decline of Competition in Congressional Elections." *American Political Science Review* 71 (1): 166–76.

Fiorina, Morris P., Samuel J. Abrams, and Jeremy C. Pope. 2006. *Culture War? The Myth of a Polarized America.* 2d. ed. New York: Longman.

Fleisher, Richard, and Jon R. Bond. 2004. "The Shrinking Middle in the U.S. Congress." *British Journal of Political Science* 34 (3): 429–51.

Galston, William A., and Elaine C. Kamarck. 2005. *The Politics of Polarization.* Washington: Third-Way.

Gulati, Girish J. 2004. "Revisiting the Link between Electoral Competition and Policy Extremism in the U.S. Congress." *American Politics Research* 32 (5): 495–520.

Hershey, Marjorie Randon. Forthcoming 2007. *Party Politics in America.* 12th ed. New York: Longman.

Jacobson, Gary C. 2003. "Partisan Polarization in Presidential Support: The Electoral Connection." *Congress and the Presidency* 30 (1): 1–36.

———. 2004a. "Explaining the Ideological Polarization of the Congressional Parties since the 1970s." Paper prepared for the annual meeting of the Midwest Political Science Association, Chicago, April 15–18.

———. 2004b. *The Politics of Congressional Elections.* 6th ed. New York: Longman

———. 2005. "Modern Campaigns and Representation." In *Institutions of American Democracy: The Legislative Branch,* edited by Paul J. Quirk and Sarah A. Binder, pp. 109–47. Oxford University Press.

———. 2006. "Competition in U.S. Congressional Elections." Paper prepared for the Cato-Brookings Marketplace of Democracy Conference, Washington, Cato Institute, March 9.

———. Forthcoming 2007. *A Divider, Not a Uniter: George W. Bush and the American People.* New York: Longman.

Koza, John R., and others. 2006. *Every Vote Equal: A State-Based Plan for Electing the President by National Popular Vote.* Los Altos, Calif.: National Popular Vote Press.

Layman, Geoffrey C., and others. 2005. "Party Polarization and 'Conflict Extension' in the United States: The Case of Party Activists." Paper prepared for the annual meeting of the Southern Political Science Association, New Orleans, January 6–8.

Levendusky, Matthew S. 2005. "Sorting in the U.S. Mass Electorate." Stanford University, Department of Political Science.

Mann, Thomas E. 1978. *Unsafe at Any Margin: Interpreting Congressional Elections.* Washington: American Enterprise Institute.

———. 2005. "Redistricting Reform: What Is Desirable? Possible?" In *Party Lines: Competition, Partisanship, and Congressional Redistricting,* edited by Thomas E. Mann and Bruce E. Cain, pp. 92–114. Brookings.

Mann, Thomas E., and Norman J. Ornstein. 2006. *The Broken Branch: How Congress Is Failing America and How to Get It Back on Track.* Oxford University Press.

Mayhew, David R. 2004. "Congressional Elections: The Case of the Vanishing Marginals." *Polity* 6 (3): 295–317.

McDonald, Michael P. 2006. "Drawing the Line on District Competition." *PS: Political Science & Politics* 39 (1): 91–94.

Ono, Keiko. 2005. "Electoral Origins of Partisan Polarization in Congress: Debunking the Myth." *Extensions* (Fall): 15–25.

Ross, Tara. 2004. *Enlightened Democracy: The Case for the Electoral College.* Los Angeles: World Ahead Publications.

Contributors

ALAN I. ABRAMOWITZ
Alben W. Barkley Professor of Political Science, Emory University

DAVID W. BRADY
Deputy director and senior fellow, Hoover Institution, and Bowen H. and Janice Arthur McCoy Professor of Political Science and Leadership Values, Stanford Graduate School of Business

JAMES E. CAMPBELL
Professor of political science, University at Buffalo, State University of New York

CARL M. CANNON
White House correspondent, National Journal

E.J. DIONNE JR.
Senior fellow, Governance Studies, Brookings Institution

GREGG EASTERBROOK
Visiting fellow, Governance Studies and Economic Studies, Brookings Institution, and contributing editor, Atlantic Monthly *and* New Republic

THOMAS B. EDSALL
Pulitzer-Moore Chair in Public Affairs Journalism, Columbia University

MORRIS P. FIORINA
Senior fellow, Hoover Institution, and Wendt Family Professor of Political Science, Stanford University

WILLIAM A. GALSTON
Senior fellow, Governance Studies, Brookings Institution

HAHRIE C. HAN
Knafel Assistant Professor of the Social Sciences, Wellesley College

GARY C. JACOBSON
Professor of political science, University of California–San Diego

ANDREW KOHUT
President of the Pew Research Center and director of the Pew Research Center for the People and the Press

MATTHEW S. LEVENDUSKY
Postdoctoral Research Fellow, Center for the Study of American Politics, Yale University

THOMAS E. MANN
W. Averell Harriman Chair, senior fellow, Governance Studies, Brookings Institution

DIANA C. MUTZ
Samuel A. Stouffer Professor of Political Science and Communication, University of Pennsylvania

PIETRO S. NIVOLA
Douglas Dillon Chair, vice president, and director, Governance Studies, Brookings Institution

THOMAS ROSENSTIEL
Director, Project for Excellence in Journalism

ALAN WOLFE
Professor of political science and director, Boisi Center for Religion and American Public Life, Boston College

Index

Abolition and abolitionists. *See* Civil War era

Abortion: election of *2004* and, 181, 182; as a litmus test issue, 64, 177; political parties and, 5–6, 12, 19, 20, 60, 62, 64, 65–66, 69, 81, 82f, 95, 178; pro-life and pro-choice movements, 4, 6, 64, 66, 81, 82f, 182–83, 264; public views of, 9, 12, 64, 65–66, 154, 182–83; Reagan, Ronald and, 179; religious factors and, 12, 22, 199; religious right and, 194; as a wedge issue, 292. *See also Roe* v. *Wade*

Abramowitz, Alan I., 12, 13, 25, 43, 72–85, 86, 92, 95–105, 107, 111–14, 272, 273, 292

Abrams, Samuel J., 8, 9, 10, 12, 51, 85, 154, 156, 272

Academia, 177. *See also individual authors and scholars*

Adams, John Quincy, 41

Affirmative action. *See* Educational issues

Afghanistan, 37, 60, 91

African Americans: Democratic Party and, 184, 188–89, 196, 203; election of *2004* and, 204; polarization and, 98–99; redistricting and, 266, 269; Republican Party and, 184, 217, 269; voting patterns of, 198. *See also* Racial, ethnic, and minority issues

"Age of low politics," 21

Agnostics. *See* Atheists and agnostics

Alford, John A., 274

Alford, Robert R., 137

Almanac of American Politics (Barone), 176

Al Qaeda, 291

America Online (AOL), 251–52

Anderson, Christopher J., 238

Ansolabehere, Stephen, 5, 280

Antiwar movement (*1960s*), 7, 8

ANWR. *See* Arctic National Wildlife Refuge

AOL. *See* America Online

Arctic National Wildlife Refuge (ANWR), 27–28

Aspire Act (*2005*), 32

Assassinations, 8

Atheists and agnostics, 202, 204. *See also* Seculars

Atlantic Monthly, 260
Atwater, Lee, 293

Baker, Wayne, 51
Balz, Dan, 178
Bangkok Post, 260
Baptists, 187, 198, 210–12. *See also*
    Religion and religious issues
Barker, David, 226
Barone, Michael, 176
Bartels, Larry M., 10, 110, 169
Battleground states. *See* States and state
    government
Baum, Matthew, 232–33
BBC, 229
Beinart, Peter, 37
Bell, Daniel, 7
Berelson, Bernard, 137
Bergen County (N.J.), 178
Big Breakfast, The (television show), 247
Blair, Tony, 149
Blogs. *See* Internet
Born-again Christians, 208, 211
Boston College, 212–13
Brady, David W., 30, 41, 119–51, 152–53,
    154, 155, 156, 159, 163, 164, 167, 279
Breaking the News (Fallows), 247
Brooks, David, 191, 205
Brooks, Preston, 120
Brown v. *Board of Education* (*1954*), 7
Bryan, William Jennings, 149
Bryson, Bethany, 51
Buchanan, James, 128
Buchanan, Pat, 49, 50, 175
Buffalo News, 260
Burton, Philip (D-Calif.), 269
Bush, George H. W., 13
Bush, George W.: class divide and, 194–95;
    Democratic themes and, 30; first term
    of, 3; immigration policies of, 31; inter-
    pretations of executive power, 50; Iraq
    war and, 167; judicial appointments of,
    38; partisan priming and, 90; as a polar-
    izing president, 8, 49, 75, 90–92,
    109–10, 165, 265, 278–79, 294, 296;
    public views of, 4, 5, 28, 110, 165, 180,
    216, 217–18; religious issues and, 180,

182, 183, 203–04, 216; second term of,
    217–18; Social Security reforms of, 36;
    stem cell research and, 147. *See also*
    Elections–*2000*; Elections–*2004*
Bush (George W.) administration, 31

CAFTA. *See* Central American Free Trade
    Agreement
Cain, Bruce, 270–71
California, 7, 20, 24, 178, 185–86, 188, 264
Campaign Finance Institute, 296–97
Campaigns: campaign activists, 70, 75, 76,
    77, 85, 99, 102, 112; candidate-centered
    campaigns, 268; fundraising and financ-
    ing issues, 273–74, 283, 296; media
    reporting on, 235–38; strategies of, 49,
    51, 294. *See also* Candidates; Political
    activists
Campbell, James E., 43, 152–62, 163
*Canarsie: The Jews and Italians of Brooklyn
    against Liberalism* (Reider), 192
Candidates: challengers, 273–74; ideological
    poles and, 71; incumbents, 25, 70, 143,
    265, 267, 268, 272, 275, 281, 286–87;
    partisanship of, 18; polarizing and non-
    polarizing candidates, 16–17; policy
    positions of, 71n45; political parties and,
    143; primaries and, 26; public accusa-
    tions of, 40–41; public polarization and,
    52; sorting and, 71. *See also* Campaigns;
    Elections; Primaries
Cannon, Carl M., 43, 163–70
Capital Gang (talk show), 240
Capital punishment, 9, 38, 55
Carmines, Edward G., 59, 106, 161, 162
Carsey, Thomas M., 291
Carter, Jimmy, 14, 35, 179, 187
Catholic Answers (religious group), 199
Catholics and Catholicism: election of *2004*
    and, 185, 189, 199, 204; political views
    of, 212, 213; presidential candidates,
    176, 180; religious divides and, 176; as a
    swing vote, 201; views of abortion and
    birth control, 210, 212. *See also* Religion
    and religious issues
CBS News poll, 168
Center on Policy Attitudes, 291

Central American Free Trade Agreement (CAFTA; *2005*), 32
Chain Reaction: The Impact of Race, Rights, and Taxes on American Politics (Edsall and Edsall), 192
Chapel Hill Herald, 198
Chicago Tribune, 260
Children's Television Workshop, 248
Civil Rights Act (*1964*), 143
Civil rights movement, 8, 19, 140, 143, 144, 154, 187
Civil War era: abolition and abolitionists, 7, 127–28; compromise solutions of, 154; Congressional voting patterns during, 126; divisions among voters, 126–27; economic issues during, 146; moral issues during, 123, 127, 128–29; political polarization during, 122, 123, 125, 127–29, 145; slavery and, 7, 126–29, 145, 153–54
Class politics, 178–79, 191–98, 217
Clecak, Peter, 177
Cleveland, Grover, 149
Clinton, Bill: "don't ask, don't tell" military policy, 147; health care reforms, 36; Lewinsky scandal and impeachment of, 21, 27, 41, 49, 70–71, 90, 166, 167, 179–80; as a polarizing president, 165; race issues and, 192; religion and, 179, 180; use of TiVo, 243; wedge issues and, 297. *See also individual elections*
Clinton, Hillary Rodham (D-N.Y.), 49, 165–66, 243, 297
CNN, 229, 230, 242, 251–52, 258. *See also* Media
Colbert, Stephen, 253
Cold War, 20, 21, 50, 143
Colmes, Alan, 253
Colorado Springs Gazette, 260
Community Action Program, 35
Congress: accountability of, 27–29; bipartisanship in, 31–32, 37, 41, 42, 138, 143, 145; bipartisan unity in, 131, 132, 133, 145, 155–56; change in seats, 24; during the Civil War era, 125; committees of, 34; competitive elections of, 25, 276–77; deliberative process of, 33–34; elections,

139, 143–44, 276–83; incivility in, 3, 33, 166, 244; legislative process in, 265; legislative record of, 29–32; moderates in, 25, 41–42; oversight of the executive branch, 34; partisan in, 140, 155; party cohesion in, 131, 133, 145, 264, 265; polarization of, 1, 18–19, 33–34, 37, 50, 73, 143, 144, 154–55, 159, 162, 166, 265, 267, 277–79, 283; positions of, 106; reforms in, 34, 283; roll-call votes in, 131n23, 155, 162; sorting in, 144, 145. *See also* House of Representatives; Political elites; Senate
Congress—specific: *55*th, 131; *73*rd, 131; *95*th, 276–78, 279f; *107*th, 130–31; *108*th, 275, 277; *109*th, 34, 155
Conservative Party (Great Britain), 149, 228
Conservatives and conservatism: characteristics of, 105–06; class politics and, 192, 193; classification of political views and, 55; compassionate conservatism, 28, 213; election of *2004* and, 181; heartland of conservative America, 206–07; ideology of, 113–14; Moral Majority and, 177–78; neoconservatives and neoconservatism, 193; numbers of, 5, 294; polarization and, 80–81, 82f, 158; public policy and, 23; regional distribution of, 178; religion and, 22, 23, 176, 209–10; religious right, 193, 194; Republican Party and, 53–54, 80, 114, 291, 293; views of cultural conflict, 50; voting patterns of, 2, 10; wedge issues and, 293. *See also* Republicans and Republican Party
Constitutional issues, 38, 257, 282
Converse, Philip E., 72, 84, 99, 105
Corzine, Jon (D-N.J.), 32
Cox, Gary W., 272
Crime, 31
Crossfire (television show), 240, 253, 254
Culture and culture wars: argument culture, 253; culture wars, 16, 40–41, 49, 50, 85, 209, 210; in the election of *2004*, 4; Hollywood culture, 177; opinion culture, 253–54, 256; partisan divisions and, 93–95; party sorting and, 69; polar-

ization and, 3–4; public views of, 51; severity of, 2, 69

Culture Wars: The Struggle to Define America (Hunter), 4

Culture War? The Myth of a Polarized America (Fiorina, Abrams, and Pope), 8, 85, 95, 108

DailyKos (website), 258

Daily Show, The (television show), 240, 247

Davis v. *Bandemer* (*1986*), 270

Day, Benjamin, 250

Dayton (Tenn.), 207

Dean, Howard, 296

Defense and military issues: partisan differences, 90–91; political parties and, 20, 81, 82f, 110, 140, 143; public views on, 98–99; as wedge issues, 292. *See also individual wars*

DeLay, Tom (R-Tex.), 38, 265, 269, 281, 283. *See also* Texas

Delli Carpini, Michael X., 105

Democracy and democratic process, 35–40, 79–80, 152

Democratic National Committee (DNC), 296, 297

Democrats and Democratic Party: African Americans and, 184, 217, 266; during the Civil War era, 126–27; class politics and, 192, 194, 217; demographics of, 137; economic factors and, 24n72, 149; election strategies and fundraising, 294–95, 296, 297; ideology, agenda, and orientation of, 13, 30–31, 87, 90, 264, 276; interpretations of executive power, 50; liberals and, 53–54, 64, 80, 114, 153, 161, 162, 166, 178, 264, 276, 291, 294–95; media choices and, 229–30; minority status of, 10, 33, 288; polarization and, 54–55, 81, 290, 294, 296; Reagan Democrats, 192; redistricting and, 266, 274, 287, 288, 290; religious and nonreligious voters, 199, 201–02, 217; sorting of, 62–67, 72–73, 161, 166; in the South, 19–20, 54, 143, 166, 176, 264; use of technology by, 295. *See also* Liberals and liberalism; Political parties; *individual elections and politicians*

Democrats and Democratic Party—specific issues: abortion, 12, 19, 178; civil rights, 187; employment, 11; health insurance, 12; homosexuals and homosexuality, 5; Iraq, 11, 20, 36–37, 91, 92; national security and terrorism, 11–12, 36; race, 130, 133, 143, 161, 192; religion, 22, 23, 93–95, 179, 187–88; role of government, 64; school prayer and, 67; September 11, 2001, 11; Social Security, 34; taxes, 31–32; trade, 31, 32; weapons of mass destruction, 92; welfare, 31

de Valera, Éamon, 148–49

Dewey, Thomas E., 137, 150

DiMaggio, Paul, 9, 51

Dionne, E. J., Jr., 42, 175–205, 206, 210, 214, 217

Districts, districting, and redistricting: competitive districts, 24, 25, 266, 268–69, 270–71, 272–74, 276–77, 278, 280, 282, 284–87, 290; Democratic Party, 266, 269; incumbency and, 268, 280; noncompetitive/"safe" districts, 1, 24n74, 70, 265, 267, 271, 274; partisanship and, 272–73, 289; polarization and, 70, 134, 156, 264, 265–66, 267, 284–85, 298; political parties and, 281; political segregation and, 12, 25; population shifts and, 270–71; post-election redistricting, 266; primaries and, 25; reforms, 271–72, 281–82, 284, 288, 290; Republican Party and, 265, 266–67; sources of decrease in balanced districts, 286t; technology and, 25, 267, 271; voting patterns in, 15, 285–86, 290. *See also* Gerrymandering

Djilas, Milovan, 193

DNC. *See* Democratic National Committee

Dole, Bob, 14

Domestic policies, 12, 21, 35, 91. *See also* Policies and policy making

Dowd, Matthew, 51, 294, 298

Downs, Anthony, 109

Dunne, Finley Peter, 163

Duverger, Maurice, 109

Dyson, Esther, 167

East (U.S.), 188, 189. *See also* Northeast
Easterbrook, Gregg, 42, 255–60
Economic issues: during the Civil War era, 127; economic crises and panics, 128; employment, 24; government management of the economy, 8, 18, 23n68, 59, 130; in the late *1800*s, 146–47; personal income, 194–97; polarization and, 153, 178; political weight of, 24; present-day issues, 147; public perceptions, 92, 93f; recessions, 24; supply side economics, 8
Edsall, Mary D., 192
Edsall, Thomas B., 42, 192, 290–98
Educational issues: affirmative action, 95; aid to parochial/religious schools, 200; class politics, 191, 192, 195; intelligent design, 23, 95; No Child Left Behind program, 30, 32; political and ideological understanding, 84, 105–06; receptivity to political cues, 17–18; school prayer, 22, 60, 65, 67, 176, 194, 292; sex education, 22, 95, 292; as wedge issues, 292
Edwards, Chet (D-Tex.), 274
E! Entertainment Television, 249
Eisenhower, Dwight D., 8, 10
Elbridge Gerry's Salamander (Cox and Katz), 272
Elections: class and, 191–98; congressional elections, 139, 143–44; cross-party voting in, 143; economic effects on, 146; effects of losing in, 238; effects of partisanship in, 143–44; election maps, 4–5, 6–7, 12; media coverage of, 235–38, 252–53; party-line voting, 92; polarization and, 4, 129, 139, 148, 156; of public officials, 69–70; reforms, 281–83; state margins of victory, 12–14. *See also* Campaigns; Candidates; Districts, districting, and redistricting; Primaries; Voters and voting
Elections (*2000*): Bush, George W. and, 14, 28, 180, 214, 294; campaign and political activists in, 100; election results, 49, 166, 274; ideology of, 277f; issues of, 4, 5–6, 28, 60, 180; polarization in, 14, 15, 16, 17n48, 178, 298; political par-

ties in, 13, 265; religion and religious factors, 22, 217
Elections (*2004*): Bush, George W. and, 6, 10, 13–14, 15, 23, 51, 181, 182, 183–84, 214, 294; campaign and political activists in, 70, 75, 85, 100, 102, 104, 111; class politics in, 194–96; Congressional elections, 24, 26; fundraising in, 296–97; gerrymandering and, 265; ideology of, 5, 181–82; issues of, 4, 5–6, 29, 31, 36–37, 60–61, 110, 181, 182–83; polarization in, 14, 15, 16, 17n48, 76–79, 80, 81–84, 96, 178; political parties in, 10, 13, 56–57, 75, 110, 134; religion and religious factors, 22, 183–90, 197–98, 199, 200–05, 214–15, 217; strategies of, 181–83; voter turnout in, 39, 114, 180; what mattered most to voters, 214–16
Elections—other specific: *1828*, 41; *1852*, 126; *1854*, 126; *1856*, 126; *1858*, 126; *1860*, 126, 127; *1880*, 120–21; *1884*, 121; *1892*, 149; *1896*, 131, 149; *1908*, 149; *1928*, 134, 176, 180; *1932*, 122, 150; *1936*, 3; *1940*, 150; *1944*, 150; *1948*, 137, 194; *1958*, 59; *1960*, 3, 14, 15, 16, 17, 176, 180; *1964*, 19–20, 187, 263–64, 288; *1968*, 187; *1972*, 15, 20, 81, 187, 193, 194; *1976*, 14, 15, 16, 17, 19, 20, 102, 104, 179, 187, 278f, 279f; *1980*, 14, 179, 187; *1984*, 19, 20, 76–77, 78, 102; *1988*, 13, 31; *1992*, 15, 17, 22, 25, 49, 104, 175, 178, 179, 297; *1994*, 26, 49, 143, 161, 166, 265, 269, 278, 287; *1996*, 6, 14, 15, 178; *1998*, 49; *2002*, 15, 29, 219, 265, 275–76, 287; *2006*, 219; *2008*, 15, 17, 297, 298
Electoral College, 4–5
Electorate. *See* Voters and voting
Ellis, Christopher, 105
Elmira (N.Y.), 137
Emerging Republican Majority, The (Phillips), 193
Energy issues and policies, 27–29, 91
Entitlements, 36. *See also* Medicare; Social Security
Environmental issues, 9, 27–28, 144

Episcopalians, 210. *See also* Protestants and Protestantism

Era of Good Feeling (*1817–1823*), 3

Ethnic issues. *See* Racial, ethnic, and minority issues

European press, 250, 251

Evangelicals, 201, 204, 206–07, 208, 212, 218–19, 293–94. *See also* Protestants and Protestantism; Religion and religious issues

Evans, John H., 9, 51

Fahrenheit 9/11 (film), 227

Fairness doctrine, 2, 21

Faith-based programs. *See* Religion and religious issues

Fallows, James, 247

Falwell, Jerry, 176, 177–78, 212

Federalist No. 10, The (Madison), 162

Felzenberg, Al, 169

Festinger, Leon, 225

Fianna Fail party (Ireland), 148–49

Fiorina, Morris P., 3, 9, 10, 12, 13, 16, 39, 40, 43, 49–71, 72–73, 75, 77, 79, 80, 84, 85–86, 87, 90, 95–112, 154, 156, 159–60, 198, 213, 292

First Amendment. *See* Constitutional issues

Florida, 49, 90, 134, 166

Ford, Gerald, 10, 14, 167

Foreign policies, 20, 35, 36–37, 42, 60, 110. *See also* Policies and policy making

Fox News, 227, 229, 230, 251, 258. *See also* Media

Franken, Al, 249, 253

Freedman, Jonathan L., 226

Free Men, Free Soil, and Free Labor movement, 128–29

FreeRepublic (website), 258. *See also* Internet

Gallup Polls, 90, 137, 168

Galston, William A., 1–47, 61, 176, 205, 295

Garfield, James A., 167

Garrison, William Lloyd, 128

Gaudet, Hazel, 137

Gay and lesbian issues. *See* Homosexual issues

Gender issues. *See* Women's issues

General Social Survey, 51, 68, 217

Georgia, 185

Gerrymandering: causes of, 284; competition and, 268–74, 277; definition of, 265, 290; effects of, 265–66, 268–69, 271, 290; polarization and, 70, 166, 266–81, 284, 285, 290, 298; redistricting and, 266; technology and, 25. *See also* Districts, districting, and redistricting

Gingrich, Newt (R-Ga.), 278

Glazer, Nathan, 194

Globalization, 147, 150–51

Goldwater, Barry, 7–8, 19, 27, 143, 187, 263–64

GOP (Grand Old Party). *See* Republican Party

Gore, Al, 14, 182, 217, 252, 294. *See also* Elections (*2000*)

Governance Studies Program (Brookings Institution), 1

Government: divided, 26; gridlocked, 29–32, 36; management of the economy, 8, 18, 23n68, 59, 98, 130, 150; public trust in, 35–36; public views of, 64, 65, 98; role of, 129, 130, 136–37, 140, 143, 145–46, 147, 150; shutdowns of *1996*, 30; unified, 26. *See also* Congress; House of Representatives; Presidents; Senate

Governors, 6–7, 109–10

Grand Old Party (GOP). *See* Republican Party

Great Britain, 149, 227–28

Great Depression, 121, 145, 149–50, 165

Great Society, 35

Greenberg, Stanley, 23

Green, John C., 93, 200–05, 207–08

Guardian (Great Britain), 260

Gulf war. *See* Iraq/Gulf war

Guth, James L., 93

Hacker, Jacob S., 28

Hadley, Charles D., 193–94

Hallin, Daniel C., 238–39

Han, Hahrie C., 41, 119–51, 152–53, 154, 155, 156, 159, 163, 164, 167, 279

Hannity & Colmes (talk show), 253

Hannity, Sean, 253
Hardball (talk show), 240, 244
Hart, Roderick P., 236–37
Health insurance, 12, 28, 30, 64, 65, 98, 99
Hertzke, Allen, 199
Hetherington, Marc J., 17
Hindus, 198, 203
Hispanics. *See* Latinos/Hispanics
Homeland Security, Department of, 30, 32
Homosexual issues: Bush, George W. and,
    181; "don't ask, don't tell" military policy,
    147, 292; election of *2004* and, 185;
    gay priests, 210; public views of, 8, 86,
    183; religious factors, 199; same-sex
    marriage and civil unions, 5, 32, 68, 95,
    177, 181, 183, 184–85, 292; as wedge
    issues, 292
Hoover, Herbert, 122, 134
Hoover Institution (Stanford University), 1
House of Representatives: bipartisan unity
    in, 131, 132, 133; competitive elections
    of, 268, 272–75; constituency opinion
    and, 275; ideology in, 87, 275–80;
    impeachment of Clinton, Bill and, 27;
    partisanship in, 140, 141, 274–75, 284;
    personal vote, 143, 144, 268, 272;
    polarization of, 1, 80, 267, 268, 277,
    285–86, 288; redistricting and, 266,
    269, 285–87; voting patterns in, 15–16,
    272, 275. *See also* Congress
Hunter, James Davison, 4, 201, 209
Huntington, Samuel P., 274–75
Huntley-Brinkley Report (television show),
    260
Hurricane Katrina, 34, 260. *See also* New
    Orleans
Hussein, Saddam, 37, 92, 110. *See also* Iraq
    war

Ideologies. *See* Conservatives and conser-
    vatism; Liberals and liberalism; Political
    parties; Voters and voting
Incumbents. *See* Candidates
Independents, 53, 84, 90, 108, 202, 229,
    251
Industrialization, 7
Inglehart, Ronald, 177

Inside Politics (television show), 242
Institute for Politics, Democracy, and the
    Internet (George Washington
    University), 296–97
Intellectuals and intellectualism, 50
Interest groups, 16, 27–28, 32
Internet: access to, 260; blogs, 252, 258,
    260, 296, 297; candidate websites, 227;
    effects of, 166–67; fundraising on, 296;
    online sources and publications, 229,
    232, 251–52, 260; polarization and, 258
Iowa, 271–72
Iraq/Gulf war (*1991*), 20, 90–91
Iraq war (*2003*–present): divisiveness of, 4,
    167; as an election issue, 6, 182, 214,
    215; factual misinformation about,
    291–92; partisan support for, 91, 168,
    293–94; political parties and, 11, 30, 37,
    60, 293–94. *See also* Hussein, Saddam;
    Weapons of mass destruction
Ireland, 148–49
Is Voting for Young People? (Wattenberg), 105
Iyengar, Shanto, 229

Jackson, Andrew, 41, 167, 252
Jackson, Jesse, 297
Jacobson, Gary C., 18–19, 42, 43, 85–95,
    108–11, 274, 284–90, 292, 298
James, Judson L., 137
Jefferson, Thomas, 41, 167
Jennings, M. Kent, 18
Jews, 22, 23, 93, 199, 203, 204, 213. *See
    also* Religion and religious issues
Johnson, Andrew, 167
Johnson, Luci, 167
Johnson, Lyndon B., 8, 35, 143, 167
Judiciary, 38

Kamarck, Elaine C., 61, 295
Kansas, 6
Kansas-Nebraska Act (*1854*), 126–27
Katz, Jonathan N., 272
Keeter, Scott, 105, 218
Kellstedt, Lyman A., 93
Kennedy, Anthony, 38
Kennedy, David, 122
Kennedy, Edward M. ("Ted"; D-Mass.), 31

Kennedy, John F., 14, 167, 176, 212
Kent State University, 8
Kernell, Samuel, 232–33
Kerry, John: election of *2004* and, 6, 10,
    15, 23, 180, 183–84, 190, 294;
    fundraising by, 296, 297; public support
    for, 5, 183, 184, 195–97, 199, 204, 212,
    216, 217; tax rates and, 31. *See also*
    Elections—*2004*
Key, V. O., Jr., 124
Klinkner, Philip A., l110
Kohut, Andrew, 42, 214–19
Korean War (*1950–53*), 91, 168–69
Kosovo, 91
Kristol, Irving, 193

Labour Party (Great Britain), 149, 228
Ladd, Everett Carll, Jr., 193–94
Lake County (Ohio), 178
Lasswell, Harold, 176
Latinos/Hispanics, 185, 189, 190, 196,
    203, 217, 266. *See also* Racial, ethnic,
    and minority issues
Layman, Geoffrey C., 291, 292
Lazarsfeld, Paul F., 137, 225
Legal issues. *See* Capital punishment; Crime
Legislative Services Bureau (Iowa), 271
Leland, John, 211
Levendusky, Matthew S., 40, 43, 49–71,
    72–73, 75, 77, 79, 80, 84, 87, 90,
    95–112, 291
Lewinsky, Monica. *See* Clinton, Bill
Liberals and liberalism: characteristics of,
    105; classification of political views and,
    55; class politics and, 191–92, 193, 195;
    culture war and, 50; Democratic Party
    and, 53–54, 64, 114, 276, 291; election
    losses and, 252; elitist liberals, 193;
    establishment and, 177; ideology of,
    113–14; modernist liberation move-
    ment, 193; national security and terror-
    ism and, 37; numbers of, 5, 181–82,
    294; polarization and, 80–81, 158;
    regional distribution of, 178; religion
    and, 22, 179, 213; shifting opinions of,
    98–99; voting patterns of, 2, 10. *See also*
    Democrats and Democratic Party

Liberator (newsletter), 128
Libertarians and libertarianism, 211
Lieberman, Joseph (D/I-Conn.), 170
Limbaugh, Rush, 226, 249, 253, 254
Lincoln, Abraham, 8, 154, 167. *See also*
    Civil War era
Lipset, Seymour Martin, 178–79
Los Angeles Times, 260
Losers' Consent (Anderson and others), 238
Louisiana, 34, 35, 185, 188–89

Madison, James, 162, 281
Mann, Thomas E., 42, 70, 263–83, 284,
    286, 288, 290
Mansbridge, Jane J., 245
Maps. *See* Elections
Marriage, 5
Marxism, 154, 193
Massachusetts, 7, 134
Matthews, Chris, 244
Mayhew, David, 268
McAuliffe, Terence R., 296
McCain-Feingold campaign finance reforms
    (Bipartisan Campaign Reform Act;
    2002), 32
McCain, John, 170, 180, 298
McCarty, Nolan, 24, 159
McDonald, Michael P., 272, 273
McGovern, George, 15, 187, 193, 194
McKinley, William, 167
McLaughlin Group, The (talk show), 240, 253
McPhee, William N., 137
Media: advertising and, 250, 259; audience
    patterns and, 227–30; availability of,
    226, 233; bracketing of acceptable opin-
    ion by, 238–40, 252–53; choice in
    sources of political news, 224–32, 249,
    251–52, 258–59; choosing whether to
    watch political news, 232–35; Christian
    communities and, 198; Clinton, Bill
    and, 71; commercial and market pres-
    sures and, 246–48, 258–59; coverage of
    elections and campaigns, 235–38,
    252–53; entertainment content and
    choice, 232, 233–35, 247, 248, 249;
    First Amendment and, 257; incivility of,
    240–45, 246–47, 257; interpretation of

information, 230–31; "new media," 224; newspapers, 227, 250, 258, 259–60; partisanship and, 21–22, 231, 232, 237–38; polarization and, 42, 52–53, 119, 166, 223, 224, 227, 229, 230–31, 232, 233, 237–38, 240–44, 245–48, 249–59; political culture and, 253–54, 255; politicization and partisan bias of, 2, 16, 225–26, 227–29, 230, 249–50; prevailing views of, 4; radio, 16, 21, 166, 229, 234, 258; religious issues and, 177; selectivity and, 224–26, 227–29, 230, 232; shout shows, 166, 240–45, 253, 255; talk shows, 16, 21, 166, 226–27, 229, 251; television, 229, 232–34, 244–45, 250, 251, 258, 259; voters and voting and, 255. *See also* Internet; *individual media outlets and personalities*
Medical issues: assisted suicide, 95; end-of-life rules, 30; health care reforms, 36; prescription drug benefit, 28, 30, 35, 41; stem cell research, 28, 30, 32, 41, 95, 147, 177. *See also* Health insurance
Medicare/Medicaid, 28, 30, 35, 42
Meet the Press (talk show), 240
Menendez, Albert J., 187
Methods: calibration of effects of redistricting, 272–73; conceptual and measurement issues in polarization, 153–56; determination of degree of partisan overlap, 139–40; differences among religiously affiliated, 200–01; establishing benchmarks for polarization, 123–29, 162; evidence of voter polarization, 157–61; examination of breadth and depth of polarization, 129–45; examination of historical time periods, 122; examination of ideological differences between party elites, 123, 129–30; examination of incivility on television, 241; examination of media choices, 233–34; measurement of district partisanship, 284; measurement of party cohesiveness, 125–26; measurement of polarization, 75–76, 80, 82, 84, 96–107, 111–12, 123, 125, 133–36, 159–60;

measurement of relative entertainment preference, 234–35; measurement of sorting, 62, 64, 107; qualitative studies, 206–13
Meyerson, Adam, 179
Michigan, 7
Michigan Survey Research Center, 137
Midwest (U.S.), 178, 188, 189
Miers, Harriet, 38
Military issues. *See* Defense and military issues
Miller, Zell (D-Ga.), 244
Minnesota, 188
Mississippi, 7
Model Cities program, 35
Moderates: districts and redistricting and; election of *2004* and, 180, 181; numbers of, 5, 25, 98, 99, 153, 159, 181, 267; polarization and, 157–60; political parties and, 294; power and leverage of, 41–42; social moderates, 205; voter turnout of, 252
Modern Republicanism, 8
Monmouth County (N.J.), 178
Montana, 7
Montana Medical Marijuana Act (*2004*), 7
Moonves, Leslie, 247
Moral and values issues: during the Civil War era, 123, 127; class politics and, 191; election of *2004* and, 6, 214–16; in the late *1800*s, 146–47; polarization and, 129, 153–54, 178; political factors, 22, 23, 293; present-day issues, 147–48, 150–51; in progressivism, 201; same-sex marriage, 5. *See also* Abortion; Civil War era; Political issues; Religion and religious issues
Moral Majority, 177–78, 179, 187, 212
Moral Sense, The (Wilson), 179
Morin, Richard, 229
Mormons, 203
MoveOn, 37
MSNBC, 251–52
Mueller, John, 170
Murdoch, Rupert, 250
Muslims, 199, 203
Mutz, Diana, 42, 223–48, 249–50, 252–53, 255–56, 259

NAFTA. *See* North American Free Trade
    Agreement
Nassau County (N.Y.), 178
National Annenberg Election Survey
    (*2004*), 185
National Association of Evangelicals, 212
National Election Pool exit poll (*2004*), 214
National Election Studies (NES): access to
    television and political knowledge, 234;
    classification of political views, 55, 56;
    engagement in political activities, 74;
    ideological positioning, 58, 80–81, 87,
    96, 114, 157; independent and apolitical
    voters, 294; party sorting on specific
    issues, 62, 66, 114; polarization, 18, 51,
    76, 80, 112, 114, 157, 160–61; policy
    areas and issues, 12, 58–59, 75; Reagan
    (Ronald) administration, 169; voter
    activism, 100–04, 112
National Energy Act (*1978*), 35
National Exit Poll (*2004*), 113
National Public Radio (NPR), 229, 230
National Review, 193
National security and terrorism: election of
    2004 and, 184; interrogation of
    detainees, 32; Iraq war and, 92, 182; lib-
    erals and conservatives and, 37; polariza-
    tion and, 22, 35, 42, 91; political parties
    and, 11–12, 37; September *11, 2001*
    and, 11; warrentless wiretaps, 91. *See also*
    September *11, 2001*; USA Patriot Act
NES. *See* National Election Studies
New Age, 177, 203
New Deal era and issues: as a class struggle,
    178–79, 191; economic issues and, 146,
    150; effects of, 122; goals of, 127,
    145–46; income-partisanship correla-
    tion, 24; polarization during, 3–4, 136,
    145, 149–50; political parties and, 59,
    60, 99, 130, 131, 133, 134, 136–37,
    149–50, 161, 263; racial and social
    issues and, 59, 60, 137, 145; religious
    and cultural issues and, 192; role of gov-
    ernment, 129
New England, 20, 178
New Hampshire, 178
New Jersey, 178

New Left, 177
New Orleans (La.), 91, 260. *See also*
    Hurricane Katrina
New Orleans Times-Picayune, 260
New Republic, 37
New Right, 177
News and newspapers. *See* Media
New York City, 193, 258
New York Daily News, 258
New Yorker magazine, 260
New York Post, 258
New York State, 7, 178
New York Sun, 250
New York Times, 236, 260
9/11 Commission, 291
Nivola, Pietro S., 1–47, 176
Nixon, Richard M.: economic issues and, 8;
    election of *1960* and, 14; election of
    1972 and, 15, 187, 193; favorable opin-
    ions of, 10; resignation of, 167
NPR. *See* National Public Radio
No Child Left Behind. *See* Educational
    issues
Nonvoters. *See* Voters and voting
North American Free Trade Agreement
    (NAFTA; *1994*), 31
North Carolina, 6
North Dakota, 7
Northeast (U.S.), 20, 178. *See also* East
Novak, Robert, 242

Oakland County (Mich.), 178
O'Connor, Sandra Day, 271
*Off Center: The Republican Revolution and
    the Erosion of Democracy* (Hacker and
    Pierson), 28
Ohio, 134, 184–85
Oklahoma, 6
Olbermann, Keith, 254
Olson, Theodore B., 38
One Nation, After All (Wolfe), 9
Oregon, 178
O'Reilly, Bill, 243, 253, 254, 258
O'Reilly Factor, The (talk show), 240, 243, 253
Ornstein, Norman, 170
Out of Order (Patterson), 235–36
Oxford English Dictionary, 120

Pacific Coast. *See* West

Pakistan Times, 260

Panic of *1857*, 128. *See also* Civil War era

Panic of *1893*, 128

Partisans. *See* Political activists; Voters and voting

Patterson, Thomas E., 235, 252

Pennsylvania, 7

Pentecostals, 207, 208–09. *See also* Protestants and Protestantism; Religion and religious issues

People's Choice, The (Lazarsfeld, Berelson, and Gaudet), 137

Perot, Ross, 25

Persian Gulf war. *See* Iraq/Gulf war

Pew Research Center for the People and the Press, 6, 11, 54, 214–15, 296

Phillips, Kevin, 193

Pierson, Paul, 28

Polarization: benefits of, 39; breadth and depth of, 129–45; causes of, 19–26, 79–80, 166, 263–64, 265–66, 292–96; choices and preferences and, 16–19; competition and, 274–80; deepening disagreements, 11–12, 49–50, 291–92; definitions, criteria, and concepts of, 75, 120, 121, 122, 123, 129, 164; economic factors and, 24, 129, 150–51; effects of, 2–4, 18, 26–27, 29–30, 35–36, 37, 39–41, 293–94, 296–98; election of *2004* and, 76–79; elite versus mass polarization, 143–44; establishing benchmarks for, 123–29, 162; history and periods of, 8, 120–29, 149–50, 152, 162, 164–66; issue divisions, 145–48; of political class/elites, 51–52, 72, 76, 85–86; religion and, 175–90; reforms and, 281–83; resolving polarization, 148–51; risks of, 35–40; sorting and, 19, 75, 79–84, 86, 99, 107–08, 111, 114, 144; symmetry of, 23; technology and, 295; territorial/spatial contours of, 12–16; trends in, 80–82, 158; visual gimmickry and, 4–5; voter turnout and, 252. *See also* Congress; Gerrymandering; Media; Methods; Political issues; Political parties; Voters and voting

Policies and policy making, 58–62, 79. *See also* Domestic policies; Foreign policies

Political activists: abortion and, 20; deepening disagreements between, 11–12; ideology of, 77, 85, 87–88; increases in, 99, 112; polarization of, 1–2, 9–10, 16, 73, 76, 82–84, 95, 109, 112–13; political engagement of, 73–75, 85; sorting and, 70; views of, 12, 109; voting patterns of, 15–16. *See also* Campaigns; Voters and voting

Political elites: bipartisanship and bipartisan unity and, 139, 140, 152; disconnect from supporters, 51–52, 71, 86, 87–90, 108–09; ideology of, 87–90, 123, 129–30, 292; polarization of, 51–52, 72, 73, 80–81, 87–90, 123–25, 139, 152, 268; political strategies of, 18, 19; positions of, 106, 107; public opinion and, 238–39; public responses to, 56–58, 109, 110–11; school prayer and, 67; sorting and, 17, 18, 55, 56–58, 67, 151. *See also* Congress

Political issues: anger level in American politics, 256–57; class politics, 191–98, 217; culture, 3–4; districts and districting, 1; issues and political agenda, 147; litmus tests, 177; morality, 4; political crises, 121; political persuasion of voters, 5; religion, 23–24, 175, 176, 197–205; sorting, 16–19, 52–69, 72–73, 86; unified government and, 26; wedge issues, 5, 22n66, 291–94, 297, 298. *See also* Congress; Polarization; *individual political entries and issues*

Political parties: activity of, 102, 103, 104; in the "age of low politics," 21–22; bipartisanship of, 31–32, 131, 133; blocs of, 10; campaign finance and; "catch-all" parties, 109; centrist policies and two-party competition, 109; choices offered by, 16–17, 27; cohesiveness of, 123, 125–26, 129, 131, 133, 136, 137, 138, 151, 263; constituents of, 123–24; definitions of, 120, 123; differences between, 11–12, 30–31, 90–91, 153, 291; domestic issues and, 21, 24n72;

gerrymandering and, 265; history of, 121–22; ideology and, 10, 53–54, 55–58, 69, 87, 109, 123, 130, 136, 138–39, 263, 277, 278, 291; in-fighting in, 148–49; minority parties, 12–13; mobilization and, 104, 111, 112, 194, 196, 275; 1950s and 1960s, 7; partisan overlap, 139–40, 141; party base, 294; party platforms, 20, 66, 121, 163, 264, 268; polarization and, 3, 18, 20, 40, 52–55, 79–80, 91, 130, 137–38, 144, 151, 153, 159, 162, 268, 277–78, 293–98; public views of, 39, 55, 55–57, 136; realignment of, 19–22, 178, 278; selection and, 277–78; sorting and, 16–19, 52–69, 72–73, 80, 86, 99, 144, 153, 166, 291; strategies of, 55; use of technology by, 295; voting patterns and, 10. See also Independents; individual parties

Politicians. See Political elites

Politics of Polarization, The (Galston and Kamarck), 295

Politics, Parties, and Pressure Groups (Key), 124

Poole, Keith T., 24, 51–52, 86, 159

Pope, Jeremy C., 8, 9, 10, 12, 51, 85, 154, 156, 279, 292

Populists and populism, 7, 149

Positive News (Great Britain), 258

Pravda (Russia), 260

Presidents: appointments of, 38; distribution of presidential votes, 133–36; elections of 2004 and, 15–16; influence of incumbent presidents, 217–18; presidential politics, 167; reforms and, 281–82; television and, 232–33

Primaries: characteristics of, 25–26, 70; Democratic Party and, 26, 279–80; districts and redistricting and, 25, 265, 279–80; ideological alignment and, 114, 279–80; incumbents and, 70, 279–80; polarization and, 70, 73, 279–80, 283, 297; reform of, 282–83; sorting and, 71, 73; turnout in, 70. See also Campaigns; Candidates; Elections; Voters and voting

Prior, Markus, 224, 232, 233, 247

Procaccino, Mario, 193

Progressives and progressivism, 146, 201, 281

Prohibition, 176

Protestants and Protestantism: conservative Protestants, 208–10; election of 1972 and, 187; election of 2004 and, 185, 204; media "smear" of, 198; political issues and parties of, 177, 199–200, 201, 203; religious divide and, 176. See also Evangelicals; Religion and religious issues; individual groups

Public, American. See Campaigns; Political activists; Voters and voting; individual ideologies and political parties

Purpose-Driven Life, The (Warren), 212

Racial, ethnic, and minority issues: affirmative action, 95; class politics and, 192–94; election of 2004 and, 184–85, 196; employment, 9; interracial dating, 8; New Deal issues and, 62, 130, 133, 162; polarization and, 190; political parties and, 140, 143, 187, 192, 217, 288; redistricting, 266–67, 271; religion and, 187; role of government, 64, 81, 82f; sorting and, 59, 64; voting decisions and, 198; as wedge issues, 293. See also individual groups

Radio. See Media

Rauch, Jonathan, 39

Reagan Democrats, 192

Reagan, Ronald: abortion and, 179; assassination attempt on, 167; budget deficit under, 110; election of 1980 and, 14, 187; favorable opinions of, 10; Republican agenda and, 20, 264; tax issues, 31

Reagan (Ronald) administration, 29, 169

Reider, Jonathan, 192

Reid, Harry M. (D-Nev.), 38

Religion and religious issues: church attendance, 185–87; degrees of conservatism, 200–01, 208; denominational factors, 176, 187; election of 2004 and, 182–90, 196–97; faith-based programs, 95; interdenominational hostility, 200, 210; megachurches, 207; political orientation,

2, 4; political parties and, 93–95, 177–78, 187–89, 201–02; religious divide, 205, 209–10; religious right, 193, 194; rise of religious conservatism, 176; role in polarization, 22–24, 175–76, 177–81, 204–05; role in politics, 175, 176, 197–98, 200, 216; school prayer, 22, 60, 65, 67, 176, 194, 292; voter responses to, 110–11; as wedge issues, 292–93. *See also individual denominations and groups*

Republic.com (Sunstein), 232

Republicans and Republican Party: abortion and, 66; African Americans and, 184, 217, 269; agenda and orientation of, 20, 28, 30–31; Christian right and, 147; during the Civil War era, 127; class politics and, 193, 217; Clinton, Bill and, 21, 27, 70–71; conservatives and, 53–54, 80, 114, 153, 162, 166, 178, 217, 264, 276, 291, 293; demographics of, 137; election strategies and fundraising, 294, 295, 297, 298; ideology and, 87, 90, 264, 276; media choices and, 229–30; Modern Republicanism, 8; during the New Deal era, 149–50; numbers of, 10; polarization and, 54–55, 81, 291, 294; political machine of, 265; primaries of, 26; redistricting and, 266–67, 274, 287, 288, 290; religious denominations and, 199–200, 201–02, 204–05, 209, 212, 218–19; sorting of, 62–67, 72–73, 166; in the South, 19–20, 154, 161, 178, 187; use of technology by, 295–96; use of wedge issues by, 293, 297; voting patterns of, 2. *See also* Moral Majority; Political parties; *individual elections and politicians*

Republicans and Republican Party–specific issues: abortion, 5–6, 12; defense and military policies, 60; economic policies, 264; employment, 11; government, 30; health insurance, 12; homosexuals and homosexuality, 5; Iraq, 11, 37, 91, 92; national security and terrorism, 11–12, 37; platform of *1880*, 120–21; race, 193; religion, 23, 93, 94, 183, 187–88;

196–97; role of government, 64; September *11, 2001*, 11; school prayer, 67; taxes, 8; weapons of mass destruction, 92

Robertson, Pat, 212

Rodin, Judith, 244

Roe v. *Wade* (*1973*), 12, 20, 176, 210, 264, 292. *See also* Abortion

Roosevelt, Franklin D., 3–4, 122, 134, 165, 167, 176, 252

Roosevelt, Theodore, 167

Roper Polls, 137

Rosenstiel, Thomas, 42, 249–54

Rosenthal, Howard, 24, 159

Rove, Karl, 49, 90, 180, 182, 293

Santorum, Rick (R-Pa.), 32

Sarbanes-Oxley rules (*2002*), 32

Saunders, Kyle, 12, 13

Schiavo, Terri, 27, 38, 91

Schneider, William, 178

Schools. *See* Educational issues

Sears, David O., 226

Seculars, 217. *See also* Atheists and agnostics

Seducing America (Hart), 236–37

Selectivity. *See* Media

Senate: advice and consent of, 38; bipartisan unity in, 131, 132; evaluations of, 109–10; "gang of 14," 42n133; ideology and approval of, 89–90; moderates in, 41–42; partisan overlap in, 140, 142; polarization of, 267, 277; voting patterns for, 15–16

"Separate Realities of Bush and Kerry Supporters, The" (survey), 291–92

September *11, 2001*, 11, 49, 291–92. *See also* National security and terrorism

Seymour, Robert E., 198

Shaw v. *Reno* (*1993*), 271

Sinn Fein party (Ireland), 148–49

Slavery. *See* Civil War era

Smidt, Corwin E., 93

Smith, Al, 176

Social issues, 206–13, 291. *See also* Moral and values issues; New Deal; *individual issues*

Social Security, 28–29, 30, 34, 36, 42, 91
Soir, Le (Belgium), 260
Sorting. See Political issues; Political parties
South (U.S.): election of 1964 and, 19–20; election of 2004 and, 188, 190; political parties in, 19–20, 40, 54, 64, 153, 155, 178, 190, 264, 286; religion in, 185, 186–87, 188, 190. See also Civil War era; Democrats and Democratic Party; Republicans and Republican Party
Southern Baptist Convention, 210–11. See also Baptists
Soviet Union, 264
Stanford University, 1
States and state government: battleground states, 5; polarization of, 267; redistricting and, 266; state margins of victory, 12–14; voting patterns in, 15–16
Steinfels, Peter, 177
Stewart, Charles, III, 5
Stewart, Jon, 240, 253
Stimson, James A., 59, 105, 161, 162
Stock market collapse (1929), 122, 128, 130
Stoker, Laura, 18
Sumner, Charles, 120
Sunday, Billy, 207
Sunstein, Cass, 232
Surveys and studies. See Gallup Polls; General Social Survey; National Election Studies; Pew Research Center for the People and the Press; World Values Survey
Sweet, Leonard, 177

Taft, William Howard, 149
Tannen, Deborah, 167, 244, 253
Tax issues, 30, 31–32, 293
Technology. See also Districts, districting, and redistricting; Polarization; Political parties
Television. See Media
Tennessee, 7
Terrorism. See National security and terrorism; September 11, 2001; USA Patriot Act
Texas, 134, 274. See also DeLay, Tom
Thatcher, Margaret, 149
Tocqueville, Alexis de, 50

Transformations of the American Party System (Ladd and Hadley), 193–94
Truman, Harry S., 137, 194

Unions, 195
United Kingdom. See Great Britain
United States (U.S.): incivility in, 244; media audience patterns in, 227–30; national identity of, 147; polarization in U.S. politics, 120–21; political conflict in, 7; polling in, 69; public political attitudes in, 7, 8, 9, 210; religion in, 206–07, 210; role of, 4; September 11, 2001 and, 11; social discord in, 256; social moderates in, 205; traditionalists and modernists in, 208, 211
USA Patriot Act (2001), 30, 32
Uslaner, Eric M., 244

Values Divide, The, (White), 4
Vietnam War (1959–1975), 20, 60, 91, 144, 167, 168–69, 239, 263
Virginia, 6
Volden, Craig, 30
Voters and voting: correlations between voter positions on two policies, 61, 63; cross-party voting, 143, 298; divisions of, 3, 137, 148, 251; economic issues and, 24, 136–37, 212; ideology and, 55–58, 69, 77, 84–85, 88–89, 105–06, 108, 113–14, 138, 144–45, 152, 159, 291, 293; nonvoters, 76, 77, 79f, 82, 84–85, 108–09, 295; party-line voting, 92; personal votes, 143–44; political engagement of, 73–79, 99–104; political parties and, 10, 20, 55–62, 64–66, 69, 105, 124, 133–38, 144–45, 149, 264, 291, 293; positions of, 105–07; in primaries, 25–26; reforms and, 282; religion and, 23n67, 216; segregation of, 12, 25, 164; sorting of, 16–19, 55–62, 64–66, 80, 90, 105, 138n38, 144–45, 151, 263, 264, 292; swing voters, 294, 296; turnout, 39–40, 41, 70, 75, 126–27, 159, 160, 204, 233, 235. See also Elections; Political activists; Political issues; Primaries

Voters and voting—polarization: Bush,
George W. and 90–92, 109–10; causes
of, 17, 109–10; districts and, 156,
285–86, 290; effects of, 51–52, 72, 294;
evidence of, 157–61; measurement of,
111–12; media and, 252; patterns and
growth of, 9–10, 72, 75–77, 138,
152–53; political engagement and,
77–79; political parties and, 124–25,
293–98; resolution of, 151; sorting and,
52–53, 79–84, 138, 144–45; trends of,
2, 8
Voting Rights Act (*1965*), 20, 264, 266, 271

Wacker, Grant, 200, 208–09
Wallace, George C., 187
Warren, Rick, 212
Warren, Robert Penn, 163
Washington Post, 178, 180
Washington State, 185–86, 188
Wattenberg, Martin P., 105
Weapons of mass destruction (WMD), 92,
110. *See also* Iraq war

Wedge issues. *See* Political issues
Welfare issues, 31, 32, 292–93
West (U.S.), 20, 178, 185–86, 187, 188, 190
Westchester County (N.Y.), 178
What's the Matter with Kansas? (Frank), 192
Wheaton College, 207
Whig Party, 126–27
White, John Kenneth, 4
Why Americans Hate Politics (Dionne), 210
Wiebe, Robert H., 136
William C. Velasquez Institute, 185
Williams, Roger, 211
Willkie, Wendell, 150
Wilson, James Q., 18, 179
WMD. *See* Weapons of mass destruction
Wolfe, Alan, 9, 42, 206–13
Women's issues, 9, 60, 62, 67, 293
Woodward, Bob, 180
World Values Survey, 51
World War II (*1939–1945*), 165
World Wide Web. *See* Internet

Yahoo!, 251–52